CROSS-FUNCTIONAL MANAGEMENT OF TECHNOLOGY

Cases and Readings

M. Dayne Aldridge

Director and Thomas Walter Eminent Scholar
Thomas Walter Center for Technology Management
Auburn University

Paul M. Swamidass

Associate Director
Thomas Walter Center for Technology Management
Auburn University

IRWIN

Chicago • Bogotá • Boston • Buenos Aires • Caracas
London • Madrid • Mexico City • Toronto

© Richard D. Irwin, a Times Mirror Higher Education Group, Inc. company, 1996

Irwin Book Team

Publisher: *Rob Zwettler*
Sponsoring editor: *John E. Biernat*
Editorial assistant: *Kimberly Kanakes*
Marketing manager: *Michael Campbell*
Project editor: *Waivah Clement*
Production supervisor: *Dina L. Genovese*
Manager, prepress: *Kim Meriwether David*
Designer: *Crispin Prebys*
Compositor: *Carlisle Communications, Ltd.*
Typeface: 10/12 *Times Roman*
Printer: *R. R. Donnelley & Sons Company*

▼▼ **Times Mirror**
◣◢ **Books**

Library of Congress Cataloging-in-Publication Data
Aldridge, M. Dayne.
   Cross-functional management of technology: cases and readings / M. Dayne Aldridge, Paul M. Swamidass.
      p.   cm.
   Includes index.
   ISBN 0–256–19429–7
   1. Technological innovations—Management.   2. Manufactures—Technological innovations—Management.   3. Technological innovations—Management—Case studies.   I. Swamidass, Paul M. II. Title.
   HD45.A5316   1996
   658.5′14—dc20   95–46606

Printed in the United States of America
1 2 3 4 5 6 7 8 9 0 DO 3 2 1 0 9 8 7 6

To John Thomas Walter, Jr., in whose honor the Thomas Walter Center for Technology Management was established at Auburn University.

Courses in management of technology (MOT) are now routinely offered in most business schools, and M.B.A. programs offering MOT as a concentration, track, or primary emphasis are growing in number each day. According to the lead article in *MBA Newsletter*, more and more M.B.A. programs are producing "techno-M.B.A.s" from universities with the two colleges of engineering and business.[1] According to this article, out of the total of 75,000 M.B.A.s graduated each year, 3,750 (5 percent) are expected to be techno-M.B.A.s; this number is expected to grow each year.

The engineering curriculum is strong in its narrow specialization, but it lacks the knowledge and skill development that are needed by engineers to function effectively within organizations. We are preparing engineers to be a excellent science-based engineers but weak business people and managers. Clearly, not all engineers will become managers and business people. But how can we lay the foundation for those who will be active on the business side to be effective business people or managers as well as effective engineers?

What about the business curriculum? Many mistakes of our manufacturing firms can be traced to an inadequate understanding of technology, product design, and manufacturing. At least partly because of the recognition given to these mistakes, many business schools are considering changes in their curriculum for both undergraduate and graduate education. The key concept in most curriculum changes is integration across disciplines within the business school. The next step should be to consider integrating the issues from engineering that are pertinent to the effective management of manufacturing firms. How can this be done?

---

[1] "Programs in Technology Management Grow as More Companies Seek Techno-MBA's," *MBA Newsletter,* August 1994. *MBA Newsletter* is a publication of Kwartler Communications, Inc., Floral Park, NY.

Technology management lies at the interface between engineering and business. It is probably the best body of knowledge that is available today to help integrate engineering and business education. One can see it happening already—many business schools have introduced courses and concentration in technology management in the last five years.

We are grateful to the business and engineering faculty, who were aware of the existence of the National Consortium for Technology in Business (NCTB) cases and encouraged us to publish them in the form of a book. We invite all users of the cases to give us feedback on improving these cases and the selection of readings.

Every case included in this book was developed by a cross-functional team of at least one faculty member from the college of business and another from the college of engineering. The cases have been tested by use in both engineering and business schools by the authors. In some instances, the cases were used in combined classes of business and engineering students, and in other instances, the cases were offered in separate classes to students from the two colleges. Either way, the content was found suitable for students in both colleges. Experience indicates that students from both colleges learn more when the cases are discussed in a classroom where both business and engineering students are present.

The chapter format of the text should provide teachers with a structure that will speed their ability to put together a course curriculum on the subject matter. In addition, we would strongly urge all teachers and students to view the readings that accompany the cases in particular chapters as being relevant to the cases in the various other chapters.

M. Dayne Aldridge
Paul M. Swamidass

A C K N O W L E D G M E N T S

This book is the compilation of the work and cooperation of many people. The editors have contributed in complementary ways to the program that sponsored the development of the cases presented here. One of us (Aldridge) developed the competitive Curriculum Development Program for Schools of Business and Engineering; the other (Swamidass) provided the vision and leadership for the publication of this text. But we both are indebted to numerous individuals and organizations that made this work possible.

A gift from the Perot Foundation made it possible for us to experiment in curriculum development through the joint efforts of business and engineering faculty under the auspices of the National Consortium for Technology in Business (NCTB). This casebook is a result of one of the projects made possible by the gift.

The Curriculum Development Program for Schools of Business and Engineering touched dozens of faculty all over the United States as case writers, proposal evaluators, case workshop attendees, and users of cases developed through the efforts of the NCTB. Further, hundreds of students in more than 10 universities were involved when their teachers/case developers tested the cases for instructional purposes. Nearly 20 businesses and organizations worked to enable 26 faculty to experience real-life business and engineering problems that they could take to their classrooms as well as describe them in their cases for the use of other faculty.

We want to express our thanks to the faculty from business and engineering colleges across the United States who participated in our competitive grant program to develop cases for use in business and engineering colleges. Out of a total of 59 proposals from 56 universities we received in the summer of 1992, 10 teams of business and engineering faculty were selected to develop 26 cases. We are grateful to the panel of experts who helped us in selecting the 10 teams for awarding grants. The experts were Carl Adams, Professor of Information and Decision Sciences, University of Minnesota; Denny Avers, formerly of IBM

Federal Systems Company; Phil Carter, Associate Dean of Business, Michigan State University; John Crisp, Dean of Engineering, University of New Orleans; Bradford F. Dunn, Dupont Field Engineering Organizations; and Bill Souder, Professor of Administrative Science, University of Alabama in Huntsville.

We acknowledge the contributions of the following faculty who participated in the NCTB grants program to develop cross-functional cases during 1992–1993:

Lehigh University: Keith Gardiner, Director, Center for Manufacturing Systems Engineering and Professor of Industrial Engineering, H. S. Mohler Laboratory; Bruce M. Smackey, Professor of Marketing, Rauch Business Center; John C. Wiginton, Professor of Industrial Engineering, H. S. Mohler Laboratory.

Morgan State University: Timothy Edlund, Assistant Professor of Strategic Management, School of Business and Management; Gee-In Goo, Associate Professor of Electrical Engineering, School of Engineering.

Northeastern University: Raymond Kinnunen, Associate Professor of Business Administration, College of Business Administration; Thomas E. Hulbert, Associate Professor of Industrial Engineering, College of Engineering.

Tennessee Technological University: John M. Burnham, Professor of Decision Science, College of Business Administration; Dale A. Wilson, Professor of Mechanical Engineering, College of Engineering; Kenneth Currie, Assistant Professor of Industrial Manufacturing Center, College of Engineering; Kathryn Langley, Graduate Student, M.B.A. Studies Division, College of Business; Gary C. Pickett, Chairperson, Department of Decision Sciences and Management; Robert R. Bell, Dean, College of Business Administration; Ramachandran Natarajan, Professor of Operations Management, College of Business; Greg Butler, Graduate Student, M.B.A. Studies Division, College of Business; Karen Ramsey-Idem, Ph.D. Student, College of Engineering, Mechanical Engineering; David Lambert, Graduate Student, Mechanical Engineering, College of Engineering; Charles W. Smith, Jr., Graduate Student, M.B.A. Studies Division, College of Business; John A. Welch, Graduate Student, M.B.A. Studies Division, College of Business.

University of Missouri–Columbia: Lori S. Franz, Department of Management; Cerry M. Klein, Department of Industrial Engineering.

University of Virginia: Robert D. Landel, McWane Professor of Business Administration, Darden Graduate School of Business; Larry G. Richards, Director, Manufacturing Systems, Department of Mechanical and Aerospace Engineering.

University of Wyoming: Lawrence Weatherford, Lead Business Faculty, College of Business; Dennis N. Coon, Lead Engineering Faculty, College of Engineering; Sam G. Taylor, Supplemental Business Faculty, College of Business; Francis M. Long, Supplemental Engineering Faculty, College of Engineering.

West Virginia University: Afzel Noore, Electrical and Computer Engineering; Ann Pushkin, Department of Accounting; Bonnie Morris, Department of Accounting; Michael Lawson, Concurrent Engineering Research Center.

Western Michigan University: Robert Landeros, Department of Management; David M. Lyth, Department of Industrial Engineering; Robert F. Reck, Department of Marketing; Liwana S. Bringelson, Department of Industrial Engineering.

Worcester Polytechnic Institute: Sharon A. Johnson, Assistant Professor, Management; Christopher A. Brown, Assistant Professor, Mechanical Engineering; Jeanne W. Ross, Assistant Professor, Management.

We commend the following businesses and organizations around the United States who worked with the faculty teams receiving our grants in developing cross-functional cases. The organizations participating in case development deserving commendation are: A. B. Chance Co.; American Saw & Manufacturing Company; Bellsouth Telecommunications, Inc.; Black & Decker Corporation; Brooktrout Technology Inc.; Durametallic; Duriron Corporation—Valve Division; Fluent Inc.; Ingersoll-Rand Company; Martin Marietta Energy Systems, Inc.; Oak Ridge Associated Universities; Oak Ridge National Laboratories; Stratus Computer, Inc.; Square D; Temic Telefunken; and Westinghouse Electric Corporation Systems Group.

We thank the participants of the First National Conference and Workshop on Business and Engineering Education, Auburn, Alabama, April 1994, who heard case writers describe their cases and provided valuable feedback to case writers. It enabled engineering and business faculty attending the workshop to hear the case writers describe the challenges of case writing and case teaching. Further, it enabled engineering faculty, who seldom use cases, to see the range of possibilities for case writing and teaching with cases. We appreciate the contribution of Drs. William Boulton, Professor, Department of Management, Auburn University; Ed Ernst, Professor of Engineering, University of South Carolina; and Gary Scudder, Professor, Owen Graduate School of Business, Vanderbilt University, who served as rapporteurs at the case workshop.

We would be remiss not to note the encouragement and cooperation of the American Assembly of Collegiate Schools of Business (AACSB) and the American Society for Engineering Education (ASEE) as cosponsors of the case development program. In particular, the help of Charles ("Chuck") Hickman, Director of Projects and Services of the AACSB, and Frank Huband, Executive Director of the ASEE, is noteworthy.

We are grateful for the excellent support provided by the editorial staff of Richard D. Irwin, Inc., and particularly thankful to Mr. John Biernat, and Ms. Waivah Clement, the editors, for this project. Linda Pattillo, of the Thomas

Walter Center for Technology Management, deserves special recognition for providing timely clerical support to complete the project on time.

The authors gratefully acknowledge the permission granted by the publishers to reprint the following outstanding articles in this book:

1. E. B. Roberts, "Managing Invention and Innovation," *Research-Technology Management* 31, no. 1 (January/February 1988).

2. S. C. Wheelwright and K. B. Clark, "Competing through Development Capability in a Manufacturing-Based Organization," *Business Horizons*, July/August 1992.

3. J. R. Dixon and M. R. Duffey, "The Neglect of Engineering Design,"*California Management Review* 32, no. 2 (Winter 1990).

4. M. Maccoby, "Teams Need Open Leaders,"*Research-Technology Management,* January/February 1995.

5. R. A. Lutz,"Implementing Technological Change with Cross-Functional Teams," *Research-Technology Management,* March/April 1994.

6. J. B. Quinn, "The Intelligent Enterprise: A New Paradigm," *Academy of Management Executive* 6, no. 4 (1992).

7. D. J. Teece, "Profiting from Technological Innovation: Implications for Integration, Collaboration, Licensing, and Public Policy," *Research Policy* 15 (1986).

8. M. M. Menke, "Improving R&D Decisions and Execution," *Research-Technology Management,* September/October 1994.

9. P. M. Swamidass, "Making Sense out of Manufacturing Innovations," *Design Management Journal*, Spring 1995.

10. "The Celling Out of America," *The Economist*, December 17, 1994.

11. M. J. Tyre, "Managing Innovation on the Factory Floor," *Technology Review*, October 1991.

12. L. U. Tatikonda and M. V. Tatikonda,"Tools for Cost-Effective Product Design and Development," *Production and Inventory Management Journal* 35, no. 2 (Second Quarter, 1994).

The authors express their sincere gratitude to the Steering Committee of the Thomas Walter Center for Technology Management, which is the headquarters for the NCTB. The Steering Committee members, Provost Paul Parks, Vice President Michael Moriarty, Dean of Engineering William Walker, and Dean of Business Wayne Alderman, all of Auburn University, provided the climate and guidance essential to the success of the various projects undertaken by the Center, including the Curriculum Development Program for the Schools of Business and Engineering. The publication of this book completes the last phase of the program, that is, the dissemination of the cases for use by interested faculty in the United States and abroad.

Thomas Walter Center for Technology Management   **M. Dayne Aldridge**
Auburn University, Auburn, AL 36849–5358   **Paul M. Swamidass**
Phone: 334–844–4333, Fax: 334–844–1678

CONTENTS

Introduction   1

Cross-Functional Management of Technology, *M. Dayne Aldridge* and *Paul M. Swamidass*   1

1   History and Overview   11

Reading 1–1   Managing Invention and Innovation, *Edward B. Roberts*   12
Reading 1–2   Common Misconceptions in Implementing Quick Response Manufacturing, *Rajan Suri*   31

2   Product Development and Team-Based Management   45

Reading 2–1   Competing through Development Capability in a Manufacturing-Based Organization, *Steven C. Wheelwright* and *Kim B. Clark*   46
Reading 2–2   The Neglect of Engineering Design, *John R. Dixon* and *Michael R. Duffey*   64
Reading 2–3   Teams Need Open Leaders, *Michael Maccoby*   74
Reading 2–4   Implementing Technological Change with Cross-Functional Teams, *Robert A. Lutz*   77
Case 2–1   Westinghouse Electronic Systems: Integrated Product Development   83
Case 2–2   Westinghouse Electronic Systems: T/R Modules   101

3   Technology in Organizations: Technology Transfer and Procurement   117

Reading 3–1   The Intelligent Enterprise: A New Paradigm, *James Brian Quinn*   118

Case 3–1 Oak Ridge Associated Universities   132
Case 3–2 Oak Ridge National Laboratory and Fluid Technology
Inc.   140
Case 3–3 Temic Telefunken: A Partner, Not a Vendor (A)   153
Case 3–4 Black & Decker's New Coffeemaker—Procuring the
Electronic Module (A)   160
Case 3–5 Temic Telefunken (B)   166
Case 3–6 Black & Decker's New Coffeemaker—Procuring the
Electronic Module (B)   168

4   Research & Development and Commercializations of Technology   172

Reading 4–1   Improving R&D Decisions and Execution, *Michael M.
Menke*   173
Case 4–1 Mountaineer: The 21st Century Incubator Project   183
Case 4–2 Brooktrout Technology, Inc.: The Commercialization
Process   209

5   Innovations in Manufacturing   219

Reading 5–1   Making Sense out of Manufacturing Innovations, *Paul M.
Swamidass*   220
Reading 5–2   The Celling Out of America *The Economist*   226
Reading 5–3   Managing Innovation on the Factory Floor, *Marcie J.
Tyre*   228
Case 5–1 Duriron Company, Inc., Cookeville Valve Division (A)   233
Case 5–2 Duriron Company, Inc., Cookeville Valve Division (B)   244
Case 5–3 Duriron Company, Inc., Cookeville Valve Division (C)   246
Case 5–4 Duriron Company, Inc., Cookeville Valve Division (D)   256

6   Costing and Technology   260

Reading 6–1   Tools for Cost-Effective Product Design and Development,
Lakshmi U. Tatikonda and *Mohan V. Tatikonda*   261
Case 6–1 Evaluation of Outsourcing Options at Stratus
Computer, Inc.   269
Technical Note: Accounting Measures of Manufacturing Costs   276
Case 6–2 American Saw and Manufacturing: Company Calculating
Cost Per Cut   281
Technical Note: Optimizing Cost per Cut   288

7   Customized Case   296

Case 7–1 The Living Case   297

8   *Appendix:* Engineering/Business Partnerships: An Agenda for Action   304

Cross-Functional Management of Technology

M. Dayne Aldridge
Paul M. Swamidass
Auburn University

The designer sat at his drafting board;
A wealth of knowledge in his head was stored,
Like, "What can be done on a radial drill,
Or a turret lathe or a vertical mill?"
But above all things, a knack he had
Of driving gentle machinists mad.

So he mused as he thoughtfully scratched his bean,
"Just how can I make this thing hard to machine?"
If he made this body perfectly straight,
The job had ought to come out first rate.
But 'twould be so easy to turn and bore
That it would never make a machinist sore.

So he'll put a compound taper there
And a couple of angles to make 'em swear,
And brass would work for these little gears,
But it's too damned easy to work, he fears,
So just to make the machinist squeal
He'll make him mill it from tungsten steel.

He'll put those holes that hold the cap
Down underneath where they can't be tapped;
Now if they can make this, it'll be just luck,
'Cause it can't be planed and can't be ground,
So he feels his design is unusually sound,
And he shouted in glee, "Success at last!
This damned thing can't even be cast."

Kenneth Lane*
General Electric

---

*Poem quoted by J. P. Haher, "A Case Study in the Relationship between Design Engineering and Product Engineering," *Proceedings of the 5th Annual Meeting of the Industrial Engineering Institute,* UCLA, 1953.

1

One can trace three major mileposts in the evolution of management during the last 100 years. First, during the second half of the last century, Fredrick Winslow Taylor originated a principle of management, dubbed Taylorism, which is founded on managers' acquiring scientific knowledge concerning the structure and content of work in order to direct workers to perform optimally through incentives and punishments. Several decades later, in the 20s, Elton Mayo, through his experiments at the Hawthorne, Illinois, factory of Western Electric, found what is known as the Hawthorne effect, which is the increase of worker productivity when personal attention is given to workers. Mayo observed that upon receiving personal attention, group members develop a sense of participation. Mayo's work is considered to have given rise to the human relations approach to management, whose influence prevails to this day. The last milepost is the present-day emergence of team-based management, particularly the rise of cross-functional teams to deal effectively with the new competitive environment of shorter-product life cycles, time-based competition, intensified global competition, and the fast-changing nature of product and process technologies.

Notably, the first two significant mileposts in management arose from a motivation to increase the productivity of individual workers. In contrast, the rise of cross-functional teams is motivated by a multitude of goals in which the goal to increase the productivity of direct workers assumes a lesser role. Firms move into cross-functional team-based management to compete effectively in product markets where product life cycles are very short, where product and process technologies become obsolete soon, and where extremely low cost and near-perfect quality are mandated by the market.

Some view the last milepost as an unparalleled paradigm shift in management. In this environment, the individual worker's productivity is no longer the central focus. Here, timeliness of getting the products to market, near-perfect quality, and lowest possible total cost (life-cycle cost) are all equally important. In this environment, the effectiveness of management, technical personnel, and other white collar employees is presumed to enhance the productivity of individual workers. Any organization that deals with products or processes involving technologies that are intensive and dynamic cannot do well in today's competitive environment without the use of cross-functional teams. This text presents several cases and readings on the circumstances that need cross-functional teams and on the effective use of these teams.

What Is Management of Technology?

Management of technology (MOT) became a topic of intense discussion during the 1980s in response to the perceived decline of international competitiveness of U.S. industries. The National Research Council (NRC) report "Management of Technology: The Hidden Competitive Advantage" probably did more than any other publication to focus and accelerate this discussion. The NRC report described MOT as "an industrial activity and an emerging field of education and research." The report provided what has become the most widely quoted definition of MOT: "Management of technology links engineering, science, and management disciplines to plan, develop, and implement *technological* capabilities to shape and accomplish the strategic and operational objectives of an organization."

Someone has said that people can understand the terms *management of employees, management of finances,* and so on, but they do not understand the term *management of technology.* The following definition, when taken together with other definitions, may help readers grasp the meaning of MOT.

> Narrowly, technology is any means of accomplishing a task; shoveling dirt is a technology. By incorporating engineering and technology management, we restrict our domain to technologies embodied in products or processes that require some engineering/scientific knowhow to comprehend. . . . MOT principally addresses three levels of analyses: who carries out technical exploration, how it is carried out, and what its impact is on the organization and its environment. (Anderson, 1993, p. 17)

MOT definition is difficult because it draws from several disciplines. "As a cross-disciplinary field, the scholarly literature on management of technology (MOT) has been 'borrowed' from related scientific fields of study such as sociology, economics, psychology, mathematics, political science, statistics, management science, systems theory, and anthropology" (Badawy and Badawy, 1993, p. 1). Some readers may add engineering, sciences, operations management, and information systems to the list of disciplines contributing to MOT. Our understanding of MOT may be enhanced if we consider how MOT is practiced; this is addressed in the following paragraphs.

How Is MOT Practiced?

A study of chief technology officers (CTOs) and their responsibilities offers an insight into what is involved in managing technology. Adler and Ferdows (1990, pp. 58–59) found that CTOs engaged in:

1. Coordination among business units' technological efforts. This included (*a*) avoiding duplication of effort in different business units, (*b*) assisting the transfer of technology from one unit to the other, (*c*) commercializing technology, (*d*) ensuring synergy between product and process technologies, and (*e*) coordinating between the business units and corporate research, across business units, and across functional areas.
2. Providing a voice for technology in the top management team. This involved (*a*) pushing for a long-term view of technology, (*b*) nurturing infant technology projects, and (*c*) providing expertise on technological questions and issues.

3. Supervision of new technology development.

4. The assessment of technological aspects of major strategic initiatives such as (*a*) new acquisitions, (*b*) joint ventures, (*c*) strategic alliances, and (*d*) long-term trends in technology.

5. The management of the external technology environment. This is a varied task including (*a*) dealings with universities and research organizations, (*b*) relations with regulatory organizations, (*c*) providing guidelines for funded research, (*d*) collecting signals about important technical developments outside the firm, (*e*) ensuring that products and processes complied with relevant regulations, (*f*) identifying regulatory trends and regulatory constraints, and (*g*) influencing the regulatory process.

Adler and Ferdows found that the management of technology within a firm may be associated with a mixture of diverse functions such as R&D, engineering, manufacturing process technology, information systems, and operations support.

Emerging Challenges in the Management of Technology

The management of technology in the 1990s in high-tech industries is faced with new and more demanding challenges. For example:

1. The inverse relationship between technological capability and price in some industries (e.g., the digital products industry). This fact is revolutionary and contradicts an established principle of commerce true in most other industries. Since the invention of transistor chips and micro chips, product capability or power goes up but product price comes down. "The cost of raw technology is plummeting toward zero" (Gross, Coy, and Port, 1995).

2. Product life cycles are very short and difficult to pace. Long-term plans (5 to 10 years) are becoming less and less meaningful in some fast-moving industries.

3. Start-up marketing costs in some products can be very high. For example, first-generation products are given away to lure long-term customers (e.g., the computer program Simply Money—1 million free copies were shipped by Computer Associates International Inc. as a tactic to enter the market).

4. Changing technology can disrupt successful product strategies. Unsuccessful product strategies in the wake of changing technology were evident in such firms as IBM, DEC, and Wang, to mention a few.

5. Product pricing is difficult when, according to a Japanese executive, "quality is perfect and nothing breaks."

When quality and price among competitors' products are comparable, competition on the basis of time emerges to the forefront. The ensuing time-based competition is enhanced by a number of things, including product and process technologies, and cross-functional management of technology.

Time-Based Competition and Technology Management

In the last 10 years or so, as time-based competition has become more prevalent, a major concern for business is the need to cut lead time continuously. One aspect of time-based competition is the reduction in the time it takes to bring a new product to market. In some industries, such as the electronics and computer-related industries, "a new product that is brought to a rapidly changing market on time but 50% over budget cuts profits only by 4% over the first five years. Yet, coming out six months late but within the development budget it will earn 33% less profit" (Gerwin and Guild, 1994, p. 679). Thus, there is a heavy price to pay for any time-to-market delay. A number of efforts are under way in organizations to cut the time-to-market cycle. Process reengineering is one popular tool to make gains in reducing lead time.

Reducing the lead time has significant impact on the management of technology. Particularly, it requires good cross-functional working within the firm. The effect of continuously reducing lead time can be felt in the following areas of MOT:

1. New product introduction.
2. R&D management.
3. New process technology implementation.
4. Product–process interaction.
5. Cross-functional teamwork and other forms of organizational adaptations.
6. The technology commercialization process.

The impact of lead-time reduction on selected areas in this list is elaborated below. In the following discussions, some of the issues relevant to managers and engineers are highlighted.

New Product Introduction

With shrinking product life cycles (PLC) and time-based competition, the importance of new product introduction cannot be overstated. New product introduction involves numerous "problem solving cycles" (Clark and Fujimoto, 1989) that involve "design-build-test" cycles until the successful product is ready for a launch. Lead-time reduction amounts to cycle-time reduction, elimination of cycles, and the overlapping of downstream and upstream cycles. For lead-time reductions in new product introductions, Gerwin and Guild (1994) recommend the following overlapping roles:

1. Manufacturing should assume a greater upstream role.
2. Design must assume a greater downstream role.
3. Manufacturing is to assume new downstream roles.
4. Design is to assume new upstream roles.

Design and development cycles require the cooperative and timely work among people from various *functions* within and outside a firm covering marketing, design, engineering, purchasing, manufacturing, planning, costing, finance, and so on. These different functions that must work together within a firm can be broadly classified as engineering oriented or as business/management oriented. Successful lead-time reduction in new product introduction can occur when people from the different functions with different orientations work smoothly and swiftly. Organizations are using cross-functional teams for that purpose.

Engineering problems frequently delay new product introductions. According to Clark and Fujimoto (1989), in companies that are very successful in lowering new product introduction lead time, the following conditions are found: (1) an organizational capability for quick engineering problem solving through overlapping linkages, (2) a strong supplier base for engineering and quality components, and (3) an innovation strategy for steady incremental changes in technology. Successful lead-time reduction in engineering problem solving occurs when:

1. Upstream and downstream relationships are made to overlap. Increased overlapping of activities and minimized sequential processing of engineering and business activities are associated with rapid new product development.
2. Tooling hardware production time is reduced.
3. Engineering changes are processed directly between engineering personnel in an informal and speedy manner without bureaucratic obstacles during the development phase before production.

Organizational Adaptation in Managing Technology

Cyert and Kumar (1994) note that more attention must be paid to the problems of organizational adaptation as part of the emerging problems associated with MOT. Within manufacturing firms there are at least three situations for organizational adaptation for superior management of technology in certain competitive environments. A demanding competitive scenario, which creates conditions ripe for organizational adaptations, consists of most, if not all, of the following: (1) product life cycles are short (about 18 months), (2) new products are introduced frequently, (3) production ramp up is very rapid, (4) there is rarely any steady state in the manufacturing cycle (ramp up and then ramp down), and (5) the quality and price of the product are at world-class levels. Many electronics and computer-related manufacturers, who are faced with these competitive environments, find that the need to adapt is critical to survival.

The first situation for adaptation concerns design engineers working in the competitive environment just described. Designers have to adapt from a culture where they have been handed detailed requirements without consultation and they were accustomed to throwing designs "over the wall" to the manufacturing function. Then, a compliant manufacturing function had the attitude that it could produce designs that were unnecessarily difficult to manufacture and that it was obligated to do so. In the newly emerging competitive environment, designers are required to adapt to a new culture: designers are expected to participate in product definition, and manufacturing engineers from the shop floor routinely impose design changes (even trivial changes) upon designers for the sake of manufacturability. Thus, prelaunch quality and manufacturability demands can justify design changes, and designers and product managers must oblige. This calls for a serious adaptation by design engineers to an organizational culture that focuses on product success in a rapidly changing competitive environment.

A second situation for adaptation concerns marketing and top management. On the matter of product launch dates, marketing or top management usually have the ultimate say. But in the competitive environment described above, where good design and manufacturability are essential for success, the time needed to attain very high prelaunch manufacturing throughput (or yield) levels (higher than 95 percent) can justify the delay of launch dates for new products. This adaptation is needed because, in our environment of short life cycles, there is no time for correcting quality problems once the product is launched.

Ultimately, the results of these adaptations can be very favorable for manufacturers. In short, product launches can be successful without quality-related problems. Further, the superior manufacturability of products, ensured during the prelaunch period, keeps costs very competitive in a market where prices normally fall every quarter (e.g., computer-related products).

The third situation for adaptation concerns the rearrangement of responsibilities between traditional functions and strong product development teams. While functional organization may not become obsolete, it needs to adapt to strong product teams by sharing or relinquishing some of its traditional responsibilities. Although functional management may still retain the responsibility to hire and train employees, strong cross-functional teams will assume more and more responsibilities for work assignment and performance evaluation in the competitive scenario described. The need for this form of adaptation is growing with the increased use of strong, cross-functional product teams in manufacturing firms today.

MOT Involves the Merging of Different Perspectives

The emergence of management of technology as a topic for research and instruction during the 1980s may be viewed as a natural response to a recognized need to solve some problems through the merging or integration of the approaches of specialists from diverse fields with highly differentiated perspectives.

The reductionistic approach of the scientific method yielded dramatic improvements in the quality and efficiencies of products and processes during the past two centuries. By dividing problems into small pieces, control and predictability have been achieved in ways not previously possible. But we are now learning that the reduction of problems into smaller and smaller pieces carries penalties—loss of the ability to control the recombination of the pieces into a coherent solution. Thus, we must constantly search for the best balance between the control and predictability of reduction, on the one hand, and the creativity and chaos of integration to respond quickly to customer needs, on the other. The individuals and organizations that learn how to find the best balance are the winners in the world of competition. This is the basis for new management strategies such as total quality management, time-based competition, and the use of cross-functional teams.

On the one hand, the practice of engineering is strongly based on a scientific, reductionistic approach to problem solving. This approach dominates the education curricula for engineers in the United States. Although a major proportion of engineers become managers, their value is perceived as rigorous, reductionistic problem solvers. It should be no surprise that designers and engineers tend to have difficulty learning to be integrators and have difficulty working across the boundaries of traditional disciplines.

On the other hand, the practice of management and business is based on knowledge that is more holistic and integrative; there is much room for experimental learning. Intrinsically, business and management involve more art and less science; business and management practices may differ from manager to manager without being "wrong." But rapid technological changes can make a manager's experiential knowledge and education obsolete. This poses a challenge to those educating undergraduate and graduate students in business.

These differing bases for the educational programs have yielded graduates from the colleges of engineering and business who are generally unprepared for employers who expect a balance between reductionistic and integrative approaches to solving real-world problems. MOT requires the merging of the two different perspectives for a balanced view of the world and yields a body of knowledge that is of value to engineers and managers. The cases and readings in this text are meant to be part of this body of knowledge common to those with engineering as well as business perspectives.

The Organization of the Book

This book is organized in seven chapters. Chapter 1 includes an article that provides a useful perspective on the history of technology management. In

Chapter 2, four articles address product development and team-based management, and the two cases on Westinghouse introduce several additional related topics.

Chapter 3 includes an article, by James Quinn, which addresses the role of technology in contemporary businesses. The five cases in this chapter address technology acquisition in an international context and technology transfer issues. Chapter 4 discusses R&D management and the commercialization of technology. Chapter 5 focuses on manufacturing innovations. Chapter 6 deals with issues of costing in manufacturing operations. Chapter 7 presents an approach to the use of field-based cases in the classroom that can be updated each time it is used in the class. In the Appendix, we present a copy of the report that resulted from the First National Conference and Case Workshop on Business and Engineering Education, Auburn University, April 1994.

References

1. P. Adler and K. Ferdows, "Chief Technology Officer," *California Management Review,* Spring 1990, pp. 55–62.
2. P. Anderson, "Toward Exemplary Research in the Management of Technology—An Introductory Essay," *Journal of Engineering and Technology Management* 10, 1993, pp. 7–22.
3. M. K. Badawy and A. M. Badawy, "Directions for Scholarly Research in Management of Technology—Editorial Commentary" *Journal of Engineering and Technology Management* 10, 1993, pp. 1–5.
4. K. B. Clark and T. Fujimoto, "Lead Time in Automobile Product Development Explaining the Japanese Advantage" *Journal of Engineering and Technology Management* 6, 1989, pp. 25–58.
5. R. N. Cyert and P. Kumar, "Technology Management and the Future" *IEEE Transactions in Engineering Management* 41, no. 4 (November 1994), pp. 333–34.
6. D. Gerwin and P. Guild, "Redefining the New Product Introduction Process" *International Journal of Technology Management* 9, nos. 5, 6, 7, 1994.
7. N. Gross, P. Coy, and O. Port, "The Technology Paradox," *Business Week,* March 6, 1995, pp. 76–84.
8. National Research Council, *Management of Technology: The Hidden Competitive Advantage* (Washington, D.C.: National Academy Press, 1987).

1   HISTORY AND OVERVIEW

READING 1–1
MANAGING INVENTION AND INNOVATION

Edward B. Roberts
Massachusetts Institute of Technology

When the Industrial Research Institute was founded in 1938, industrial research in the United States had experienced 20 years of dramatic growth, despite the shock of the Depression, and was poised on the brink of World War II expansion that gave it the form and scope we see today. MIT historian Howard Bartlett reported that from 1921 to 1938 the number of U.S. companies with research staffs of more than 50 persons grew from 15 to 120 [1].

Despite continued rapid increases in industrial R&D involvement and resource commitment over the following 25 years, in 1962, when we founded the MIT Sloan School of Management's Research Program on the Management of Science and Technology, we encountered an academic tradition that for the most part had paid little attention to the organization and management of large-scale technology-based programs. Indeed it was for the purpose of bringing academic research-based insights to bear on such technological enterprises that James Webb, the visionary administrator of the National Aeronautics and Space Administration, urged us with exhortation and funds to begin our research program.

Prior to our start, academics had concentrated largely on two themes: historical romanticism about the lives and activities of great "creative inventors," like Edison and Bell, and psychological research into the "creativity process." While those writings made interesting reading, in my judgment neither track contributed much usable knowledge for managers of technical organizations. Indeed with such rare exceptions as Jewkes et al. [2], the few university researchers who were focusing at that early time upon issues of R&D management were not paying much attention to organizational variables or to innovation as a multistage, multiperson, complex process. Perhaps not surprisingly, industry in the early 1960s appeared rather unenthusiastic about social science attempts to probe the underpinnings of effective research, development, and technology-based innovation. In contrast, I sense broad acceptance in the 1980s

Source: Reprinted with permission from *Research Technology Management* 31, no. 1 (January/February 1988).

of the results of many academic studies of RD&E, with the Industrial Research Institute especially noteworthy in its efforts to advance collaboration in the field of management of technological innovation.

Invention and Innovation

Roundtable discussions at the 1970 annual IRI spring meeting provide a useful starting point for this review—a set of definitions of the invention and innovation process:

> Innovation is composed of two parts: (1) the generation of an idea or invention, and (2) the conversion of that invention into a business or other useful application.... Using the generally accepted (broad) definition of innovation—all of the stages from the technical invention to final commercialization—the technical contribution does not have a dominant position. [3]

This leads me to a simple definition of my own, but nonetheless one that I feel is critical to emphasize:

> Innovation = Invention + Exploitation

The invention process covers all efforts aimed at creating new ideas and getting them to work. The exploitation process includes all stages of commercial development, application, and transfer, including the focusing of ideas or inventions toward specific objectives, evaluating those objectives, downstream transfer of research and/or development results, and the eventual broad-based utilization, dissemination, and diffusion of the technology-based outcomes.

The overall management of technological innovation thus includes the organization and direction of human and capital resources toward effectively: (1) creating new knowledge; (2) generating technical ideas aimed at new and enhanced products, manufacturing processes, and services; (3) developing those ideas into working prototypes; and (4) transferring them into manufacturing, distribution, and use.

Technologically innovative outcomes come in many forms: incremental or radical in degree; modifications of existing entities or entirely new entities; embodied in products, processes or services; oriented toward consumer, industrial, or governmental use; based on various single or multiple technologies. Whereas invention is marked by discovery or a state of new existence, usually at the lab or bench, innovation is marked by first use, in manufacturing or in a market.

Most organized scientific and engineering activity, certainly within the corporation, is beyond the idea-generating stage and produces not radical breakthroughs but rather a broad base of incremental technological advance, sometimes leading cumulatively over time to major technical change. Academic research in the area of technology management has focused primarily on incremental product innovations oriented toward industrial markets. (Interestingly, academic marketing research has focused primarily on incremental product innovations aimed at consumer markets.) Neither the less frequently arising areas of radical innovation nor process innovation has received much systematic attention from academia, unfortunately.

One of my favorite visual aids is Figure 1, portraying a process view of how technological innovation occurs, and emphasizing two key generalizations. First, technological innovation is a multistage process, with significant variations in the primary task as well as in the managerial issues and effective management practice occurring among these stages. Figure 1 presents six stages, but the precise number and their division are somewhat arbitrary. What is key is that each phase of activity is dominated by the search for answers to different managerial questions.

At the outset, for example, emphasis is on finding a motivating idea, a notion of possible direction for technical endeavor. Coming up with one or more technical and/or market goals that stimulate initiating a research, development, and/or engineering (RD&E) project is the task undertaken during Stage 1. The relevant managerial question for this stage is, How do more and better targets get generated? Which people, which structures, which strategies can be employed toward more effective idea generation for these objectives? Good managerial practice at this stage frequently involves loose control, "letting many flowers bloom," pursuing parallel and diverse approaches, fostering conflict or at least contentiousness, stimulating a variety of inputs. Critical at this early stage is ready access to small amounts of R&D financing, free of heavy and discouraging evaluative procedures. A major mistake is to set up stringent formal processes for approval of the small sums needed to try out an idea. Distributing small "pots of gold" for first- or second-level R&D supervisors to dispense at their discretion, akin to Texas Instruments' heralded "$25,000 money," makes good sense.

Later, the Stage 5 commercial development for example, the task involves in-depth specification and manufacturing engineering of ideas that have by now already been reduced to an acceptable working prototype. The managerial issues in this stage involve coordinating a number of engineers of different disciplinary backgrounds toward achieving, within previously estimated development budget and schedule, a predefined technical output ready for manufacture in large volume, reliably, and at competitive production costs. Effective managerial practice in this stage might well involve tight control, elimination of duplication, strong financial criteria for resource use accompanied by formal evaluation, single-minded even somewhat rigid adherence to plan, especially in regard to those resources—in many ways the opposite of what is encountered in Stage 1!

The next generalization embodied in Figure 1 is that innovation occurs through technical efforts carried out primarily within an internal organizational context, but involving heavy interaction with the external technological as well as market environment. Proactive search for technical and market inputs, as well as receptivity to information sensed from external sources, are critical aspects of technology-based innovation. All studies of effective innovations have shown significant contributions of external technology and have found success heavily dependent upon awareness of customer needs and competitor activity. Indeed one of the most important trends in industrial innovation activity during the 1980s is the continuing increase in the use of external sources of technology as critical supplements to internal R&D efforts.

The details of Figure 1 specify a set of key flows and decision points that occur during the process of innovating. A number of major managerial elements that are embodied in those details will be treated in the remainder of this article. Two aspects of the diagram, however, are potentially misleading and deserve immediate mention. First, for ease of presentation all stages are shown at equidistant intervals, inappropriately suggesting perhaps the similarity of these phases from a time duration

FIGURE 1

The process of technological innovation can take as long as 20–30 years, according to some studies, but for most industrial product innovations the duration from initial idea to market is more likely to be three to eight years

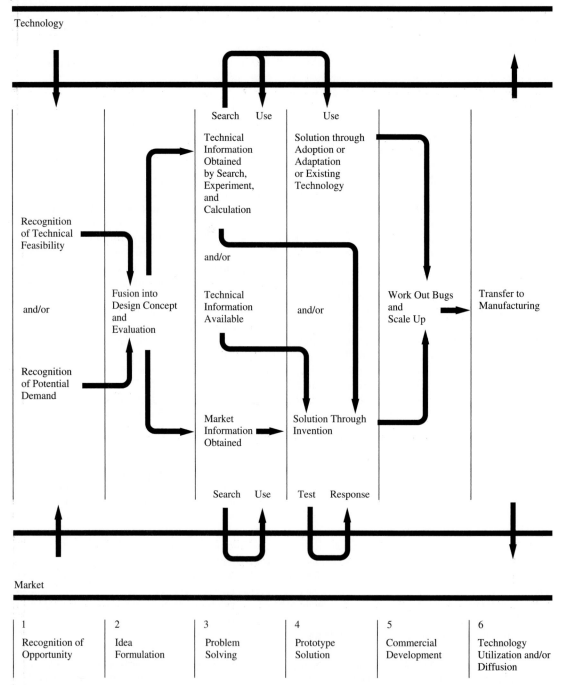

Source: *Reprinted with permission from E. B. Roberts and A. L. Frohman, "Strategies for Improving Research Utilization,"* Technology Review 80, no. 5 (March/April 1978).

and/or resource consumption perspective. This is by no means true. In particular, while each technical field is characterized by quite different schedule and resource requirements, Stage 5, commercial development, usually takes as long as the several earlier stages combined and requires more resources than most of the other stages together. That is the reason for tight financial standards being properly applied immediately prior to a project's entry to this stage.

Second, for simplicity's sake no feedbacks are pictured in Figure 1 from later stages back to earlier ones. Yet, inevitably, these feedbacks exist and cause reiteration to occur among the stages. For example, involvement in the problem-solving process, Stage 3, generates new insights as to alternative idea formulations, Stage 2; and efforts at transfer into manufacturing as part of technology utilization, Stage 6, often create new requirements for problem-solving, Stage 3. Indeed a recent article by Kline [4] argues that the multiple feedback loops are the essence of the innovation process. Thus the real process of technical innovation involves flows back and forth over time among differing primary activities, internal and external to the dominant innovating organization, with major variations arising throughout the process in regard to specific tasks, managerial issues, and managerial answers.

Beyond my descriptive perspective on how innovation occurs is Peter Drucker's [5] prescriptive advocacy as to how it ought to happen: "Systematic innovation . . . consists in the purposeful and organized search for changes, and in the systematic analysis of the opportunities such changes might offer for economic or social innovation." Drucker identifies seven sources for innovative opportunity, listed in Table 1. Most challenging to those of us committed to the development and use of new

---

TABLE 1   Seven Sources for Innovative Opportunity

The unexpected
The incongruity
Process need
Changes in industry or market structure
Demographics
Changes in perception, mood, and meaning
New knowledge, both scientific and nonscientific

Source: P. F. Drucker, *Innovation and Entrepreneurship: Practice and Principles.* New York: Harper & Row, 1985.

science and technology is Drucker's assertion that "contrary to almost universal belief, new knowledge—and especially new scientific knowledge—is not the most reliable or most predictable source of successful innovations." As with most Drucker "truths," this one is intuitively attractive, as well as unverified in any systematic manner. Whether or not new science is a critical "source" of successful innovations no doubt depends on how you define both *science* as well as *source*. But there is no doubt that advances in science and technology are instrumental to the development and implementation of almost all successful product and process innovations. It is the rare case that a success stems from merely a re-packaging of previously existing science and technology.

Rather than focusing at this point on the claimed sources from which innovations arise, the remainder of this article concentrates on three dimensions—staffing, structure, and strategy—each subject to managerial influence and/or control. (I will discuss innovation sources much more in the section on structure.) . . . Taken together, improved management of these dimensions contributes critically to achieving successful institutionalized innovation. Throughout the article I shall be seeking to blend the findings from academic research on the management of invention and innovation with the experiences and observations of successful industrial and government technology managers.

Staffing Considerations

Two primary issues arise in regard to staffing the technological organization: what kinds of people need to be involved for effective technical development, and what managerial actions can be taken to maximize their overall productivity. In regard to people requirements, as explained by Roberts and Fusfeld [6], a number of "critical behavioral roles," not just technical skills, must be practiced by the people involved in a technical development. By combining the management of technological innovation literature with our own consulting experiences, we identified five key roles for achieving successful innovation, which we have been able to use to enhance RD&E organizational performance. Following us, others have since added to this list, generating as many as 12 key roles needing separate monitoring and support.

Critical Innovation Roles. First are *idea generators,* the creative contributors of new insights that both initiate projects and contribute to problem solutions throughout technical projects [7,8]. Ideas can be drawn from the "market pull" of sensing real or potential customer needs or demands, or from the "technological push" of envisioning the possible extension of technological performance of a material, component, or system. Ideas include not just those which lead to project initiation, but also the many throughout an innovation-seeking endeavor which contribute importantly toward invention or innovation outcomes. Thus idea generators for technical projects may be scientists or engineers, sales or marketing persons, or even managers! The rare but valuable idea generators are those who come up with multiple ground-breaking ideas over their careers, such as S. D. Stookey at Corning Glass Works who among other successes came up with key ideas for photosensitive glass and Pyroceram [9]. Individual differences that are either innate or developed over long periods no doubt account for many of the distinctive characteristics of effective idea generators. But many sources of heightened idea creativity arise from managerial influences, for example, from the internal organizational climate or environment and especially from supervisory practices. These are discussed in greater detail in my later section on individual and organizational productivity.

There are, however, significant differences between "idea-havers" and "idea-exploiters"—those who come up with ideas and those who do something with the ideas they have generated [10,11]. This holds true whether the ideas are born in universities, government labs, or in industry. The generally low rate of energetic pursuit of newly created RD&E ideas mandates the requirement for the second key role in technical innovation-seeking activities, that of the *entrepreneur* or *product champion*. Entrepreneurs advocate and push for change and innovation; they take ideas, whether their own or others', and attempt to get them supported and adopted. Most major studies of factors affecting product success have found the active presence of a product champion to be a necessary condition for project success [12]. For example, in recent years the late Ken Estridge gained widespread repute as the product champion behind IBM's successful development and launch of its personal computer. Lew Lehr rose to the presidency of 3M as an eventual outgrowth of his own championing of 3M's health products business [13]. And despite not being a family member of the closely-held Pilkington Glass company, Alistair Pilkington became "process champion" for the revolutionary float-glass process

which dramatically changed the company and the industry and again, not incidentally, led this "champion" into the chairmanship of the firm.

As I reported in my first *Research Management* article, the entrepreneurial "role" is the same, whether carried out internally in existing organizations or "externally" in their own newly founded companies [14]. But the mode of behavior and what is needed for "internal" versus "external" entrepreneurial success may well be different, as expanded by Maidique [15]. My own studies of "internal entrepreneurs" found that they needed to be sensitive to company politics and the latest corporate "buzzwords" in order to gain internal support, and as indicated below required a high-level "sponsor" to lead them through the corporate jungle. Lehr [13] argues that strong entrepreneurial efforts are needed even within companies that have long traditions of fostering entrepreneurship, in order to overcome inevitable managerial resistance.

A third required role in effective innovative activities is the *program manager or leader*, sometimes strangely called the "business innovator," supplying the support functions of planning, scheduling, monitoring and control, technical work supervision, business and financial coordination relating to the R&D project [16,17]. This is the one "role" which is also usually an assigned job in the organization, the other roles being incidental to an individual's specific work assignment.

Gatekeepers, or special communicators, are the fourth critical role identified, the link-pins who frequently bring information messages from sources outside of a project group into that group [18]. These human bridges join technical, market, and manufacturing sources of information to the potential technical users of that information. Gatekeepers may bridge one technical group to another within the same company, or may link university research activities to a corporate advanced technology center, or may tie customer concerns into a supplier's design team.

Tom Allen's pioneering empirical studies of the functioning of the technical gatekeeper have been extended by many other academics and broadly accepted and applied throughout industry and government. For example, a study of so-called bridge scientists at Stanford Research Institute found that such individuals are rare but easily identified [19]. Effective "bridgers" were found to be interpersonally able (e.g., good listeners), have depth in at least one discipline, have a wide range of interests, and be oriented toward problem solving. As

I have argued repeatedly [6], a vital extension of the concept is the recognition that some gatekeepers can "bridge" to market or manufacturing inputs, rather than just technical information, often bringing in raw or processed information, or points of view, that are otherwise lacking within the R&D organization itself.

The final key role is that of the *sponsor* or *coach,* performed usually by a more senior person who is neither carrying out the R&D itself nor is directly and personally aggressively championing the change. The role is one of providing encouragement, psychic support, facilitation to the more junior people involved in the task implementation, often including important help in "bootlegging" the resources needed by those trying to move technological advances forward in an organization [14]. My research data affirmed the logical—the higher up in an organization a sponsor was located, the higher the probability of success of internal efforts to generate new product lines. Sponsors are often needed for idea generators, project managers, and especially for entrepreneurs. A good example of the effectiveness of the "ultimate sponsor," the corporate chief executive officer, is Chapman's sponsorship of Gorman's work on "available light motion pictures" at Eastman Kodak [20]. But CEOs as project sponsors can be organizationally dangerous too! Who is to turn off the CEO's pet project when it runs amok?

These several critical roles are all needed within or in close contact with each internal working group in order for it to achieve successfully the goals of an innovative outcome. But in addition, the effective development and maintenance of a technical organization requires recognition of these differentiated roles in order to create and implement appropriate people management processes, including recruiting, job assignment, personnel development and training, performance measurement, and rewards.

Individual and Organizational Productivity. Beyond the people and role behaviors needed for effective staffing are the principal managerial acts that can affect staff creativity, inventiveness, and productivity. The 30 years of *Research Management* reveal plentiful discussions of approaches for stimulating creative idea-generating among scientists and engineers, including such techniques as brainstorming, Synectics, and morphological analysis. (See 21 and 22 for extensive reviews.) Despite the enthusiastic testimony in the various articles, I remain unconvinced that systematic evidence supports the use of these methods, which, frankly, I view as mainly gimmicks. As documented below, effective individual and group supervision, including proper maintenance of group diversity and task challenge, seem to me more likely to produce usable ideas.

Stages of a scientist's or engineer's career, and the composition of his/her immediate work group are primary influences upon technical productivity (or creativity or inventiveness, if you prefer). This generalization rests upon a broad foundation of research into the performance of technical people and project groups. Katz [23] has demonstratd that technical professionals evolve through three career stages, which he labels socialization, innovation, and stabilization. As with the different stages of a project cycle, each stage of an individual's career provides a new set of managerial challenges for maximizing personal productivity. The setting of work norms, providing task direction, and joining new employees into the internal technical communications network are managerial issues confronted during the socialization or job "break-in" stage. In contrast, maintaining the employee's earlier motivation and renewing technical skills are among the very different sort of questions needing treatment in the stabilization or job maturity phase.

But personal and group productivity are not just influenced by the individual's job cycle. The nature of the immediate work group, its composition and supervision, matter greatly. In general what Kuhn [24] called creative tensions, a mix between comfort-reinforcing stability and conflicting challenge, seems desirable. For example, multidimensional diversity among technical colleagues in a project team heightens technical performance [7]. Variations in age, technical background, even personal values, correlate with enhanced group productivity. This need for internal challenge is further reflected in the findings that the average years a group has worked together significantly impacts upon that group's technical productivity [25]. The long-term stable technical group apparently becomes too self-secure, diminishes its outside technical contacts, and decreases its performance. Supervisory intervention at the technical group or RD&E project level seems able to affect this performance, however. For example, technical skills of the first-level group leader, and not human relations skills, enhance a group's effectiveness [26]. And even the stable technical team can be moved to high-performing status with proper leadership, in this case requiring strong direction and control by the project manager [17]. Thamhain and Wilemon [27] support the importance of the project manager's technical expertise and reliance upon work challenge as major sources of effective technical performance.

Organization Structure

The design of organization structures that will enhance technological innovation requires focusing on both the organization's inputs and its outputs. Effective RD&E organizations need appropriate technical and market information inputs, and their outputs need to be integrated toward mission objectives and transferred downstream toward their ultimate users.

Market Inputs. Managerial research has repeatedly demonstrated that 60 to 80 percent of successful technical innovations seem to have been initiated by activities responsive to "market pull," that is, forces reflecting orientation to perceived need or demand [28–30]. Of particular note is the recent IRI study of basic research in industry [31], which among many other interesting conclusions produced the unsought finding that "most innovations come about as a result of the recognition of a market need or opportunity. While the push of new technology is also important, it plays a distinctly secondary role." These studies less frequently indicate how technical organizations uncover these needs. Sometimes one person's personal "hobby-horse" forces "market" consciousness to initiate and sustain a technical program, especially when coupled with that individual's entrepreneurial drive and skills, as in Peter Goldmark's successful pursuit of the long-playing record. As Goldmark exclaimed, "My initial interest in the long-playing record (LP) arose out of my sincere hatred of the phonograph . . . it seemed to violate what I thought the quality of music should be" [32].

In organizations less dominated by one key figure, "market gatekeepers" or customer liaison personnel frequently aid the technical organization to better understand its customers' requirements, priorities, or preferences. For example, Corning Glass supposedly discovered the need for optical waveguides as a result of one of its staff visiting the British Post Office. Organizing to gain meaningful market inputs for research and engineering use may depend upon explicit assignments of such responsibilities to cooperating marketing staff or to RD&E people themselves. The product development cycle should be organized, as suggested in Figure 1, to

bring market inputs into design repeatedly, during the early product specification stage and again during prototyping, through active involvement of selected customers. As a sharp contrast to desirable practice, in one consulting project for a major chemical company I found the sales organization prohibiting R&D people from visiting "their" customers, lest the R&D people agree with customer complaints!

A special prospective customer for innovations, often overlooked when R&D does occasionally seek market inputs, is the company's own manufacturing activity. Yet depending on the company and industry, the manufacturing organization turns out to be the eventual "customer" of anywhere from one- to two-thirds of the company's technological developments. Manufacturing, similar to an outside unrelated potential product customer, has to decide whether or not it wants to "buy" an internally developed improvement in materials, components, manufacturing equipment, or overall production process, for its own internal "consumption." That prospective in-house manufacturing "customer" deserves at least the same degree of involvement with the design and development process as does an outside firm or individual. If R&D's "market-oriented" ties to its own manufacturing group can be improved, the potential for significantly impacting company performance is high, especially given the recent IRI study results that show R&D aimed at process innovation as far more likely to succeed than that targeted toward new and improved products [33]. But I am convinced that overcoming the gap between the central lab and a major plant installation usually needs special efforts and sometimes creative organizational designs, in particular when important process changes are contemplated.

Rather than seeking collaboration to provide market information to the RD&E process, many companies have ill-advisedly substituted marketing-oriented control of RD&E. Organizational subordination of research and engineering to "product managers" (inevitably marketing or sales people) or tight budgetary control of RD&E by these units may force market-based criteria to dominate technical project selection. But this is usually accompanied by a short-term quick-fix orientation, erosion of technical capability, and gradual destruction of product/process competitiveness. Analyses by Souder [34] have demonstrated that strong and positive relations between R&D and marketing organizations significantly improve the track record on new product introductions. In my experience this is best achieved by welding partnerships among equals, rather than by extracting compliance from subordinates. Good examples of such R&D/marketing partnerships are evident in the team structures used by both Hewlett-Packard and 3M in their new product pursuits.

Market research techniques have long been used to help define consumer preferences in new product designs [35]. These methods have been less helpful for developing industrial goods. Recently von Hippel [36] has demonstrated that potential industrial customers whose needs place them at the leading edge of technological demands can be used to specify detailed desired performance characteristics and features for as yet nonexisting products. Military or space research requirements are frequent sources of such "leading edge" requirements. Fusfeld [37] has long used this insight in developing forecasts of the rate of market penetration of new technologies. The problem, however, is to distinguish a customer demand that is truly in the vanguard of future broader market needs from the "cry for help" from what amounts to the "lunatic fringe" that exists in almost every technical field. That fringe also has needs that are real and extraordinary, but unfortunately not representative of future growth opportunities.

Technical Inputs. Despite the presumed dominant role of "market pull" as a source of innovative projects, "technology push," that is, undertaking projects for advancing the technical state-of-the-art in an area without anticipation of the specific commercial benefits to be derived, is also the critical source of many significant product and process successes. The many studies cited earlier still show these technology-push successes to be in the minority, but unfortunately do not clearly indicate the relative worth of the two approaches. One confusion leading to arguments is to assert that if market pull is the key, then market research should be more effective than it has proven to be! Collier [38] for example quotes Barnes' listing of "Neoprene, nylon, polyethylene, silicones, penicillin, Teflon, transistors, xerography, and the Polaroid Land camera" as not resulting from "a market research study of what people *said* they wanted." While market research is not the only or even the primary indicator of market pull, many research directors especially sympathize with Collier's point of view. Guy Suits [39], long-time leader of General Electric's research efforts, cites Langmuir's work on hydrogen dissociation, leading to a new type of welding, as a good example of technology push. Indeed, Casey [40] goes

further, arguing that misleading market research was a contributor to the long period required for commercial development of high-fructose corn syrup. More logs are heaped on this fire when one cites the supposed market research studies (often claimed to have come from the same large consulting organization!) that demonstrated no meaningful market prospects for computers, instant photography, or the dry copier.

When technical advancement is the goal, managers have long understood that professional depth in an organization is achieved by grouping people together in their own area of specialization, with work assigned and performance supervised by a more accomplished person of the same specialization [41]. This approach is called functional or discipline-based or specialty-oriented organization. It is the traditional organization structure of the craft guild and of the university. Multiple specialists working together interact comfortably, using the same general knowledge base, analytic skills and tools, and vocabulary. When technical people are organized in functional arrays, their natural interplay brings depth of specialized capabilities to bear on technical problems. Indeed, Marquis and Straight found that technical groups organized in functional forms have the highest technical excellence [42].

But in any nontrivial technical field the vast majority of applicable technical knowhow exists outside of a performing technical organization. For technical effectiveness even a strong functional team needs to draw upon the preexisting technical knowledge that is in the outside world, whether in the technical literature, in already developed products and processes, or especially in the minds of other technical professionals. For example, as illustrated in Table 2, several studies point out that for innovations eventually developed within a firm, about 60 percent of the sources of the initial technical ideas had outside origins [28]. Allen [43] has demonstrated the relative differences among channels for technical information input to an organization, distinguishing what is readily accessed from what is used most effectively in coming up with high-rated problem solutions. His work, as well as that of others [44, 45], indicates the minor role played by the literature, especially in contributions to engineering and development, in contrast with personal contacts, experience, and training.

One factor that inadvertently has significant effect on technical inputs to RD&E groups is the architectural layout of their work space. Early observations by Jack Morton, then vice president of semiconductor research

TABLE 2   Sources of Ideas for Innovations Developed within the Firm

Author	Study	N	% from Outside the Firm
Langrish et al.	Queen's Awards	51	65
Mueller	Du Pont	25	56
Myers/Marquis	5 Industries	157	62
Utterback	Instruments	32	66

Source: From data contained in J. M. Utterback, "Innovation in Industry and the Diffusion of Technology," *Science* 183 (February 15, 1974).

at Bell Laboratories, led to his concern for the physical separation between technical organizations that were intended to relate to each other [46]. Research at MIT by Muller-Thym in the early 1960s empirically established spatial effects on the frequency of communication among engineers and scientists in the same laboratory. These concepts have been well developed by Allen [18] into careful findings on specific design elements of RD&E architecture. The distance between two potential communicators, vertical separation, walls, and other architectural features importantly influence technology flows.

Thusfar I have addressed what affects technical inputs in support of an organization's internal invention activities, the first element of the two-step innovation process I defined initially. What about technical inputs not aimed at invention but rather at innovation directly? Clearly, technological solutions (inventions) already exist elsewhere, and an innovating organization might merely adopt or adapt them by slight modification for a new purpose. This would permit skipping the first stage of invention and going directly to the exploitation stage. An early U.S. study determined that 22 percent of key successful innovations had been adopted or adapted [44] while comparable U.K. data indicated a 33 percent adoption rate [45]. Japanese data on license fee payments for foreign technology show a long-established pattern of heavy use of outside technology. A small study of Taiwanese innovations found adoptions to have accounted for the bulk of successes [47]. While specific percentages no doubt have changed in recent years, adoption or adaptation of prior outside inventions is a major source of innovation worldwide, but apparently still substantially underutilized by U.S. firms. In recent years the growth of research consortia, effective or not, and the rapidly growing number of "strategic alliances" between large corporations and new firms in areas of emerging technologies indicate that more looking to the outside for technology is taking place, even by U.S. companies. I will discuss this development further in the section on strategy.

One unique source of potential adoptions is the user. Von Hippel [48] has shown that users frequently create and implement innovations for their own use, followed later by manufacturer adoptions of those innovations for large-scale production and distribution. His research on scientific instruments and several areas of manufacturing equipment demonstrated that heavy percentages of new products had been user-developed.

Technical organizations need to be designed to facilitate accessing these several different sources of technical information inputs, whether as contributions toward internal inventions or as sources for adoption more directly as innovations. A variety of approaches are suggested, ranging from such simple considerations as ensuring that at least some salespeople have technical skills and/or incentives so that they bring back a customer's ideas in addition to his orders. Much more ambitious are the IBM marketing department's several "applied science centers" across the United States, established adjacent to concentrations of innovative users to learn about new software and hardware developments and transfer that technical information back into IBM's product development groups. IBM's Cambridge operation in Technology Square, working closely with MIT's pioneering Project MAC, thus became the source of IBM's first commercial computer time-sharing system, a field adaptation of an innovative user's development. As one approach to overcome biases against outside sources of technology, increasingly corporations are establishing the position of chief technical officer or vice president of technology, with broad responsibility for both internal technology development as well as external technology acquisition. Organizational experiments to enhance both technical and market information inputs are underway across a broad front.

Output-Focused Organization.   Just as the functional organization structure maximizes technical inputs, the project, program, mission, or product organization is intended to integrate all inputs toward well-defined outputs. By placing in the same group, under a single leader, all the contributors toward a given objective, the project organization maximizes coordination and control toward achieving output goals. The Marquis and Straight study [42] cited earlier supports these findings. But project structures have a fundamental flaw that seriously affects many technical organizations. The project form tends to remove technical people from organizational groups in which they interact with colleagues of their own scientific or engineering discipline. Furthermore, the project manager may be technically expert, but inevitably in only one of the disciplines of his or her subordinates, not all of them. If the project has long duration, especially when the technology base is rapidly changing, the technical skills of the project members erode over time due to lack of stimulating technical reinforcement and supervision.

This dilemma has led to the creation of an organization that is intended to be a "compromise"—the "matrix" structure in which technical performers are supposed to maintain active membership in two organizations, their original discipline-based functional group as well as the focused project group. In theory the "matrixed" person thus has two bosses, one functional and one project, each of whom will extract his appropriate "due," thereby attempting simultaneously to maintain the technical skills and performance of the individual, more or less, while orienting his loyalty and contributions toward the project's output goals, more or less! However, most technical "matrix" organizations are only "paper" matrices, not "real" matrices—they appear to be matrices on organization charts but do not strongly pull the engineer between two conflicting masters.

If one wanted to obtain truly matrixed individuals, the influences that push a technologist's time and attention toward competing sets of objectives (e.g., functional excellence versus project schedule demands) would have to be roughly balanced between those objectives. A technical contributor's priorities are influenced by: (*a*) who is responsible for his/her performance evaluation and reward distribution, (*b*) who makes the individual's specific task assignments, (*c*) where is the individual physically located relative to the two "competing" managers, (*d*) what is the longer-term career relevance of the competing groups, and (*e*) what is the relative persuasiveness (whether based on personality or power) of the two managers. Achieving even a rough balance among these influences would be practicable only by dominance of the functional manager on some of these dimensions, dominance of the manager on

others, and perhaps rough equivalence of the two managers on still other influences upon matrixed persons. The absence of reasonable balance in most "paper matrixed" cases leads the actual situation to its "default" condition, with the achieved results reflecting the characteristics of the dominant organization form, either functional or project but seldom both. Recent studies suggest that certain patterns of dominance among these contending influence sources achieve better performance of matrix organizations [25].

Output Transfers.   But in addition to generating outputs, the technical organization needs to be designed to enhance output transfer downstream toward eventual customers and users. Downstream is where innovation takes place and where benefits are realized! A consulting survey of prestigious major corporate research laboratories has indicated a high degree of dissatisfaction with the extent and effectiveness of transfer of results to potential recipient groups [49, 50]. Three different clusters of bridging approaches were found helpful in increasing transfer in those labs—procedural, human, and organizational. Most organizations used a variety of these approaches, often several simultaneously. My findings have been reaffirmed by recent comparative case studies by an internal task force at IBM [51] and by a consulting project at Union Carbide [52], among others.

Procedural methods include: joint planning of RD&E programs by the performing group and the organization that is expected to be the receiver, often resisted by R&D as an "invasion" of its turf; joint staffing of projects, especially pre- and posttransfer downstream; and joint project appraisal after project completion, done cautiously if at all after failures in order to avoid destructive fingerpointing.

Human bridges are the most effective transfer mechanisms, especially the upstream and downstream transfers of people. Movement of people upstream: (*a*) brings with them information on the context of intended project use, (*b*) establishes direct person-to-person contacts that will be helpful in later posttransfer troubleshooting, and (*c*) creates the image that the project eventually being transferred has involved prior ownership and priority inputs from the receiving unit. Later movement of people downstream: (*a*) carries expertise for posttransfer problem-solving, and (*b*) not unimportant, conveys the risk-reducing impression that the receiving unit will not be stuck with solving posttransfer problems by itself. Other human bridges that are widely used include rotation programs, market gatekeepers, joint problem-solving sessions, and other formal and informal meetings.

Organizational techniques for enhancing transfer are usually more complicated to design and implement than procedural or human bridge approaches. "Integrators," sometimes named transfer managers, or integrating departments are frequently appointed to tie together the sending and receiving organizations. This person or unit is given the responsibility for moving the project from the sender into operating condition in the receiver organization, either lacking authority in one or the other organization or being matrixed between both.

More ambitious organizational approaches include dedicated transfer teams, established solely for the period during which technical results are being transferred to their "customers," done especially for moving purchased process technology. Venture teams, discussed further below, are also employed to reduce functional organizational transfer issues, shifting leadership responsibility among the many-disciplined team members as the primary phase of the project shifts from research to engineering to manufacturing to sales.

Strategy

Strategic management of technology includes both strategic planning and strategic implementation aspects at either of two levels: (*a*) overall, for the entire technology-dependent firm, government agency, division or product line, or (*b*) more focused, for just the technology development/acquisition process/department/laboratory of the entire organization. As recently as 10 years ago neither of these levels of strategy was the subject of much serious scholarship, or even management consulting practice. Few researchers carefully studied the overall management of the technology-intensive company. And fewer still addressed the questions of how to incorporate technological considerations into overall business strategy.

Strategic planning focuses upon the formulation of an organization's goals and objectives, and upon developing the policies needed to achieve those objectives, including identification of the organization's primary resources and priorities. But developing corporate strategy with such a global perspective, including technological dimensions, is quite new. Indeed the evolution of corporate strategic planning as a field of practice is divisible more or less into three decades: the 1960s,

during which multiyear budget projects became the earliest forms of financial planning, sometimes mislabelled *long-range planning:* the 1970s, when market growth/share matrices and market attractiveness considerations added a new dimension to strategic analysis; and the 1980s, during which technology as a strategic factor became so widely acknowledged as to cause firms and even countries to realize that financial, marketing, and technological considerations needed to be integrated in overall strategy development [53].

Strategic Thinking and Planning. Horwitch and Prahalad [54] provided an early set of perspectives at the overall strategic level, differentiating the key issues of technology-oriented strategic management among three modes: the small, usually single-product, high-tech firm; the large, multimarket, multiproduct corporation; and the multiorganization, even multisector societal program. For each of these, Horwitch and Prahalad find a primarily nonoverlapping set of strategic issues and priorities. More recent writing has focused upon similarities between the first two "modes," the entrepreneurial smaller firm and the successfully innovative larger corporation [55–58; see also 14]. Maidique and Hayes conclude that to be innovative the large corporation needs to manage the "paradox" of chaos versus continuity, similar to the "creative tensions" required for the innovative technical person [7, 24].

In moving from strategic thinking toward strategic planning we need principals for developing more detailed technology strategies. But what are the underpinnings of technological change, especially as it relates to the corporation, upon which overall technology strategy should be based? Three general observations seem critical here, all linked to the dynamics of technological innovation processes: (1) there are characteristic patterns over the life cycle of a technology in how frequently product versus process innovations occur; (2) each stage of a technology has differing critical implications for innovation, including type, cost, degree of invention, and source; and (3) an organization's efforts to generate technological innovation create almost inevitable internal dynamics in the allocation of R&D efforts, generating multiple management problems. Each of these is discussed more fully below, with suggestions of related technology planning and strategy development approaches.

Utterback and Abernathy [59] demonstrated that a technology tends to evolve in three stages. Most technologies move from an early "fluid stage," dominated by frequent product innovations, through a "transition stage," characterized by significant process innovation and the emergence of a dominant product design, into a "specific stage," featuring lower rate of and more minor product and process innovations. While variations in this pattern of course occur, some of which are already well understood [60, 61], this generalization becomes one important basis for developing a company's or a product line's technology strategy.

One of the most significant findings from this research has been the reaffirmed role of the smaller firm as the dominant source of innovation during the earliest emerging stage of a technology, with the locus of innovation shifting toward larger companies in the transitional and more mature stages of a technology [59]. Most studies that have sought to find differences in R&D productivity as a function of company size have not made this critical distinction as to the stage of technology or type of innovation. Consequently, the findings of these economic analyses have varied unconvincingly all over the lot, from some that have asserted the large company is most productive of innovations to others that have claimed the exact opposite, to still other studies that have found nonlinear ties between size and R&D results.

The potential stability or predictability in patterns of technology evolution is the rationale for attempting to use technological forecasting techniques as part of technology planning and strategy development. Most technology forecasting methods are simple, often inadequate for the task [62, 63]. Indeed, despite recent "rediscovery" by some consultants of technology S-curves for forecasting and planning [64], the intellectual development of the technology forecasting field more or less stopped over a decade ago [65, 66]. Yet some corporations have benefited enormously from thoughtful application of technology forecasting methods to their strategic analyses. Tracy O'Rourke, the chief executive officer of Allen-Bradley, for example, cites a comprehensive technology forecast as the basis for planning his company's successful transition from electromechanical to solid state electronic devices [67].

Each stage of a technology is associated with different strategic implications. The earliest stage in a technology's life cycle tends to feature frequent major product innovations, heavily contributed by small entrepreneurial organizations, often closely tied to lead user needs. The development of frozen orange juice concentrate by the National Research Corporation and its spinoff companies is one such example [68]. The present rash of biotechnology discoveries is coming primarily from university laboratories directly or from young small enterprises, leading irresistibly to the explosion of biotech alliances between large companies and the new start-ups. The same alliance pattern has evolved in the areas of machine vision and artificial intelligence.

The intermediate stage of a technology's life cycle may include major process innovation, with continuing but lessened product variation occurring, with increasing numbers of competitors, both large and small. To achieve the dominant product–process design during this stage, large corporations sometimes undertake long-term development programs that combine many elements of applied research and engineering. For example, General Motors's successful efforts in developing its two-cycle diesel engine included more than 10 major developments needed for the final system [69].

The late stage of a technology features less-frequent minor product and process innovations, contributed primarily by large corporations, motivated mostly by cost reduction and quality improvement operational objectives. As illustrated by Hollander's [70] careful analysis of Du Pont rayon innovations, shown in Table 3, these numerous minor innovations can produce dramatic cumulative impact upon costs. In fact the so-called learning curve (i.e. decreasing unit manufacturing cost as cumulative production increases) results primarily not from the volume itself but rather from the usual continuing allocation of engineering efforts to incremental cost reduction projects as a product line's volume increases. Management of the technical investment is the primary source of the so-called learning curve competitive advantage, not the share of market.

These key dimensions of a technology described above should strongly influence choices made by a firm or government agency in developing its technological strategy. A company's detailing of its "product innovation charter" [71], or its application of project selection principles or techniques [72] as part of technology planning, ought to reflect at least general consideration of the current stages of its principal technologies. In particular, the late stage of one technology usually corresponds to earlier stages of other potentially threatening technologies. Most corporations fail to anticipate or even appropriately respond to these technological threats [64, 73].

TABLE 3   **Cost-Reducing Innovation in Du Pont Rayon Plants**

Plant	Contribution of Minor *Technical Change* to % of Net Reduction in Unit Costs Due to *Technical Change*
Spruance II-A	83
Spruance I	80
Old Hickory	79
Spruance III	46
Spruance I	100

Source: From data in S. Hollander, *The Sources of Increased Efficiency* (Cambridge: MIT Press, 1965).

Technology life cycles occur in an industry as a whole, thus providing an "environmental" set of influences upon a single organization's strategy. A different kind of cycle, however, is produced within a firm by its own attempts to develop and commercially exploit technology. As a major project moves downstream through a multistage research-design-development-production engineering-field trouble shooting technical organization, decisions on acquisition and allocation of technical resources can cause major instability in overall performance, including in the rate and character of new product releases and resulting sales and profits [74, 75]. For many small firms the resulting "boom then bust" often spells disaster. Similar though less-evident problems arise at the product line level of large corporations and government agencies. Self-induced cycles of primarily discovery followed then by primarily exploitation seem to have plagued the growth years of Polaroid Corporation, for example, contributing to its financial crises of the late 1970s.

Large-scale and realistic computer simulation models have been developed and increasingly employed in recent years for helping to cope with this aspect of technology and overall organizational strategy development [65, 74–76]. While these computer modeling methods are primarily strategic support tools, the technological forecasting and project selection techniques that were mentioned principally enhance tactical and operational aspects of technology planning and management. Other approaches to technology planning have been developed and successfully applied at both the tactical and strategic levels. For example, Crawford [71] has conceptualized a "product innovation charter" that contains five major areas for inclusion in a formal strategy statement, with each of the five subdivided into finer categories. Crawford argues for taking into account explicitly the company's target business arenas, objectives of product innovation, specific program of activities, the degree of innovation sought, and any special conditions or restrictions on the strategy.

Another most impressive technique for technology planning is "competitive product profiling," in which an organization's product line is compared to its key competitors in terms of seven technology-based measures: functional performance, acquisition cost, ease of use, operating cost, reliability, serviceability, and system compatibility [77]. IBM adds "availability" to this list of competitive measures, making "reliability, availability, serviceability" (RAS) a critical element of its internal technology planning. Extending this approach to analysis of competitive manufacturing processes has been attempted, but with less success due to relative lack of competitor data. Fusfeld [77] has tried to overcome this limitation and bring technology planning to the level of assessment of overall organizational capability. He uses in his analytical framework the "technology planning unit," the level of generic technology in the organization as it is being applied to a particular market opportunity, and tries to evaluate relative technical strength. Further developments of technology planning approaches, especially at the strategic level, are needed and can be expected during the coming decade [78].

Strategic Implementation. But beyond strategic planning must come strategic implementation. Tactics and operations are the means of implementation of strategy. Not much has yet been written about specific implementations of technology strategies. At the national level, Johnson [79] has concluded that, relative to American firms, Japanese industry has more heavily invested in applied rather than basic research, adopting and improving on preexisting products and technologies, in already well-developed market areas. He cites government policies in regard to patents, subsidies, and tax incentives as important in both countries. In his recent survey studies while at MIT, Hirota [80] has developed strong empirical evidence on U.S.–Japanese technology strategy differences, supporting but going beyond Johnson's observations. However, recent Japanese pioneering efforts in such areas as compact-disk technology and more advanced semiconductor memories suggest that Japanese R&D strategy may be in transition toward what has been a dominant U.S. approach [81].

Although now also of increasing interest to nontechnical industries, the so-called venture approaches have been a unique means for implementing overall strategies seeking accelerated technology-based new business development for growth and/or diversification. These venture approaches involve larger organizations in attempts to emulate or couple with smaller entrepreneurial units. The spectrum of possible strategic and organizational alternatives includes venture capital investments in young "emerging technology" companies, sponsored spin-offs of new product development-commercialization groups, "new-style joint ventures" that feature alliances between large and small companies, internal ventures, and integrated venture strategies [82]. Collaborative undertakings among U.S. firms are growing dramatically, involving new linkages with universities and especially new investment/development/commercialization ties with young high-technology companies [83, 84].

A subject of active study and industrial practice off and on since the early 1960s, venture approaches have recently become increasingly attempted by companies and even countries as part of their strategies for intensifying their technological industrial base. Venture strategies require long-term persistence for effective implementation and dramatic differences in management style and policies from traditional mainstream approaches. These demands for "managerial innovation" are seldom adequately met, producing high failure rate among corporate venturers [85, 86]. Yet the occasional dramatic success, such as Texas Instruments' entry into the semiconductor business [87] or IBM's Personal Computer venture or 3M's "Post-Its," offer sufficient upside attraction to keep companies making new venture attempts.

The variety of venture alternatives for entering new businesses has raised issues as to means for selecting among them. Roberts and Berry [88] have devised a research-based matrix reflecting primarily the organization's "familiarity" with the market and technology aspects of the new business. The Roberts/Berry framework, supported by a field test in a large diversified U.S. firm, concludes essentially that the further the new area is from the firm's base "familiar" business, the less

resource-intense the venture approach to be taken. An unpublished Japanese analysis of corporate venture success and failure and a host of studies performed by members of my mid-career MIT Management of Technology Program have strengthened the data support for "familiarity" as a powerful determinant of business development. Further reaffirming this emphasis upon "familiarity" as a key variable for eliciting strategic direction are the recent findings by Meyer and Roberts [89] that the more successful small high-technology companies pursue product development strategies that are focused upon moderate degrees of technological and market change. Much more research is needed to test the applicability of these results in other industries and with larger companies.

With the exception of its brief mention above in regard to U.S. and Japanese R&D investments, the role of government policies and actions in affecting technology strategy has been ignored thusfar. Yet government regulatory activities in regard especially to health and safety have had significant positive and negative influences on technological innovation [90–92]. But, as pointed out by Abernathy and Chakravarthy [93], government's strategic role has also included actions to create technologies directly (via the Horwitch/Prahalad Mode III, for example, 54) as well as indirectly through market modifications [94]. In a sense the variety of alternatives facing governments for influencing technological change are equivalent to the corporate venture alternatives described previously.

In Conclusion

Recent work by Gobeli and Rudelius [95] provides a fitting basis for finishing this article. In their integrative comparative analysis of five firms in the technology-intensive cardiac-pacemaker industry they observe the differing competitive impacts that have come from the multiple stages of the innovation process. Managing at the creativity phase is not enough, nor even is managing manufactured quality sufficient, nor is managing that is focused primarily upon any other single aspect of innovation. They reaffirm the importance of key innovation-supporting people roles. Gobeli/Rudelius describe the importance of market–technology linkages, effective program management, government intervention, and appropriate goal setting, planning, and risk taking for firms in this medical electronics industry.

Technological innovation can provide the potential for altering the competitive status of firms and nations. It can contribute to increased corporate sales and profits, as well as individual and national security and well-being. But its purposeful management is complex, involving the effective integration of people, organizational processes, and plans. Only recently have some companies undertaken bold and broad action steps to try to institutionalize an effective product and process innovation program. Two firms in particular, long known for effective innovation, have publicized ambitious multifaceted endeavors. 3M has based its attempts heavily upon a so-called intrapreneurship approach, while Corning Glass has developed a more broadly based effort, including redesigning organization structures, changing incentive programs, and undertaking widespread management involvement and educational change activities. In both cases leadership for these multiyear institutional change programs came from the CEO's office. Other companies would be wise to consider whether top-down companywide commitments to accelerate and enhance effective innovation might not also apply to them.

This article has argued a host of generalizations about managing the process of invention and technological innovation, each supported by literature, empirical research, and practitioner experience. Some of these generalizations have already been widely diffused into practice, such as recognition of the gatekeeper's impor-

tance to information flow and nearly everyone's efforts to stimulate internal entrepreneurship. Some of my other contentions may still be subject to debate, modification, and even rejection as we learn more.

Both academics and technology managers need to join in this continuing search for clearer managerial insights about technological invention and innovation and more effective organizational performance. The National Research Council's recent report, *Management of Technology: The Hidden Competitive Advantage,* summed up the goals: "Effective work in the field of management of technology can play a crucial role in devising the strategies and imparting the skills and attitudes to U.S. engineers and managers that they will need in the future technology-dominated economy" [96]. It listed eight challenges of critical importance to industrial competitiveness: how to integrate technology into the overall strategic objectives of the firm; how to get into and out of technologies faster and more efficiently; how to assess/evaluate technology more effectively; how best to accomplish technology transfer; how to reduce new product development time; how to manage large, complex, and interdisciplinary or interorganizational projects/systems; how to manage the organization's internal use of technology; how to leverage the effectiveness of technical professionals. Hopefully, more light will be shed on these key industrial needs prior to the IRI's Diamond Jubilee!

Summing Up

- Technological innovation is a multistage process, with major differences needed for effective management of each stage of activity.

- To achieve effective innovation, an organization requires that "critical role-players" collaborate in a formal or informal team relationship. These critical roles include the idea generator, the entrepreneur, the program manager, several types of gatekeepers, and the sponsor.

- Group diversity is a major influence upon technical performance. A group that stabilizes its membership for too long not only decreases its productivity but tends to become insular and to evidence "Not Invented Here" behavior.

- Highest product development success rates are produced when marketing and R&D organizations work in close collaboration.

- "Market pull" far more frequently leads to successful innovations than does "technology push," although both sources of initiating projects account for success and failure alike.

- Users not only furnish critical "market needs" input data to designers, but in some industries supply the actual innovations that manufacturers later adapt, improve, and commercialize.

- Downstream transfer of RD&E results can be improved through use of multiple procedural, human, and organizational "bridges." Human bridges are the most effective transfer mechanism, and people movements, rotations, and face-to-face meetings should be used routinely and frequently.

- Most technologies move through evolutionary stages: an early one dominated by frequent product innovations, a transition characterized by increased process innovation and the emergence of a dominant product design, and a mature stage featuring much lower rate and more minor degree of both product and process innovation. A firm's innovation strategy and technological resource allocations should differ markedly depending upon the stage of its primary technology.

- "Competitive product profiling" is a useful method for initiating technical planning in a company, comparing the key technical performance characteristics of a product line with competitors' related products.

- Recent growth of venture capital and alliance methods reflects increasing recognition of the need to link external technologies with internal capabilities.

- Top management commitment is essential to assure success of broad-based programs aimed at institutionalizing the development of effective product and process innovations.

References

1. H. R. Bartlett, *The Development of Industrial Research in the United States* (Washington, D.C.: National Research Council, 1941).

2. J. Jewkes, D. Sawers, and R. Stillerman, *The Sources of Innovation* (London: Macmillan, 1958).

3. "Top Research Managers Speak Out on Innovation," *Research Management,* November 1970.

4. S. J. Kline, "Innovation Is Not a Linear Process," *Research Management,* 1985.

5. P. F. Drucker, *Innovation and Entrepreneurship: Practice and Principles* (New York: Harper & Row, 1985), pp. 35–36.

6. E. B. Roberts and A. R. Fusfeld, "Staffing the Innovative Technology-Based Organization," *Sloan Management Review* 22, no. 3 (Spring 1981).

7. D. Pelz and F. M. Andrews, *Scientists in Organizations,* rev. ed. (Ann Arbor, MI: University of Michigan Press, 1976).

8. F. M. Andrews, "Innovation in R&D Organizations: Some Relevant Concepts and Empirical Results," in E. B. Roberts et al., eds., *Biomedical Innovation* (Cambridge: MIT Press, 1981).

9. S. D. Stookey, "History of the Development of Pyroceram," *Research Management,* Autumn 1958.

10. D. Peters and E. B. Roberts, "Unutilized Ideas in University Laboratories," *Academy of Management Journal* 12, no. 2 (June 1969).

11. E. B. Roberts and D. Peters, "Commercial Innovation from University Faculty," *Research Policy* 10, no. 2 (April 1981).

12. A. H. Rubenstein, A. K. Chakrabarti, R. D. O'Keefe, W. E. Souder, and H. C. Young, "Factors Influencing Innovation Success at the Project Level," *Research Management,* May 1976.

13. L. W. Lehr, "Stimulating Technological Innovation: The Role of Top Management," *Research Management,* November 1979.

14. E. B. Roberts, "Entrepreneurship and Technology: A Basic Study of Innovators," *Research Management* 11, no. 4 (July 1968).

15. M. A. Maidique, "Entrepreneurs, Champions, and Technological Innovation," *Sloan Management Review* 21, no. 2 (Winter 1980).

16. D. G. Marquis and I. M. Rubin, "Management Factors in Project Performance," MIT Sloan School of Management Working Paper, 1966.

17. R. Katz and T. J. Allen, "Project Performance and the Locus of Influence in the R&D Matrix," *Academy of Management Journal* 26 (1985).

18. T. J. Allen, *Managing the Flow of Technology* (Cambridge: MIT Press, 1977).

19. J. Gartner and C. S. Naiman, "Overcoming the Barriers to Technology Transfer," *Research Management,* March 1976.

20. L. J. Thomas, "Available Light Movies—An Individual Inventor Made It Happen," *Research Management,* November 1980.

21. W. E. Souder and R. W. Ziegler, "A Review of Creativity and Problem-Solving Techniques," *Research Management,* July 1977.

22. H. Geschka, "Introduction and Use of Idea-Generating Methods," *Research Management,* May 1978.

23. R. Katz, "Managing Careers: The Influence of Job and Group Longevities," in R. Katz, ed., *Career Issues in Human Resource Management* (Englewood Cliffs, NJ: Prentice Hall, 1982).

24. T. S. Kuhn, *The Structure of Scientific Revolutions* (Chicago: University of Chicago Press, 1963).

25. R. Katz and T. J. Allen, "Investigating the Not Invented Here (NIH) Syndrome: A Look at the Performance, Tenure, and Communication Patterns of 50 R&D Project Groups," *R&D Management* 12, no. 1 (1982).

26. G. F. Farris, "The Technical Supervisor: Beyond the Peter Principle," *Technology Review,* 1973.

27. H. J. Thamhain and D. L. Wilemon, "Leadership, Conflict, and Program Management Effectiveness," *Sloan Management Review* 19, no. 1 (Fall 1977).

28. J. M. Utterback, "Innovation and the Diffusion of Technology," *Science* 183, no. 4125 (February 15, 1974).

29. A. Gerstenfeld, "A Study of Successful Projects, Unsuccessful Projects, and Projects in Process in West Germany," *IEEE Transactions on Engineering Management* EM-23, no. 3 (1976).

30. R. Rothwell, C. Freeman, A. Horsley, V. T. P. Jervis, A. B. Robertson, and J. Townsend, "SAPPHO Updated-Project SAPPHO Phase II," *Research Policy* 3 (1974).

31. W. C. Fernelius and W. H. Waldo, "Role of Basic Research in Industrial Innovation," *Research Management,* July 1980.

32. P. C. Goldmark, "How the LP Record Was Developed—Or the Case of the Missing Fuzz," *Research Management,* July 1974.

33. N. R. Baker, S. G. Green, and A. S. Bean, "The Need for Strategic Balance in R&D Project Portfolios," *Research Management,* March–April 1986.

34. W. E. Souder, "Effectiveness of Product Development Methods," *Industrial Marketing Management* 7 (1978).

35. G. L. Urban and J. R. Hauser, *Design and Marketing of New Products* (Englewood Cliffs, NJ: Prentice Hall, 1980).

36. E. A. von Hippel, "Lead Users: A Source of Novel Product Concepts," *Management Science,* July 1986.

37. A. R. Fusfeld, "How Not to Fall on Your Face in Technological Forecasting," *Inside R&D* 7, no. 2 (January 1978).

38. D. W. Collier, "More Effective Research for Large Corporations," *Research Management* 12, no. 3 (May 1969).

39. C. G. Suits, "Selectivity and Timing in Research," *Research Management* 5, no. 6 (1962).

40. J. P. Casey, "High Fructose Corn Syrup—A Case History of Innovation," *Research Management,* September 1976.

41. P. R. Lawrence and J. W. Lorsch, *Organization and Environments* (Boston: Harvard Business School, 1967).

42. D. G. Marquis and D. L. Straight, "Organizational Factors in Project Performance," MIT Sloan

School of Management Working Paper #133-65, 1965.

43. T. J. Allen, "Performance of Information Channels in the Transfer of Technology," *Industrial Management Review* 8, no. 1 (Fall 1966).

44. S. Myers and D. G. Marquis, *Successful Industrial Innovation* (Washington, D.C.: National Science Foundation, 1969).

45. J. Langrish, M. Gibbons, W. G. Evans, and F. R. Jevons, *Wealth from Knowledge* (London: Macmillan, 1972).

46. J. A. Morton, *Organizing for Innovation* (New York: McGraw-Hill, 1971).

47. A. Gerstenfeld and L. H. Wortzel, "Strategies for Innovation in Developing Countries," *Sloan Management Review* 19, no. 1 (1977).

48. E. A. von Hippel, "Has a Customer Already Developed Your Next Product?" *Sloan Management Review* 18, no. 2 (Winter 1977).

49. E. B. Roberts, "Stimulating Technological Innovation: Organizational Approaches," *Research Management* 22, no. 6 (November 1979).

50. E. B. Roberts and A. Frohman, "Strategies for Improving Research Utilization," *Technology Review* 80, no. 5 (March/April 1978).

51. H. Cohen, S. Keller, and D. Streeter, "The Transfer of Technology from Research to Development," *Research Management,* May 1979.

52. J. J. Smith, J. E. McKeon, K. L. Hoy, R. L. Boysen, L. Shechter, and E. B. Roberts, "Lessons from 10 Case Studies in Innovation," *Research Management* 27, no. 5 (September–October 1984).

53. E. B. Roberts, "Strategic Management of Technology," in *Global Technological Change: Symposium Proceedings* (Cambridge: MIT Industrial Liaison Program, June 1983).

54. M. Horwitch and C. K. Prahalad, "Managing Technological Innovation—Three Ideal Modes," *Sloan Management Review* 17, no. 2 (Winter 1976).

55. J. B. Quinn, "Technological Innovation, Entrepreneurship, and Strategy," *Sloan Management Review* 20, no. 3 (Spring 1979).

56. T. J. Peters and R. H. Waterman, *In Search of Excellence* (New York: Harper & Row, 1982).

57. M. A. Maidique and R. H. Hayes, "The Art of High-Technology Management," *Sloan Management Review* 25, no. 2 (Winter 1984).

58. J. Friar and M. Horwitch, "The Emergence of Technology Strategy: A New Dimension of Strategic Management," *Technology in Society* 7, nos. 2 and 3 (Winter 1985/1986).

59. J. M. Utterback and W. J. Abernathy, "A Dynamic Model of Product and Process Innovation," *Omega* 3, no. 6 (1975).

60. J. M. Utterback, "Systems of Innovation: Macro/Micro," in W. N. Smith and C. F. Larson, eds., *Innovation and U.S. Research* (Washington, D.C.: American Chemical Society, 1980).

61. J. M. Utterback and L. Kim, "Invasion of a Stable Business by Radical Innovation," in P. R. Kleindorfer, ed., *The Management of Productivity and Technology in Manufacturing* (New York: Plenum Press, 1986).

62. E. B. Roberts, "Exploratory and Normative Technological Forecasting: A Critical Appraisal," *Technological Forecasting* 1, no. 2 (Fall 1969).

63. A. R. Fusfeld and F. C. Spital, "Technology Forecasting and Planning in the Corporate Environment: Survey and Comment," in B. V. Dean and J. L. Goldhar, eds., *Management of Research and Innovation,* TIMS Studies in the Management Sciences, vol. 15 (North-Holland, 1980).

64. R. N. Foster, *Innovation: The Attacker's Advantage* (New York: Summit Books, 1986).

65. E. B. Roberts, *The Dynamics of Research and Development* (New York: Harper & Row, 1964).

66. J. P. Matino, *Technological Forecasting for Decision Making* (New York: Elsevier, 1972).

67. T. O'Rourke, Presentation at Pugh-Roberts Associates, Inc., Workshop on Critical Issues in Technology Management, April 15, 1986.

68. D. H. Peters, "The Development of Frozen Orange Juice Concentrate," *Research Management* 11, no. 1 (January 1968).

69. R. A. Richardson, "Research toward Specific Goals: Development of the Light-Weight, Two-Cycle Diesel," *Research Management,* Summer 1958.

70. S. Hollander, *The Sources of Increased Efficiency* (Cambridge: MIT Press, 1965).

71. C. M. Crawford, "Defining the Charter for Product Innovation," *Sloan Management Review* 22, no. 1 (Fall 1980).

72. M. R. Baker and W. H. Pound, "Project Selection: Where We Stand," *IEEE Transactions on Engineering Management* EM-11, no. 4 (December 1964).

73. A. C. Cooper and D. Schendel, "Strategic Responses to Technological Threats," *Business Horizons* 19, no. 1 (February 1976).

74. E. B. Roberts, "Research and Development System Dynamics," in E. B. Roberts, ed., *Managerial Applications of System Dynamics* (Cambridge: MIT Press, 1978).

75. H. B. Weil, T. A. Bergan, and E. B. Roberts, "The Dynamics of R&D Strategy," in E. B. Roberts, ed., *Managerial Applications of System Dynamics* (Cambridge: MIT Press, 1978).

76. K. G. Cooper, "Naval Ship Production: A Claim Settled and a Framework Built," *Interfaces* 10, no. 6 (December 1980).

77. A. R. Fusfeld, "How to Put Technology into Corporate Planning," *Technology Review* 80 (May 1978).

78. M. E. Porter, *Competitive Advantage: Creating and Sustaining Superior Performance* (New York: Free Press, 1985).

79. S. B. Johnson, "Comparing R&D Strategies of Japanese and U.S. Firms," *Sloan Management Review* 25, no. 3 (Spring 1984).

80. T. Hirota, "Environment and Technology Strategy of Japanese Companies," MIT Sloan School of Management Working Paper #1671-85, June 1985.

81. M. A. Cusumano, "Diversity and Innovation in Japanese Technology Management," in R. S. Rosenbloom, ed., *Research on Technological Innovation, Management, and Policy* (Greenwich, CT: JAI Press, 1986).

82. E. B. Roberts, "New Ventures for Corporate Growth," *Harvard Business Review* 59, no. 4 (July–August 1980).

83. D. Dimanescu and J. W. Botkin, *The New Alliances: America's R&D Consortia* (Cambridge: Ballinger Publishing, 1986).

84. "Strategic Alliances: New Competitive Muscle," *Business Week,* October 6–7, 1986.

85. E. B. Roberts and A. Frohman, "Internal Entrepreneurship: Strategy for Growth," *Business Quarterly* 37, no. 1 (Spring 1972).

86. N. Fast, "A Visit to the New Venture Graveyard," *Research Management,* March 1979.

87. P. E. Haggerty, "Strategy, Tactics, and Research," *Research Management* 9, no. 3 (1966).

88. E. B. Roberts and C. A. Berry, "Entering New Businesses: Selecting Strategies for Success," *Sloan Management Review* 26, no. 3 (Spring 1985).

89. M. H. Meyer and E. B. Roberts, "New Product Strategy in Small Technology-Based Firms: A Pilot Study," *Management Science* 32, no. 7 (July 1986).

90. W. M. Capron, ed., *Technological Change in Regulated Industries* (Washington, D.C.: The Brookings Institution, 1971).

91. T. J. Allen, J. M. Utterback, M. S. Sirbu, N. A. Ashford, and J. H. Hollomon, "Government Influence on the Process of Innovation in Europe and Japan," *Research Policy* 7, no. 2 (April 1978).

92. O. Hauptman and E. B. Roberts, "FDA Regulation of Product Risk and its Impact upon Young Biomedical Firms," *Journal of Product Innovation Management* 4, no. 2 (June 1987).

93. W. J. Abernathy and B. S. Chakravarthy "Government Intervention and Innovation in Industry: A Policy Framework," *Sloan Management Review* 20, no. 3 (Spring 1979).

94. J. M. Utterback and A. E. Murray, "The Influence of Defense Procurement and Sponsorship of Research and Development on the Development of the Civilian Electronics Industry," MIT Center for Policy Analysis Working Paper CPA-77-2, June 1977.

95. D. H. Gobeli and W. Rudelius, "Management Innovation: Lessons from the Cardiac-Pacing Industry," *Sloan Management Review* 26, no. 4 (Summer 1985).

96. National Research Council, *Management of Technology: The Hidden Competitive Advantage* (Washington, D.C.: National Academy Press, 1987).

READING 1–2
COMMON MISCONCEPTIONS IN IMPLEMENTING QUICK RESPONSE MANUFACTURING

Rajan Suri

Many managers believe their companies need to improve efficiency to deliver products to customers quickly. They believe machines and people must be kept busy all the time to get products out sooner. But with these beliefs, they may find their lead times getting longer, not shorter. Some have heard that Quick Response Manufacturing (QRM) techniques will improve production times and speed to market, but are not sure what the term means. This paper will define QRM and correct some of the misconceptions that surround it.

During the 1980s, manufacturing firms realized they had to focus on quality improvements to achieve world-class status in their industry. Today, management in most manufacturing firms understands the strategic importance of quality improvement. But speed has again become a key element of competitiveness, in addition to quality; firms that do not recognize this risk falling behind.

Using speed to gain advantage is also known as time-based competition, delivering products or services faster than one's competitors.[1] "Time is becoming the main battlefield—and weapon—of competition."[2] But more is involved. Simply looking for ways to speed up existing procedures can yield benefits. One company found that efforts to reduce throughput time were closely linked to other improvements.[3] "Everything we wanted to do to improve operations had something to do with squeezing time out of our processes. The deeper we probed, the more opportunity we saw."

While time-based competitive strategies can be applied to any business, this paper will focus on its application in manufacturing. This specific time-based strategy is called Quick Response Manufacturing (QRM). For manufacturing firms, competing with speed primarily means reducing lead times: the time to bring new products to market and the time to manufacture an existing product from its raw materials. Efforts to reduce these times can result in significant competitive advantage.

Implementing QRM techniques can bring substantial reductions in lead time—75 percent in new product introduction time and 90 percent in time to fill orders for existing products. When they are successful, lead time reduction programs result in quality improvements and cost reductions as well.[4] QRM techniques can help create an enterprise that simultaneously achieves low cost, high quality, and rapid delivery.

However, implementing QRM is not easy. Competing on speed has received plenty of publicity, and several articles and books have been written on the subject, but our experience with several firms shows that much remains to be learned about how to achieve successful implementation of QRM in a manufacturing enterprise.

This paper will discuss the main issues related to implementing QRM and dispel some misconceptions about speed in manufacturing. First, before discussing these issues, we will explain the benefits of QRM techniques for manufacturing firms.

Benefits of QRM

Reductions in lead time, both for new product introduction and for delivery of existing products, can bring significant benefits. Some are obvious; others are less well-known but equally important.

Benefits of Quick Response in Innovation. If a firm's lead time to bring new products to market is shorter than that of its competition, it can beat the competition to market and gain a substantial market share while the competition catches up (Figure 1). It may even be able to charge high prices when there is no competing product. Both of these can result in excellent profits.

Source: Reprinted with permission from *The Journal of Applied Manufacturing Systems,* Spring 1995. A version of this paper is published in the Autofact '94 Conference Proceedings, published by the Society of Manufacturing Engineers.

Rajan Suri is Professor of Industrial Engineering at the University of Wisconsin–Madison and Director of the Center for Quick Response Manufacturing. He received his bachelor's degree from Cambridge University (England) and his M.S. and Ph.D. from Harvard University. His interests include modeling and decision support for manufacturing systems, specializing in time-based competitiveness. He was the Editor in Chief of SME's *Journal of Manufacturing Systems* from 1989 to 1994.

FIGURE 1

Beating the Competition to Market

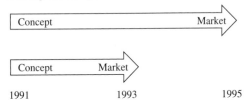

1991   1993   1995

FIGURE 2

Reaching the Market at the Same Time, but with Newer Technology

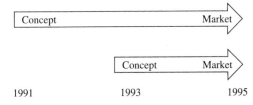

1991   1993   1995

However, a different benefit is less frequently appreciated. A firm with a shorter time to market may reach the market at the same time as its competitor with similar product; yet its product will contain newer technology.

Consider the example in Figure 2. There are two firms, on with a four-year time to market and the other with a two-year time to market. Both firms wish to introduce a new product in 1995, aimed at a similar market niche. However, the second firm is able to start development two years later than the first. Most design and manufacturing decisions are made in the first 5 percent to 20 percent of the total lead time. As a result, while the first firm is locked into 1991 technology, the second firm will use 1993 technology.

As examples of the advantages to the product, the second firm's product designs could incorporate microprocessor and control technologies that were not developed in 1991, as well as plastics and other new materials that were not available then. It could also plan its production based on new injection molding or other processes that were not known in 1991. These and other decisions will result in a product that will be received by consumers as more up-to-date and having greater functionality than the first firm's product. The product is also likely to be of superior quality and lower cost. The likely result is a successful product offering.

This strategy was used very profitably by Japanese automobile manufacturers during the 1980s. While Western manufacturers thought the Japanese advantages lay in lower labor costs, better quality, or government subsidies, their greatest strength lay in rapid product introductions. Japanese firms in other sectors soon adopted similar practices. The inability of Western firms to understand this strategy allowed Japanese domination of several additional markets, such as consumer electronics.[5]

Another benefit, often underestimated, is that many firms have been able to cut product introduction lead times while using fewer resources for development and introduction processes. In some cases, firms have cut lead times in half and used half as many people[6]—a fourfold improvement in productivity. Because most resources used in product introduction are considered overhead and not direct costs, this results in a tremendous reduction in overhead costs.

All the above factors result in excellent profits for a firm that successfully implements quick response in innovation.

Benefits of Quick Response in Production. Reducing the time used to produce and deliver existing products also has advantages. This does not refer only to manufacturing—it includes all the steps from receipt of order to shipping. Responding quickly increases customer satisfaction and may assist in taking orders away from competitors if they are slow to respond. If a customer has an urgent need for a firm's product, the firm might even charge a price premium and further add to its profits.

Less obvious, but in some ways more important, is the fact that implementing QRM leads to improved integration of an entire enterprise. To deliver products faster, an organization must be streamlined. Searching for ways to save time in the whole process reveals sources of quality problems and wasted efforts. Fixing these results in higher quality, lower work-in-process (WIP), less waste of all types, and lower total operating costs. The result is a leaner, more competitive company. Implementing QRM makes a company's future more secure.

Results of Quick Response Strategies. Firms successful in implementing QRM become formidable competitors in their markets. These firms can offer customized products, faster delivery, competitive prices, and high quality. Such capabilities leave little or no room for competitors to gain advantage. QRM-based companies achieve impressive financial results. These firms grow three times as quickly as the industry average and are twice as profitable.[7]

Equally important to consider is the possible cost if a firm does not use QRM techniques and a competitor does. Implementing QRM is not easy, and transforming an organization for QRM can take several years. If a competitor has already implemented QRM, a firm may lose substantial market share by the time it catches up. While trying to catch up, a firm may even lose so much market share that it goes out of business altogether.

Misconceptions about QRM

Misconception: Everyone must work faster, harder, and longer to get jobs done sooner.

Many organizations continue efforts to reduce standard times for their operations. But this is the worst way of trying to increase speed. Production and clerical staff, accustomed to efficiency studies based only on performance time, eventually become wary of the word "speed."

Manufacturing firms would do better to find entirely new ways of completing a job, focusing on lead time minimization. This requires major organizational restructuring as most organizations are designed to manage scale and cost. The CEO of Northern Telecom says of its journey toward QRM, "The deeper we probed, the more opportunities we saw. Ultimately we didn't just change our existing processes. We looked at them in totally new ways and redesigned our entire organization."[8]

To fully comprehend the need for restructuring, we must understand how most manufacturing companies are organized today. This will provide a perspective on many existing manufacturing/management systems that must be redesigned for QRM. We start by describing the evolution of postwar U.S. manufacturing strategy.[9]

The Eras of Scale and Cost Strategies.   During the 1960s, the world economy was growing quickly due to the ongoing recovery from World War II. At the same time, industrial countries were still rebuilding their industrial capacity, which had been devastated by the war. The United States was the only industrially advanced nation that could supply global markets, and the

opportunities seemed limitless—the more a firm produced, the more it could sell. U.S. firms dominated world markets and manufacturing was driven by "scale" (Figure 3). This encouraged firms to build the largest factories possible. Many large U.S. corporations, such as General Motors, Ford and IBM, grew and flourished during this era.

As European and Japanese firms entered world markets more effectively in the 1970s, their economies were still less developed than the U.S. economy, so they were able to produce goods more cheaply, though not necessarily better. Low-cost (and often low-quality) products entered world markets. To maintain market share, U.S. firms focused their competitive strategies on issues of cost and price.

These first two steps in postwar competitive strategy laid the foundation for management systems that are firmly entrenched today. Organizational structures, manufacturing layouts, manufacturing systems, management methods, reporting systems, performance measures, and reward systems are all based on managing scale and cost. This has significant implications; we will discuss specific examples later.

Two Major Paradigm Shifts

The 1980s brought the first postwar paradigm shift in manufacturing. Primarily through the results of Japanese firms, the manufacturing world realized that cost and quality were not tradeoffs: if one focused on improving quality, cost competitiveness would follow. This realization did not come without significant pain. Many U.S. firms lost substantial market share and closed plants before their management fully understood the importance of this focus on quality.

FIGURE 3

The Evolution of Postwar Manufacturing Strategy

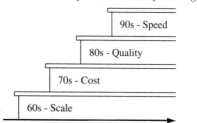

Now another paradigm shift has occurred, leading to a focus on speed. Taking quality a step further, competing on speed can result in both quality and cost improvements—in addition to shorter lead times. In other words, a manufacturing firm that successfully implements QRM can supply its customers with better quality products, at lower cost, faster than anyone else—a truly formidable competitive advantage.

The promise of QRM seems too good to be true, and many managers find it hard to believe. They assume improving speed means buying new machines, allocating more resources, or compromising quality. To reduce lead times, they believe, costs will go up and quality will go down. But time-based competitors can achieve cost and quality advantages along with greater speed.

Searching for ways to improve lead times can uncover other inefficiency and quality problems. As these are eliminated, costs decrease and quality improves. Such firms as Beloit Corporation and Ingersoll Cutting Tool have discovered the deeper an organization looks, the more opportunities it finds. For instance, an initial study at Ingersoll suggested that order processing time could be reduced by 20 percent; but with further exploration, reductions of as much as 70 percent became possible. Finally, the implementation team devised ways of achieving a 90 percent reduction in lead time.[10] To gain a complete perspective on today's manufacturing systems, we need to review one more concept.

The Planning Loop: A Legacy of Scale-Based and Cost-Based Management

The key to implementing QRM is breaking the planning loop.[11] A direct outgrowth of scale and cost management strategies, the planning loop is part of almost every manufacturing enterprise. Modern manufacturing companies are complex organizations that require long lead times to resolve conflicts between activities that need the same resources.

For example, if a customer order for 1,000 parts must be milled before it is painted, the milling department must have sufficient capacity to perform the milling. Lead time is allowed for the order to reach the milling department, for a machine to be set up, and for the pieces to be milled. Any given order may go through several departments, each with a need for sufficient lead time. The result is a long total lead time.

Long lead times require sales forecasts to assist in planning. Labor, equipment, and materials expenses

A Basic Quiz on Implementing QRM

Find out if your organization is ready to embark on the QRM journey. For each statement below, ask yourself: "Would the key managers in my company consider this statement to be True or False?" Mark your responses in the boxes, then compare them with the correct answers at the end of the paper. If you're a real QRM veteran, write down one or two sentences explaining why you think each statement is True or False.

1. Everyone will have to work faster, harder, and longer hours, in order to get jobs done in less time.
   ☐ True   ☐ False

2. To get jobs out fast, we must keep our machines and people busy all the time.
   ☐ True   ☐ False

3. In order to reduce our lead times, we have to improve our efficiencies.
   ☐ True   ☐ False

4. We must place great importance on "on-time" delivery performance by each of our departments, and by our suppliers.
   ☐ True   ☐ False

5. Installing a Material Requirements Planning (MRP) System will help in reducing lead times.
   ☐ True   ☐ False

6. Since long lead time items need to be ordered in large quantities we should negotiate quantity discounts with our suppliers.
   ☐ True   ☐ False

7. We should encourage our customers to buy our products in large quantities by offering price breaks and quantity discounts.
   ☐ True   ☐ False

8. We can implement QRM by forming teams in each department.
   ☐ True   ☐ False

9. The reason for implementing QRM is so that we can charge our customers more for rush jobs.
   ☐ True   ☐ False

10. Implementing QRM will require large investments in technology.
    ☐ True   ☐ False

must be planned several months before actual orders are received. As lead times lengthen, such forecasts become less accurate. So manufacturers keep reserve inventories of raw materials, components, subassemblies, and finished goods. When forecasts are incorrect, some inventory is not used as expected. As a result, inventories rise.

Some unscheduled orders create the most planning difficulties. Unexpected orders from important customers management wishes to satisfy. These jobs may be put into the factory and expedited, crowding out scheduled jobs. Regularly scheduled jobs are delayed, leading to longer delivery times. When customers complain because deliveries are late, management discovers that every area's lead times are longer than planned lead times. It finds no clear indication of inefficiency; in fact, it probably finds high use of machines and labor, with many departments working overtime to clear backlogs.

The organization decides these longer lead times are a truer indicator of its performance capabilities and incorporates the revised, longer lead times into its quoting, planning, and release policies. The longer lead times then result in even worse forecasts, leading to more inventory, more unscheduled jobs, and regularly scheduled jobs being late even with these longer quoted lead times; and the spiral continues.

During the late 1970s and early 1980s, lead times at many corporations increased several times over because of this planning loop. The author personally witnessed the quoted lead time for a company in the aerospace industry go from six months to nine months, then to 15 months, and finally to 24 months as the spiral grew.

This planning loop is a legacy of scale-based and cost-based management systems because in making items on a large scale and at reduced cost, companies performed operations of a given type in one department. For example, the milling department did the milling on all products. This enabled them to economize in several ways. First, by pooling the demand of all products, companies could even out production irregularities. This allowed for the use of fewer machines and laborers so that the right number of resources were used nearly 100 percent of the time. Second, with many products requiring similar components, companies could build those components economically by using one setup, storing the components for later use. Third, companies could train their workers in only the skills needed to operate in one department. Lower skill levels meant lower hourly rates and total payroll. This organization is the logical evolution of Henry Ford's assembly line ideas from

1914 (e.g. see the book by Womack et al),[12] but adapted for more general fabrication operations.

As manufacturing competition evolved, this organization developed several disadvantages. Products requiring many operations suffered long and tortuous routes through factories. Departments lost sight of their customers. Low skill levels led to low quality and "quality by inspection." Because many products were made using general purpose machines, setups tended to be long. Coupled with the desire to minimize handling across long routes, this led to a preference for large batches. Lead times became correspondingly long. All the elements were in place for the planning loop to spiral out of control.

This planning loop cannot be controlled; it must be eliminated. Companies that try to control the planning loop by using sophisticated material planning or scheduling systems only make it worse (the reason is explained later in this paper). The planning loop can only be eliminated by reducing the consumption of time throughout the system. Instead of asking how much time they need to do a task, firms must ask why a task takes so long and what can be done to finish it in less time.

Taking time out of the system requires implementing quick response in three areas:

- In production (this includes everything from order entry to the shopping dock).
- In sales and distribution.
- In new product introduction.

In this paper we will focus on production aspects with some discussion of new product introduction. For more on sales and distribution, see the book by Stalk and Hout.[13]

Reducing the consumption of time is far from trivial. Manufacturing and management systems today are focused on cost reduction, not on time reduction. Correspondingly, attitudes are based on cost rather than time. As a result, many organizations have had their lead time reduction programs stalled soon after initiation. This is because the tradition of cost-based management leads to misconceptions and misunderstandings about how to implement speed in manufacturing. This makes reorganization of production for QRM that much more important.

Implementing Quick Response in Production

This section reviews the key ideas behind implementing QRM for delivery of existing products. The aim is to reduce the lead time from receiving an order to shipping the completed product. This involves all the processes in this cycle, including inside sales, order entry, engineering and process planning (if product customization is necessary), manufacturing planning, materials procurement and preparation, fabrication and assembly processes, inspection, packaging, and shipping.

Reducing the lead time for existing products requires major restructuring involving three key departures from cost-based manufacturing strategy:

1. *The organization of process components must be changed from a functional basis to a product-oriented basis. This includes both white collar and blue collar work.*

Most firms are organized with all orders entered by one department, all milling done by another, and so on. Instead of this, firms should organize all the process components necessary to deliver a finished product (or a family of related products) into one department, usually called a cell. If the number of processes is so large as to make this department unwieldy, it can be split into smaller departments. It is important to make each department responsible for an identifiable sub-product, with a clearly defined hand-off to the next department.

For example, inside sales, order entry, design engineering, process planning, manufacturing/materials planning, and shop ticket printing might be organized into one cell. A second cell would take the shop tickets and perform material preparation, rough turning, finish turning, face milling, grinding, inspection, and packaging. The work force in each of these departments, whether white or blue collar, must be cross-trained so that each person can perform several operations for the department. This ensures that the cell can operate even if some people are absent due to sickness or vacation. It also enriches each person's job, helps to motivate them and results in many productivity improvements over time.[14]

2. *As the factory is transformed into a number of product-oriented cells, complex, centralized scheduling and control systems can be replaced by simpler, local scheduling procedures.*

In the traditional functional layout, a job would pass through several departments. As far as each department was concerned, the jobs appeared from somewhere and disappeared somewhere else after they were done. No department had responsibility for, or even much visibility of, the overall product routing and delivery schedule. Its goal was simply to do a good job in its own function. In such an organization, each department had to be told by a central scheduling system which jobs to work on next.

In a cellular organization, inventory and schedules are clearly visible. The team operating the cell does not need a schedule for each piece of equipment in the cell. It just needs to be given the final delivery schedule, and it takes responsibility for scheduling equipment, labor, and priorities. The central system now assigns overall delivery schedules, orders and allocates material, and coordinates among cells if necessary.

This system is far simpler than centralized scheduling of every piece of equipment for every order in the factory; this simpler system works better as well. Detailed schedules produced by complex scheduling systems often do little to help the shop floor because changes caused by expedited jobs, machine failures, or material shortages can make a schedule obsolete before it is even printed.

Supervisors then ignore the detailed schedules and set priorities informally. Their decisions make the detailed schedule even less usable because the schedule's assumptions are no longer true. A centralized scheduling system cannot succeed in such an atmosphere, and the enterprise returns to expediting urgent jobs manually. A cellular factory allows for manual scheduling of jobs within each cell, and with its simpler task of coordination, the central system can be quite effective.

3. *As each cell begins to operate smoothly, efforts are focused on how to run smaller and smaller batches.*

Each cell is now responsible for a single product or a small family of products. Setups on each machine can be tailored more closely to this family and made much shorter than in a functional layout. The proximity of all machines in the cell also encourages the use of smaller transfer batches, leading to overlapping operations. With a cross-trained group of operators working as a team to deliver the product, additional setup reductions and many other improvements can be realized.[15]

As a result, products that were made in lot sizes of 100 will soon be made economically, rapidly, and with high quality, in lot sizes of 20, 10, or even one. Reductions in lead time will be phenomenal. Some firms with cellular organization can now make products to order in one or two days that once had a two-month lead time and were stocked in large quantities.

The three steps above must be seen as sequential implementations; attempting the third step first would be counterproductive. During the early 1980s, many Western managers visited Japanese factories and returned with the idea that a lot size of one was ideal. They cut lot sizes in their own factories without implementing any other changes (the factories were still organized in a functional layout). Huge bottlenecks and even worse delivery performance resulted.

Even with setup reduction in place, functional layouts offer limited gains. The amount of material handling necessary discourages the production of small batches, and other improvements in quality and setups are impossible without a product-oriented team, as in a cell. Proper implementation of cells, however, takes more than just the restructuring above. It requires a whole new attitude toward three key concepts in manufacturing management, as discussed next.

The QRM Approach to Lot Sizes, Lead Times, and Utilization

Misconception: to assist in getting jobs out fast, we must keep our machines and people busy all the time.

For manufacturing managers, keeping machines and labor busy is synonymous with good management. Yet planning or aiming for 100 percent machine and labor utilization can have a disastrous effect on lead times. As the planned use of any resource approaches 100 percent, the queue for that resource gets longer and jobs spend more time waiting (consider any highway at peak traffic loads, or any supermarket on a Saturday afternoon). Cost strategies and scheduling philosophies of the 1970s taught managers to run large lots to reduce setup cost and save time on scarce resources. These also created long lead times.

Ironically, firms that want short lead times must strategically plan to operate at 80 percent or even just 70 percent capacity on critical resources. While it may seem that these resources are being wasted, this idle capacity should be viewed as a strategic investment that will pay for itself many times over in increased sales, higher quality, increased prices, lower total costs, and higher overall profitability.

Misconception: To reduce lead times we have to improve our efficiencies.

Most measures of efficiency work counter to lead time reduction. For example, consider measures of productive output for a work center. Only good pieces produced contribute to the measure. Supervisors and machine operators are encouraged to run large lot sizes, minimizing setup time and maximizing the number of pieces produced in a given period.

When an operator has achieved a "good setup," in which a machine is producing pieces faster than the standard time, there is every incentive to keep producing the same part since this will have a positive effect on efficiency. However, large lot sizes have long lead times. There is also no incentive to help other people keep a job moving. If a machine operator stops work to assist another operator, the first operator's efficiency will be reduced.

Using QRM techniques, total lead time becomes the principal measure of performance. Other traditional measures such as efficiency, utilization, and others, should either be rethought with lead time in mind, or abandoned altogether. While this may appear severe, the benefits of taking this bold step are described clearly in a case study at Beloit Corporation, where such a change resulted in lead times for one product line being reduced from 36 days to six days.[16]

The preceding points on lot sizing, lead times, and utilization are summarized by the graphs in Figure 4.

Understanding the Dynamics of the Shop Floor. The traditional view of capacity, as described by MRP and other capacity planning systems, is simple—a company has enough or it doesn't. So a production schedule is either feasible or infeasible. The modern view, however, is that the tradeoff between capacity utilization and lead times gradually worsens. Comparing the upper and lower graphs on the left side of Figure 4 helps explain many problems of large firms.[17] Because manufacturing managers were judged on their use of capacity, they tended to operate their resources at close to 100 percent utilization, which resulted in long lead times and high work-in-process. They often needed expensive overtime to catch up on past due jobs.

The two graphs on the right show another piece of the same story. The efficiency measure mentioned previously only gave credit for actual run time. Time taken for setup was considered wasted, so manufacturing managers ran the largest lot sizes they could. Efficiency appeared to increase with lot size (upper right graph); but the lower right graph shows the effect of this mistaken strategy—large lot sizes result in long lead times and high work-in-process. This explains the U-shape of this graph.[18]

The graph goes up on the right because large batches occupy each machine in their route for a long period, and thus have long production times. If all the batches in a factory are large, all the queue times at machines become very long as well, since each part has to wait

FIGURE 4

Understanding Lot Sizes, Lead Times, and Utilization

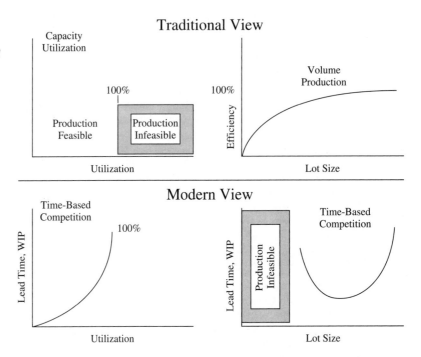

behind several other large batches with long machining times. The graph goes up on the left because as lot size decreases, setups increase, leading to higher utilization and higher waiting times.

On the other hand, if lot sizes are reduced too much, production becomes infeasible. Somewhere between the two extremes is a "good" lot size, which reduces lead times and WIP. This "good" lot size bears little relation to the value calculated by the Economic Order Quantity formula (EOQ, also called Economic Lot Size). Nor can it be predicted by an MRP system, which assumes fixed queue times regardless of workload. Each factory must determine what lot sizes are good for its products.

A new computer-based factory modeling approach based on Rapid Modeling Technology (RMT)[19] is a useful guide for manufacturing decision-makers in setting lot sizes and resource utilization for QRM.[20] RMT enables a manufacturing line or cell to be modeled, and key decisions to be evaluated, quickly and easily. One company used RMT to identify which setups to reduce and what lot sizes to run in order to reduce lead times by 75 percent.[21] Others have used it to justify running key resources at less than 100 percent capacity.[22]

The Hidden Errors in EOQ.   Because planning based on the EOQ formula is still widely practiced, or lot sizes set by EOQ are still used, it is important to know why EOQ is incompatible with a QRM strategy. The EOQ formula trades setup cost for WIP holding cost, but it does so for a single product, without estimating the dynamics and interactions of the shop floor. Queue times change with lot sizes, large lot sizes of one product can affect the queue time of other products, and quality factors influence over-all lead times. As a result, EOQ fails to consider several effects and costs when it calculates the order quantity for a part. These include:

- Costs of poor quality: In spite of the best inspection procedures, part defects are not always discovered before a downstream fabrication or assembly operation is attempted. When parts are made in big lots, this can result in a large quantity of parts being scrapped or reworked, with a correspondingly high cost. Or a consumer may discover the defect, in which case warranty costs are incurred. An EOQ calculation does not incorporate these costs.

- Costs of obsolescence or engineering changes: Similarly, when parts are made to stock in large quantities, whole batches of parts can be made obsolete by a design change. Parts must be scrapped or reworked, again with a correspondingly large cost. The cost of this possibility is also not taken into account when the large batch size is set by the EOQ calculation.

- Costs of long lead times: Large batches result in long lead times. The EOQ formula does not account for the fact that it can lead to a factory full of large lots that stall traffic, leading to long delivery times, late deliveries, and unhappy customers. The company actually incurs costs of expediting, high WIP, or even costs of lost sales, none of which are in the EOQ calculation.

- Market value of responsiveness: Ingersoll Cutting Tool Company cut one month out of lead time for a line of products and found its sales more than doubled.[23] Profits that may result from short lead times are not factored into the EOQ formula.

- Costs of a longer planning loop: Large lot sizes result in long lead times, which in turn result in a longer planning loop. As described above, the planning loop brings a host of associated costs. None of these are factored into the EOQ formula.

Put bluntly, nothing can be salvaged from the EOQ formula for use with QRM. In the short term, analysis tools such as RMT can help set good lot sizes. In the long term, the only correct approach is to ask constantly how lot size for a product can be reduced further, and then to make the improvements necessary for that reduction.

Material Planning and Control under QRM

This section discusses factors that relate to both internal and external supply of materials in the context of QRM implementation.

Misconception: We need to place great importance on "on-time" delivery to each of our departments and suppliers.

Nothing is wrong with on-time performance, only with overemphasizing it. Departments will commit to as late a time as possible, to be sure they can meet their deadlines. Instead of every unit in the organization trying to reduce its lead times, they will pad them as much as possible so their on-time deliveries look good (the discussion on MRP systems below gives another reason for padding). Suppliers react similarly. All this padding results in long overall lead times and, worse still, creates a longer planning loop with all its problems.

Instead, managers should measure the reduction of lead times and emphasize this as the most important performance measure. On-time deliveries will begin to improve when lead times start decreasing throughout the organization. Shorter lead times will counteract the planning loop effect and, as a result, delivery problems will also decline.

Misconception: Installing a Material Requirements Planning (MRP) system will assist in reducing lead times.

Nothing could be farther from the truth. MRP systems serve the important function of assisting with materials supply: for example, determining when more stock needs to be ordered from vendors. However, an MRP system will not assist in lead time reduction; if anything, it will foster an increasing spiral of lead times.

This is because MRP systems work with fixed lead times for each department. To be on time, a department manager needs to quote a lead time that will be feasible no matter how busy the department may be. Lead times in an MRP system, then, assume the worst case. This results in wasteful time estimates and long total lead times. Long lead times, in turn, extend the planning loop, resulting in even longer lead times. Despite budgeting more time, companies find they are late. As a further attempt to fix the problem, managers start pressing departments for "on-time" performance, which only exacerbates the problem.

MRP systems are useful in providing high-level planning and coordination of materials. But to reduce lead times, a company must restructure its manufacturing organization into simpler product-oriented cells. A firm should not use MRP systems for micromanagement of every work center. Let teams run their own cells, managing their work centers with short lead times as their objective. If necessary, provide these cells with simple analysis tools to plan and manage their capacities to preserve shot lead times.[24]

Customer and Supplier Relations and QRM

Supplier relationships have been discussed in books on quality, and are essential to QRM as well. Although more has been written about the importance of quality in selecting and building partnerships with suppliers, this section will focus on lead time and delivery issues more specific to QRM. Note that points made in the previous section about on-time delivery and assumptions of fixed lead times apply to suppliers as well.

Misconception: Because long lead time items must be ordered in large quantities, purchasers and managers should negotiate quantity discounts with suppliers.

Suppliers work in the same ways as manufacturers. Buying large batches encourages suppliers to make large batches. Because suppliers' factories are likely managed on cost-based philosophies, suppliers prefer to run large batches at (apparently) lower cost. These large batches result in long lead times at their factories, which in turn requires customers to order parts in large batches. Most purchasing agents are encouraged by management to negotiate price breaks and quantity discounts from suppliers, so a manufacturer has another built-in incentive to order in large quantities.

Emphasis on large lots results in reduced quality, higher costs, and longer lead times from the supplier. This is to the detriment of the manufacturer's production responsiveness and costs. Obsolete inventory presents another, hidden cost, which a customer risks incurring with every large order. A final hidden cost is that these long lead times lengthen the customer's own planning loop, with all its attendant costs.

However, if suppliers become familiar with QRM principles and implement QRM methods, they will be able to produce smaller lots at lower cost and better quality, with shorter lead times. Likewise, purchasing departments should be aware of the pitfalls of ordering large quantities.

When both purchasers and suppliers apply QRM techniques, cost reductions will follow, along with lower in-house stocks and more responsive supplies providing higher-quality goods. Achieving this requires working with suppliers over a long term; these results are not possible overnight. Retraining a purchasing staff can be difficult. They have been pressured for years to look for price break opportunities, and may find it hard to believe this new approach will work.

Misconception: We should encourage our customers to buy our products in large quantities by offering price breaks and quantity discounts.

This is the reverse of the above situation. Now the manufacturer's performance will suffer, with its customers enduring the resulting negative effects. To prevent this, a company implementing QRM techniques must educate its customers about its QRM program. If customers are willing to accept smaller lots at reasonable prices, a manufacturer can implement a QRM program sooner and with greater confidence.

Customers need to understand how they will benefit by production and purchase of smaller lots at lower cost. However, they need to be patient while the manufacturer embarks on QRM reforms and order smaller lots. If a customer insists on ordering in large lots, the manufacturer should produce the order in several small batches. This may seem unreasonable. If the customer wants to place a large order, filling it all at once seems to make the most sense.

But a large order can get in the way of other customers' orders, blocking access to a critical resource from other orders, delaying them and creating dissatisfaction among the company's other customers. Breaking up the large order allows other jobs to get through critical resources. This also addresses the other costs of large lots listed earlier. For a firm implementing QRM, these costs exceed those of multiple setups.

Products delivered to an end consumer pass through a chain of suppliers, from the mining of minerals to the final retailer. This is known as the supply chain. The above efforts, relating to both supplies and customers, should be communicated throughout the chain, building a partnership of suppliers that is extremely responsive to the consumer. In the end, everyone will benefit as quality improves, stocks are eliminated, costs go down, and the consumer's orders are filled rapidly at low prices.

Quick Response in White Collar Work

The Role of Teams in a Quick Response Organization. Manufacturing cells and related ideas discussed above do not apply only to the shop floor. A good portion of a firm's lead time may be in the white collar part of the organization. To reduce lead times, some firms have attempted to implement teams here as well.

Misconception: We can implement QRM by forming teams in each department.

Forming teams in each department may not improve QRM implementation or overall performance. A team with all its members in one functional department may be useful for efforts such as SPC or process improvements, but will do little to reduce lead times.

A better idea is to form a closed-loop, multifunctional, cross-trained team responsible for a family of products. The team should be located in one place, provided with the ability to obtain all the information it needs locally, and authorized to make necessary decisions. This is the only way to get significant reduction of lead times for such tasks as estimating and quoting, processing orders, design and drafting, and other white collar jobs required to complete an order. "Closed-loop" means all necessary processing steps can be done within the team—ideally, the order never leaves the team's area.

To create such a team, a company must cut across functional boundaries and change reporting structures. If orders require so many steps that a team would be too large, the steps should be partitioned into logical subsets with a team for each subset. Each team should be able to define its "product," be self-contained with respect to that product and have the full responsibility of delivering that product to the next team in the shortest lead time possible; it should view the next team as its customer in all respects.

Note the point about cutting across functional boundaries. Firms that try to keep organizational structures unchanged while creating cross-functional teams will be disappointed. Such teams, consisting of members based in their own functional departments, will meet often and have some minor impact, but will not even approach the full potential of QRM.

On the other hand, cross-functional, closed-loop teams that work together regularly will substantially restructure or reinvent tasks, combining or eliminating steps, leading to 50 percent or greater lead time reductions.[25] In addition, using a Kaizen outlook, such teams will continuously reduce their lead times and improve their quality.[26] Ingersoll Cutting Tool Company recently implemented such a closed-loop team to process orders for one line of cutter bodies. In doing so, it reduced order processing lead time by 90 percent, from 10 days to less than one day.[27]

Another problem in white collar departments is the belief that Quick Response Manufacturing, by nature of its title, is only a manufacturing issue. Some staff members are uninterested in QRM because their job duties do not involve manufacturing. This belief is wrong for three reasons. First, a significant portion of lead time is often consumed in order entry, engineering, estimating, and other premanufacturing operations. Second, manufacturing lead time is often affected by decisions made prior to manufacturing. Third, many support functions and policy decisions have significant impact on manufacturing performance.

These functions may still be driven by the cost-based philosophies, which will then influence manufacturing decisions and performance. To support a QRM program, its implementation should be seen as the responsibility of the entire organization, and the organization as a whole must embrace time-based decision-making. The Ingersoll Cutting Tool case study illustrates these points effectively.

Quick Response in New Product Introduction. Cross-functional teams can be especially effective in

reducing lead times for new product introduction. This includes all the steps from the product's concept stage to the time it reaches the first set of customers. The team must perform several functions, including marketing and sales, accounting and finance, product design, process engineering, tooling, manufacturing, purchasing, and shipping. External vendors may even be involved in early planning stages. This approach is known as Concurrent Engineering (CE) or Simultaneous Engineering.

CE can help reduce time to market, but this subject has been well covered elsewhere, so we will not dwell on it here.[28] However, one important observation deserves mentioning: implementing CE is far from easy. Companies that have attempted to introduce CE teams have encountered many obstacles. Among these are incomplete or ineffective implementation and prevalence of a cost-based mindset within the organization.

Incomplete implementation occurs when team members remain based in their original functional departments. This limits possible improvements, as mentioned earlier. Prevalence of a cost-based mindset can also seriously impair CE implementation. Traditional cost-based functional departments reward their employees for doing well on tasks narrowly defined to improve the efficiency of that department. In many cases, these incentives run counter to lead-time reduction efforts.

For example, a design department may be evaluated by the number of new designs it produces each month. In such a case, designers have an incentive to create new designs even though similar part designs may already be available. Designing a new fastener, for instance, may take less time than rummaging through file cabinets to find an appropriate existing fastener. Because the new design is rewarded and reusing the old design is not, the new design prevails.

On the other hand, the predominance of new designs can delay a new product introduction, because new designs need new process routings, tooling and fixtures, quality checks, and possibly debugging of the new processes. Use of the old design would have enabled immediate use of existing tooling and established manufacturing processes. Similar examples can be found in all functional departments. Unless the organizational culture adopts a time-based mindset, teams will have little opportunity to cut through traditional barriers and implement time-saving ideas.

Creating the Mindset for QRM

Misconception: The reason for implementing QRM is so that we can charge our customers more for rush jobs.

For QRM to work, everyone in an organization must understand why it matters and what purpose it serves. QRM provides some benefits that some may mistake for its purpose; companies must keep a clear distinction between the two. For example, although QRM techniques will allow a company to respond more rapidly to short-notice orders, the point is not to charge customers more for rush jobs. Although customers may pay more for speed, this is not the main reason for engaging in QRM.

Increased customer satisfaction is another benefit of QRM, but is not its main goal either. A QRM strategy must be founded on creating value for the customer. This will result in increased customer satisfaction, and customers may even be willing to pay more. A recent article by Stalk and Weber warns of the dangers of implementing a time-based strategy without considering whether it is creating value for the customer.[29]

At the same time, a more fundamental reason for implementing QRM is that it leads to improved integration of the whole enterprise. A QRM strategy results in higher quality, less WIP, less waste, lower costs, higher profitability, and higher sales. The result is a truly competitive company with large market share that will be very hard to beat. Embarking on the QRM journey strengthens a company and helps secure its future.

Stalk and Weber mention that certain domestic Japanese markets have so many time-based competitors that this strategy has reached its limits. This is not a concern for most U.S. companies; most U.S. firms have not yet adopted QRM strategies, so the few that do so first stand to reap tremendous gains.

Misconception: Implementing QRM will require large investments in state-of-the-art technology.

Many new technologies, such as rapid prototyping and CAD/CAM, offer great opportunities for time reduction. While these are important to consider, several steps must precede them. The biggest obstacle to successful implementation of QRM is not technology, but outlook or "mindset." Through training provided to everyone in the firm, from shop floor workers to top management, a company can help its employees understand its mission and methods.[30] Demonstrating lead time reductions through inexpensive solutions creates interest and helps assure employees of the value of QRM. Implementation will be easier if employees feel the techniques are worthwhile.

Because QRM requires people to disregard so many accepted rules about what is "right" in manufacturing and management, the entire organization's mindset must change. This is only possible through education. Without training, all other efforts will fail. However, many first-cut reductions in lead time can be achieved through low-cost or no-cost solutions. A few early successes will create a positive outlook, and people will be willing to try other QRM ideas. Higher-cost technological solutions should be brought in only after early initiatives are successful and low-cost solutions have been explored thoroughly.

Conclusions

Lead Time Reduction: Problem or Opportunity? Clearly, lead time reductions cannot be made tactically; they must be part of an organizational strategy led by top management. To significantly reduce lead times, firms must change many traditional ways of operating. This will necessarily affect the organization's structure. Such change has companywide implications and cannot be accomplished without the total commitment of top management. Senior managers cannot simply order their staffs to cut lead times in half, delegate responsibility, and expect it to happen. If reducing lead times was that easy to accomplish, most companies would have done it already.

Implementing speed is still timely. A substantial competitive opportunity remains available to most companies willing to implement QRM techniques. Firms that can find ways to successfully implement QRM will have created a profitable enterprise as well as a significant threat to the competition.

Key Points to Remember

- Companies that successfully implement QRM techniques find they are able to achieve superiority simultaneously in speed, cost, and quality.

- Implementing QRM does not mean everyone must work faster and longer; it means finding whole new ways of doing the job.

- QRM is not about 10 percent or 20 percent improvements (as is common with efficiency programs). It is about 50 percent, 70 percent, or even 90 percent reductions in lead time.

The results of implementing QRM can be very satisfying indeed: successful speed-based competitors find themselves growing at three times the industry average, with twice the industry average in profitability. The greatest obstacle to implementing QRM is not financial resources or technology, it is mindset. Companies that understand this and invest in creating the right mindset have the greatest success in using QRM techniques.

End Notes

1. G. Stalk, Jr., "Time—The Next Source of Competitive Advantage," *Harvard Business Review,* July–August 1988, pp. 41–51.
2. T. Peters, "Tomorrow's Companies," *The Economist,* March 4, 1989, pp. 19–22.
3. R. Merrills, "How Northern Telecom Competes on Time," *Harvard Business Review,* July–August 1989, pp. 108–114.
4. Stalk, "Time—The Next Source of Competitive Advantage."
5. G. Stalk, Jr., and T. M. Hout, *Competing against Time,* (New York: Free Press, 1992). Stalk and Hout's book is full of David and Goliath stories—small firms that used speed as a strategy to gain market share against large, established companies.
6. C. Charney, *Time to Market: Reducing Product Lead Time* (Society of Manufacturing Engineers, 1991).
7. Stalk, and Hout, *Competing against Time.*
8. R. Merrills, "How Northern Telecom Competes on Time," *Harvard Business Review,* July–August 1989, pp. 108–114.
9. Stalk, "Time—The Next Source of Competitive Advantage."
10. J. V. Owen, "Time is the Yardstick," *Manufacturing Engineering,* November 1993, pp. 65–70. Additional details can be found in *ManuFax* 3, no. 1, Manufacturing Systems Engineering Program, University of Wisconsin–Madison, 1994.
11. While some of these ideas were discussed by J. W. Forrester in "Industrial Dynamics: A Major Breakthrough for Decision Makers," *Harvard Business Review,* July–August 1958, a formal treatment of the planning loop in the context of time-based competition was first given by Stalk in "Time—The Next Source of Competitive Advantage."
12. I. P. Womack, D. T. Jones, and D. Roos, *The Machine That Changed the World* (New York: HarperPerennial, 1991).
13. Stalk and Hout, *Competing against Time.*
14. N. L. Hyer and U. Wemmerlöv, "Group Technology and Productivity" *Harvard Business Review,* July–August 1994, pp. 140–49. Also see the note on Kaizen under item 3.
15. The Kaizen (continuous improvement) philosophy provides a concrete framework for encouragement

and implementation of numerous employee-generated ideas for productivity improvement (e.g., see M. Imai, *Kaizen,* McGraw-Hill, 1986.) Note therefore that creation of a Kaizen mindset in the organization assists the successful implementation of QRM.
16. J. V. Owen, "Time Is the Yardstick."
17. More detailed explanation of the graph on the lower left side of Figure 4 can be found in any textbook on industrial engineering or queuing theory.
18. Readers interested in the mathematical theory behind this graph should see the article by U. Karmarkar, "Lot Sizes, Lead Times and In-Process Inventories," *Management Science,* 1987, pp. 409–18.
19. R. Suri, "RMT Puts Manufacturing at the Helm," *Manufacturing Engineering* 100, no. 2 (1988), pp. 41–44.
20. R. Suri, "Lead Time Reduction through Rapid Modeling," *Manufacturing Systems,* July 1989, pp. 66–68.
21. A. Rehman and M. B. Diehl, "Rapid Modeling Helps Focus Setup Reduction at Ingersoll," *Industrial Engineering,* November 1993, pp. 52–55.
22. S. de Treville, "Time Is Money," *OR/MS Today,* October 1992, pp. 30–34.
23. *ManuFax* 3, no. 1.
24. R. Suri, "Lead Time Reduction through Rapid Modeling."
25. Restructuring of tasks has recently been called "Business Process Reengineering" (BPR); see M. Hammer and J. Champy, *Reengineering the Corporation* (New York: HarperBusiness, 1993). While BPR is a general approach that looks at improving any business activity, our focus is on lead time reduction in a manufacturing enterprise, and we are able to make more specific comments for this situation.
26. See footnote 15 on Kaizen.
27. J. V. Owen, "Time Is the Yardstick." Additional details can be found in *ManuFax* 3, no. 1.
28. For example, see C. Charney, *Time to Market: Reducing Product Lead Time* (Society of Manufacturing Engineers, 1991), and the large number of other references in that book.
29. G. Stalk, Jr., and A. M. Weber, "Japan's Dark Side of Time," *Harvard Business Review,* July–August 1993, pp. 93–102.
30. Owen J. V., "Time is the Yardstick."

Answers to the Quiz

All the statements are false. Add up your score and compare with the guide below.

9–10 correct	Your firm is a veteran of implementing QRM.
6–8 correct	Your firm has the ability to implement QRM successfully with more training and education.
0–5 correct	It will take a lot of groundwork to implement QRM in your firm. Without creating the proper foundation, you may find lead times getting longer when you embark on your QRM programs.

Do not be alarmed if your firm did not score well. Managers and supervisors in most firms give incorrect answers to several questions in the quiz, which leads to setbacks when they attempt to implement QRM. Through our work at the Center for Quick Response Manufacturing, we have found that despite extensive background reading many people continue to think that at least some of the assertions are true. As a result, lead-time reduction efforts in their companies have little effect, or worse still, lead times get longer and not shorter. The benefits of adopting a QRM strategy and the perils of not doing so, however, should have convinced you that implementing QRM ought to be a priority for your firm.

2   PRODUCT DEVELOPMENT AND TEAM-BASED MANAGEMENT

READING 2-1

COMPETING THROUGH DEVELOPMENT CAPABILITY IN A MANUFACTURING-BASED ORGANIZATION

Steven C. Wheelwright
Kim B. Clark

In a competitive environment that is global, intense, and dynamic, developing new products and processes is increasingly a focal point of competition. Firms that get to market faster and more efficiently with products that are well matched to the needs and expectations of target customers create significant competitive leverage. Firms that are slow to market with products that match neither customer expectations nor the products of their rivals are destined to see their market position erode and financial performance falter. In a turbulent environment, excelling at product and process development has become a requirement for being a player in the competitive game; doing development extraordinarily well can provide a sustainable competitive advantage.

INDUSTRIAL COMPETITION AND DEVELOPMENT REALITIES

The importance of product and process development is not limited to industries or businesses built around new scientific findings with significant levels of R&D spending, or where new products have traditionally accounted for a major fraction of annual sales. The forces driving development are far more general and apply in virtually all manufacturing environments. Three are particularly critical for firms that historically have viewed the United States as a large, mature, primarily domestic market:

• *Intense international competition.* In business after business, the number of competitors capable of competing at a world-class level has grown at the same time that those competitors have become more aggressive. As world trade has expanded and international markets have become more accessible, the list of one's toughest competitors now includes firms that may have grown up in very different environments in North

Steven C. Wheelwright is the Class of 1949 Professor of Business Administration, and Kim B. Clark is the Harry E. Figgie, Jr., Professor of Business Administration, both at the Harvard Business School, Cambridge Mass. Reprinted with permission from *Business Horizons*, July–August 1992. Copyright 1992 by the Foundation for the School of Business at Indiana University.

America, Europe, and Asia. The effect has been to make competition more intense, demanding, and rigorous, creating a less-forgiving environment.

• *Fragmented, demanding markets.* Customers have grown more sophisticated and demanding. Levels of performance and reliability previously unheard of are today the expected standard. Increasing sophistication means that customers are more sensitive to nuances and differences in a product and are attracted to products that provide solutions to their particular problems and needs. Yet they expect these solutions in easy-to-use forms.

• *Diverse and rapidly changing technologies.* The growing breadth and depth of technological and scientific knowledge has created new options for meeting the needs of an increasingly diverse and demanding market. Developing novel technologies and understanding existing technologies increase the variety of possible solutions available to engineers and marketers in their search for new products. Furthermore, the new solutions are not only diverse but also potentially transforming. New technologies in areas such as materials, electronics, and biology have the capacity to fundamentally change the character of a business and the nature of competition.

These forces are at work across a wide range of industries. They are central to competition in young, technically dynamic industries, but they also affect mature industries in which life cycles historically were relatively long, technologies mature, and demands stable. In the world auto industry, for example, the growing intensity of international competition, exploding product variety, and diversity in technology have created a turbulent environment. The number of world-scale competitors has grown from fewer than 5 in the early 1960s to more than 20 today. But perhaps more important, those 20 competitors come from very different environments and possess a level of capability far exceeding the standard prevailing 25 years ago.

Much the same is true of customers. Levels of product quality once considered extraordinary are now a minimum requirement for doing business. As customers have grown more sophisticated and demanding, the variety of products has increased dramatically. In the mid-1960s, for example, the largest selling automobile in the United States was the Chevrolet Impala. The platform on which it was based sold approximately 1.5 million units per year. In 1989, the largest selling automobile in the United States was the Honda Accord, which sold about 380,000 units. Thus, in a market that is today larger than it was in 1965, the volume per model has dropped by a factor of four. Currently more than 600 different automobile models are offered for sale on the U.S. market.

Similarly, technological change has had dramatic consequences. In 1970, one basic engine–drive train technology (a V8 engine, longitudinally mounted, water cooled, carbureted, hooked up to a three-speed automatic transmission with rear wheel drive) accounted for close to 80 percent of all automobile production in the United States. Indeed, there were only five engine–drive train technologies in production. By the early 1980s that number had grown to 33. The growing importance of electronics, new materials, and new design concepts in engines, transmissions, suspensions, and body technologies has accelerated the pace and diversity of technological change in the 1980s. Simply keeping up with those technologies is a challenge, but an often straightforward one in comparison with having to integrate them in development efforts.

Similar forces have been at work in other traditional, mature industries. In textiles and apparel, for example, firms such as Benetton and The Limited have used information technology to create a production and distribution network that links retail outlets directly to distribution centers and back into factories and suppliers in the chain of production from fiber to finished product. The thrust of these networks is the ability to respond quickly to changing customer demands at relatively low cost.

Fueled in part by availability and in part by growing demands for differentiated products, product variety has expanded significantly. In plant after plant, one finds vast increases in the number of styles produced and a sharp decline in the length of production runs. These are not changes of 10 or 20 percent: in the 1980s, it was common for apparel plants to experience a four- to fivefold increase in the number of styles produced. These increases in garment variety have pushed back into the textile plants as well. For example, the average lot size for dying at Greenwood Mills, a U.S. textile firm, declined in the 1980s from 120,000 to 11,000 yards.

Changes in markets and technologies for automobile and textile firms have accentuated the importance of speed and variety in product development. But changes in competition, customer demand, and technology have also had dramatic effects on newer, less-mature industries in which product innovation has always been an important part of competition. In industries such as computer disk drives and medical equipment, already short life cycles have shrunk further and product variety has increased. In addition, competition has placed increased pressure on product reliability and product cost. In disk drives, for example, the market for Winchester-technology hard disks has expanded from a base in high-end systems for mainframe computers to include a spectrum of applications ranging from laptop personal computers to large-scale supercomputers. Even within an application segment, the number of sizes, capacities, access times, and features has increased sharply. In addition to this explosion of variety, firms in the hard disk drive industry have had to meet demands for dramatic increases in reliability (10-fold in five years) and decreases in cost (5 to 8 percent quarterly). These have been met in part by incremental improvements in established technologies and in part by introducing new design concepts, production technologies, materials, and software.

Much the same has been true in the market for new medical devices. Innovation has always been important in creating new medical devices, but by the 1980s success required the ability to follow an innovative product with sustained improvements in performance, application to new segments, improved reliability, and lower cost. In the case of devices for angioplasty (a surgical procedure using a balloon on a small wire to expand closed arteries), the initial innovation was followed by a variety of developments that offered the physician greater control of a smaller device, making access easier and creating additional applications. In concert with process changes that substantially improved or reduced variability of performance characteristics, changes in the product have opened up new applications and treatment of a more diverse set of clinical problems and patients, worldwide.

The Competitive Imperatives.   Rigorous international competition, the explosion of market segments and niches, and accelerating technological change have created a set of competitive imperatives for the development of new products and processes in industries as diverse as medical instruments and automobiles, textiles and high-end disk drives. Figure 1 identifies three of these imperatives—speed, efficiency, and quality—and suggests some of their implications.

To succeed, firms must be responsive to changing customer demands and the moves of their competitors. This means that they must be fast. The ability to identify opportunities, mount the requisite development effort, and bring to market new products and processes quickly is critical to effective competition. But firms also must bring new products and processes to market efficiently. Because the numbers of new products and new process technologies have increased while model lives and life cycles have shrunk, firms must mount more development projects than has traditionally been the case—utilizing substantially fewer resources per project. In the U.S. automobile market, for example, the growth of models and market segments over the last 25 years has meant that an auto firm must mount close to four times as many development projects simply to maintain its market share. But smaller volumes per model and shorter design lives mean that resource requirements must drop dramatically. Effective competition requires highly efficient engineering, design, and development activities.

Being fast and efficient is essential but not enough. The products and processes a firm introduces must also meet demands in the market for value, reliability, and distinctive performance. Demanding customers and capable competitors mean that the ante keeps going up—requirements of performance, reliability, ease of use, and total value increase with each product introduction. When competition is intense, firms must attract and satisfy customers in a very crowded market. More and more this means offering a product that is distinctive, that not only satisfies but also surprises and delights a customer. Moreover, attention to the total product experience and thus to total product quality is critical.

The Opportunity and the Challenge

Firms that step up to the challenge and meet these competitive imperatives enjoy a significant advantage in the marketplace. Developing outstanding products not only opens new markets and attracts new customers, but also leverages existing assets and builds new capability in the organization. Getting a succession of distinctive new disk drives or a string of new medical devices to market quickly and consistently requires solving technical problems that builds know-how. Moreover, it stimulates the creation of greater capability in problem solving, prototype construction, and testing that can be applied in future projects.

All of these skills and capabilities enhance a firm's ability to compete. But there is more. Successful new products also unleash a virtuous cycle in reputation and enthusiasm within and outside the organization. Inside, successful new products energize the organization; confidence, pride, and morale grow. The best employees remain challenged and enthused. Outside, outstanding new products create broad interest in the firm and its products, enhance the firm's ability to recruit new employees, and facilitate the building of relationships with other organizations. The organization's momentum builds and reinforces itself.

Whereas the potential opportunities to be realized in developing new products and processes are exciting,

FIGURE 1

The Development Imperatives

Required Capability	Driving Force	Implications
1. Fast and Responsive	Intense competition; changing customer expectations; accelerating technological change	Shorter development cycles; better targeted products
2. High Development Productivity	Exploding product variety; sophisticated, discerning customers; technical diversity	Leverage from critical resources; increased number of successful development projects per engineer
3. Products with Distinction and Integrity	Demanding customers; crowded markets; intense competition	Creativity combined with total product quality; customers integrated with truly cross-functional development process

making them happen is a demanding challenge. New product or process development entails a complex set of activities that cuts across most functions in a business, as suggested by Figure 2, which lays out the phases of activity in a typical development project—a new product. In the first two phases—concept development and product planning—information about market opportunities, competitive moves, technical possibilities, and production requirements must be combined to lay down the architecture of the new product. This includes its conceptual design, target market, desired level of performance, investment requirements, and financial impact. Before a new product development program is approved, firms also attempt to prove the concept's viability through small-scale testing, constructing models, and often, speaking with potential customers.

Once approved, a new product project moves into detailed engineering. The primary activity in this phase of development is designing and constructing working prototypes and developing tools and equipment to be used in commercial production. At the heart of detailed product and process engineering is the "design-build-test" cycle. Both products and processes are laid out in concept, captured in a working model (which may exist on a computer or in physical form), and then subjected to tests that simulate product use. If the model fails to deliver the desired performance characteristics, engineers search for design changes that will close the gap and the design-build-test cycle is repeated. The conclusion of the detailed engineering phase of development is marked by an engineering "release" or "sign-off" that signifies that the final design meets requirements.

At this time the firm, typically, moves development into a pilot manufacturing phase, during which the individual components, built and tested on production equipment, are assembled and tested as a system in the factory. During pilot production many units of the product are produced and the ability of the new or modified manufacturing process to execute at a commercial level is tested. At this stage all commercial tooling and equipment should be in place and all parts suppliers should be geared up and ready for volume production. This is the point in development at which the total system—design, detailed engineering, tools and equipment, parts, assembly sequences, production supervisors, operators, and technicians—comes together.

FIGURE 2

Typical Phases of Product Development

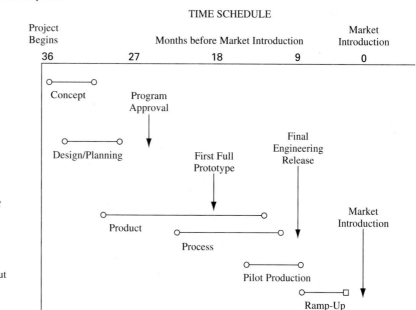

The final phase of development is ramp-up. The process has been refined and debugged but has yet to operate at a sustained level of high-yield, volume production. In ramp-up, the firm starts commercial production at a relatively low level of volume; as the firm develops confidence in its (and its suppliers') abilities to execute production consistently and marketing's abilities to sell the product, the volume increases. At the conclusion of the ramp-up phase, the production system has achieved its target levels of volume, cost, and quality. In this phase, the firm produces units for commercial sale and, it is hoped, brings the volume of production up to its targeted level.

An obstacle to achieving rapid, efficient, high-quality development is the complexity and uncertainty that confronts engineers, marketers, and manufacturers. At a fundamental level the development process creates the future, and that future is often several years away. Consider, for example, the case of a new automobile. The very best companies in the world in 1990 could develop a new car in three to three and a half years. At the outset of a new car development program, therefore, designers, engineers, and marketers must conceive of a product that will attract customers three years into the future. But that product must also survive in the marketplace for at least another four to five years beyond that. Thus the challenge is to design and develop a product whose basic architecture will continue to be effective in the marketplace seven to eight years after it has been conceived.

The problems that uncertainty creates—different views of the appropriate course of action, new circumstances that change the validity of basic assumptions, and unforeseen problems—are compounded by the complexity of the product and the production process. A product such as a small copier, for example, may have hundreds of parts that must work together with a high degree of precision. Other products, such as the handle of Gillette's Sensor razor, appear to be fairly simple devices, but because of very demanding performance requirements are complex in design and come out of a manufacturing process involving sophisticated equipment and a large number of operations.

Moreover, products may be evaluated across a number of criteria by potential customers. Thus, the market itself may be relatively complex with a variety of customers who value different product attributes in different ways. This means that the firm, typically, draws on a number of people with a variety of specialized skills to achieve desired yet hard-to-specify levels of cost and functionality. To work effectively, these skills and perspectives must be integrated to form an effective whole. It is not enough to have a great idea, superior conceptual design, excellent prototype facility, or capable tooling engineers; the whole product—its design system, production process, and interaction with customers—must be created, integrated, and made operational in the development process.

But an individual development project is not an island unto itself. It interacts with other development projects and must fit with the operating organization to be effective. Projects may share critical components and use the same support groups (model shops, testing labs). Additionally, products may require compatibility in design and function: models of computers use the same operating system, and different industrial control products conform to the same standards for safety. These interactions create another level of complexity in design and development.

Critical links also exist with the operating organization. A new design requires developing new tools and equipment and uses the skills and capability of operators and technicians in the manufacturing plant. Further, it must be sold by the sales group and serviced by the field organization. Of course, new products (and processes) often require new skills and capabilities, but, whether relying on new or old, the success of the new product depends in part on how well it fits with the operating units and their chosen capabilities. Thus, effective development means designing and developing many elements that fit and work well as a total system. Our work suggests that the degree to which such integration is achieved in the new product (or process) depends on the patterns of work and communication that take place throughout the development effort.

ACHIEVING CROSS-FUNCTIONAL INTEGRATION

The extent to which problem solving is integrated in product and process development shows up most forcibly in relationships between individuals or engineering groups where the output of one is the input for the other. An example is the relationship between a design group responsible for the design of a plastic part and a process engineering group responsible for designing the mold that will be used in producing the part. The upstream group—in this case, the part designers—establishes the physical dimensions of the part, how it will interface with other parts within the system, the surface characteristics of the part, and the particular material to be used in its construction. All of these decisions—dimensions, tolerances, interfaces, surface characteristics, and materials—become inputs into the downstream organization's design problem—in this case, the design of molds to be used in the production of the part. The mold designer's problem is to create a mold (or set of molds, particularly if the part is to be produced in volume) that will give the part its shape and surface characteristics, but will also be sufficiently durable, cost-effective, and operational so that the part can be manufactured in volume (can withstand repeated use, without breaking or sticking) reliably at low cost. How these two engineering groups work together determines the extent and effectiveness of integration in the design and development of the part and its associated mold.

Patterns of Communication.   A critical element of the interaction between the upstream and the downstream group is the pattern of communication. The choices firms make about communication between upstream and downstream groups play an important role in shaping the nature of cross-functional integration. But there are also choices about how to link the actual work in the two groups in time. The key issue is the extent to which work is done in parallel. Figure 3 puts the communication patterns together with different approaches to parallel activity to create four modes of upstream-downstream interaction.

The first mode is what we call the serial mode of interaction. In this classic relationship, the downstream group waits to begin its work until the upstream group has completely finished its design. The completed design is transmitted to the downstream group in a one-shot transmission of information. This one way "batch" style of communication may not convey all of the important nuances and background to the final design, nor does it necessarily comprehend the strengths and opportunities afforded by the downstream group. In that sense, the problem solving that lies behind the design of the product and that will produce the design of the mold is not integrated.

The second mode—what we call early start in the dark—links the upstream and downstream groups in time but continues to employ a batch style of communication. This mode of interaction often occurs when the downstream group faces a deadline it feels cannot be met without an early start on the project. But the upstream group communicates only at the end of its work, so the downstream group may be surprised by the design and experience a period of confusion as it tries to adjust its work to the upstream design. Although the net result may be some reduction in overall lead time, the extent of the surprise and confusion can often be sufficient to actually make the process longer than in mode one. Although the downstream group works in parallel with the upstream group, and in this sense they are "concurrent," in actuality they operate without information, and the problem-solving cycles in the two organizations are not linked.

The third mode—what we call the early involvement mode—begins to move toward real integration. In this mode, the upstream and downstream players engage in an interactive pattern of communication. The upstream group, however, is still involved in the design of the part well before the downstream group begins its work. Thus, while the downstream group develops insight about the emerging design and participates through feedback and interaction in the design process, it waits until the design is complete before undertaking problem solving in its own domain. The pattern of communication we envision here not only occurs earlier than it does in modes one and two but involves two-way communication of preliminary, fragmentary information. For example, instead of waiting until the design is complete, engineers in the upstream group share preliminary analysis, alternative designs, and tentative proposals with their downstream colleagues. Similarly, the downstream group shares its views about capabilities of the downstream process, the constraints it faces in designing the molds, and the relative merits of alternative concepts under discussion. Although it waits to begin work on the mold design until the part design is complete, the downstream group benefits from early involvement in two ways. First, the part design reflects a much better understanding of the issues confronting the process engineers than was true in either modes one or two. Second, the mold designers themselves have a much better sense of the issues and objectives embodied in the design. The net effect is that they are able to complete their work with fewer delays and downstream changes. In this sense, problem solving in the downstream and upstream groups is much more integrated.

The last mode in Figure 3—what we call integrated problem solving—links the upstream and downstream groups in time and in the pattern of communication. In this mode, downstream engineers not only participate in

FIGURE 3

Four Modes of Upstream-Downstream Interaction

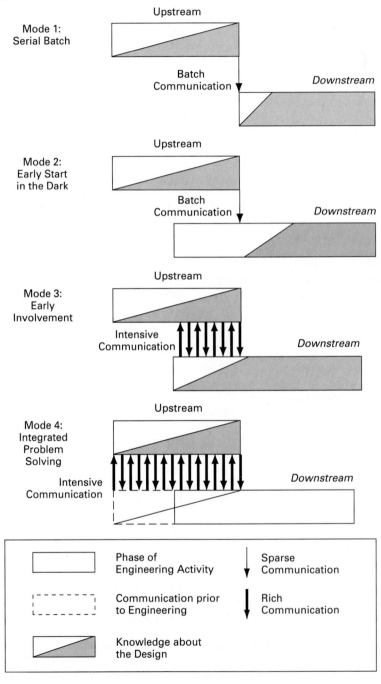

a preliminary and ongoing dialogue with their upstream counterparts, but use that information and insight to get a flying start on their own work. This changes the content of the downstream work in the early phases of upstream design, and is also likely to change fundamentally the content of communication between the two groups. Whereas in mode three the content of feedback from downstream engineers must rely on past practice, theoretical knowledge, and engineering judgment, under integrated problem solving that feedback will also reflect actual practice in attempting to implement the upstream design.

Communication that is rich, bilateral, and intense is an important, even essential, element of integrated problem solving. Where problem solving between upstream and downstream groups is intimately connected, the practice of "throwing the design (blueprints) over the wall"—inherent in mode one—will not support timely mutual adaptation of product and process design. What is needed to capture the nuance and detail important for joint problem solving is face-to-face discussion, direct observation, interaction with physical prototypes, and computer-based representations. Moreover, that intimate, rich pattern of communication must occur in a timely way so that action may be taken to avoid costly mistakes downstream.

The essence of mutual adjustment is real-time coordination between upstream and downstream groups. In this way design engineers take into account the preliminary results of process engineering problem solving to make products easier and less expensive to manufacture. Likewise, process engineers shape their problem-solving efforts to deliver the capabilities required by the upstream design. But this kind of mutual adjustment begins only after downstream problem solving has begun.

Capabilities and Relationships.   Integrated problem solving relies on early action by the downstream group; dense, rich dialogue between upstream and downstream participants; and a style of problem solving that is broader and more comprehensive than one experiences in the more narrow functional focus inherent in mode one. Indeed, effective integration places heavy demands on the organization. The engineering process must link problem-solving cycles in time; communication must be rich, precise, and intense; and the relationship between upstream and downstream groups must support and reinforce early and frequent exchange of constraints,

ideas, and objectives. Moreover, because problem solving across traditional functional boundaries occurs in real time, the capacity for quick and effective action is critical. Thus, effective integration relies on a specific set of capabilities, attitudes, and relationships.

Upstream Capabilities.   From the perspective of the upstream engineering group, the challenge is to meet performance objectives in a way that complements downstream work and makes use of what the downstream can do. Making this happen requires skills and capabilities that go beyond the narrow technical ability to accomplish the upstream task. Three capabilities seem particularly important.

Downstream-Friendly Solutions.   The first challenge is to create what we call downstream-friendly solutions. Upstream engineers must be knowledgeable about downstream constraints and capabilities. They must learn to use techniques for promoting early and continued communication with the downstream group and acquiring relevant knowledge and experience from previous projects. A variety of methods have been developed in recent years, including design for manufacturability, value engineering, failure mode and effects analysis, and Taguchi methods®. Each of these is designed to enhance the upstream group's ability to predict the consequences of its actions and to devise solutions to its own problems that are downstream-friendly.

The objective here is not simply to make life easy for the downstream engineers. It is true that ignorance of downstream constraints hampers integrated problem solving, and may create very expensive and time-consuming engineering changes. It is also true, however, that excessive attention to downstream problems may hamper the commercial appeal of the design. Overemphasis on manufacturability or overreliance on simple parts may reduce downstream problems but render the product less attractive. Thus, downstream constraints must be carefully balanced with issues of design quality to maximize the total customer experience inherent in joint upstream–downstream solutions.

Error-Free Design.   With an emphasis on creating downstream-friendly solutions, upstream engineers can have a substantial impact on the number of engineering changes and the time required to complete downstream work. But many such changes and much expensive time wasted are not due to lack of knowledge of downstream constraints or capabilities, but simply to outright mistakes—errors in copying documents, typing a "6" instead of a "9," sending a document to the wrong location, and so forth. Such minor details often have insidious consequences. In the first place, if not caught early, such errors require downstream engineering changes that are costly and time-consuming, but add no value to the overall quality of the product. Second, such errors are often very difficult to track down once they have been propagated in the system. Third, they erode the mutual respect needed for groups to work as peers.

For all these reasons, error-free design is critical in achieving integrated problem solving. Designing it right the first time is a matter in the first instance of attention to detail, and discipline in the activities of individual engineers. But effective design reviews, testing, and engineering discipline can dramatically reduce or eliminate mistakes and errors.

Quick Problem Solving. Even when solutions are relatively friendly and careless mistakes have been eliminated, disagreements and conflict between upstream and downstream groups are inevitable in situations in which the product is complex and customers are demanding. When differences arise, dealing with them effectively is enhanced by quick problem-solving capabilities in the upstream group. Faster design-build-test cycles in the upstream facilitate short feedback loops and quick mutual adjustment. When a problem arises in the downstream that requires upstream adjustment, the speed with which the upstream group can effect a new solution is critical in achieving responsive, fast action. Time is of the essence in this context. Since problem solving is mutual, getting to new alternatives quickly allows the downstream group to maintain its focus and complete its work in an integrated fashion. In organizations that have achieved integrated problem solving, there is a major difference between having a preliminary design done in two weeks rather than in four. In a slow organization those two weeks are not very important. In this case quick action supports integration.

Downstream Capabilities. Among downstream engineers, the challenge is to get a flying start on development before getting complete information. Moreover, that flying start must not create so many constraints on the design that it loses its appeal in the market. Moving fast but effectively in the downstream depends on three capabilities.

Forecasting from Upstream Clues. To start quickly, downstream engineers must begin working on solving problems that have not been well defined. In that context, it is essential that downstream engineers develop the ability to forecast what the upstream group is likely to do. This requires that the downstream group develop skill in finding and using clues about upstream work. In combination with insight and understanding about previous patterns of upstream behavior, these clues become the basis for downstream action. For example, mold designers may know that the part designers are particularly worried about the strength of the part. They may also have learned from conversations with the part engineers that the alternative solutions include changes in the internal structure of the part. And given the manner in which the part designers have approached these issues in the past, the concern about strength means that the part is likely to have internal ribs. These clues can therefore be the basis for initial mold design and planning.

Regular and close communication between upstream and downstream engineers is essential to finding clues and to using them effectively. But the downstream engineers need not be passive in this process. Once they discern a particular issue and a particular design direction, they may offer suggestions or counterproposals. If those suggestions are focused on helping upstream engineers solve their part design problems effectively— "If you want to go with small ribs, we can give you very tight tolerances that will cut down flash"—and are not simply expedients to make life in the downstream simple—"Small ribs won't work; go with large ribs, they are easier to make"—the ideas from downstream are much more likely to improve overall design and enhance the achievement of an integrated solution. Furthermore, active downstream involvement is likely to increase the quality of the clues and thus the forecasts they generate.

Managing Risk. Starting quickly based on a forecast of likely upstream action is a course fraught with risk. Downstream engineers must know how to make tradeoffs between the risk of a given change and the benefit of an early start. Moreover, they need to be skilled in managing the tradeoff so that the early start is made in a way that reduces risk. Take, for example, the case of process engineers trying to develop molds. Based on early clues from the part designers, and intensive discussion, mold engineers may identify sections of the part that are unlikely to undergo significant adjustment and change. Other sections of the part, however, may be less firm. This gives them the ability to begin mold design and construction by establishing the basic configuration and then using cutting margins (excess material that can be pared back once the final dimensions have been established) to allow a flying start. There is a significant amount of know-how involved in making such knife-edged tradeoffs. This implies that integration of problem solving requires significant skill in applying deliberate and detailed analysis and calculation in support of fast action.

Coping with Unexpected Changes. Even the best forecasters and the most clever downstream engineers will encounter unexpected changes in design. Given this fact of life, the downstream group needs to be flexible and skilled at quick diagnosis and quick remedy. Just as fast action in the upstream group facilitates mutual adaptation and integration, quick adjustment to unexpected changes on the part of the downstream group is essential to avoiding long delays and idle resources in development.

The ability to move quickly in reacting to unexpected changes relies on skill in problem diagnosis, and organizational capability in mobilizing resources and focusing attention and effort on the important problems. But there is also the matter of raw engineering talent. It is one thing to get an organization to run tests quickly, build tools rapidly, and have decisions made promptly. But it is quite another to be able to size up a situation, identify a solution, and designate the appropriate test. Simply stated, downstream organizations that are fast and effective have many excellent engineers. Downstream (and upstream) groups that are slow have a few very good engineers and many others that only follow routine procedure and look up specifications in handbooks. Although these groups may arrive at solutions given enough time, the name of the game in integrated problem solving is speed. In this case, there is no substitute for competence.

Attitudes toward Integration. Effectively deploying upstream and downstream skills and capabilities in achieving integrated problem solving depends on fundamental attitudes that affect the relationship between upstream and downstream groups. People in the upstream group, for example, must be willing to share early preliminary information with their downstream colleagues. A perfectionist mentality, an attitude of "I won't give you anything now, because I know I'll have to change it later and I know I'll take the blame for it," is anathema to integrated problem solving. Likewise, people in the downstream must be willing to take risks based on their best forecast of the future. They must be comfortable in a very ambiguous environment. A "wait and see" attitude, an attitude of "Don't talk to me until you are absolutely sure the design is done," may appear to minimize the risks of change but is in fact a cultural obstacle to effective integration.

Mutual trust and joint responsibility are essential to integrated problem solving. Once product engineers have worked hard to reduce unnecessary changes, they must trust the manufacturing process group's willingness and ability to cope with the changes that might emerge in the course of development. If process engineers trust product engineers to help them overcome manufacturing difficulties, they will be more willing to get, and more capable of getting, a flying start.

Mutual trust hinges on mutual commitment to one another's success. Without such commitment, engineers are less likely to expose themselves to the personal risks inherent in integrated problem solving. And there are risks. Integration requires that engineers in the upstream and downstream let their colleagues see what actually goes on in their respective departments. It exposes weaknesses and mistakes and makes clear the limits of their ability much more than does the sequential batch mode of operation.

Effective integration is also built on shared responsibility for the results of upstream–downstream collaboration. Where integrated problem solving prevails, the objective of the upstream group cannot simply be a completed design, nor can the downstream group focus its attention solely on a well-conceived set of tools or processes. Both groups must recognize that the objective is a high-quality, low-cost part that fits well with other parts under development, comes off the production line at commercial volume levels with the styling, surface finish, cost, and structural integrity to satisfy customer expectations, and is available for the targeted market introduction. This is a very complex objective that neither the upstream nor the downstream group completely controls. To achieve the objective, therefore, there must be joint responsibility for joint output.

The Fast-Cycle Competitor

Effective cross-functional integration is just one of many skills a firm must develop to compete through development capability. Other important themes that characterize outstanding development include clarity of objectives, focus on time to market, high-quality prototypes, and strong leadership. These capabilities lead to rapid, efficient development of attractive products and manufacturing processes. The power of such capabilities lies in the competitive leverage they provide.

A firm that develops high-quality products rapidly has several competitive options it may pursue. It may start a new product development project at the same time as its competitors, but may introduce the product to the market much sooner. Alternatively, it may delay the beginning of a new development project to acquire better information about market developments, customer requirements, or critical technologies, introducing its product at the same time as its competitors but bringing to market a product much better suited to the needs of its customers. Furthermore, if it has also achieved speed and quality in an efficient way, it may use its resources to develop additional focused products that more closely meet the demands of specific customer niches and segments. Whatever the mix of customer targeting, speed to market, and product breadth the firm

chooses to pursue, its advantages in fundamental capabilities give it a competitive edge. The competitive interaction between two electronics firms, which we shall identify as Northern and Southern Electronics Companies, clearly illustrates the nature of such a competitive advantage.

Northern Electronics exemplifies a firm, not unlike many others we've seen, in which slipped development schedules, budget overruns, late design changes, and problems with field failures or factory yields following market introduction were common occurrences. For such a firm, competing against a company capable of rapid but effective product development was a bewildering, discouraging, and ultimately unprofitable experience. Figures 4a and 4b illustrate just such an episode in Northern's history. Consider first Figure 4a, which graphs the price, cost, and product generation experience of Northern and its principal competitor, Southern Electronics Company, from 1979 until 1985.

Until 1985, both Northern and Southern followed standard industry cycles in new product development, pricing, and manufacturing costs. With a product

Figure 4a

Standard Competitive Patterns for the Compact Stereo Market

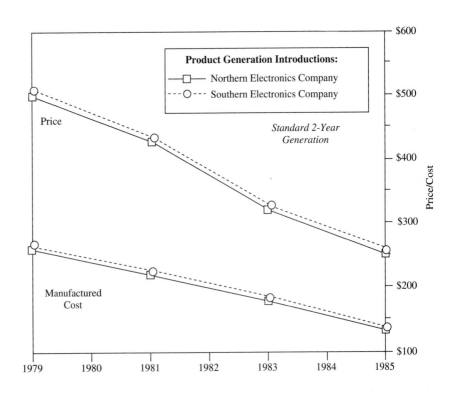

Figure 4b

Competition on Rapid Development Capabilities in the Compact Stereo Market

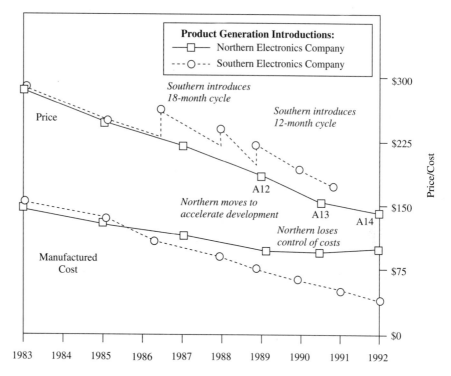

development cycle of 18 to 20 months, both firms introduced a new generation of product every two years. Between major generational changes in products there were frequent model upgrades and price declines as the cost of key components and manufacturing fell with increasing volume. Thus, until the mid-1980s, both Southern and Northern had prices and costs that tracked each other closely, and both mirrored industry averages.

Improvement Efforts at Southern Electronics. In the early 1980s, changes in Southern laid the foundation for a significant change in the nature of competition in the industry. Stimulated by the efforts of Greg Jones, the new vice president of engineering, Southern embarked on a concerted effort to reduce its product development lead time. Without compromising quality, Jones and the entire organization began to develop the characteristics sketched out in Column 3 of Figure 5. Stronger leadership, more effective cross-functional integration, greater attention to issues of manufacturability and design, more effective prototyping, and a revamped development process gradually led to a reduction in develop-

ment lead time from 18 to 12 months. By 1986 Southern could develop a comparable compact stereo system about six months faster than Northern.

As Figure 4b suggests, Southern began to use its new development capability in early 1986. At that point it broke with industry tradition and introduced its next generation of stereo products about six months sooner than expected. With a more advanced system and superior performance, Southern was able to achieve a premium price in the marketplace. Although Northern followed six months later on a standard cycle, its next generation stereo was unable to command its traditional market share. As a result, Northern's volume increased more slowly than expected and its cost position began to erode slightly relative to Southern.

Southern Electronics introduced its next generation product 18 months later in the fall of 1987. Once again the product achieved a premium price in the marketplace. However, Southern did not fully exploit its premium pricing opportunity. Instead, it lowered prices somewhat to further increase its market share. At that point, not only was Northern behind in product features

FIGURE 5

Central Themes in Ineffective and Effective Development Projects

Problematic Projects		Outstanding Projects
Characteristics	*Consequences*	*Selected Themes*
• Multiple, ambiguous objectives; different functional agendas	• Long planning stage; project becomes vehicle for achieving consensus; late conflicts	• Clear objectives and shared understanding of project's intent throughout organization; early conflict resolution at low levels
• Focus on current customers and confusion about future target customers	• Moving targets; surprises and disappointments in market tests; late redesigns; mismatch between design and market	• Actively anticipating future customers' needs; providing continuity in offerings
• Narrow engineering focus on intrinsic elegance of solutions; little concern with time	• Slipping schedules; schedule compression in final phases	• Maintaining strong focus on time-to-market while solving problems creatively; system view of project concept
• Reliance on engineering changes and manufacturing ramp-up to catch and solve problems; "We'll ECO it when we get to manufacturing"	• Poor, unrepresentative prototypes; many late changes; poor manufacturability; scramble in ramp-up; lower-than-planned yields	• Testing and validating product and process designs before hard tooling or commercial production; "design it right the first time"
• Narrow specialists in functional "chimneys"	• Engineering "ping-pong"; miscommunication and misdirected effort; use of time to substitute for integration	• Broad expertise in critical functions, team responsibility, and integrated problem solving across functions
• Unclear direction; no one in charge; accountability limited	• Lack of a coherent, shared vision of project concept; buck passing; many false starts and deadends	• Strong leadership and widespread accountability

and technology, but Southern's aggressive pricing posture put even more pressure on Northern's sales volume and margins. Although Northern fought back with price discounts, increasing advertising, and promotions to dealers, it was unable to stem the erosion of its historical market position. The result was an even greater disparity in the cost positions of Northern and Southern Electronics.

Northern's Competitive Reaction. In late 1988, Northern introduced its next generation stereo system, the A12. Developed under the motto "Beat Southern," the A12 would be the product to regain their former competitive position in the market, Northern's executives felt. Much to their surprise, however, the rollout of the A12 in early 1989 was met by Southern's introduction of its next generation stereo system: Southern had moved to a 12-month product introduction cycle in late

1988. At that point Northern was a full generation of technology behind Southern in its market offerings. Northern's management determined that the only course of action open was to accelerate development of the next generation system, the A13. They thus embarked on a crash development effort to bring the A13 to market in early 1990. At the same time they began development of the A14, which they targeted for the Christmas 1990 selling season. The A14 was to get them back into the competitive ball game on solid footing—a "close the gap" strategy.

While Northern's strategic intent was to catch up to Southern with accelerated product development, the reality was much different. Northern brought the A13 to market in early 1990, but the development process was so hectic and the ramp-up in manufacturing so strained that the company effectively lost control of its costs. The product came to market but was much more expensive and less effective than the company had planned. Because of its many problems, scarce development resources that were to have been moved to the A14 in early 1990 were focused instead on correcting problems and cleaning up the A13's design. To make matters worse, Southern continued to follow its 12-month introduction cycle and actually beat Northern to the market with its next generation product. The result for Northern was a further erosion in margins and market position.

Without making fundamental changes in its development process, which management considered neither necessary nor within the charter of those working on the A14, Northern's attempt to push ahead with the A14 for the 1990 Christmas season was a dismal failure. The A14 product had so many problems in the field and was so expensive to manufacture that the product line became a serious financial drain on the company.

The Sources of Advantage.   The key to Southern's success in the compact stereo market was its consistent ability to bring excellent products to market before its competitors. This ability was rooted in fundamental changes that Jones and others had made in its development process. These included obtaining broad-based organizational and individual buy-in to key project goals at the onset, and empowering and encouraging development teams to modify the development process while developing the needed products. In addition, it harnessed that capability to a marketing and pricing strategy that was well targeted at Northern's weaknesses. In effect, Southern changed the nature of competition in the industry; Northern was forced to play a game for which it was ill suited—a game Northern never fully comprehended until it was years behind in capability.

Southern Electronics' ability to bring a competitive product to market more rapidly than its chief rivals created significant competitive opportunities. How Southern chose to exploit those opportunities depended on the nature of its competition and its own strategy. But the ability to move quickly in product development created at least three potential sources of advantage:

• *Quality of design.* Because Southern had a 12-month development cycle, it could begin the development of a new product closer to the market introduction date than its competitors. Whereas Northern had to begin 18 to 20 months before market introduction, Southern's designers and marketers could gather and refine an additional six months of information before

setting out to design a new product. In a turbulent environment, designers face a high degree of uncertainty in the early stages of development about which set of product characteristics will be most attractive to target customers. Additional time to secure feedback on the most recently introduced generation and learn about market developments and emerging customer preferences may mean the difference between winning and mediocre products. Although the product may use the same basic technologies, additional market information may yield a much better configuration. The product's features and aesthetics may be fresher, more up to date, and more closely matched to customer expectations. Thus, Southern could exploit its lead-time advantage by waiting to launch its development effort until more and better market information became available. Even though its product would arrive on the market at the same time as its competitors, its product would offer the customer a superior experience.

• *Product performance.* A much faster development cycle gave Southern Electronics the opportunity to launch a new product program well in advance of its competitors. It could use that lead to introduce the next generation of product technology. In this case, the advantage of speed lay not in superior market or customer intelligence, but in the ability to exploit technological developments and bring them to market faster than its competitors. The gap in performance this created is depicted in Figure 6 for a single product generation. As illustrated, a six-month jump on competitors in a market accustomed to 18- to 24-month design lives can translate into as much as three times the profit over the market life of the design. Conversely, being late to market with a new product can lead to break-even results and zero profit. This provided Southern with the leverage to control not only its own profits and returns, but also those of its chief competitor, Northern.

Putting a sequence of such developments together further widens the competitive gap, as depicted in Figure 7. The slow-cycle competitor brings new technology to market every two years. The fast-cycle competitor, in contrast, achieves the same performance improvement every 12 months. Whereas the initial advantage of the fast-cycle competitor is relatively small, the ability to move quickly to market eventually creates a significant performance gap. To the extent that customers can discern the difference in performance and to the extent that the gap offers them valuable improvements, a faster time to market creates a superior product.

FIGURE 6

*The Impact of Market
Introduction Timing
on Lifetime Profits of
a Major New Product*

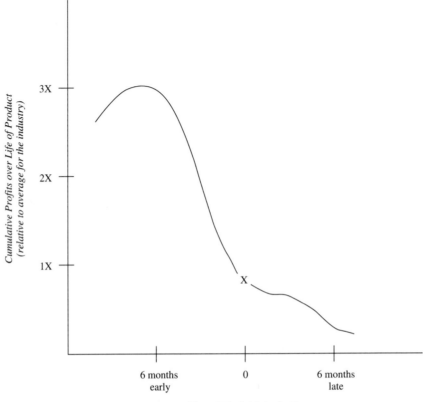

*Time of Market Introduction
(relative to competitors)*

• *Market share and cost.* A better product design and superior product performance gave Southern the opportunity to achieve premium prices in the market. However, a firm may also choose to price its product to create superior value for its customers, thereby translating advantage in design and performance into increases in market share. When lower costs are driven by growth and increases in volume, increases in market share may translate into improved cost position for the fast-cycle competitor. Thus, even if two competitors operate on the same learning curve, the fast-cycle competitor will achieve a cost advantage.

However, it may also be the case that the capabilities that underlie fast development cycles create a steeper learning curve. Speed in development is rooted in the ability to solve problems quickly and to integrate insight

and understanding from engineering with critical pieces of knowledge in manufacturing. This set of capabilities likewise is critical in achieving cost reductions in established products. Thus, when costs are sensitive to volume and fast-cycle capability enhances a firm's overall learning capacity, the fast-cycle competitor enjoys double leverage in improving its manufacturing costs.

How a fast-cycle competitor chooses to exploit the potential advantages in design, product performance, and manufacturing cost will depend on the competitive environment and the firm's strategy. In the case of Southern Electronics, all three dimensions of advantage were important. Initially, Southern used its six-month advantage in lead time to obtain better market information and still introduced its 1986 compact stereo about six months before its competition. In the second generation, however, Southern accelerated its model introduction and

FIGURE 7

Fast Cycle Development and the Technological Gap

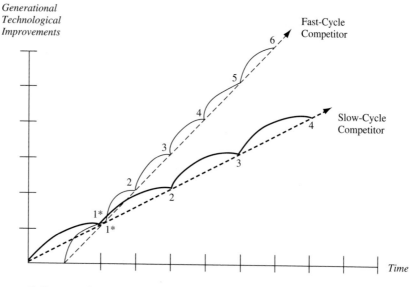

*Indicates product generation.

began to exploit is development capacity to achieve superior product performance. By 1990, Southern was a generation ahead of its competitors in product technology. It used its superior design and performance to achieve some price premium in the market, but it did not raise prices as much as its performance advantage warranted. The result was a superior value for customers, increases in market share, and steeper slopes on its manufacturing learning curve. Thus, Southern used its advantage in performance and cost both to expand its market share and increase its margins.

But perhaps the most powerful effect of Southern's fast-cycle capability was its ability to change the nature of competition. By improving its development productivity and shortening the time between product generations, Southern forced Northern to play a competitive game that Northern was not prepared to play. Northern would have faced competitive difficulties no matter how it responded to the Southern challenge, but it compounded its problems by failing to change fundamentally its approach to product development. By attempting accelerated development in the context of its traditional systems, Northern created internal confusion, strained its resources, and actually reduced the effectiveness of its development organization. In addition, previously enthusiastic, capable, and hard-working product

managers became frustrated and disappointed. Thus, at the start of the 1990s, Northern Electronics faced the challenge of undertaking a major overhaul of its development process while its margins were eroding, market position was slipping, and morale among some of its best development people was declining. Southern's fast-cycle capability had clearly put Northern and its other major competitors at a significant competitive disadvantage while generating additional enthusiasm and competence among people such as Jones and individual project contributors. Southern was continuing to build momentum as Northern and other competitors continued to lose it.

Conclusion

Achieving competitive advantage through effective development capability is not just a theory. Effective, fast-cycle competitors have emerged in a wide range of industries. Companies such as Honda in automobiles, Compaq in personal computers, Applied Materials in semiconductor production equipment, ACS in angioplasty, Sony in audio products, Matsushita in VCRs, The Limited in apparel, Phillips in computer monitors, Hill-Rom in hospital beds, and Quantum in disk drives have made the ability to bring outstanding products to market rapidly a central feature of their competitive strategy. Once achieved, an advantage built around fast-cycle capability seems to be strong and enduring. In the first place, the advantage is based in capabilities—human and organizational skills, processes and systems, and know-how—that are difficult to copy. Moreover, effective, rapid development creates superior products and offers customers superior value. It therefore helps to create a market franchise and brand equity. A real product advantage rooted in difficult-to-copy capabilities and a translation of that product advantage into a fundamental market franchise that reinforces its own momentum is a powerful combination. Although product development is difficult, doing it well confers significant advantage. Furthermore, the more challenging the development requirements, the more dramatic the potential impact.

This article is adapted from Chapters 1 and 7 of the authors' *Revolutionizing Product Development: Quantum Leaps in Speed, Efficiency, and Quality* (New York: Free Press, 1992).

References

W. J. Abernathy, K. B. Clark, and A. M. Kantrow, *Industrial Renaissance* (New York: Basic Books, 1983).

T. Bailey, "Technology, Skills, and Education in the Apparel Industry," Technical Paper No. 7, Conservation of Human Resources, Columbia University, November 1989.

C. M. Christensen, "The Development of the Magnetic Information Storage and Retrieval Industry, 1960–1987: An Analytical History," unpublished paper, Harvard Business School, December 1990.

K. B. Clark and T. Fujimoto, *Product Development Performance* (Boston: Harvard Business School Press, 1991).

T. Fujimoto, "Organizations for Effective Product Development," unpublished D.B.A. dissertation, Harvard Business School, 1989.

P. G. Smith and D. G. Reinertsen, *Developing Products in Half the Time* (New York: Van Nostrand Reinhold, 1991).

G. Stalk, Jr., and T. M. Hout, *Competing Against Time* (New York: Free Press, 1990).

J. P. Womack, D. T. Jones, and D. Roos, *The Machine That Changed the World* (New York: Rawson Associates, 1990).

Reading 2-2
The Neglect of Engineering Design

John R. Dixon
Michael R. Duffey

The proper study of mankind is the science of design.

—Herbert Simon

The competitive difficulties with U.S. manufactured goods have been attributed to a wide range of problems, including trade regulations, lack of overseas marketing, short-term financial strategies, labor costs, interest rates, and the value of the dollar. Recent attention has mostly focused on physical manufacturing itself; that is, the failure to invest in new manufacturing facilities and processes, the neglect of manufacturing education and research, and poor management of manufacturing operations. Many of these issues are discussed in the excellent study from MIT entitled *Made in America.*[1] However, another fundamental—yet largely overlooked—problem is our long-standing neglect of engineering design. High quality and low cost cannot be manufactured-in unless they are first *designed*-in.

It is becoming common for analysts to cite the "80/20 rule" first publicized 20 years ago in a British aerospace study: that 80 percent of manufacturing costs are committed during the first 20 percent of the design process.[2] However, the implications of this observation are still often ignored, and management continues to search principally for remedies in manufacturing operations. To regain world manufacturing leadership, we need to take a more strategic approach by also improving our engineering design practices. Unfortunately, just what engineering design is—and its role in the "stream" of product development, manufacturing, and use—seems to be obscure to most economic and business analyses, and consequently often poorly effected by U.S. management.

Our intent here is to present a view of discrete product manufacturing from the perspective of engineering design and to describe the current state of design research, education, and practice in the United States. Repair of our design infrastructure is an essential strategy for U.S. revival in manufacturing competitiveness.

Roots of the "Crisis in Manufacturing"

When attention first focussed on the "crisis in manufacturing" in the 1970s, most attempts at a solution were directed at downstream production operations. This is where money is spent and products take physical form. With a concern for reduced labor costs, many companies invested heavily in manufacturing automation (such as robotics) without a longer, strategic plan. In many cases—for example, GM's Saturn plant—the results were discouraging. Even when factory floor automation has been implemented successfully, it has rarely yielded a sustained market advantage. Labor costs are not a large percentage of the sales price of most manufactured goods and, in any case, our competitors, especially the Japanese, are still ahead on this score.

More recently, attention has focussed on manufacturing activities slightly upstream of product fabrication, such as tooling and process engineering—what we've termed in Figure 1 the design-manufacturing transition. Much of the current interest in quality concerns this stage of the life cycle; for example, the use of statistical techniques proposed by Deming and others to identify and improve critical process parameters.[3] Lester Thurow has written about the importance of improving such manufacturing process technologies.[4]

It is in the earlier stages of engineering design, however, where the major decisions are made that dictate the downstream cost and quality of the final product. This importance of early design commitments is beginning to be recognized in the form of design for manufacturing initiatives at Ford, IBM, Xerox, and elsewhere. Researchers such as Don Clausing[5] and Kim Clark[6] are examining the role between engineering design and management practices. Dr. H. Barry Bebb, Vice President of Xerox and one of the few senior advocates for design engineering in industry, has rightly called design the "missing link in U.S. competitiveness."[7]

A Definition of Engineering Design

By *engineering* design, we mean the development of a product from its technical conception through detail

FIGURE 1

The Product Life Cycle: An Engineering Design Perspective

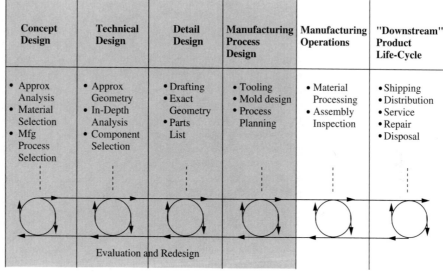

	Concept Design	Technical Design	Detail Design	Manufacturing Process Design	Manufacturing Operations	"Downstream" Product Life-Cycle
Examples	• Approx Analysis • Material Selection • Mfg Process Selection	• Approx Geometry • In-Depth Analysis • Component Selection	• Drafting • Exact Geometry • Parts List	• Tooling • Mold design • Process Planning	• Material Processing • Assembly Inspection	• Shipping • Distribution • Service • Repair • Disposal

Market Opportunity

New Technology Concept

Engineering Design

Evaluation and Redesign

design, and the design of the related manufacturing process and tooling. It is mechanical design, as opposed to electronic design, that is considered to be a major problem for manufacturers. While both require reasoning from basic scientific principles and the use of analysis techniques, mechanical design practice is in general complicated by the following four issues:

- The wide range of materials available to mechanical designers.
- The complex and sensitive role of manufacturing concerns on mechanical designs.
- The nonmodularity of mechanical designs.
- The role of complex 3-D geometry.

Mechanical design includes initial design and redesign for function, structural integrity, manufacturability, use, serviceability, repair, disposal, and other product life-cycle considerations. We also distinguish engineering design from what is often called industrial design; the latter is centrally concerned with important issues of styling. Industrial design is a part of, or runs parallel to, engineering design.

Engineering design can be broadly grouped into four phases, as shown in Figure 1: concept design, technical design, detail design, and the manufacturing process

design. The *concept design* phase involves the initial technical conception and "back of the envelope" engineering of the product, incorporating input from upstream (new technologies, marketing assessments, aesthetic and ergonomic design considerations, etc.) and also—at least ideally—initial input from downstream manufacturing concerns. During the *technical design* phase, more precise analytical techniques and engineering knowledge are used to meet the increasingly complete and accurate specification. *Detail design* is the process of documenting (usually in 2-D drawings, bills of material, etc.) the more or less complete description of an already fully designed product. The *manufacturing process design* includes the design of molds and tooling, fixturing for machining, assembly devices, workcell configuration, and process planning.

A single pass through the above design phases is rarely adequate. Design is fundamentally an *iterative* process in which redesign can be driven by both upstream (e.g., marketing reassessment) and downstream activities (e.g., redesign for assembly, ease of repair). Redesign early in the product life cycle, when the costs of changes are minimal, is healthy and desirable. But redesigning to correct substantial deficiencies discovered in detail design, and particularly during manufacturing planning or production, can be extremely costly and time-consuming.

Engineering design includes both *new product* design and the *incremental* design of existing products to meet changes in marketing, manufacture, functional deficiencies, and so on. The Polaroid Land camera is a classic example of the engineering design of a new product. Following Edwin Land's research into novel photochemical-processing techniques, it was necessary to design such things as entirely new battery elements, roller mechanisms, optics, and shutters to transform this technological and scientific advance into a commercial product. While the United States has been and continues to be *the* world leader in science and new technology development (e.g., superconductivity, computers, high-definition television, medical instrumentation), Japan and other competitors are beating us to the marketplace with successful new or improved products. Roland Schmitt has emphasized the role of *incremental* engineering redesign of existing products: the Japanese and others, he says, are effecting shorter redesign cycles in a wide range of electromechanical products which result in significant competitive advantage.[8] "There probably aren't a lot of differences between initial designs here and in Japan," says Michael Poccia, an engineer who troubleshoots mechanical design process and product problems at Kodak. "The major difference seems to be their commitment of resources to continuing improvement."

The Role of Design in Manufacturing Competitiveness

By looking at the issue of manufacturing competitiveness from the viewpoint of engineering design, we assert the following:

- *In terms of long-range strategy, the factors of cost, quality, and time-to-market are design problems more than manufacturing problems.* Product cost *has* been reduced by increasing factory floor efficiency and—at least temporarily—by the lower value of the dollar. But further cost reductions, as well as quality and time-to-market improvements, will be driven not by downstream manufacturing, inspection, or inventory control, but by the strength of engineering design practices. Recent "design for manufacturing" initiatives at Ford, IBM, NCR, Xerox, and elsewhere seem to bear this out. Most manufacturing costs are

mandated by the design. Quality can be manufactured *out* by poor practice (unusual), but quality can't be manufactured *in* or inspected *in* unless it is present in the design itself.

- *Market loss by U.S. companies is due to design deficiencies more than manufacturing deficiencies.* From power tools to construction equipment to automobiles, foreign products have gained market share due to better design more than to any other factor. One of the most ominous market losses is in manufacturing equipment. In many important applications, U.S. designs of machines used to manufacture metal and plastic products have been bettered by those in Japan, Korea, Germany, and elsewhere. Typically, this industry's problems are attributed to "management,"[9] but the bottom line is surely design, and perhaps management of design. The textile machinery industry in this country virtually ceased to exist when U.S. textile manufacturers turned to better designed machinery from Germany and elsewhere in the 1970s.[10] Except for a few bright exceptions, the U.S. machine tool industry and many others may be headed on this same path.

- *Manufacturing processes themselves are designed.* For example, injection molding—the manufacturing process predominantly used for plastic components—requires an intensive design of the die. Locating gates and runners for the molten plastic, cooling lines, redesigning the part geometry for proper draft angle and side actions are intensive design efforts. Neglect of design at this phase causes extremely costly and time-consuming iteration of die cutting and adjustments to the mold machine parameters. Assembly systems—whether automated indexing devices or a sequence of manual operations—are also designed, as are process plans for machining and metal forming. To effectively commercialize U.S. advances in materials, VLSI and other technologies will require intensive design efforts for processing machinery.

- *Many technical product problems commonly associated with manufacturing processes are traceable to design problems.* In this country, traditional barriers between design and manufacturing, and the lack of knowledge about manufacturing processes by designers have limited attention to manufacturing problems early in the design cycle. The Design-For-Manufacture Workshops developed by Boothroyd, by Hitachi and others are attempting to close this gap.[11] Tolerancing problems on a part, for example, are best—but least often—remedied by a redesign rather than pushing the limits of the manufacturing equipment.

- *Opportunities to surpass foreign competitors are best found in engineering design.* As more countries gain sophistication and aggressiveness in the discrete product markets traditionally held by U.S. companies, design becomes an even more crucial competitiveness weapon. We may use improved manufacturing to catch up, but we can only regain the lead by dramatically improved design. Our ability to commercialize new technologies such as superconductivity depends on improving our engineering design knowledge and practices. Also, mature industries such as machine tools and automobiles can only sustain competitive advantage by superior incremental design.

Assessing the U.S. Design Infrastructure

Most practitioners would strongly agree with Barry Bebb's assessment that the U.S. design infrastructure is broken. In May 1988, the Design Theory and Methodology Program at the National Science Foundation (NSF) sponsored a Workshop on Engineering Design. Sixteen nationally recognized experts in design from industry and academia concluded that

> engineering design is not taught, researched, or practiced as effectively as needed by American industry.... Much of the world's best existing design knowledge is not available to U.S. designers.... There is a need to convert the present "art form" of design into a theory-based and repeatable professional discipline. Perpetuation of the art form leaves major issues of competitiveness, education, and utilization of national resources to chance.[12]

The engineering design infrastructure consists of our engineering design education programs, our research

effort, and the design knowledge tools and practices used in manufacturing firms.

Engineering Design Education. The historical roots of the current neglect of design education go back to before World War II. During the war, it was observed that scientists who had a firm background in physics and other basic sciences were often more adept at design and other engineering skills that those with a traditional engineering education. Based largely on findings of studies done in the decade after World War II, engineering educators completely revised the engineering curriculum to include much more basic science and analytical techniques. This was probably a correct step, but in the process, design was not changed and was relegated to a very low priority. Of the 250-odd engineering schools in the U.S., design is still generally taught only in the context of a few "machine design" courses, which traditionally stress analytical design techniques more than actual design.

The NSF Workshop on Engineering Design concluded that there are two sources of curriculum problems:

- There is no foundation for a science of design.
- There are few opportunities for undergraduates to explore realistic design problems from industry.

The industry-backed engineering accrediting organization (ABET) is committed to legislating more and better design courses into the curriculum. However, faculty with the education and experience to teach design as needed to revitalize U.S. industry design practices are simply not present in sufficient numbers to make any widespread, permanent improvements. A few valiant but geographically scattered design-oriented faculty members have developed and taught excellent courses, but without a large and vibrant faculty constituency, design education remains generally in the doldrums.

Today's engineering faculty have all been educated in the post–World War II era in which design has been neglected. New faculty will also have matured in highly science- and analysis-oriented graduate programs. The realities of academic life require the Ph.D., but there are *very* few graduate programs in engineering design in the United States. Hence there is no viable source of new faculty to teach the kind of design needed. A realistic program that could attract academically qualified, industrially experienced people to move from industry to academia does not exist. Nor does any significant national program exist for getting faculty out to industry to gain the needed experience. (It must be the *right* experience or we will simply perpetuate the current problems!)

Cost is an enormous problem for colleges and universities that might wish to respond to ABET and improve their engineering design education. Even if the knowledge and the experienced people were available to teach modern, realistic design courses, such courses are extremely demanding of faculty time and energy. It is simply easier and less expensive to teach analytical methods than it is to teach design. Without adequate budgets, schools cannot afford the cost of true engineering design education.

Thus, it is useless to talk about changing engineering design curricula unless provisions are made for providing a continuous source of appropriately educated and experienced faculty to teach, update, and provide political support in academia for design. We have no such source. Our engineering design education infrastructure is indeed severely broken.

Research in Engineering Design.   Research in a technical field does two important things: it produces new people for the field, and it generates new knowledge. Thus, a strong case can be made that the primary cause of our broken engineering design infrastructure is the neglect of research. If adequate support for research in engineering design were available, graduate programs would naturally form around this research. Not only would new knowledge be developed, but also new people would be educated to carry the knowledge and a design orientation into industry and into courses and faculty meetings.

A vivid example of this process at work is the field of materials. Two decades ago, fundamental research in materials became the focus of Department of Defense and other government agencies. The result is that today we not only have prosperous industries in new materials, but we also have exciting new materials graduate and undergraduate education programs. There is a large pool of very well educated materials scientists and engineers for both industry and faculty positions. In contrast, it is almost impossible to find qualified people in engineering design.

New Knowledge.   In addition to the people that research in engineering design could generate, new knowledge derived from research is just as desperately needed and the potential benefits are enormous. The kind of research needed in engineering design stretches along a spectrum from short-term, very applied projects for specific companies to long-term, very basic research into design theory and methodology. In between, there is research that is intermediate-term and of a *precompetitive* nature. This is applied research in the sense that it deals with real issues that concern designers on a regular basis, but it is not specific to a company or to a particular type of product.

An example of a basic research need is development of the basis for a new generation of computer-aided mechanical design systems.[13] There is a strong consensus—at least among end users in industry—that current computer-aided design (CAD) systems have very limited application in engineering design and manufacturing environments. Although complex 3-D modeling software exists, most companies continue to use their CAD systems solely for two-dimensional detail drafting; a relative few are performing more sophisticated but highly constrained finite element analysis and tool path generation functions. The real benefits— simulation of product and process operations, making downstream manufacturing information available to designers at early stages, integration of optimization and other mathematical tools, and increased communication among design, manufacturing, and other departments— are not realized. (Interestingly, current research programs in integrated manufacturing—such as the Automated Manufacturing Research Facility at the National Institute of Standards and Technology—are being impeded by the lack of a robust, flexible computer representation of the product design.)[14] This is due to a number of reasons, the most important being that the required software does not yet exist, even though the computer hardware needed is available and relatively inexpensive. The software doesn't exist because the research on which it can be based is not complete. The *lack of a theoretical basis for design processes* is also inhibiting the development of other useful CAD tools for designers. The relation between basic research and application is commonly acknowledged in other scientific and engineering disciplines. But the status of design as an "art" more than a "science" inhibits serious study and support for research in design theory.

Precompetitive research in design can be sponsored jointly by companies with common applied research needs. For example, cost analysis models for early design stages that are sensitive to downstream life-cycle issues are currently sought by a wide range of companies. Also, industrywide research and dissemination of the design-for-quality methodologies pioneered by Genichi Taguchi could and should have been undertaken when these ideas were first introduced from Japan 10 years ago.[15]

Sources of Research Support.   Where can the financial support be found for design research? Clearly, specific product research should be sponsored by industry or done by the companies themselves. Most companies, in fact, do this, though they tend only to be able to do those projects that resolve some obvious, immediate crisis. It is difficult for universities to be able to do this kind of research, though it can be done where there are very close university–industry relationships.

There is a question about U.S. industry's interest in longer-term design research. Does industry in general have the vision and will to invest in it? Many visitors to the few existing design research labs in the United States are not from U.S. companies, but from Japan, Germany, France, and other foreign countries. After comparing notes with other design researchers, one of the authors found that foreign visitors to these labs usually arrive in groups that have carefully studied the technical publications and ask prepared questions. This contrasts sharply with the occasional visitors from U.S. companies. One academic researcher, respected for basic work in design for manufacture applications, recently sent a prospectus to a prominent, very large U.S. manufacturer to inquire about possible financial support. The reply was that yes, the research was certainly worthwhile in the long term, but why should they pay for basic design research when they can read the results in available technical publications? However, they won't read it because, without support, the work cannot be done. Precompetitive research needs industrial support.

In Japan, it is common for industrial firms to have their own software teams developing application software specific to the company needs. In the United States, this role is usually assigned by default to software vendors, but this doesn't work. Unless there is potentially a very large multicompany market for software, the risk simply does not justify the large development cost. The result is that the application software does not get developed. Universities—through sponsored research projects—can develop application soft-

ware up to what is called the proof-of-concept stage. However, graduate students cannot finish the job of making the software ready for actual use in industry. This transition from research software to field-ready software is not especially difficult but it is time-consuming and expensive. There is no real mechanism in our society for getting this job done.

The longer-term, more-science-oriented research should be the province of government, especially the National Science Foundation. Until four years ago, however, there was no design program at NSF. With great foresight, a program was initiated by MIT's Nam Suh in 1985. However, today that program, called Design Theory and Methodology, still has a budget of only about $3 million (about a quarter of 1 percent of the NSF budget) and is under fire within NSF. Even if the program survives politically, $3 million is only a very small portion of the money needed to repair the damage done by previous decades of neglect in basic research in engineering design. Moreover, it may be noted that Japan's Hitachi spends more money on design-related research than the entire NSF budget.

Defense Department Involvement.   The Department of Defense (DOD) has also sponsored research in design topics related, of course, to specific defense products. Recently, however, DOD, through the Defense Research Projects Agency (DARPA), has undertaken to sponsor work that is somewhat less product-specific. In a program called DICA—the DARPA Initiative in Concurrent Engineering—a consortium of defense industries and university researchers is attempting to develop an approach to design called *concurrency* into a more formal, computer-supported methodology. Concurrent design means that, in addition to the function of a product or device, manufacturing concerns and indeed all life-cycle concerns are taken into account from the very beginning of the engineering design process. The DICE program is an excellent example of intermediate-term, precompetitive research that can pay off handsomely. A possible criticism is that progress may be limited because some of the basic research on which to build a concurrent design system is not being done, and there is little patience among the defense contractors involved for this kind of longer-term research.

In the fall of 1988, a Defense Studies Board report suggested that DOD might be given prime responsibility for sponsoring research to rejuvenate our manufacturing industries. The main argument for using DOD for this is that there is no other agency that could get the funds from Congress to do it. We have no National Engineering Foundation, and NSF is not going to do the job, though the funds available there can make a significant impact if used to support the right set of fundamental studies.

DOD has a pretty fair track record in basic research sponsorship. The field of material science noted above is a case in point. However, there are three concerns about DOD sponsorship of research in design and manufacturing. One is whether the proper relationship between design and manufacturing will be reflected in the funding goals and policies; that is, will their program reflect the fundamental role of design? The second concern is whether the more basic scientific issues will be given appropriate attention. The successful materials program included a great deal of basic research. Design and manufacturing researchers, however, are under much greater pressure from industries with urgent short-term needs. Can a suitable balance between long- and short-term research issues be attained by a DOD program? Third, can Congress fund DOD sponsored research in design and manufacturing without exerting adverse political influence on the use of funds? However we do it, research is the key to new people and new knowledge that can repair design education and reform design practices.

Management of Design. Despite the design buzzwords beginning to become common in industry literature (e.g., *design for manufacture, concurrent design, design for quality*), changes in the management of engineering design are slow to come. For while the *recognition* of design's importance in keeping U.S. industries competitive in global markets has begun to increase, the actual *response* continues to be almost entirely in manufacturing: automation of existing processes, material and labor cost reductions, quality control, and so on.

Within U.S. manufacturing organizations, there are at least three reasons for this, which are symbiotically linked to the lack of research and education resources described above. They are:

- The lack of technical understanding about engineering design by management.
- Inadequate metrics for evaluating the engineering design process.

- Outmoded organizational structures which are unresponsive to the importance of good design for cost, quality, and time-to-market.

Lack of Understanding. The lack of understanding by management of emerging engineering technologies and organizational structures is particularly true for design. Clark and Hayes have cited the loss of product and process design know-how by managers and engineers since World War II as central to our manufacturing decline.[16] According to Xerox's Bebb, this is a major reason for our failure to learn from the successes of Japanese industry:

> The implications of many of the "experts" about Japanese processes that success is due to manufacturing effectiveness and management practices is dangerously misleading. A primary factor in Japan's success is development and utilization of new engineering design methodologies that are not yet broadly understood by U.S. engineers, much less by U.S. corporate management.[17]

Among other things, U.S. management tends to blur the distinction between *new technology concepts* and *engineering design* of new products. Many corporate R&D laboratories have been well staffed for "Big Science" technical innovations, but lack the resources and mandate to pursue more practical issues of product development.

As with engineering schools, business schools lack a pool of experienced faculty to teach the management of design. While Don Clausing and others have made a promising start in developing appropriate management methods, these initiatives remain far from the mainstream of traditional business school curricula on discrete product manufacture.[18]

Metrics. Managers and economists have failed to construct and implement evaluation procedures for manufacturing that are sensitive to the role of design. There are a number of reasons for this. First, there is a natural tendency to look where money is actually spent (in downstream manufacturing) rather than to where the commitment to spend is in fact made. The former is easy to identify; the latter is more diffuse and obscure, but more important. Second, there is a very strongly ingrained tradition in industrial management—going back to Frederick Taylor and Henry Ford—to measure product value only in terms of labor and material costs.[19]

Manufacturers must also find ways to include the *value of the design itself* as a part of the product value equation.

Xerox's Bebb and others have described some innovative work in the past few years in "competitive benchmarking" that includes assessment of engineering design on cost and quality. One study comparing plastic parts found that Japanese supplier costs were 50 percent less than U.S. costs. Half of this cost difference was due to higher resin costs and mold and other processing expenses. The other half was due to differences in design engineering: less multifunctionality of parts, tooling design, finishing, tolerances, and other design factors. As Bebb has noted, "The Japanese were simply outdesigning us."

Perhaps even less understood than evaluation of product designs is the *evaluation of the design process itself.* For example, time cycles for evaluating design value and design costs are typically tied directly to manufacturing cycles, and even to cycles for financial and tax statements. One problem that results from ignoring design cycles is cost increases by subcontractors. In many cases, a vendor for a particular part makes a successful low bid knowing that later design changes will allow it to increase the actual part cost, thus skewing the entire costing process. New accounting methods such as those proposed by Kaplan are beginning to address these issues.[20]

Organization.   In most U.S. industries, the responsibility for design, manufacturing, field service, and other functions is divided into companywide departments instead of being grouped by product. "In a lot of companies," says Kodak's Poccia, "you'll just be ignored if you tell a product group that they need to make a design change to avoid difficulties for the customer service department later on." Reorganization along product lines—spearheaded by efforts at Kodak, Xerox, IBM, and others—is starting to make a difference. In the past five years, both Xerox and Kodak have reorganized design and manufacturing along product lines.

A number of U.S. companies have in recent years experimented with design-for-manufacture (DFM) teams to address manufacturing issues early in the design process (the IBM Proprinter and Ford Taurus are probably the best-publicized examples; AT&T, NCR, Digital, and others are also using DFM teams). While a significant step in the right direction, many DFM efforts—in contrast to the Japanese—still focus on cost first and quality second. Another team concept known as The House of Quality—originally developed at Mitsubishi in Japan and adopted by Ford, Xerox, and others—has been used to bring together design engineers and marketing personnel early in the engineering design process.[21] In general, there still remains much to learn from the Japanese regarding organization for design: for example, Japanese design teams tend to stay assigned to a product well into production, but the norm in U.S. companies is to reassign design engineers soon after production has begun.

Xerox, as much as any other U.S. corporation, has taken dramatic steps to improve their design infrastructure. Ten years ago, spurred by the need to survive in the face of severe competitive pressures on cost and quality, Xerox commissioned a study to compare Japanese-made copiers with their own. Their conclusion—after much disbelief and rechecking within the company—was that Japanese copiers were being manufactured at half the cost and with significantly higher quality, and in half the time to market than their own. Since then, an intense program of fundamental changes in design practice has been instrumental in bringing cost and quality back to competitive levels (though time to market still remains longer than that of foreign companies), but only after a massive restructuring of management and engineering processes.

Design management and practice innovations such as these are still quite novel outside of a relatively few high-tech electromechanical industries. However, similar initiatives by a broad spectrum of discrete product manufacturers are critical to the long-term prospects of U.S. industry.

Conclusion

There are many causes, and hence many fixes, to our competitiveness problems in manufactured products. Most of these causes—the dollar, interest rates, bureaucratic issues—have been widely discussed. The current favorite cause is manufacturing itself. However, a critical problem, and an essential part of any long term-solution, is being neglected in the discussion. That problem is engineering design.

As a nation, we have neglected engineering design education and practice for decades, relying on old education courses and old design methods. Most importantly, we have also neglected engineering design research; as a result we have not generated the new people and new knowledge to revitalize our design education and practices. Economists, managers, and business schools have also neglected engineering design by failing to understand it, value it, and account for it appropriately.

We can no longer afford this neglect of such a fundamental field. The well-being, if not the survival, of our manufacturing base is threatened. A tactical, short-term, catch-up response via improvement of manufacturing alone is necessary but inadequate. We must also fix our broken engineering design infrastructure: education, practice, and especially research.*

Acknowledgements—We are indebted to Dr. H. Barry Bebb of Xerox for his ideas on engineering design in industry, and in particular for his suggestions for this article. Thanks also to Michael Poccia of Kodak, as well as the many other design engineers whose conversations with the authors in the past year contributed to this article.

References

1. M. L. Dertouzos, R. K. Lester, and R. M. Solow, *Made in America* (Cambridge, MA: MIT Press, 1989).

2. W. G. Downey, "Development Cost Estimating," Report of the *Steering Group for the Ministry of Aviation,* HMSO, 1969, reference from D. J. Leech and B. T. Turner, *Engineering Design for Profit* (New York: John Wiley, 1985).

3. Myron Tribus, "Deming's Way," *Mechanical Engineering,* January 1988.

4. Lester C. Thurow, "A Weakness in Process Technology," *Science,* December 18, 1987.

5. Don Clausing and John R. Hauser, "The House of Quality," *Harvard Business Review,* May/June 1988.

6. Kim B. Clark and Robert H. Hayes, "Recapturing America's Manufacturing Heritage," *California Management Review,* Summer 1989.

7. H. Barry Bebb, "Quality Design Engineering: The Missing Link in U.S. Competitiveness," keynote address to the 1989 National Science Foundation Engineering Design Conference, Amherst, MA, June 11–14, 1989.

8. Roland Schmitt, introductory comments to the 1988 National Science Foundation Grantee Workshop on Design Theory and Methodology, Rensselaer Polytechnic Institute, Troy, NY, June 3–5, 1989.

9. Seymour Melman, "How the Yankees Lost Their Know-How," *Technology Review,* April 1987.

10. Michael J. Piore and Charles F. Sabel, *The Second Industrial Divide* (New York: Basic Books, 1984).

11. Geoffrey Boothroyd and Peter Dewhurst, *Product Design for Assembly Handbook* (Wakefield, RI: Boothroyd Dewhurst, 1987).

12. Workshop on Engineering Design, May 25–26, 1988. Sponsored by Design Theory and Methodology Program, Division of Design, Manufacturing and Computer Integrated Engineering, National Science Foundation.

13. Michael R. Duffey and John R. Dixon, "A Program of Research in Mechanical Design: Computer-Based Models and Representations," *Mechanism and Machine Theory* (1990).

14. Preprints, Workshop on Manufacturing Data Preparation Technology, National Institute of Standards and Technology, Gaithersburg, MD, June 29–30, 1988.

15. Genichi Taguchi, *Introduction to Off-Line Quality Control* (Dearborn, MI: American Supplier Institute, 1980).

16. Clark and Hayes, "Recapturing America's Manufacturing Heritage."

17. Bebb, "Quality Design Engineering."

18. Clausing and Hauser, "The House of Quality."

19. Robert S. Kaplan, "One Cost System Isn't Enough," *Harvard Business Review,* January/February 1988.

20. Robert S. Kaplan and H. Thomas Johnson, "Activity-Based Information: Accounting for Competitive Excellence," *Target,* Spring 1989.

21. Clausing and Hauser, "The House of Quality."

READING 2–3
TEAMS NEED OPEN LEADERS

Michael Maccoby

There is no teamwork without considerable openness about sharing information, surfacing criticism, and resolving conflicts. So, if openness is so good, why don't we have more of it?

The simple answer is lack of trust. If I am open, the other person may take advantage of me. If I am honest about my costs, another person may not be and thus gain an advantage in the budget meeting. After all, we may share company goals, but we are also competing with each other. If I am honest about what I don't know, or admit a mistake, others may think I am out of touch or inadequate. If I criticize someone else, I may make an enemy. If I am open about bad news or openly disagree with the boss, I may be punished.

Only credible leadership can dampen these fears. To achieve openness in the team, the leader must *be* open and *encourage* openness in others by establishing and following rules and practicing values of respect and helpfulness.

Limits to Openness

We should keep in mind that all openness is not useful. In any company, there are initiatives that should remain secret, so that potential deals do not fall apart. In personal relationships, there are truths, which if told, are not helpful. For example, Freud criticized "wild analysis" in which analysts made interpretations that caused defensiveness. The patient was not prepared to understand these truths.

In the 1960s and 70s, some companies sponsored "sensitivity groups" in which managers were encouraged to "let it all hang out" and tell others what they thought of them. The result was that, for some people, these became insensitivity groups, where barbed comments wounded people. Instead of building trust, some of these sessions provoked rancor, resentment, and paranoia.

Michael Maccoby is president of The Maccoby Group, Washington, D.C.–based consultants for strategic development. He currently consults to AT&T's Workplace of the Future. Reprinted with permission from *Research Technology Management,* Jan.–Feb. 1995.

Openness requires respect for others, tact, and a focus on sharing information and critical comments that everyone can acknowledge as useful for improving teamwork and organizational performance. There should be a common understanding and acceptance of the reasons why openness is desirable. Furthermore, openness takes time. People must test the waters before diving in.

The Swedish Bank Team

In working with the executive team of Swedbank (*Sparbanken Sverige*), I have experienced openness pushed to the limits with positive results. Two years ago, the bank was created by a merger of 11 Swedish savings banks (700 branches), some of which were in danger of going under due to the Swedish savings-and-loan crisis. A new executive team was formed, composed of 17 managers from the central bank and savings banks. The CEO, Goran Collert, asked me to help the team to define their goals, roles, and relationships.

I began the process by interviewing each manager separately about their views of their roles and each other. They all saw a need to know one another better. Some had critical views about others as team members. They also all believed that this team was too large, and that it was essential for Collert to select a smaller team of 5–10 members who would meet regularly to deal with strategic issues. But what should be the criteria for inner group membership? Team members were concerned about being left out.

Eighteen Months, Seven Meetings

We held seven two-day meetings over a period of one-and-one-half years. At each meeting, we increased openness through exercises that asked participants to share their experiences and aspirations and also to evaluate one another's performance.

At one of the early meetings, I led the team in describing the bank as a social system. They then defined the bank's seven Ss: strategy, structure, systems, skills, style, shared values, and stakeholder values; they discussed how these Ss needed to be aligned in order to achieve their goals. (See "To Create Quality, First Create the Culture," *RTM,* September–October 1993, pp. 49–51.)

At the third meeting, we did a priority-setting exercise. This exercise caused team members to begin challenging one another. In one dramatic encounter, an executive accused another of being lazy and not using his considerable talents to benefit the bank. The executive accepted the challenge and began to take a more active and productive role after the meeting.

We continued the priority exercise at the next meeting. Collert again raised the issue of forming the smaller inner circle with which he could work more easily in shaping strategic issues. The group described how they expected the inner circle to behave so as to guarantee that it was not forming a new hierarchy.

At the next meeting—the fifth—Collert challenged the group to raise the level of openness. He offered a choice: Either he would choose the inner team members by himself, or the group could participate in the decision by defining the qualities for membership, evaluating one another, and recommending who should be on the team. Although Collert would make the final decision, he promised to be influenced by the group's recommendations.

Portraying the Ideal Leader

The group also discussed the ideal qualities required of the bank's leadership. They agreed that the vision of the bank as a flat, decentralized organization required top managers to be synthesizers (see "From Analyzer to Humanizer: Raising the Level of Management Thinking," *RTM,* September–October 1994, pp. 57–59). As a step toward selecting the inner team, they brainstormed a list of 14 qualities required for top management:

1. Concern and understanding of the whole bank as a social-economic system.
2. Personal integration—social competence, judgment, and motivation.
3. Business orientation and customer focus.
4. Integrity as a leader—"walking the talk."
5. Commitment, energy, and ambition.
6. General knowledge and experience with the bank's different units.
7. Listening and learning "humbleness."
8. Self-awareness, knowing oneself.
9. Enabling others to succeed, being supportive and cooperative.
10. Generosity and openness.
11. Intuitive as a strategic thinker.
12. Wisdom, good judgment, creating trust.
13. Courage.
14. A good representative of the bank.

Although somewhat redundant, this list focuses on the combination of business management skills and personal qualities that the group expected from the ideal leader. Two qualities that could have been added are "an interactive change agent" and "a good communicator." However, the list proved useful in initiating the process of mutual evaluation.

Choosing the Inner Wheel

The next exercise provoked controversy. I proposed that team members rank-order eight executives whom they would support as members of the inner wheel. Some were reluctant. One said the exercise might be too hurtful to those who were not selected. It might drive a wedge between group members. Others supported the process. They argued that without this exercise, Collert would select the inner team by himself, and they would lose the chance to influence him. In any case, some argued that they needed to raise the level of openness and maturity to work together as a team.

I suggested a compromise. Only Collert, Christer Sandahl (a Swedish consultant), and I would see the results, and we would report back the names of those executives who received votes from at least 14 colleagues, 80 percent of the team. Everyone assented to this exercise, and as it turned out, one person received 100 percent while two others received all but two votes.

The group then discussed the leadership qualities they saw in Collert and the three who had received 80 percent of their votes. I asked them to relate any concerns they had about these four individuals and to describe the improvements they would like to see in their behavior. This process did, in fact, raise the level of openness and maturity. By being the first to be evaluated, Collert modeled openness and nondefensiveness. Viewpoints about the four that I had heard in private conversations became open.

At the sixth meeting, Collert announced that he had selected two more members of the inner wheel. One of these had been close behind the top three in the voting and had been scored high on leadership qualities. The other had not received such strong support, but Collert argued that his competence was needed in the inner wheel. The group openly discussed this executive's strengths and weaknesses.

This open discussion had a positive impact on the manager who had heard the criticism before, but had not understood how widely and deeply it was shared by his peers. Open evaluation was now experienced by the group as helpful feedback, and all the other team members asked to have their turn. This proved especially useful for team members who were disappointed at not having been chosen and wanted to know why.

At the seventh meeting, the group decided it wanted to continue to focus on long-term strategy combined with personal development. One issue suggested was information technology. It was also decided to expand the larger team to include six more top executives who would be introduced to the team by mentors who volunteered to describe what we had done and were trying to achieve. Team members recognized that in order to improve teamwork, they could not rely on these quarterly meetings, but had to create smaller projects and to spend time with one another outside the workplace.

Openness Elsewhere?

How generalizable is the experience of the Swedbank executives? Does this kind of openness depend on national culture? Are Swedish managers more open than those in other countries?

The answer is not simple. It would probably be more difficult to achieve this degree of openness with such a large group in many other cultures. Even in Sweden, it takes exceptional leadership and skillful facilitation to develop openness. It is true that in many American companies, managers are very "political" and tend to say what the boss wants to hear, but this depends to a great extent on the boss and the organizational values he or she affirms.

Where leaders practice values of respect for individuals, and where everyone understands common goals, it is possible to achieve considerable openness. Sometimes this starts out with exercises such as 360° evaluations from the boss, peers, subordinates, and customers. However, where there is insecurity, fear of reprisal, and tolerance for disrespectful, humiliating behavior, no one should be surprised that people play it safe.

An article in *Business Week* (September 26, 1994) describes how the top management of Chase Manhattan Bank used a mutual evaluation exercise to start a change process. The unanswered question raised by the article is whether or not this led to sustainable organizational improvement. Unless openness is carefully managed, euphoric instant intimacy does not last very long.

It may be more difficult to develop openness in Asian culture, because of sensitivity about criticizing anyone and causing loss of face. However, when I interviewed technical managers in China, Taiwan, Singapore, Hong Kong, Malaysia, Indonesia, Thailand, and the Philippines, I found them to be very open in private conversation, once they were convinced that my purpose was to strengthen the organization and that they would not be directly quoted. In this, they were no different from technical managers in Europe, the United States, Canada, and Mexico. It remains to be tested how much openness can be achieved with Asian managers who are given good leadership. Taiwanese engineers told me they would like to have more open discussion on sensitive personal issues.

Payoff

In summary, there is always resistance to being more open. Some kinds of resistance are realistic, others are irrational. Both types of resistance need to be made conscious, analyzed, and worked through. Everyone encounters limits to openness; there is only so much of reality any of us can bear. But for the individual as well as the team, stretching oneself pays off in greater awareness and ability to make informed choices.

No leader, in my experience, has suffered from being too open. By sharing knowledge, showing vulnerability, and creating a spirit of helping each other succeed, the open leader develops trust and brings out the best qualities in team members.

READING 2–4
IMPLEMENTING TECHNOLOGICAL CHANGE WITH CROSS-FUNCTIONAL TEAMS

Robert A. Lutz
President and Chief Operating Officer,
Chrysler Corporation

Chrysler's first turnaround, the company's storied comeback of the early- to mid-1980s, is a familiar story by now. But our more recent turnaround (which is still going on) is, I believe, an equally impressive story. What makes it impressive, in my view, is the degree to which we have been successful in implementing "teamwork" concepts into virtually everything that we do—including our research and development.

Traditionally, Chrysler, like virtually all other Western automakers, was organized around vertically oriented, "chimneylike" functional departments (Figure 1).

Source: Adapted from his address to the Industrial Research Institute Annual Meeting in Hot Springs, Virginia, May 1993. Reprinted with permissiion from *Research Technology Management,* March–April 1994.

Each department—design, engineering, procurement & supply, and so forth—was pretty much a world unto itself—a silo, if you will.

The Design Department, working more or less in a vacuum, would design a car and then (as represented by the larger arrows in Figure 1) "shove it out the door" to the Engineering Department. But, because engineering hadn't been fully involved in the process, changes for feasibility would invariably be required—resulting in what I call "re-do loops" (the broken lines).

Then, engineering, in a vacuum itself, would engineer the car and shove it out the door to procurement & supply to buy parts and components from suppliers. But again, there would be more re-do loops, because our suppliers had been in a vacuum of their own.

FIGURE 1

Vehicle development at Chrysler used to be a sequential, component-based process, where chimneylike functional departments (design, engineering, procurement) were pretty much worlds unto themselves

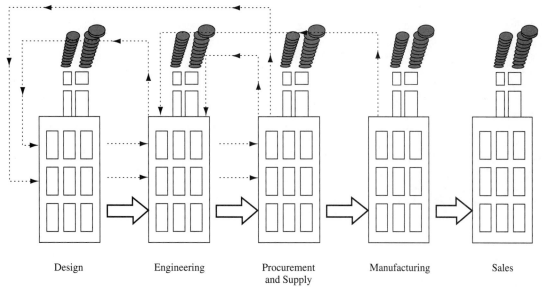

Design   Engineering   Procurement   Manufacturing   Sales
                                     and Supply

⋯⋯ "Re-do" Loops

The same thing would happen all the way down the line until, finally, all of the re-do loops started to look like a massive fur-ball!

The results, sadly, were mammoth costs, uncompetitive product development times, and, last but by no means least, "lowest-common-denominator" cars and trucks. That's because, even though there were intense turf battles all along the way, the sense of "ownership" for a *complete* vehicle was so diffuse it was almost as if nobody was responsible for it!

Toppling the Chimneys

After a lot of soul-searching, we took a brave pill and radically restructured out company's organizational system. Figure 2 illustrates what we did: Essentially we toppled the old functional chimneys and replaced them with *cross-functional* product development teams— what we call our platform teams.

We have four major platform teams in place: one each for small cars, Jeep vehicles and pickup trucks, minivans, and large cars. Each of these teams is made up of specialists from all the old functions, including our key suppliers. Indeed, our suppliers are critically important to us, both because they provide us with no less than 70 percent of our parts, and because they also supply us, more and more, with a whole lot of R&D. They feel safe about doing that because of the way we treat them.

In fact, I would maintain that the relationship we have with our suppliers is widely considered to be the closest in the domestic auto industry—what some have called an "American-style *keiretsu.*" The term I like to use is "virtual enterprise"—it really is as if we are becoming one big, seamless value-added chain.

Of course, a lot of companies have had so-called matrix organizations, but often without a lot of success. One reason for that, in my view, is that those organizations are often merely "coordinating functions" trying to help guide projects through the all-powerful "system." They are sort of like tug boats trying to push a battleship around. But at Chrysler, we have basically traded in both the tug boats *and* the battleship on four nimble destroyers!

Importantly, on the bridge of each of these ships is what the business-school textbooks might call a "Big L" leader (or what the Japanese would call a *shusa* leader). This is a leader who is truly empowered to make decisions without needless interference or meddling from the top of the house.

FIGURE 2

Chrysler replaced its functional chimneys with cross-functional product development "platform" teams that carry out a concurrent, whole-vehicle-based process

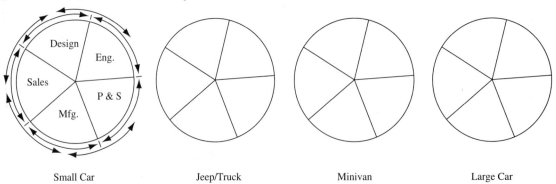

Small Car   Jeep/Truck   Minivan   Large Car

◀――▶ Decision Tradeoffs

New Cars—Faster, Cheaper

To try and quantify the difference this makes, consider Figure 3. This is sort of a "textbook" look at how platform teams are helping us at Chrysler to introduce products more quickly and at less cost. The horizontal axis of this graph represents the *time* it takes to develop a new car or truck. And the vertical axis represents *product spending*.

As the line beginning at the far left shows, under a traditional organization, spending on new product development, typically, began very *early* on the time axis. That's basically because we were afraid to wait! Spending then continued upward until, finally, it skyrocketed as we approached actual Job One production. That's due to all those re-do loops involving overtime, tooling changes, and so on.

To make matters even worse, spending continued even *beyond* Job One production, because we were changing things even after the cars were coming off the line.

The result was absolutely huge total costs—all that area in black. Of course, that's not to mention the opportunity cost of a slow response to the market, or the cost of bad quality due to all the last-minute changes.

Compare that to the spending curve in grey. Under our new set-up, spending begins much *later* along the "time" line. In other words, while positions are being debated and tradeoffs hammered out, hardly any money at all is being spent.

However, once a consensus is achieved within the cross-functional group, spending can ramp up much more quickly than in the past. It then remains consistently strong through the now-shorter development period. Then it ramps down fairly rapidly as well, finally ending (as it should) as Job One approaches.

Here are a couple of real-world examples.

1. Our newest sports car, the Dodge Viper, isn't exactly a technology showcase. It has no air conditioning, no CD player, no sophisticated electronics to speak of; in fact, it doesn't even have side windows or exterior door handles! What the Viper *does* have is a 400/horsepower, 8-liter, all-aluminum V-10 engine, plus some other, equally awesome, mechanicals. The car can go from zero to 60 in 4.3 seconds, and from zero to 100 *and back to zero* in just 14 1/2 seconds.

However, what makes the Viper most important to Chrysler is a different kind of speed. In January 1989, this car was merely a "one-of" concept car at the Detroit Auto Show. Exactly three years later, actual production Vipers were out on the streets.

Bringing the Viper to life in this almost-unheard-of development time was a highly focused, cross-functional team—in this case, made up of just 85 people. They called themselves Team Viper, and they

FIGURE 3

Under traditional product development (black), spending begins early and skyrockets as changes continue to be made to cars coming off the line. By initiating spending later, when the platform has achieved consensus, total costs are much less

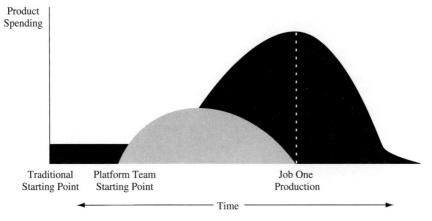

did the job not only in just three years but also for only $70 million (which in the car business usually won't even buy a decent change of grille and tail lamps!).

But, importantly, Team Viper wasn't so much a "skunk works" for us as it was a *test bed*—a test bed for our larger platform teams that are now in place. Aided by what we were learning from the Viper experience, we began making cross-functional teamwork the hallmark of *all* Chrysler product-development projects.

2. One of the most significant success stories thus far has been our new trio of 1993-model four-door family sedans—the Chrysler Concorde, the Eagle Vision, and the Dodge Intrepid—available at prices starting at $16,000. Unlike the Viper, these "LH" cars are loaded with modern-day technology like multivalve V-6 engines, ABS brakes, traction control, and standard dual air bags—not to mention what is considered in the industry to be a revolutionary overall vehicle design that we call cab forward.

Table 1 compares our 93 LH project with the original Taurus and Sable models introduced by the Ford Motor Company in 1986. Both programs spawned almost the same number of new vehicles, and both also involved the development of all-new powertrains. However, under our platform team setup, we were able to develop our cars in just three and one-fourth years, versus a reported five and six years for Taurus/Sable.

The total cost for the entire LH program was just $1.6 billion, including $600 million for plant modernization alone. That's at least $1 billion *less* than what was reportedly spent on Taurus/Sable. And we did it with a team of only 744 people!

That is the power of teamwork. What we are finding, frankly, is that having fewer people and limited resources doesn't have to be a liability—not if those resources are properly focused, and not if your people are organized so that they are genuinely turned-on and feel that their contributions really *do* make a difference.

The Viper team, for instance, consisted of volunteers who were wildly enthusiastic about cars. They were rewarded in the usual monetary sense, but they were also recognized in nonmonetary ways. Viper team members were the celebrated heroes of Chrysler, and many articles praising their accomplishments were written. Also, Lee Iacocca and I frequently went to visit them, and they received several other forms of recognition.

R&D on the Platform Teams

How does R&D fit into all this? In the old days, our advanced R&D group at Chrysler was itself a "chimney." (Perhaps a more apt description might be a very narrow, very bright, *stovepipe* branching off from the main engineering chimney.) This kind of setup is common in American industry. A group of scientists are off in a corner inventing things—but the problem is, they may not be inventing the *right* things for the market. Or, if they *are* the right things, they may be impractical—or too costly—to manufacture.

Even if they meet all of the other criteria, they may still never see the light of day simply because of the "Not-Invented-Here" syndrome and other psychological barriers to technology transfer.

At Chrysler, just as we have attempted to blur the line between our designers and our engineers and our manufacturing people, and just as we have also tried to blur the lines between ourselves and our suppliers, we have also intentionally blurred the lines between our advanced R&D people and our production people. We have done that by putting most of our R&D people onto our platform teams, right along with everybody else.

For instance, our entire electric vehicle project fell under the auspices of our minivan platform team. We feel that makes sense because minivans, with their people-carrying capabilities, are a logical type of vehicle for the alternative-fuel market (such as commuter vehicles for the Los Angeles basin). As we develop alternative-fuel vehicles to meet a growing list of state and federal regulations, we think it's just common sense to do our best to make sure that these vehicles are not just *technology*-driven, but also *market*-driven.

TABLE 1   Development Comparison

	1986 Taurus/Sable	*1993 LH Sedans*
Vehicles	Two sedans Two wagons	Four sedans
Powertrain	All-new	All-new
Development time	Five–six years	3.25 years
Cost	$2.5 billion (est.)	$1.6 billion

The Power of Tech Clubs

How do we avoid duplication of effort—or, even worse, the hoarding of information—when we have our platform teams working separately on R&D projects? How do we prevent, for instance, one platform team from inventing one kind of passive restraint system and another group from inventing a different one? The answer is that we have encouraged the formation of a very informal network inside the company that we call Tech Clubs.

These Tech Clubs have no formal charters, no minutes are taken, and no reports or white papers are prepared, or anything like that. In fact, we're not even sure exactly how many Tech Clubs we have! We want to get to the point where top management is no longer capable of drawing the company's organization chart! We want to stress a total horizontal and vertical flow of information, to the point where an organization chart becomes largely irrelevant.

All these Tech Clubs are, for instance, the brake engineers from the four platform teams, plus perhaps a purchasing person and maybe a supplier or two, getting together once a month or so over coffee to discuss their common problems, their common needs, and, most important, how each of them is coming up with *solutions*. They do this freely, because they know that the new system rewards collaboration, not competition (or at least not *internal* competition!).

Once in a while, there is a problem or a need that is just too big to be solved inside the Tech Clubs. So the Club members go to the general managers of their respective platform teams who, in turn, discuss with each other what to do. Once again, the system encourages them to collaborate.

What usually happens next is that the platform general managers, in collaboration with the Tech Clubs, agree among themselves on the logical platform team to be assigned the project. We don't worry about whose budget the money is applied to. In the old days, nobody would assume anything because it might get on their budget! This requires new thinking on the part of the finance department, which now needs to measure financial parameters horizontally to the point where we capture the cost of the vehicle from inception to customer delivery. That's very different from focusing vertically on the little salami slices of cost, which is the way our traditional systems were built.

To get this kind of change, you have to take a lot of impediments and fear out of the system. As a result, for instance, when these general managers get together to decide which platform team is going to deal with a particular problem, they help arrange whatever assistance or outside expertise may be needed.

Selecting General Managers

We look for people with good technical skills to be general managers, although they don't have to be specialists in combustion processes or anything like that. They do, however, have to be very goal-oriented, be very active, have good interpersonal skills, and be capable of motivating and building teams. We do not want the "Bull of the Woods" kind of people who rule by intimidation; we want people who manage the new way—by teaching and coaching (but not abdicating). And they have to have a strong desire to get the job done.

Scientific Research

Our small—but excellent—scientific research activity is not assigned to any platform team. In fact, this is where a lot of that so-called outside expertise comes from. It is a team of just 69 people, and they work closely with both the platform teams and the Tech Clubs. They are vitally interested in entirely new ways of fabricating automobiles, as well as in looking at advanced engine transmissions and bodies. But again, it is in the platform teams themselves that most of our advanced engineering and preprogram work gets done.

Proximity and Learning

In deciding where to locate our platform teams, we recognize that there are two forms of proximity. One is psychological proximity, or psychological cohesion of an organization: people identifying with the same thing and working on the same project willingly and in a team-oriented way, including working with suppliers. Obviously, the other type of proximity is physical. It is when you add the psychological proximity to the physical co-location that things really start to happen.

We put each platform team in a separate wing of a building, with escalators connecting them to the physical labs and the fabricating shops where the suppliers' representatives and our own people build assembly prototype parts. In that way, the platform people can grab a supplier's representative, and maybe their buddy from manufacturing and their buddy from design, and go down the escalator together until 30 seconds later they are looking at and feeling hardware. Then, when the hardware is assembled, they can drive it right onto a test track.

There is also an intensive learning process as each new platform team sits down with the team that preceded it. There is none of that "We're the big heroes and we don't want you guys to be better than we were, so you will just have to find out on your own." Instead, teams review the *entire* program, and they say, "Here's where we made a mistake; here's where we started something too early; here's where we started something too late; we had a bad experience with this supplier and we would suggest you not use him," and so forth. In this way, time and money are constantly being squeezed out. So far, the most friction-free development process at the

lowest cost and the greatest speed, with the largest number of absolutely perfect preproduction vehicles, has been our new Neon. The Neon team beat nearly impossible cost and weight targets, and they did that by studying the Viper team, the LH team, the Grand Cherokee team, the Dodge Ram Pickup team, and so on.

To sum up, we need to keep erasing that line between the people who *innovate* and the people who *implement*. We need to make *everybody* feel that they have the freedom to innovate and invent—just as we also need to make sure that our scientists, who are at the forefront of new technology, feel a keen sense of responsibility to the marketplace and to real, live customers.

It really is, I submit, all about teamwork. Teamwork is working at Chrysler, and I think it can work in R&D as well.

CASE 2–1
WESTINGHOUSE ELECTRONIC SYSTEMS: INTEGRATED PRODUCT DEVELOPMENT

John W. Kamauff, Jr.
Robert D. Landel
Larry Richards

In the summer of 1993, Robert T. Barnes, general manager of the Manufacturing Operations Division for Westinghouse Electric Corporation's Electronic Systems (ES), was reconsidering the organization's approach to integrated product development (IPD). He knew IPD had exciting possibilities for overcoming chronic deficiencies in the company's traditional serial approach to product development, but he was concerned about its effectiveness in several recent projects. Since 1990, ES had invested significant resources in investigating and understanding IPD and had developed guidelines for program managers and IPD cross-functional teams. An integrated development approach had been adopted, to varying degrees, in such major developmental projects as transmit/receive modules, modular radar, and low-temperature cofired ceramics. In reviewing progress to date, Barnes was attempting to identify what aspects of the multifunctional team approach really worked well and, more importantly, he hoped, how to institutionalize an IPD approach within ES.

Westinghouse Electric Corporation

Westinghouse Electric Corporation was a world leader in the development of advanced products and services for government, industrial, and commercial applications for more than 100 years. In 1992, however, the corporation reported a net loss of over $1.2 billion, despite generating an operating profit of $750 million, on sales and operating revenues totaling nearly $8.5 billion.

Source: This case was developed by Professors John W. Kamauff, Jr., Robert D. Landel, and Larry Richards of the University of Virginia based on field research initially conducted by Mr. Richard J. Frank, Jr., UVA, MBA 1992. Mr. Steve Kramer of Westinghouse Electronic Systems assisted in the research activities. Copyright © 1994 by the National Consortium for Technology in Business, c/o the Thomas Walter Center for Technology Management, Auburn University.

Recipient of the "one of the best cases" award at the preconference workshop at the First National Conference on Business and Engineering Education, Auburn University, Auburn, Alabama, April 5, 1994.

Westinghouse Electronic Systems

Westinghouse ES, considered to be one of the corporation's core businesses, generated approximately 31 percent of the company's annual revenues. With sales of over $2.87 billion in 1992 and a backlog of nearly $4 billion, ES continued to be a world leader in airborne and ground-based surveillance radar and other high-technology defense systems. Although headquartered at Baltimore-Washington International Airport, ES had other facilities both nationally and internationally. The group's primary customers were large institutional buyers representing the U.S. government and international agencies; ES worked closely with the Department of Defense (DOD), Federal Aviation Administration, National Aeronautics and Space Administration, and the U.S. Postal Service, and with prime contractors and commercial airframe and ship manufacturers to "turn advanced technology into advanced products, rapidly and efficiently." The approximate 1993 distribution of customer orders is shown in Table 1. According to *Westinghouse Today: A Special Report* (1993):

> ES has the resources to transform technical problems and market challenges into solutions our customers can depend on. Our strengths begin with our human resources: more than 14,600 highly skilled people, including nearly 5,000 engineers and scientists. They are equipped with the state-of-the-art research facilities and the tools needed to maintain our leadership in key technologies from sensors to

TABLE 1   1993 ES Customer Base

Customer	Percent (by $ volume)
Department of Defense	64%
Foreign military sales	6
Commercial	15
Government	8
Foreign	7

software. Westinghouse can exploit technological advances as they develop.

As shown in Exhibit 1, ES had adopted a management structure oriented around four product families: Aerospace and Anti-Submarine Warfare (ASW); Command, Control Communications, and Intelligence; Information and Security Systems; and Integrated Logistics Support. The Design Engineering and Manufacturing Operations Divisions (DEMOD) provided matrix support to the programs. Computer-integrated systems helped transform design engineering and manufacturing into a single, unified process. The ES flexible, distributed-manufacturing plants made it a low-cost producer of high-quality systems even in limited production quantities. Westinghouse also supported its manufactured products throughout the systems' operational life cycles.

Overall, in 1993, ES was continuing its strategy to strengthen its commercial electronics operations while maintaining its defense market-share. Key contract awards in mobile satellite communications, transportation-management systems, and international air traffic control had positioned the group to compete for key infrastructure projects in the 1990s. In conjunction with its continuing diversification into a wide spectrum of nondefense needs in commercial and civil markets, ES was also attempting to increase its global penetration by establishing strategic positions and joint ventures around the world.

DEMOD Background

In addition to supporting its program management with a matrix organization, ES was one of the first U.S. companies to treat design engineering and manufacturing as a single, continuous practice by combining, in 1984, Design, Producibility, and Engineering Division and Manufacturing Operations Division (MOD) under a single general manager. The manager who spearheaded the move summarized his role as follows: "I'm the embodiment of concurrent engineering."

After nearly a decade of being under a single senior executive, in 1993, the DEMOD was structured as shown in Exhibit 2. Permanent functions in the key disciplines of product design, manufacturing, quality assurance (QA), logistics, human resources, and information systems retained authority and responsibility for the technical performance and professional standards of their functional units. Project management teams were

created, as needed, to complete the work on specific programs.

R. T. Barnes, MOD general manager, cited the matrix organization as a competitive capability:

> The ES matrix organization enables us to design and build our products with maximum efficiency. The matrix structure forms a network of functional and program responsibilities and allows us to apply our engineering and manufacturing resources equally to the common elements of every ES system, whether for defense or commercial use.

To ensure a smooth transition from development to manufacturing, ES had also established producibility and transition assurance centers in 1988. This strategy had cut transition times between concept design and manufacturing up to 50 percent and more. Another innovative ES concept had cut its materials acquisition cycle time an astonishing 600 percent. ES had built an automated Material Acquisition Center (MAC) in 1982 to unify all the functions in acquiring, preparing, and distributing materials for manufacturing. The MAC's integrated information systems received and transferred manufacturing data throughout ES.

ES also developed a Manufacturing Systems and Technology Center (MS&TC) to develop the systems needed for manufacturing advanced products. For instance, ES engineers pioneered the computer-integrated manufacturing systems in use at their Electronic Assembly Plant (EAP). Located in College Station, Texas, this $55 million plant demonstrated the power of Westinghouse manufacturing technology. Its flexible manufacturing systems had reduced cycle times for printed wiring assemblies by 85 percent, while increasing first-time-through yields to a full 90 percent. In addition to EAP, ES operated specialized manufacturing centers in the Caribbean and Europe. Services ranged from cable fabrication to systems integration and test. This distributed manufacturing system enabled ES to build world-class products on a global scale.

Despite these accomplishments in integrated-design engineering and manufacturing, concerns remained that the existing organization did not adequately address the most difficult programmatic issues such as cost, schedule, and performance. According to Bill Newell, a supervisory engineer in Hybrid Engineering:

> Our culture is driven by programs and, as a result, we are weak in the area of manufacturing collaboration. Operations is seen here as a stepchild, to simply support the programs. While we do accomplish some fantastic things in

EXHIBIT 1

Westinghouse Electronic Systems (ES)

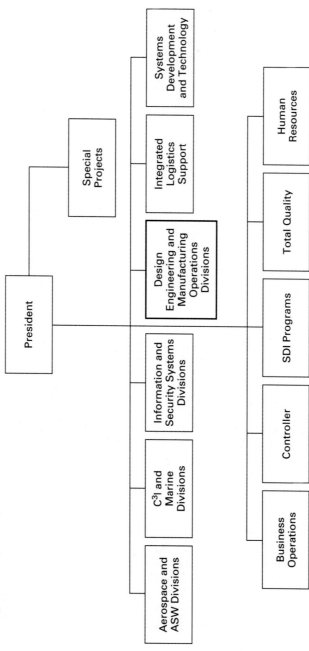

EXHIBIT 2

Design Engineering and Manufacturing Operations Divisions (DEMOD)

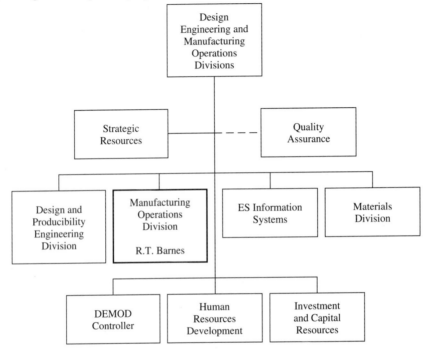

Source: Westinghouse.

manufacturing, there is no vision that we could be a manufacturing-driven company.

Recognizing such concerns about the matrix organization's ability to support programs, ES began to investigate the concept of IPD.

Integrated Product Development (IPD)[1]

IPD is a process of using a systematic, structured approach to consider all stages of the product's life cycle during the initial design stage; product cost and performance are engineered to meet the customer's objectives. The basic principle is to integrate the design of a product with the design of its manufacturing,

[1] Much of this section is based on *Results of the Aeronautical Systems Division Critical Process Team on Integrated Product Development* (WPAFB, OH: Aeronautical Systems Division, Air Force Systems Command, November 1990).

operation, support, and training processes; the goal is to achieve low-cost development, production, operations, and support within the shortest schedule and with robust quality of the products and services. In this context, IPD capitalizes on a systems perspective and structured program:

- Product and process alternatives are considered early to assure that the most cost-effective alternatives are chosen for further development.
- Using multidisciplined teams ensures producibility and performance from system design to field support.
- Teams use quantifiable technical and management tools.

The IPD approach requires the simultaneous, rather than sequential, integrated development and qualification of all the elements of a total system (Exhibit 3). It focuses on establishing Integrated Product Teams at the

Exhibit 3

Sequential versus Integrated Product Development

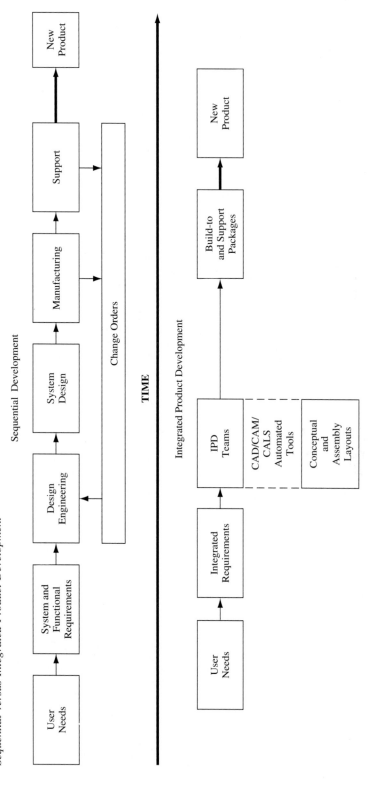

"doing level" to ensure that all functional and special-interest groups are "integral contributors" rather than "monitors" in the process. For IPD to be successful, the development process must change what people do and when they do it so that they actively participate by creating products that incrementally define the total system. IPD provides a structure to increase the emphasis on, and ownership of, the products and processes, improve horizontal communications, establish clear lines of responsibility, delegate authority, and institute clear interfaces with suppliers and customers.

The IPD Group

The general manager of Systems Development and Technology cited the turbulent nature of the ES marketplace as a major driver for change:

> In our business, we need a flexible factory and a close interaction between design and manufacturing. In the 1950s, our manufacturing was characterized by a dictatorial supervisor who mandated what got done; now it's tough to distinguish between the design engineering and manufacturing people. When you combine that with IPD—which is simply good common sense—you get all the people together to design and build. For years (and even still), we have pushed the design, and our "macho factory," to not be outdone by design, got the job done. But it was hard work and often at the expense of the people involved.

Barnes's MOD was significantly affected by the effectiveness of product development planning. By the 1990s, there was great pressure to compress product development cycle times from the 36–48 months that had typified efforts in the late 1980s to 12–24 months. In addition, the products were experiencing ever increasing cost competition. In traditional serial development, when MOD was ready to produce, the product had reached a very-high-value-added state. Marketing and design had finished their inputs and had begun focusing on new projects. Any changes in product design at the production stage were costly in terms of time and money. The IPD concept appeared to be an excellent way to implement total quality management in MOD's core functions while avoiding cost overruns, missed schedules, and systems integration performance failures.

These factors spurred Barnes to initiate an IPD effort in the transmit/receive (T/R) module project, and IPD evolved with each succeeding development project. A dedicated IPD facilitation/support group was eventually formed in 1991 with a cadre of eight people:

> It's been an issue of survival . . . when you are #1 on the DOD list and the Berlin Wall comes down, you scramble. Industry won't stand by so that you can build a program. We were world class in DOD and "also-rans" in commercial applications. IPD was our way to get ahead.

This group was charged with facilitating IPD activities within the existing organization and implementing process control and optimization (especially in manufacturing operations). In addition, the group was asked to develop and implement IPD training initiatives. These goals alone provided significant technical and cultural challenges, but in the words of Jeff Tucker, IPD group leader, "The [technical] tools are easy, but the real challenge for us is in implementation of cultural change."

The size of the IPD group had fluctuated since its inception in 1991, but including the manager, it consisted of eight people in 1993 (two of whom were on leave attending graduate engineering programs). Over time, the group had evolved to serve two primary roles: (1) facilitator for process control and optimization and (2) integrated product development liaison for key products.

In its role of product development liaison, the IPD group represented manufacturing and operations concerns to the design function. One group member saw the ideal IPD group tasks as evolving from these current roles:

> The IPD group would maintain its position as a technical support organization for process control, but the support would expand beyond the manufacturing division. In an ideal situation, the group's role as manufacturing liaison to design would be transferred to the relevant manufacturing group involved in each specific project. The IPD group would then act as a facilitator behind the scenes to help the process of IPD rather than do it themselves.

Some individuals within the IPD group were frustrated by the group's current position in the organization. Because the group resided *within* MOD, it faced difficulties in influencing the other functional divisions and truly integrating the various product development activities. Other divisions were frequently unaware of the existence of an IPD organization, and even when told, they often seemed uninterested in consulting IPD.

Expanding IPD

After considerable discussion, senior ES management decided that IPD offered enough benefits that the approach should be adopted in selected program situations.

As with all major initiatives to modify organizational behavior, however, the new product development strategy found advocates and opponents, and many issues centered around the relatively new IPD group.

The IPD Guide. To support the spread and acceptance of IPD, Barnes authorized the development of a user-friendly IPD guide that would solidify Westinghouse IPD concepts and also serve as a learning tool for program managers and the IPD teams that would consequently be formed for each project. This guide, published internally in July 1992, was developed by a quality improvement team composed of seasoned department and program managers and based on their experiences. Members of the IPD group did not participate in the preparation of the guide but were given the opportunity to critique the results.

The guide included a commitment statement ("We are committed to the Integrated Product Development process. We will assist the program manager and IPD team leader in understanding the use of this guide in their programs") and a sign-off by the general managers of all supporting matrix divisions, including MOD (Barnes), Systems Development and Engineering, Design and Producibility Engineering, and Quality Assurance.

The System Team. The guide introduced the ES product development "wheels" (Exhibits 4 and 6), in which all functional areas were served equally by the team leader who occupied the center of the wheel. The guide's purpose was to lead users through the complete cycle of subsystem product development. It adhered to a typical DOD process flow, from contract award through first-piece production and did not specifically address preproposal or system level activities. It provided a list of IPD group members to help in IPD training and give "specialty guidance for the various disciplines."

The guide proposed a tiered approach. The system team (Exhibit 4) was responsible for the entire product system. It was led by the program manager who worked with the subsystem team leaders and support managers. The key task was the development and management of the comprehensive program plan (CPP):

> The *program manager* is responsible for generating the CPP with appropriate division level general managers within one month after receipt of contract award. The CPP defines the product subsystems, the events necessary for the

Exhibit 4

System Team

Source: Westinghouse.

program to meet its requirements, and the support resources needed. The output of the CPP is required input for the IPD team leaders. The major components of the CPP are shown in Exhibit 5. The *program manager* also works with marketing and IPD team leaders to assure that the system (hardware/software) meets market needs.

The IPD Team. The second-tier teams, the subsystem IPD teams, represented by the IPD wheel (Exhibit 6), would support the program launch team. Each IPD team would take responsibility for specific subsystems such as the power supply, antenna, transmitter, or receiver. These teams consisted of an *integrated team leader* and members of the following core disciplines, as appropriate, for each specific subsystem: system design, product design, manufacturing, QA, test, materials, suppliers, and integrated logistics support. The guide spelled out the responsibilities of each team member as follows:

> The *integrated team leader* is responsible for planning and managing the team activities to meet the requirements and goals for a segment of the contract/product; cost (both nonrecurring and recurring), schedule, technical goals and objectives; application of resources and tools; team

Exhibit 5

Comprehensive Program Plan (CPP)

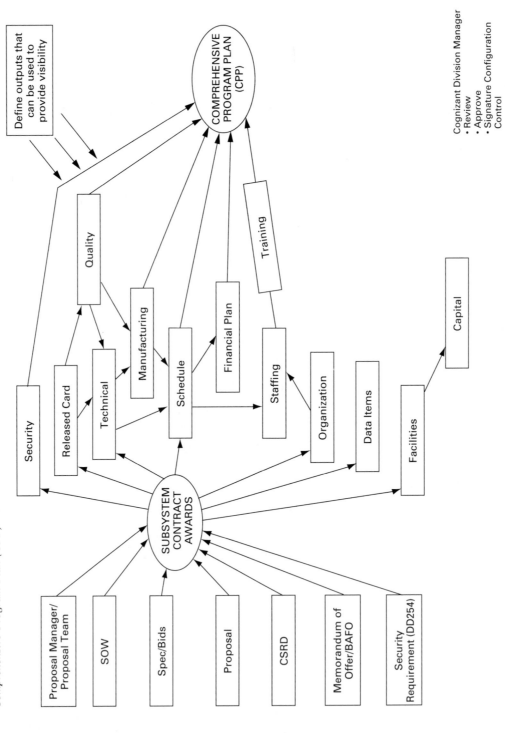

Exhibit 6

Integrated Product Development (IPD) Team

Source: Westinghouse.

effectiveness and implementation processes. The leader must also work with the program manager and marketing to assure that the subsystem meets market needs.

System design is responsible for systems analysis, system requirements, system hardware/software partitioning, system test and verification, documentation, and control of all systems requirements.

Product design is responsible for specification and design of all operational hardware and software elements of the system; incorporating quality, reliability, maintainability, producibility, and other specialty disciplines into the designs of all commodities in the system; documenting and controlling all design data; product design planning and managing; and engineering test equipment.

Manufacturing is responsible for manufacturing planning, product quality, production control, industrial engineering and process development, tool development and fabrication, assembly and test, manufacturing management, generating product cost data, and process source selection.

Quality assurance is responsible for quality flow-down and reporting; planning and managing

quality systems; quality-related training; process and personnel certification; and product acceptance.

Test is responsible for test planning and process development, test hardware and software development, design and acquisition, test equipment and use documentation, test equipment maintenance, calibration, and configuration control.

Materials is responsible for purchased material quality, acquisition planning, requisition release, cost and schedule availability, supplier identification, requirements flow-down, subcontract negotiations, and subcontract management. *Materials* also participates in the design-to-cost activity to contribute to accurate target pricing.

Suppliers participate in an integrated product design activity. They extend in-house capabilities to provide product (material) in support of program requirements. They are responsible for requisite planning and operations execution to ensure timely delivery of compliant product at a reasonable price.

Integrated logistics support (ILS) is responsible for analysis, Life Cycle Cost Analysis, spares provisioning, training, handbooks, field engineering and support, repair and maintenance services, ILS planning and management, and support and test equipment.

The IPD team was also to consult with other disciplines or, if conditions warranted, include them as full-time team members: internal and external customers, contract partners, management or technical specialists, analytical process facilitators and/or marketing. The roles of these groups were as follows:

Customers, both internal and external, are often considered to participate in making team decisions and tradeoffs. If a positive environment can be maintained on an ongoing basis, the IPD suggests that this relationship "be one of the most effective team arrangements." It is essential that contract *partners* are involved in each other's team activities. If the interface is major, it may be necessary that individual disciplines be represented by all partners. In addition, there will be times when *management or technical specialists* in specialty disciplines such as technology innovators, estimators, and management information systems developers will provide critical assistance to a specific team. Similarly, *analytic process facilitators* help to facilitate team problem-solving activities using such techniques as quality function deployment, Pareto analysis, and Taguchi methods (or designed experiments). Finally, *marketing* works with program management and IPD team leaders to ensure that future market options for the system are vigorously pursued.

IPD Team Assessments

The new IPD team concept was applied to many new product efforts, including transmit/receive (T/R) modules, modular radar (MODAR), and low-temperature cofired ceramics (LTCC). One of the issues that plagued a definitive analysis of the IPD efforts was that none of the programs had yet entered into full-scale production. Barnes was able to point to the establishment of the IPD group and the preparation of the IPD Guide as tangible evidence of applying the IPD approach at ES. He was also keenly aware that the lack of a clear, undisputable IPD success story contributed to varying views about the IPD process. Barnes believed each program had to be reviewed in detail, however, to get a clear understanding of the degree to which IPD could be successfully applied.

T/R Modules.   Radar system technology had changed substantially from the traditional mechanically steered antennas and the relatively inefficient passive phased arrays to active phased arrays. Active phased arrays are stationary antennas made up of up to several thousand radiating elements. Each element is directly attached to a T/R module. Each T/R module includes its own small transmitter and receiver, which are phase-adjusted so that (a) their transmissions combine in only one direction (a radiated beam) and (b) received signals are combined but from only one direction.

Since radar systems were ES's main products, and the T/R modules were the key determinants of the radar system performance and/or costs, these modules were critical to the success of each product. In order to control costs and ensure radar performance, ES designed and manufactured the T/R modules in-house. T/R modules were also used in electronic warfare systems. T/R modules had evolved into a generic commodity that could be sold to others, and these modules provided the stepping stones to enter new commercial markets.

Because one radar system could use thousands of T/R modules, the quantities needed for all ES systems could total millions of units per year. In addition, ES had decided to invest in developing advanced manufacturing methods to provide these low-cost, high-volume microwave assemblies to other radar companies. However, according to Barnes, who oversaw the effort: "This transition to high-volume commercial manufacturing (e.g., in million-size lots) has been a radical departure for us. IPD is the only way to do it; we have to integrate these technologies very early on."

The T/R module program was thus the first major project to incorporate the new IPD concepts into the product development activities, although the formalized IPD integrated team activities were not begun until 1990. Starting in 1987, Bill Newell, Manufacturing Engineering Lead, and Dr. Ted Foster, the Microwave Engineering Manager, spent an average of five hours a day for four to five months defining the integration tasks. In this time, they formulated an umbrella developmental strategy for the project that was still being used in 1993. The strategy included commitments, initially, to such philosophies and methodologies as concurrent engineering, variability reduction, statistical process control (SPC), and subsequently the IPD approach. During 1988–89, integrated product/process development activities were investigated under the auspices of the U.S. Air Force T/R Module Manufacturing Technology program, and the IPD team concept was actually written into the F-22 radar proposal for the advanced tactical fighter, which was subsequently awarded in 1990 to the team of Westinghouse and TI.

The T/R module IPD team was composed of representatives from design, manufacturing, materials, factory test, components, quality, and variability reduction. Customer relations were handled on multiple levels: Top management interacted directly with the customer's top management. At a lower organizational level, the systems team translated specific product performance requirements into subsystem requirements, and the subsystem engineers worked directly with the customer's engineers to resolve problems that arose.

Realizing the importance of an integrated effort from the supplier to the customer, Westinghouse trained its suppliers in TQM techniques. Initially, some suppliers realized only a 5 percent yield, which was completely unsatisfactory for the aggressive cost goals required by the F-22 contract and set by the IPD team. The variability reduction training provided by ES, however, contributed to eventual supplier yields ranging from 95 percent to greater than 99 percent. The T/R module team also experimented with supplier relations by bringing a supplier into the design review. This approach had never before been tried but the results were significant. As the materials manager explained, "The supplier said the design would not work, and this resulted in a design change." Supplier relationships thus proved to be especially rewarding in the T/R module project.

Quality function deployment (QFD) proved to be a useful tool in the T/R modules. It was used, for example, in the translation of the housing or interface requirements into design guidelines. Team members used QFD to identify customer needs and determine the engineering tradeoffs between different customer requirements. Using the tool was not always easy, however, according to Robert Horner, the IPD group member who facilitated supplier partnerships: "QFD is a very good tool, but it is not much fun. Getting together for a consensus is really tough. We did try to include the customer in these meetings."

Design of experiments (DOE) was also considered to be vital by the IPD teams to the project's success. Every process relied on a controlled experimental foundation. Between 1990 and 1992, 30 DOEs were performed at an average cost of $30K each and resulted in at least a 10-fold reduction in defects in each of five critical assembly processes. Formal SPC was not used, but data for future use were collected and stored in a database. According to Horner, "SPC should not be necessary if the proper work is done up front with QFD and DOE."

Manufacturing analyses were also used where practical. No other T/R modules were available for direct comparison, but ES conducted comparative assessments of the individual components of the T/R modules. ES determined the technical needs for each purchased component, then went to the suppliers and asked how each planned to meet those needs. This method helped with the initial selection of suppliers.

Despite the apparent valuable contribution of IPD tools and techniques in some areas, their use was not universal. During 1990, ES embarked on an investigation of the process of benchmarking led by Steve Kramer, a senior manufacturing engineer and IPD group member. The initial results of his benchmarking efforts were disseminated throughout the IPD group but were not totally embraced by the team members.

Feelings about the matrix management support of IPD were mixed. Horner explained: "Matrix management is both a friend and a foe. It is good for sharing the wealth of knowledge between projects, but it is also a drain on getting things done." The major concern was that IPD team members frequently moved between projects, and the transitions took time and promoted inefficiency. Furthermore, team members were not evaluated by team leaders but by their functional supervisors. The concern was voiced that "an individual could do well on a project but not be properly rewarded." On a more positive note, most team members believe that product-development duplication was reduced: "Wheels are not being reinvented in every project." Newell commented: "If you asked me if it is

working, I would have to say yes. We get incredible results while being significantly understaffed . . . upper management loses sight of how hard people are working."

Consistency of effectiveness proved to be a problem in the early IPD efforts. The IPD teams had different abilities and achieved different results. The F-22 operations manager, and a team member, attributed much of the disparity to "the differing abilities of the leaders." Indeed, leadership was often seen as the critical component for a successful team. In the T/R module project, team leaders were chosen based on past performance in the "old management system" and were given little or no training in the new methods.

MODAR.   The MODAR program was intended to provide low-cost predictive wind shear and improved weather detection in an expanded airborne radar market.

The key to the MODAR program was to develop a new product line by overcoming significant challenges in modularity, flexibility, and guaranteed high reliability in a short development time. The potential problems were exacerbated by the fact that limited nonrecurring development funds were available. In addition, MODAR was designated to be a dual-use product, built to commercial standards but applicable in both the military and commercial markets. With this product, ES was entering a highly competitive market where performance had to be cost-justified.

Launched in 1991, shortly after the T/R module program, MODAR adopted an IPD approach in order to meet a diverse set of objectives. For the most part, the goals were well defined and communicated throughout the teams. "Aggressive target pricing" was embraced as key to MODAR success. Extensive tradeoffs were made in establishing the design requirements and tolerances before 10 percent of the project was completed, and the baseline requirements did not change significantly for the remainder of the project.

The success of many Westinghouse projects often depended on the organization being able to learn new technologies and simultaneously learn to serve new markets. Unlike those projects, MODAR drew from a familiar technology (airborne fire-control radars). The MODAR program only had to extend an existing technology to a new, albeit commercial, customer base, which in this project eliminated a significant amount of uncertainty.

According to Rita Herlihy, a mechanical design engineer and IPD team member, the MODAR IPD team was composed primarily of design and manufacturing staff with quality and reliability staff playing minor roles. Prior to Jeff Tucker's assignment as IPD group leader in 1992, he served as a manufacturing engineer in the IPD group that facilitated the MODAR IPD process. While some people wanted to conduct general training in IPD tools for the entire MODAR staff, Tucker believed that such training would waste valuable time because everyone would not be using all the tools and techniques. According to Bob Jelen, engineering manager for MODAR, "Jeff brought a sense of reality to the program by introducing only the tools which were needed and could be used at the time."

The key elements introduced during MODAR were CPP (Comprehensive Program Plan), phased product build, quantitative tools/methods, cross-functional teams, team ownership/accountability, and training and development. In addition, the developers embraced proactive manufacturing participation, added purchasing coordinators to each IPD team, set "no purchase over cost" goals, established partnerships with suppliers, provided timely feedback on the status of cost goals, and used "prototype" hardware built by production facilities/personnel.

The MODAR project eventually used a variety of IPD tools and techniques, as shown in Table 2.

Notwithstanding the debate over the use of tools, the initial program results were dramatic, providing a reduction in the product development cycle time of over 50 percent when compared with previous efforts (see Table 3), which translated directly into reduced nonrecurring engineering costs. MOD was also able to automate 96

TABLE 2 MODAR Productivity Tools

Quantitative Tools and Measures

QFD
Functional analysis
Failure mode and effect analysis
Value analysis engineering
Design-to-cost
Design of experiments
Design for assembly
Competitive cost comparisons
Structured problem solving
Capability studies/SPC

TABLE 3 MODAR Cycle-Time Reduction

	Typical Program (months)	*MODAR (months)*
First processor hardware	10–12	5
First prototype system	14–18	6½
First flight	18–24	8½
First production delivery	24–30	14

percent of the circuit card assemblies by designing to process and standardizing the criteria for component selection. The Advanced Manufacturing Technology Center, which was dedicated to high-volume production, increased process yields from 80 percent to 99 percent and, in one department, decreased defects by almost 80 percent in one year.

The IPD teams were credited with much of this success through their abilities to inculcate a holistic view of the product-development effort, obtain early manufacturing participation, and facilitate communication with the teams. Mike Fahey, a manufacturing engineering manager, stated "The MODAR project was the first time in my life that I had seen a design change before it went into manufacturing."

Despite these early successes, some observers noted that IPD teams could have performed better in some areas. Supplier nonrecurring engineering needed to be fully planned, for example, and the condensed schedule caused higher rework labor and material on the initial systems. The IPD teams met weekly to ensure that all groups were working toward the same goals and working well together. These meetings proved to be a source of frustration for some people, however. Herlihy explained those involved in MODAR noted a number of weak areas in the process. Accountability between task and schedule was criticized, for example. Jelen also noted a problem when the time came for the transition to production: "Some of the design engineers simply did not want to let go of the product." Additionally, while communication within teams was strong, communication between IPD teams was weak.

The team approach was touted as a great idea, but the meetings often went off track. They would get bogged down in a few details which could have been solved by a few individuals. Major conflicts were resolved with a few key people. The decision-making process seemed to be hampered by the new team process. The emphasis on consensus decisions often acted as a detriment to decisive action. Furthermore, the team composition, especially in leadership positions, was criticized as being poorly planned. According to Herlihy: "Electrical engineers made up the majority of IPD leaders, but they did not really lead. I do not think they understood their roles; they were expecting to be in more of a technical position."

Barnes knew that team members were still struggling with team life cycle. Although the teams were technically intact in 1993, they had not really worked together since the assembly drawings had been created and delivered to manufacturing during the previous year. Herlihy believed that "the team should not fall apart after design is done. Members should still continue the contact."

Unlike in other IPD efforts, little conflict occurred between the functional matrix and IPD team leaders. Herlihy explained that she had devoted full time to the MODAR project during the early stages and used functional management as a consulting resource. Unfortunately by 1993 she had been assigned to two other jobs that demanded equal time and this caused problems.

In addition, the transition to production had not gone smoothly, some assembly and workmanship issues were noted in high-quantity production, and Barnes had recently begun to encounter some significant problems:

> On MODAR, we did great on the up-front planning, but then we unleashed our young people and told them to go do it. We lost the necessary discipline to get it done and did not ask enough critical questions throughout the process. We have, in essence, "empowered" our people without preparation. We failed to enforce the programmatic discipline. Everything went fine until we put it together . . . from an overall systems viewpoint we failed to stay close enough to it. Our 25- to 40-year-old workforce had not been prepared adequately for the tasks.

LTCC. Low-temperature cofired ceramics (LTCC) was a new technology that formed electronic elements or networks on a supporting substrate. It had emerged as a viable alternative to other packaging and interconnection methods because of its ability to integrate digital, analog, radio-frequency buried microwave and components in a hermetic, monolithic unit.

The LTCC development project followed the T/R module and MODAR IPD efforts and offered the greatest opportunity for introspection because it drew significantly on the learning from previous IPD efforts. Relying on the experiences of the past, the LTCC project used such tools as QFD, benchmarking, and cost modeling in the early stages to lower overall costs in the long run. To achieve the specific program goal of developing, demonstrating, and implementing a low-cost, high-throughput (250,000 square inches per week), and flexible LTCC manufacturing process, the IPD team developed a comprehensive methodology consisting of six tasks: state-of-the-art review, manufacturing-system requirements definition, benchmark study, process simulation and cost modeling, manufacturing-system concepts generation, and manufacturing system concept selection. The task interactions are shown in Exhibit 7. Recognizing that the six tasks were interdependent, the IPD team opted for close interaction between the parties responsible for each task. To facilitate daily communication, members were colocated in one office area.

As illustrated in Exhibit 7, state-of-the-art review, requirements definition, and benchmarking provided information for the generation of two potential LTCC *manufacturing-system concepts.* An iterative process involving the cost and simulation models, technical feasibility analysis, and risk analysis was used to determine the most effective low-cost, high-throughput, flexible LTCC manufacturing system.

The early results of the LTCC IPD teams had been mixed. Tim Parr, the manager of Printed Wiring Assembly Manufacturing Engineering and the LTCC team leader, told Barnes: "The LTCC project has been the most frustrating in my career at ES. The transition from design to manufacturing has been difficult, since design engineering has been reluctant to give up the design." Parr believed that an integrated team required that "team members have experience in both manufacturing and design, or team members from design and manufacturing need to understand their disciplines and be willing to hand off to the next discipline at the appropriate time." He believed the LTCC project faced a situation in which the good design engineers were unwilling to hand off to the somewhat inexperienced manufacturing engineers. Parr's concern with inexperienced manufacturing personnel was exacerbated by the fact that, although most of the team consisted of unquestionably dedicated industrial and manufacturing engineers, they had spent most of their time in ES labs prior to the LTCC project.

Parr's views on IPD tools were varied. He said, for example, "I hate the term DOE . . . it's a buzz word . . .

EXHIBIT 7

LTCC Methodology

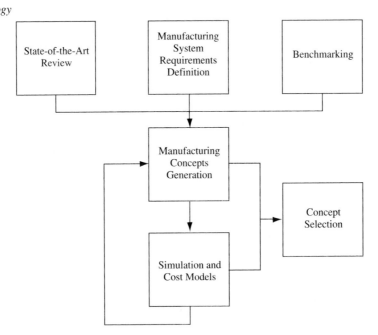

Source: Westinghouse.

but I love the concept." Parr was also a strong supporter of benchmarking when it was used judiciously. Although his team used QFD to identify the customers' needs and translate into specific product and process specifications, Parr remained skeptical: "I feel that QFD is grossly overrated. It consumes a great amount of time, and you must measure the benefits against the input. It may be appropriate in some cases and LTCC may be one of those cases, but they try to use it everywhere. Sometimes it cannot be justified."

Barbara Mae, a senior manufacturing engineer, who led the QFD effort, was also suspicious of QFD's utility in the LTCC project:

I think QFD was unsuccessful in the LTCC effort. The houses [of quality] were too big and should have been scaled down. Furthermore, management kept pulling people off QFD; it was the lowest thing on everyone's priority list. QFD was further frustrated by management's misunderstanding that QFD could be accomplished in a short period of time. They simply did not understand that time between sessions was required for research.

QFD (quality function deployment) did further the LTCC effort. Different pockets of people contributed to LTCC development, and QFD brought these people together in one room. QFD helped form team relationships.

Training was also designated by Mae as a limiting factor in the LTCC application. Mae had been put in charge of several QFD efforts without any prior training, and although she had learned QFD (by self-education and experience), she desired some formal training. She believed the training needed to be accomplished at three levels: management, among QFD team members, and for the QFD leader. "Management needs to understand the requirements and limitations of QFD. Team members and team leaders need training to understand the concept and their respective roles." One team member, Stephanie Caswell, a manufacturing engineer, also liked the concept of QFD but was having problems with the mechanics and had hoped for additional training.

Of all the IPD tools used in the LTCC project, benchmarking, which was facilitated by Steve Kramer, a senior manufacturing engineer in the IPD group, may have been the most appreciated by all participants. IPD team members and process owners (those who would eventually be responsible for implementing the manufacturing-system concept) participated in visits to investigate how other organizations approach problems similar to those encountered at ES. According to Caswell, one of the process owners, it was valuable to see how other people have solved similar problems. "You can lean a great deal just by looking around, but you have to see it. You cannot benchmark over the phone."

Cost control was an important element of the LTCC project. In its transformation from a government contractor to a commercial competitor, ES found that it had to pay much closer attention to the production costs of its products. The traditional military contract concentrated on higher performance at lower production quantities. The private sector spurred ES to begin an aggressive design-to-cost strategy to increase the cost viability of high-technology products which also carried over to the military sector.

The LTCC project used a process simulation and a spreadsheet cost model to assist with the design-to-cost effort. The ultimate goal was to simulate the manufacturing of a product design. The model considered the technical difficulty of the design and the material/labor requirements and then calculated the manufacturing cost of each product. A single simulation took about three hours, however, and according to a manufacturing engineer, "When it takes that long to run a simulation, it really is not a useful tool anymore."

One potential weakness of the preproduction planning, which included QFD, benchmarking, and cost modeling, was noted by Caswell:

> The study is primarily a paper study which aims to identify the optimal manufacturing facility. Unfortunately, Westinghouse faces incredible time pressures and is very reactionary in its response to this pressure. A result is that some equipment has been ordered prior to the identification of the optimal configuration. They try to get the study team involved, but in some cases, they simply could not wait for advice.

Views from the Functional Areas

Barnes recognized that the existing matrix structure at ES had a significant impact on the effectiveness of IPD

teams. Individuals reported to their respective teams and also to their functional leaders. The functional structure served as an important resource to all teams and team members. Each function had the dual responsibility of staying abreast of all developments in the functional area and also serving as technical support to the individuals who were members of project teams. The IPD efforts had a tremendous effect on all ES functions; instead of keeping all projects within the boundaries of the functional areas, functions were now expected to lend their members to project teams. The different functional leaders expressed different views of the effect of IPD on ES and their specific functions.

Marketing. The marketing department for ES consisted of 20 people who obtained additional support at the division level. Because of ES's historical focus on the military market, the marketing department concentrated more on strategic issues, such as which markets to pursue, than on day-to-day relationships with the customers. As Steve Winchell, marketing manager, explained: "Our engineers work with our customers only a daily basis. This is not bad, since they work with the customers' [the military] engineers." Winchell was clearly concerned that "this will not work as well in the commercial world."

Although marketing did not work closely with IPD teams on a daily basis (not designated on the IPD wheel of Exhibit 6), Winchell believed that his people were indeed a part of the teams.

> In product development, marketing must bring the initial idea. Marketing people are charged with looking for new opportunities and they do that to support the team effort. However, when they find a new opportunity, they are immediately looking for other opportunities. There simply is not enough time or enough people to work on the old one.

Winchell added that "most design and manufacturing engineers don't come in contact with marketing. Some don't even know we have a marketing group."

Manufacturing. In the 32 years in which he had been involved primarily in mechanical design and manufacturing engineering, Mike Fahey had seen many changes. Fahey viewed IPD as being much broader than concurrent engineering: "It is an integrated methodology." Despite his support for cross-functional team empowerment, Fahey did see some potential pitfalls in team management:

> If you get a participative system that becomes inert because people are so participative, you are headed for trouble. You need a leader who will keep them on track, and he needs to be autocratic in this regard. He needs to say "[The task] will be done by this time." A participative manager must put pressure on people.

Fahey noted a major structural problem which interfered with the IPD process: "All budget money came through the functional management, and this fact weakened the power of the IPD team leaders." In his eyes, to be truly effective as a leader, the leader should be responsible for both team member evaluations and funding. The functional leaders could then concentrate on ensuring that their function was on the leading edge of its technology.

In terms of current acceptance of IPD, Fahey felt that much needed to be done. "I do not believe that there is a universal support of IPD. The only person who has given a blank check to IPD is Bob Barnes . . . I think you need to get a little autocratic to institutionalize this system. We need to say that this is the way DEMOD will do business."

Design Engineering. According to Jim Redifer, general manager of the Design and Producibility Engineering Division: "A matrix organization leads to technical competence because mentoring is available, but the environment can be sheltered from the rest of the world. On the other hand, an IPD framework yields greater self-reliance and interplay with other functions, but people need to learn to ask for help when it is needed; it also requires a greater emphasis on interpersonal skills." In his opinion, IPD teams necessarily "make life more difficult for our functional managers—since they have to be able to reach out to a somewhat more spread out group of people—and somewhat easier on our program managers, but that's probably the way it should be."

Because they furnished 80–90 percent of the IPD team leaders, design had a unique perspective on the role of the team leader position. Team leaders had found the position to be extremely frustrating. According to Jerry Beard, manager, Signal Generation and Reception: "Vivian Armor, DEMOD Human Resources manager, conducted a survey of all team leaders. When asked if they would like to be a team leader again, only 1 of 14 responded positively." Beard felt that management had

mismatched people to the job. "Although some did the job well, none were trained and no one knew how to train them. In the old days, we had a design leader who was primarily technical with technical responsibilities. The position now is more of a program manager and less of a technical role. People are falling by the wayside."

Beard felt that upper management wanted the functional organizations to be held responsible for product failures. This situation understandably created a reluctance on the part of functional managers to turn responsibility over to IPD teams. An example can be seen in the development of nonstandard parts. ES wished to reduce the number of parts it produced to reduce inventory and to facilitate automation. Upper management pressured the functions and required that functional management—not the teams—must approve all nonstandard parts. John McClure, Mechanical Design and Development manager, agreed and noted that "functional managers would often grab the team back since they didn't want the team to stumble."

Regarding functional managers, Redifer was not convinced: "You *can't* teach an old DOD dog new tricks!" In the first two years he headed Design Engineering, all of his department managers retired, died, or were laid off, so he was able to build a cadre of people committed to his vision of greater interaction between design and manufacturing. In general, he was not sure if you can train someone with the necessary expertise to run IPD teams: "People need to have an innate ability to lead."

ES has a dual track for management and technical promotion, but according to Redifer:

> Functional people never viewed a move into program management as a desirable step in their vertical track careers. Now, because of flatter organizations and integrated efforts, we need much more lateral movement and adaptability to new environments, including a greater emphasis on interpersonal skills such as communicating to a scattered functional group. In any case, because of program autonomy, it's still difficult to get them to listen to you. IPD has been personally driven rather than implemented by management or a steering committee.

Systems Design and Development. Noel Longuemare, general manager, Systems Development and Technology, viewed the IPD process as consisting of potential tradeoffs in terms of innovation, a structured methodology, and risk management:

From our own experiences, defense engineers can very readily adapt to the commercial environment, but they have to understand the new ground rules. It's not an instant transition. Contrary to the military approach where there is a set of requirements, in the commercial world the number one issue is the price of the product as an independent variable; everything else is a dependent variable. We have to give these people a tool set that enables them to translate their actions into costs. We have shown that once a price is set, it is possible to develop the performance accordingly. It is, however, much more difficult to invert the process.

In his opinion, the application of oversight and discipline within the DOD had gotten out of hand—no tradeoffs were allowed; in the commercial world, the customer who has to sell the product can readily make these tradeoffs. He hoped that IPD would help ES to adapt to this emerging environment. "We have found IPD to be successful beyond our expectations when we use it properly, so we are diligently pursuing ways to make it the norm. We have seen no disadvantages . . . it's a win–win."

Regarding tools, Longuemare believed the single largest failing was in providing enough depth in the requirements.

Understanding the relationships was important before we went off to do something. In the military, it always took them longer to get the contract written, so we were behind the power curve to begin with; we marched off smartly and typically had to backtrack in order to match the changing requirements. Few were willing to invest the requisite time to do the up-front planning. One of the main advantages of the IPD process is that it is conducive to doing just that.

To do IPD, a fundamental importance is to have collocation for the core team. It is also important to give the team local authority to get the job done, particularly so that they do not have to fall back upon preexisting systems. At ES, one of the biggest mountains yet to be climbed is the development of the necessary systems to facilitate IPD work. Until recently, it has not been possible to bulk our costing for separate items. We had to segregate for different uses.

Quality Assurance.   Terry Hart, Quality Assurance manager, suggested that the IPD process had run into problems as teams began to cut corners.

Terry Hart tried to ensure that there was a flowdown of quality objectives to all teams so that they are all heading in the same direction: "The key is understanding what the mission of the team is. We need to understand the purpose of the team and staff it

accordingly—it could be based on experience or a variety of other factors." Hart also contended that the problem of measuring engineering was still paramount: "How do you measure engineering? It's the most difficult area to measure . . . let's do it like we've always done it. We seem to learn the same lessons over time. Recently, we have tried to measure the profile of engineering change notices over time, but we are not convinced this will work."

Bob Glanville, DEMOD QA manager, supported the IPD effort, but in his opinion, several changes were required before IPD would become an effective force in QA. He believed the organization had not yet realized the full benefits which IPD could provide. QA was the last group to see the product before it reached the customer, but Glanville believed quality awareness needed to move back through the organization, "We must do our quality work up front. This means meeting the customer requirements and minimizing variability." He was convinced that one part of a good IPD process was design and manufacturing working together to develop a process with a high yield. Unfortunately, the current situation was one in which "we measure a few processes, but manufacturing does not measure, or even understand, many processes."

Others in QA emphasized the importance of prioritizing customer requirements. Glanville added: "It is essential that we distinguish key functional requirements from other requirements. Often the customer does not differentiate key requirements. Hopefully, IPD teams can help us to prioritize what the customer really needs."

Summary

Barnes knew the sentiment about IPD, both pro and con, was running high. Clearly, it was a topic of debate—one that generated significant emotion in the functional areas, the programs, and especially the increasing number of people who had actually been involved on teams. For example, many program personnel had begun to focus on the difficulty of MODAR making the transition to production:

The initial shock of IPD was that we took our best artisans and then put them together under young technical leaders; this was something new, and the resistance was, "You want me to go and do this?" The thing that has me concerned is that some of the dinosaurs are saying, "See, IPD does not work."

Longuemare echoed this belief:

Now we must have the greatest degree of personal interaction and quick decisions in our programs. That does not imply that there is not a discipline in the approach. There are some fundamental problems that remain. How do you create an environment that encourages innovation while maintaining discipline and configuration control while designing a product that can be built? No individual is necessarily best at all things ... most of the time you cannot find people who can create and maintain discipline.

We frequently take someone who is innovative and put them into a position that requires them to maintain discipline ... and often have to endure the consequences.

Barnes was an ardent champion of IPD and believed that the benefits could be captured only if all of ES embraced it. Therefore, he had to act quickly to demonstrate its viability for integrating product development before opinions opposed to IPD became entrenched.

CASE 2-2
WESTINGHOUSE ELECTRONIC SYSTEMS: T/R MODULES

John W. Kamauff, Jr.
Robert D. Landel
Larry Richards

By May 1989, the most recent development phase for the transmit/receive (T/R) module had been successfully completed by a multifunctional team at Westinghouse Electric Corporation's Electronic Systems (ES). One thousand complex, highly integrated microwave modules were produced with minimal rework, and at less than 20 percent of the first lot cost in 1988. The T/R modules were destined for a prototype, state-of-the-art, phased-array radar system for the U.S. Air Force's (USAF) next-generation fighter aircraft, the Advanced Tactical Fighter (ATF). The T/R module program was the first major project in which Westinghouse's new integrated product development (IPD) concepts had been incorporated into the project development activities.

The IPD team for the T/R module had reached its cost and production quantity goals for demonstration/validation phase of the program. Bill Newell, lead manufacturing engineer, knew the team had an objective of making the T/R devices a "throwaway" (replace versus repair) product by the end of the decade. Newell wondered how the team could possibly achieve this goal. What were the most significant barriers to reaching the program vision of a throwaway module?

Newell speculated on the future phases of T/R module development:

> There is so much room for improvement in our product development approach. The challenge is to make the whole development activity robust—the organization, the processes, the design, even suppliers. Every nook and cranny has to be examined. We have to make the key drivers of the product and our process tolerant of significant variation in the manufacturing environment. In short, we have to identify the drivers of cost, performance, and schedule and optimize and improve them continuously.

Source: This case was developed by Professors John W. Kamauff, Jr., Robert D. Landel, and Larry Richards of the University of Virginia, based on research initially conducted by Mr. Walter J. Sedlazek, UVA, MBA 1991. Mr. Steve Kramer of Westinghouse Electronic Systems assisted in the research activities. Copyright © 1994 by the National Consortium for Technology in Business, c/o the Thomas Walter Center for Technology Management, Auburn University, Alabama.

Recipient of the "one of the best cases" award at the preconference workshop at the First National Conference on Business and Engineering Education, Auburn University, Auburn, Alabama, April 5, 1994.

Background

Westinghouse Electric Corporation is a Pittsburgh-based manufacturing company with a rich tradition. It celebrated its 100th year of business in 1986 and was a global, $12 billion company with operations in 44 countries. Westinghouse was organized into three manufacturing lines of business and a financial group. The defense business, Electronic Systems (ES), was a $3.2 billion business with 23,000 employees in 1990. The other two manufacturing lines were industrial products and the nuclear-power-plant business.

The core business for ES is radars for the military, and it is the global leader in airborne fire control radar. Westinghouse radar dated to Pearl Harbor and was used in military equipment ranging from the Airborne Warning and Control System (AWACS) to the F-16 fighter aircraft. In the 1980s, ES had tripled its annual sales and quadrupled its operating profit while keeping the size of its workforce stable. To support this productivity growth, ES had invested in its organization and facilities.

In 1988, the Westinghouse's nuclear division had been one of the first three companies to win the Malcolm Baldrige National Quality Award honoring American businesses whose goods and services have attained "preeminent quality leadership." As a result, a renewed quality awareness had spread throughout the corporation. An internal competition modeled on the Baldrige Award, called the George Westinghouse Quality Award, was begun. At the same time, the U.S. Department of Defense (DOD) instituted a policy on total quality management for its contractors. As a consequence of these developments, ES established a goal to win the George Westinghouse Award in 1993 and the Malcolm Baldrige Award in 1994.

Mid-1980s Development Environment at Electronic Systems

The ES-designed and -produced military airborne radars were of the highest quality in performance and durability. The group's top market share indicated the military's approval of ES's technical ability. ES was also recognized as being expensive in product development, requiring long lead times to develop and deliver its products.

In the mid-1980s, ES had an engineering-driven culture and was organized in a matrix structure. The functional areas included systems design, product design, manufacturing, quality assurance, materials, administrative, and logistics support groups. The technical management of each development project was led by a program manager who had members of the key engineering disciplines matrixed to the project. The conceptual, prototype, and product development phases of a project were frequently led by a manager from product design. Project teams were staffed primarily with design engineers and supported by the other functions and skilled technicians. Later development stages were headed by manufacturing personnel with the other engineering functions supporting ramp-up and volume production.

The attention to high-performance product characteristics in ES radars gave the electrical engineering function a leading role in product development. Engineering was perceived to be an "elitist" organization. Confidence in the manufacturing organization was not high, as evidenced by the common practice of using engineering technicians as a manufacturing group to perform highly specialized, low-volume assembly work during the prototype and development phases of a project. Sometimes these technicians were used even for production of low-volume, deliverable equipment. One prevalent attitude was expressed by a senior product design manager:

> Design engineers did not understand the production process but thought that they did. Design engineers resented manufacturing for not understanding their needs, for instance, not knowing why their designs required the specifications they defined. As a result, designs were difficult to make and the routine factory workers could not do any sophisticated prototype work because it was kept in design engineering.

Another design engineer added: "Design engineers owned the whole process of new product development. Design it, paste it up (layout), shoot it, get mechanical engineering consultancy for packaging, and finally build and test the prototype in the design laboratory area." He continued:

> Manufacturing was the "other" division. You even had to go and find the mechanical engineers because they were on a separate floor. There was not much thought about the

process of building the final design; design decisions were all made using *performance-based* criteria. The product was redesigned for producibility after we released the drawings to manufacturing and sourcing.

The design engineer, typically, would have already been assigned to the next development project and necessarily isolated from production activities once the design had been released to production. Manufacturing and process engineers were responsible for producing it, manufacturing technicians were responsible for troubleshooting the design in production, and a test engineer was responsible for resolving all but major design flaws. The design engineers thus did not find themselves on the production floor resolving time-consuming production problems caused by their designs unless they had made a major error.

Design engineers, who claimed that their view was "always right," seldom considered input from the production floor. Factory operators and supervisors were perceived by some arrogant engineers as not being able to add anything because they were "dumb." Other design engineers believed manufacturing had "no good ideas" so "why solicit their help?"

The suggestion system used on the manufacturing floor was ineffective. It was dollar based, and some machine operators believed management actually discouraged awards for usable suggestions by tolerating a lengthy process for approving and implementing ideas.

The factory floor did not concentrate on process improvement. Each manufacturing operator, building the radar units, was skilled at basic, manual assembly operations. Training was aimed at developing correct assembly techniques in order to meet product certification requirements. Quality control was performed by visual inspection to meet military standards and achieved through 100 percent screening/testing and rework.

The Opportunity

In 1985, the USAF was about to begin its next generation of fighter aircraft, the ATF. It called for the design of a high-performance radar based on phased-array radar (PAR) technology. Traditional radar physically steered a specially designed flat plate antenna to transmit and receive electromagnetic energy in the form of radio frequency (RF) signals. PAR had up to thousands of small antennas physically built into an array that could be electronically altered to simulate an antenna being mechanically steered to transmit and receive RF signals. The current generation of PAR, in which a number of vendors were competitive, had a centralized system to transmit and receive RF energy through the antenna array. The ATF program presented an opportunity to decentralize the transmit/receive system to individual, microprocessor-controlled transmit/receive (T/R) modules for each antenna array element (see Exhibit 1), significantly increasing radar capability and reliability.

Senior managers at ES considered capturing the contract for the ATF radar system development a strategic necessity. The technology developed for the ATF would have wide application in future radar systems and would give the winner an advantage in future contracts. Westinghouse's leading position in airborne radar would be threatened if it lost this contract.

The concept of a phased-array radar using individual T/R modules was a high-risk approach. Exhibit 2 shows the cost of a complete radar system at 10 percent of the total aircraft cost and shows that a T/R module would have to be produced in volume at a cost of $400. Additionally, the T/R module would have to be the size of a finger and produced at a rate of one per minute.

Although full-scale production would not occur for over a decade, the technology required for the T/R module was unproven. The estimate was that with *existing* product and process technology, a single module would cost $1 million and take several months to be produced. The challenge, therefore, was to demonstrate the cost viability of new technologies in the form of T/R modules. The challenge was formidable and the USAF customer was skeptical of both the technological and cost risks. Westinghouse was perceived as having the design expertise to manage the technical risk, but its manufacturing capability for (relatively) high-volume production was questionable in the customer's mind.

Sugar Cube

The initial Westinghouse design for the T/R module, called the sugar cube, was a crucial step toward winning the contract. The goal of the sugar cube was to take existing state-of-the-art technology to a new level. A functioning prototype would demonstrate the design concept. More importantly, Westinghouse's strategy called for manufacturing engineers to become involved during the transfer of the design concept to a function-

ing module. This involvement by manufacturing was atypical; as noted, prototypes were normally prepared in the electrical and mechanical engineering design groups.

The sugar cube led to a joint venture with a competitor: Texas Instruments (TI). The competitive strategy was to capitalize on TI's manufacturing capability and win the USAF's confidence in minimizing the cost risk. The Westinghouse/TI team was selected as a sole supplier on the first phase of the ATF program. Having a single source was an unusual decision for the early stage of a major military program and a major victory for ES, given its relative inexperience in high-volume manufacturing.

Dr. Ted Foster, the ES T/R Module manager explained the situation:

> The environment was in flux during the bidding. There was the concern of losing Westinghouse's radar systems development expertise to a competitor—TI. TI was to provide producibility expertise. It had large-volume production experience in monolithic microwave integrated circuit (MMIC)—the technology on which T/R modules were based. It would be key in successfully transferring the design to a manufacturable state.

The T/R module was a highly integrated, complex electronic module similar to a very large-scale integrated circuit (VLSI), a relatively mature technology. Exhibit 3 on page 106 shows the scale and the major subassemblies (transmitter, receiver, and microprocessor controller) of the module. All three subassemblies fit within the housing of the largest subassembly, the T/R module.

Although the T/R module was similar to VLSI, the design and manufacturing issues were more complex. VLSI circuits processed low-power digital signals at moderately high frequencies. T/R modules, except for the microprocessor controller, would process higher-power RF signals at microwave frequencies. T/R modules were also made from gallium arsenide, a very difficult material with which to work compared with VLSI's silicon.

RF technology, on which T/R modules were based, was commonly referred to as "black magic" by electrical engineers. The performance and reliability of units based on RF technology were extremely sensitive to interactions between materials, components, interconnections, tolerances, and the environment. To have any opportunity of a reasonable production yield, a robust design had to be intricately linked to a manufacturing process that emphasized variability reduction.

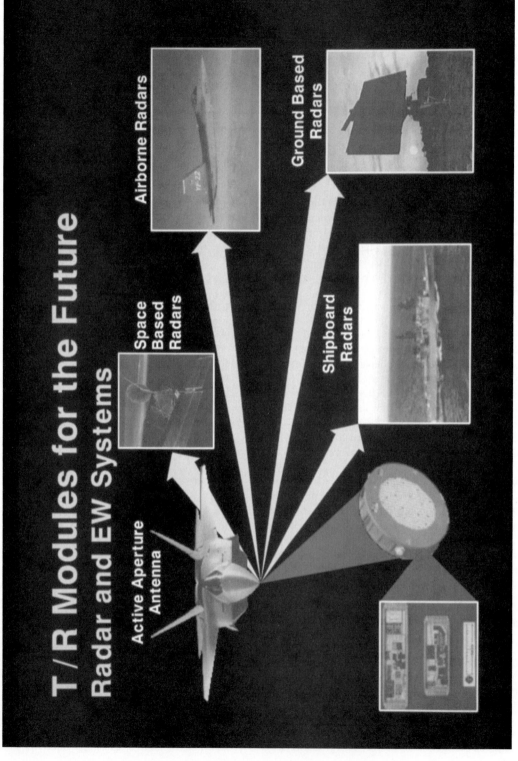

Source: Westinghouse.

EXHIBIT **2**

The Importance of Module Price

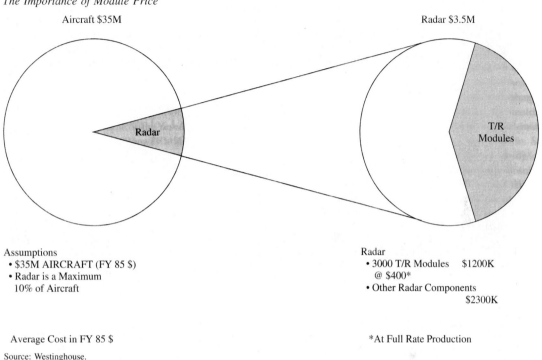

Aircraft $35M

Radar $3.5M

Radar

T/R
Modules

Assumptions
• $35M AIRCRAFT (FY 85 $)
• Radar is a Maximum
  10% of Aircraft

Radar
• 3000 T/R Modules $1200K
  @ $400*
• Other Radar Components
                 $2300K

Average Cost in FY 85 $

*At Full Rate Production

Source: Westinghouse.

The proposed miniature scale, high volume, and projected low cost of the T/R module compounded the design and manufacturing issues. Process yield would be critical to both volume and cost. Automated, precise, and nonvisual techniques for production and quality control would also be necessary. The skills required to deal with variability, scale, volume, and yield would challenge the capabilities of the entire ES organization.

The Vision

The sugar cube provided only a starting point for Westinghouse's development. As one electrical design engineer, explained: "The sugar cube was awarded the corporate gold signature award, which was a design achievement award. It was *not producible;* it was an engineering feat. It helped to win the contract, but did not provide the capability to fulfill it." The program was viewed by some as an Olympian quest, in essence "a

challenge to be the best." In the electrical engineer's eyes:

> We saw the ATF radar system as the first of its kind to be flown in the U.S. and the most advanced in the world. It was a very clear and effective motivator to the people involved in the project . . . they had a big role to play in the business going forward.

ES had much at stake in this project because the future of their radar business depended on it. It was also an opportunity to develop a strong leverage point to increase and consolidate a mainstay business for the divisions. This vision, however, was predicated on producibility.

The T/R module team was determined to chart a path to their cost-target goal. Exhibit 4 shows what ES would have to achieve, in terms of a learning curve, to obtain that goal. Bill Newell, lead manufacturing engineer, commented, "We had to plan for both a revolution and

EXHIBIT 3

The Scale of Major Subassemblies

T/R Modules Have Progressed Significantly With IPDs

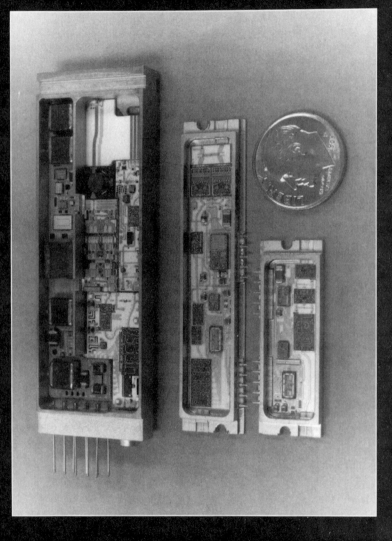

Source: Westinghouse

Exhibit 4

Learning Curve (T/R Modules)

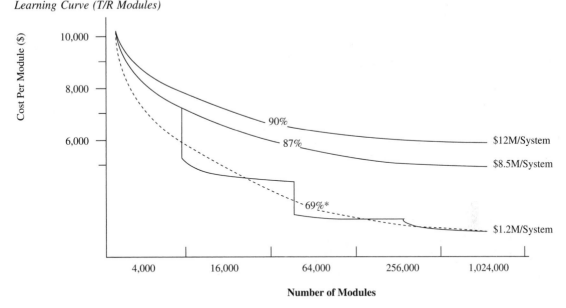

Number of Modules

*** 69% Equivalent Learning Curve Accomplished
through Cost / Producibility Initiatives**

Source: Westinghouse.

an evolution in order to stay on a 69 percent learning curve over the next decade."

To drive this effort, the team investigated the use of the process capability metric, the C_{pk}, which provided guidance on variability reduction and targeted performance. It was a predictor of the ultimate yield of the production process as a result of manufacturing process capability and design specifications. C_{pk} defined the quality level of the T/R module's product and process design in terms of expected defects per process step. The quality of vendor-supplied parts, the number of process steps, and their process capability, as defined through C_{pk}, would be clear indications of the yields the T/R module would generate and, ultimately, its costs and producibility.

This planning was then transferred into a series of milestones that would have to be reached in order to accomplish the project goal. Exhibits 5 and 6 show the specific, measurable goals and technological advances necessary for the project to be successful.

These distinct and unambiguous goals were translated in terms of functionally integrative metrics, such as the number of parts and process steps (see Exhibit 6). The metrics were intended to create a product that was easily manufacturable and cost-effective and that would generate high yields through low defects. The thinking was: the fewer the parts and process steps involved in producing the product, the less overhead, people, and equipment that would be required. Minimal parts and processes also reduced the opportunity for things to go wrong.

The team also explicitly identified the critical risks that would have to be managed in the program. Recognition of risks early and by the whole project team would result in prioritizing and focusing efforts on ensuring the project's outcome. The critical risks were identified as follows:

- Module complexity driven by functional requirements.
- Availability/affordability of RF components.

EXHIBIT 5

Evolutionary and Revolutionary Process Developments

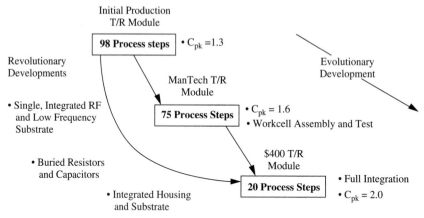

- Component variability.
- Process variability.
- Test complexity.
- Automation feasibility.
- The inappropriateness of military specifications for volume production.

After the project team explicitly defined criteria for success and clarified the critical risks, these factors became guidelines for actions and setting priorities in decision making; additionally, they provided a focus for discussions and supported the producibility vision. Because the goals and issues were broad rather than detailed action plans, they were easily understood by the project team.

Based in part on the success of the ATF radar program, the USAF Manufacturing Technology Directorate awarded the Westinghouse/TI team a contract to accelerate the cost reduction of T/R modules.

Expectations

Ted Foster described what would be involved in reaching the cost, yield, and volume milestones and in managing the risks:

> We had to gear people up. It was to be a cultural change exercise. No one had ever done this before. We had to

investigate and challenge the obstacles to our vision. We had to look at what keeps Westinghouse, even American industry, from doing what we had set out to do.

There was a common understanding that we had to leave the old environment behind and do things faster and cheaper. We had to produce at 50 to 100 times faster than we were capable of doing at that point, and do it with an immature technology at an "unheard-of" cost. Collectively, we understood that change was required. Our ability to control variation was going to be critical.

A manufacturing engineer described the T/R project as a new program requiring new skills and processes:

> Everybody was expected to do what it takes. You had to pull your weight in the project and to take a risk. The environment was new, open, different. People were encouraged to do things that made sense (a commonsense approach). The product required new, advanced technologies for the processes and the design. It was much harder to work with than digital microelectronics. The newness was traumatic.

A mechanical design engineer described the program as having a *"break-the-rules"* mentality to push things as far as they could go. "Management was constantly urging us on. They made a concerted effort to make this thing work."

Newell described the leadership expectations of Foster as follows: "Ted gave people the authority and responsibility to meet the goals of the program. He

EXHIBIT 6

Concurrent Engineering Is Required to Reach Goal: $400 T/R Module

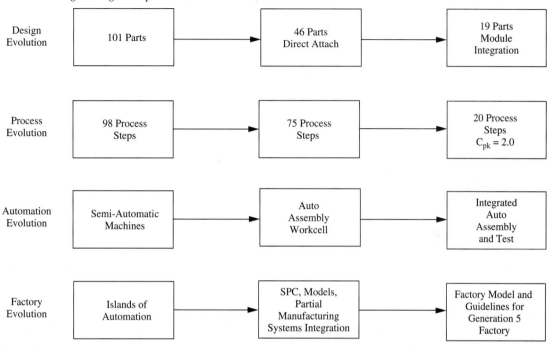

Design Evolution	101 Parts	46 Parts Direct Attach	19 Parts Module Integration
Process Evolution	98 Process Steps	75 Process Steps	20 Process Steps $C_{pk} = 2.0$
Automation Evolution	Semi-Automatic Machines	Auto Assembly Workcell	Integrated Auto Assembly and Test
Factory Evolution	Islands of Automation	SPC, Models, Partial Manufacturing Systems Integration	Factory Model and Guidelines for Generation 5 Factory

Source: Westinghouse.

expected you to do the same. Attention to your people, communications, commitment, taking care of the details, that is how it was expected to work."

Management Approach

The ES management approach to the mapped revolutionary path and the expectations it had raised for the project consisted of several elements:

- Concurrent engineering (CE).
- Taguchi methods for robust design (TM).
- Statistical process control (SPC).
- Quality function deployment (QFD).
- Supplier partnerships.

CE was directed at the need for all relevant functional disciplines to work together to achieve producibility and increase productivity. The approach was a contrast to the separate, sequential, "hand-off" method of development that had characterized product development in the past. It entailed the concurrent development and design of products, process, and equipment and the early involvement of all the relevant players in the project's design decisions. The highly interdependent nature of the T/R module development increased the potential for anticipating risks.

The general manager of manufacturing operations explained the application of CE this way.

> We intend to use CE as a way of speeding up development time and reducing life-cycle costs. It is a form of risk abatement for our strategically important programs. One recent radar program cut its typical development time from 36 months to 12 months when we tried a CE approach. We understand that process development is just as critical as design and that they are best approached together, as early in the program as possible.

CE, with its cross-functional representation early in the development decision making and communication of needs and trade-offs, was expected to have a positive impact on: functional design complexity, process and component variability, automation feasibility, sourcing of RF components, military specifications on the production rate, and producibility test complexity.

TM attacked the causes and interactions of variation. This methodology was to provide guidance in improving the design of the product and process through experimentation in order to achieve a robust product. The search for producibility was expected to be expedited by TM's structured approach to design through experimentation and the use of statistical tools. TM further defined quality as a function of variability and targeted performance, and encouraged the use of data and statistical tools for analysis and problem solving.

SPC was intended to maintain control of critical processes once they had been optimized through Taguchi analysis. It was also intended to introduce problem solving based on quantifiable data throughout the operations function team, from operators to management. The lead manufacturing engineer described SPC this way: "Its mission was to expose and encourage the idea of data collection and problem solving and to *stop* subjective analysis and others constantly tweaking our processes."

This message was well communicated. One operator talked about how the training in SPC was more than just the typical class: "They took the time to explain why it was being used and how it could help me in my work. I really appreciated that."

QFD was expected to bring the "voice of the customer" into all of the critical design decisions. QFD is a structured methodology that starts with customer requirements and ends with design and process selections and specifications explicitly tied to the most critical customer needs. The intended end result is to develop a product with the customer's voice driving all the project's decisions and tradeoffs.

The inclusion of suppliers was critical to program success. The ultimate yield and final cost of the T/R module depended on the quality of the materials and component parts supplied. Newell explained, through the use of an example, the impact a supplier could have on the program:

> The microprocessor subassembly, 3/4 inches square, with 256K of memory, was experiencing less than a 50 percent yield in its first electrical test. There was a schedule to meet, and the classical response would be to double production to meet schedule. I had a hunch that it was not a problem with the process. I went to Foster and explained the situation in detail. We took this idea to our internal customer [program manager], and jointly developed a plan to isolate the problem. More people were assigned to the project, and failure analysis was performed with teams of chip design engineers, electrical engineers, and test and manufacturing engineers. A two-month schedule slip occurred. The problem was traced to a supplier part. The supplier was brought in but would not change its inspection methods. So we developed an internal screening process for the part and yield went to 90 percent the first time. The throughput rose from 25 a week to 250 a week. The entire contract was then completed in only 10 weeks.

Project Team

The project team assigned to T/R modules was hand picked in 1987. The criteria for the team members were effective personalities, technical expertise, and commitment to the project. The key members of the team had a history of interaction that gave the group a sense of stability in the new and challenging environment they were facing.

Newell described the T/R module team as "a team of team players. Each brought different gifts to get the overall job done. It was a talented team who had special qualities. Its members were very good at what they did." Mike Appleby, senior manufacturing engineer, added: "The T/R team was seen as a select group of very ambitious people. They were the cream. There was a wide set of experiences across disciplines. The team had a lot of visibility. Respect preceded the decision to join for many of the team members."

Dottie Gantt, an operator, had a similar view. "The team project [was] composed of [a] certain type of people who were dedicated to their work, worked hard, and didn't have a chip on their shoulder. They were willing to do and try new things."

Advanced Manufacturing Technology Center (AMTC)

Because state-of-the-art results were being pushed in the design and manufacturing areas, Foster decided that a "culture of reliance" between the groups of engineers was essential. His first step was to bring together the key engineering functions—systems, mechanical, electrical, manufacturing, and quality and colocate them by "pushing their desks together." He also encouraged people involved in the project to get to know each other. Previously, a typical relationship was based only on seeing and interacting with someone from another area at meetings. Now Foster encouraged informal interaction and personal knowledge of the others. They were able to break down barriers in communications and develop relationships.

The same idea was used when the program moved into the production stage. A dedicated facility, the AMTC, was constructed in 1988 for the manufacture of the T/R module. All the main activities were collocated there. Test and production-floor activities, which were traditionally separated, were tightly coupled. Similarly, engineering offices and meeting rooms were conveniently located to the production floor and the test area to encourage interaction.

The AMTC was designed for the transition of the prototype to the low-rate production phase. It would eventually be used to prove the high-rate production, as well. The plan was to develop in the AMTC as much of the prototype design and processes as possible and to abandon the design engineers' labs for the actual operating environment at the earliest possible date.

In addition to reducing the inherent risks in handoff and ramp-up, the transition from design to production would be expensive and, more importantly, take valuable time. The operator skills that were proven and developed in the AMTC would be directly transferrable to the next phase, so significant training was not required. Management and engineering would know the operator skills required for operators for each development phase.

A senior manufacturing engineer, expanded on the usefulness of the AMTC idea:

> The start-up production of the program was done by technicians and operators that worked on the floor, not engineering lab technicians with different skills and training. This way, workers who had the "floor perspective" communicated to the engineers what made them most effective, given their skill set. The engineers learned to understand these operators and translate this learning into their designs and processes. The AMTC was an effective communications tool and relationship builder.

A manufacturing engineer mentioned that the proximity and accessibility of the engineers to the operators led to enhanced communications and commitment:

> An operator did not have to [literally] disrobe [the AMTC was a clean room] to talk with the engineers. All of the

engineers—quality, electrical, manufacturing, mechanical—worked on the floor or were in the offices. The informal setting allowed discussions to take place easily. The collocation also reduced the need for expediters because each individual was responsible for movement of the product. Even when dealing with backlogs, the test function made sure to test up-to-date product to allow assembly to keep moving.

> Another example was when manufacturing engineers would perform an operator's job (wirebonding) to keep things moving. This was not the most desirable "quality control" thing to do, but it captured the spirit of trying to keep product moving and having everyone share the same space.

The AMTC environment allowed for much tighter reporting between the engineers, technicians, and operators, so a feedback loop developed among them. The traditional isolation of the design engineers from the floor was removed. Relationships developed that were less formal and problem laden than usual: "finger pointing" and confrontation rarely occurred.

Team Building—Relationships—Communications

The cultivation of informal relationships and the enhanced communications between the groups did not occur overnight. Participants in the process usually described it as incremental, although major events also changed attitudes. Newell described the incremental process and how trust and teamwork were solidified and significant problems were solved:

> Each day, Foster and I discussed what was "hurting" progress. Each of us initially tried to control the other, to get our "way." Six weeks into the program, a feeling of mutual trust and teamwork began to evolve. The time we invested in each other was critical. Problem solving and responsiveness developed. Listening and consensus were created.

> The big event was an art work change. There was a wirebond-yield problem in production of an assembly with 280 wirebonds. The bond pads were designed to 8 mil, but the process developed 6.5-mil pads. This created problems on every part, and 80 percent of the parts were defective. A change to a 10-mil pad could have easily been incorporated into the design, but the art work documentation had to be changed. This was a time-consuming pain in the neck for the design engineer, but the change allowed the process to develop an 8-mil pad. Yields went to 99.5 percent with the change.

A manufacturing engineer shared this view of the contribution of relationships to success:

> People development was critical to our success. "Paying attention to people" was required. Allowing people the freedom of alternative ways of doing things was important. *Showing* them that doing things differently was the way to reach our goal was perhaps most important.

Newell demonstrated this leadership with the group: "The process starts with a couple of key people leading the way. Eventually, momentum builds as everyone begins to understand what the expectations are for their behavior." Problems were solved together, and the use of teams slowly became a practiced approach to problem solving.

Appleby, a manufacturing engineer with an electrical engineering (EE) background, interpreted the jargon between the design engineers and the manufacturing groups and acted as liaison between the design and production groups until they developed a common language. The diversity of backgrounds in his group (which included physicists and chemical, industrial, and mechanical engineers) had already made his group somewhat flexible and unusually willing to take a fresh look at things. Thus CE approach was an extension of what was going on in his group.

Appleby commented on how engineering and manufacturing were able to work together and what resulted:

> The process was evolutionary. Our outlook was the key: To do the project cost effectively was the spur to change. It was done as a team in a central location. There was team responsibility accepted for the project. We were in this together and we learned to talk together. T/R modules presented a new technology in terms of manufacturing and design, so there were many bugs to work out. We had daily informal meetings to work out the bugs.
>
> The work processes of the electrical design engineers experienced the most significant change. Manufacturing engineers' methodologies did not change much; we had always interacted with the design engineers. Now, they relied on and utilized us. The electrical designers became more ready to describe why they did things; they went to manufacturing; they realized there was value there.
>
> Evan Deoul was the role model for the design engineers: He was a good communicator and checked with us before a decision was made.

Deoul, a design engineer, described the perspective on CE shared by some of his peers in design:

CE is an evolution of a mindset. It did not happen overnight. It resulted from a growing appreciation of the goal for our product. We started realizing that performance was not the only goal: producibility was just as critical. We started talking more about producibility, and the manufacturing people began talking more about design.

Deoul cautioned that some design engineers believed that they now "had a producibility perspective" and believed they could now incorporate it into their designs and go back to business as usual:

> They think it is easier for a design engineer to understand producibility than for a manufacturing engineer to understand microwaves. Their attitude is: "We have the capability to best understand producibility. We don't need the manufacturing people any more. We always drove this process, and should reassert this control now that we can show manufacturing that we are sensitive to their problems."

As one design engineer explained it:

> We held onto the project very closely, in our minds at least, through the first build in the AMTC. The first 25 units were fully tested by us in our labs. We felt intimately involved with the success of the project and put in long hours during this time. We gained confidence in the product over this period.
>
> Our controlling role was gradually released to the test engineers, and we eventually acted as a support function to the testers. We had to learn how to back up and respect the test engineers. This occurred during the ramp-up stage of production. In retrospect, the involvement of the test engineers at such a late stage was a problem. Their concerns could have been incorporated in the design phase and would have made their job easier.

CE also included the operators. Gantt shared her relationship with the project:

> The T/R program experience was very positive. You were made to feel a part of it. There was a sense of teamwork because of engineering proximity and feedback. There were meetings with everyone (management-type meetings) that gave the group a sense of what was expected and where we were going. It was an indication of taking the time to help you understand what you were working on and why.

Gantt received recognition for her personal efforts through letters from senior management. The first letter she received was signed by someone of whom she had never heard. Someone had to tell her the writer was one of the division general managers. This letter represented the first time, in her 22 years at Westinghouse, that a senior manager had recognized her accomplishments. She shared the story of what prompted the letter:

> A part kept failing a test, but there was nothing wrong with the part. I knew it had to be a problem with the test. After watching how the test was being performed, I saw why the test was failing. The test fixture was not being prepared properly for the test, and it, not the part, rattled during the test. The rattle gave the false reading. I showed the engineer, who been working on the problem for some time, what I though the problem was. He substantiated it. At first, I thought he was going to take credit for it. Then I received the letter. The general manager thanked me for solving a problem that was having a major scheduling impact on the job.

Team Problem Solving

The manufacturing engineers extended team problem solving to their interactions with the factory operators. Operator meetings with manufacturing engineers in attendance were instituted at the start of the production phase. The meetings were intended to create a means of communicating the collegial aspect of this project: operators would be expected to solve problems and their input would be counted on and would be used. One manufacturing engineer described the meetings:

> They began as gripe sessions. We would take the constructive input and act on it. Originally, 90 percent of the operators showed up, but most were not there in spirit—they didn't believe Westinghouse would act on their suggestions.
>
> As time went on and we acted proactively on their comments, all of a sudden, operators became part of the solution. There was a realization that problems were not limited to any individual or group. Teams began to form naturally in attacking problems. A problem was attacked after a group consensus, by people talking about it and agreeing that it was a problem. Volunteers would take responsibility for the problem and recruit critical skills to be added to the group.

This change in behavior took months to develop. Meetings began as daily sessions and had been reduced to three times a week.

At this point, however, Foster announced the formation of total quality teams (see Exhibit 7). Some believed that the momentum that had been created by the previous approach was slowed by this decision. One engineer explained:

EXHIBIT 7

T/R MODULE TEAM

* * * NEWS * * *

Thanks for all your ideas and efforts! Just to give you an idea of some of the team accomplishments over the past six weeks, here are some highlights.

PRODUCT QUALITY TEAM

- Working to clarify the criteria used to define product quality for the DEM/VAL phase.
- Exploring the possibility of using a nondestruct pull test to supersede visual criteria when the wire integrity is in question.
- Designing a vacuum spatula to improve the handling of logics. This tool will allow handling of the backside of the substrate, therefore reducing the frequency and magnitude of wirebond damage.

TEAM MEMBERS

Darlene Crawll	Dottie Gantt	Wyatt Luce	Will Pierson
Ruth Daly	Sandy Garcia	Angela Martin	Al Simon
Dave Dimmick	Steve Kramer	Porter Newton	Harolyn White

Source: Westinghouse.

These total quality teams were not allowed to develop naturally and create a buy-in by the members. Some groups did not understand the problems they were asked to solve because they did not understand the problem definition. There was also an "I do not want to be on this team" mentality. These situations caused frustration within the groups.

Gantt shared this evaluation about her team:

I was part of the inspection team (the product quality team in Exhibit 7). It was not as successful as some other teams because we did not understand what we were supposed to be doing. The T/R product was a prototype, and it did not fit into the traditional military inspection standards we were accustomed to in their production area. We were working on a problem that probably was not a problem.

A senior test technician talked about the initial lack of trust between the engineers and the operators. He believed they talked down to him, but that they had a lot to learn from him: "The technicians are the most *critical* link in the process of production. They are the ones who find what is wrong and make the initial decision on what to do." The technicians dealt with both the engineers and the operators and ultimately had to find a way to bridge the communication gap to get the product manufactured correctly.

There is a gap between the theory of paper design versus the real-world problems inherent in the production process. I showed the engineers the problems with the product and described why the design was causing the problems. Mostly, it was due to the variability of the real world. I had to build the trust of the engineers, and I had to learn to trust them. The trust had to be earned, *especially* on the engineers' side.

Another perspective the technician offered was management's appreciation and use of the operators' *thinking* capabilities. Time was taken to explain things and let the operators know why they were doing certain things:

Management has to lead the change; they are the ones with the power to make the change. The use of the AMTC facility and the appreciation of the people in the T/R program was an attempt by management at changes for the better. Operators could not be expected to have the influence to make the AMTC happen. Alone, we also couldn't get the engineers to work with us.

Measurements

Deciding on measurable goals became a way of reporting the T/R module work activities. For instance, the manufacturing group established realistic output quotas in collaboration with the operators during production. Individuals measured their work and recorded it on a work sheet, where it was compiled by the manufacturing engineers. Results were displayed on charts in the AMTC. A manufacturing engineer thought the procedure worked well: "We all knew what the schedule was, and we had to find a way of getting there. We agreed on our goals together. By displaying our efforts, we saw how we were doing. It was simple—*post it, you know it.*"

The goal of an affordable, throwaway T/R module was approached from a producibility perspective. The engineering groups used a set of metrics to guide in product development. The manufacturing group provided direction on product cost drivers. Drivers such as number of parts, process steps, and connections between subassemblies were identified and shared with the design engineers. Targets were negotiated and set. This project was the first time design engineers had signed up for such objectives. Having measurable targets for producibility required a system of tracking and measuring. Deoul commented: "The goals were very visible to the team and to those watching the team. They became a very effective motivator."

Robust Design

The design-of-experiments (DOE) methodology was used at various points in the program to develop a solution that accepted or controlled variability in parts or processes. DOE was used in formulating a robust solution for a tuning subassembly. Following the DOE principles, the tuning stub was taken through multiple new design and process iterations to find a solution that was tolerant to a controlled range of widely varying process and part deviations. The work was carried out in the design engineers' labs, which set up equipment and processes that were identical to the tuning subassembly and T/R module final assembly in the AMTC. This setup was selected because it was early in the production run-out stage, and many "unknown" production problems were being attacked at this time.

Deoul remarked that the "sensitivity testing" design engineers performed on their computer-aided design systems was another form of the DOE methodology:

When we run our circuit simulations, or when the mechanical engineers run their stress and heat simulations, we vary critical parts and parameters using a very structured approach. We have learned that simulations are very helpful in discovering bugs in the design before we get to production.

Outcomes

Exhibit 8 depicts how the T/R module team documented its cost reduction progress for the program. The reduction of variation and control of the processes was a major element in the success. Steve Kramer, a senior manufacturing engineer, reflected on the deployment of the various tools:

> There was not a strong push behind the use of tools in the program. DOE was not really used to its fullest extent. Some SPC charts for critical processes were developed. The problem is that it takes a while for people to buy into these advance methods.

A manufacturing engineer tended to agree: "SPC was not utilized as much as it could have been." She emphasized that the operators' skills were an important area for potential improvement. Having the best attitude could not succeed alone. She reflected on what happened:

> There was a conflict between research money [process development funding independent of the program] and having a job to do [T/R module production]. It ended with T/R research competing with production. The pace of the program was intense. In the month that AMTC came online, prototype modules were being cranked out. There was no time taken to iron out the line and do a capability study. If we had, we might have attained better performance.

She also believed that the lack of real-time feedback to operations—yield data were received too late to make

Exhibit 8

ATF T/R Module Cost

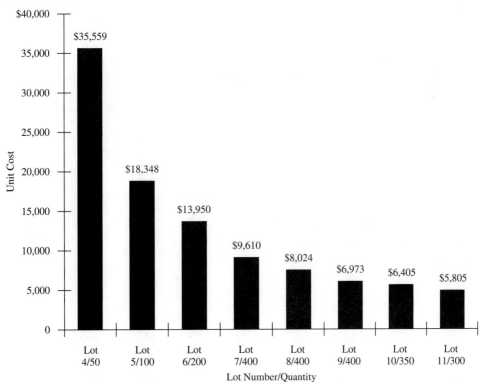

Source: Westinghouse.

incremental adjustments—caused lower yields than might have been possible.

A quality engineer observed that the early stages of production revealed a number of product defects. Some others expressed the opinion that the immaturity and newness of the technology made the concurrent engineering approach difficult to pull off because of the uncertainty of the environment. One said, for example, "We struggled through the design period because we tried to please everybody."

Others felt that pressing the technological envelope was the reason why it had worked so well. The design engineers had to rely on the manufacturing engineers to know what the machines could do, and the manufacturing engineers had to know what the design engineers were doing to design the processes. Newell was pleased with the outcome of what had been accomplished thus far:

> After production ramp-up, we were producing modules at 95 percent yield and the last 1,000 of the 2,500 modules we made were produced without offline rework. If rework was necessary, we did it in-process. This achievement and action was a far cry from the mindset in which we started.

A general manager agreed. He wrote a memo that claimed the T/R module program was the most advanced example of CE in the division.

Reflections

The demonstration/validation phase of the ATF Program was completed and the prototype proven, in terms of producibility. The next step was to build a next-generation device, called the advanced prototype, within two years. This was to be followed by low-rate production or full-scale development and finally, a high-volume production phase at the end of the 90s.

Deoul believed that there was an up-front investment involved in the approach to a program like the T/R modules: "It pays for itself over the course of the program, but it takes vision and courage to do it." Newell remarked that the program was "an evolution and a revolution." It had been a five-year journey. Now that Ted Foster was no longer leading the T/R module program, what would a successor do to continue the program's successes? What should the important initiatives toward variability reduction and targeted performance be? Tools like QFD, TM, and SPC were underused in an attempt to leverage results from CE. Was the culture established well enough that these techniques could now be more fully deployed? What would be required for their deployment? Was the culture itself responsible for the success in variability reduction and could it accommodate the future challenges?

Kramer summarized the concerns about instituting the learning outcomes from CE:

> How are we to close the loop? The experiences and lessons are only with the people involved with the program. What if more leave, like Foster? Management does not know where they are with this. Peers seem to work well together and accept it, but management is not as committed to the ideas.

ES had a strong, decentralized culture. For Newell, the major issue was determining under what circumstances the integrated approach used in the T/R module development program would be appropriate in other programs. Could it be adopted on a divisional scale? What about the skills called for in programs like T/R modules? What skills needed to be upgraded for the future phases of the T/R module project? Will the reward and recognition systems have to be changed under a CE approach? What about the organizational structure? Will it be affected by a CE approach? How would suppliers fit into the future of the program?

As Newell reflected on the program, he was aware that the integrated approach to T/R modules had undoubtedly raised more questions than it had resolved. His immediate dilemma was determining what initiatives to pursue in order to institute the success of the early T/R module efforts.

3 TECHNOLOGY IN ORGANIZATIONS

Technology Transfer and Procurement

Reading 3–1
The Intelligent Enterprise

A New Paradigm

James Brian Quinn

At their core, most successful enterprises today can be considered intelligent enterprises, converting intellectual resources into a chain of service outputs and integrating these into a form most useful for certain customers. Clearly, enterprises providing law, accounting, financial, architectural, applied research, health care, education, consulting, design, and most forms of entertainment services primarily sell the skills and intellect of key professionals. But in manufacturing as well, materials without human inputs have little intrinsic value, and—as analysis will demonstrate—most of the processes which add value to materials derive from knowledge-based service activities. In the past, investors—and particularly venture capitalists—shied away from companies with a strong service orientation, "because their assets could walk away any night and leave you with nothing." They wanted "solid assets to offset downside risks." Now that view is changing.

Rewards Come from Intellect, Not Bricks and Mortar

In manufacturing today, most venture capitalists recognize that investments in bricks and mortar provide little security and warrant only mortgage rates of return. They make their money by: (1) investing in the special skills and intellect which only highly motivated, knowledgeable people can provide, and then (2) leveraging this intellect in the marketplace through a few "best-in-world" internal systems and the integrated management

James Brian Quinn is the Buchanan Professor of Management at Amos Tuck School, Dartmouth College. His most recent book is *Intelligent Enterprise: A Knowledge and Service Based Paradigm for Industry* (New York, Free Press: 1992), which explores in greater depth the issues discussed in this article.

Source: Reprinted with permission from *Academy of Management Executive* 6, no. 4 (1992).

of many outsourced activities. Virtually all high technology start-ups work in this fashion today. Venture capitalists try to keep conventional plant and equipment investments limited—in part because they can be so quickly supplanted by new technologies—and focus their client companies' management talent and investments on effectively building the intellectual assets and personal attitudes most important to the needs of a selected customer group. Unless the facilities and manufacturing technologies are themselves part of the core competencies of the company, strategy dictates that they *should* be limited—and be selectively outsourced—whenever feasible. This is not an argument against facilities investment per se. It does suggest, however, that those fixed facilities that remain should, themselves, ordinarily embody as much of the firm's uniqueness and critical intellect as possible.

Every few years *Inc.* or *Venture* magazine runs a special article in which they feature the garages in which today's great companies started, as a reminder that companies start small and that ideas and intellect—not physical assets—build great companies. TA Associates, one of the longer-running and more successful venture capital groups with high-tech manufacturing firms, now actively looks for service companies "having good cash flows, low overheads, and steady revenues from service customers." One venture capitalist summarized the issue clearly: "We don't want to invest in hard assets. They are too short lived and risky. We certainly don't want to invest in bureaucracies. We want to invest in people who have a clear viable concept, who can manage outside contracts with the best sources in the world, and who can concentrate their internal energies on that small core of activities which creates the real uniqueness and value-added for the company. That's where the action is today, but it's a tough sell against traditional thinking."

- Novellus Systems Inc., the most profitable and fastest growing company in the semiconductor production equipment field, provides an interesting example. With only 12 shop floor personnel, Novellus concentrates on design and engineering of advanced chemical deposition equipment. It disdains internal "metal bending" activities in favor of long-term strategic relations with a few trusted and specialized parts and subsystem producers. In addition to design, Novellus controls all assembly, test, customer contact, and postsales service work and uses partners and suppliers to leverage its inhouse capital and design resources. In a notoriously cyclical industry, Novellus' profits grew 20 percent during the 1991–92 recession on sales of $350,000 per employee—almost double the industry's average (*Business Week,* January 27, 1992).

Many large manufacturing companies (like Sony, Nike, Honda, Apple, Matsushita, Polaroid, Liz Claiborne, Genentech, or IBM) initially succeeded by following the intellectual holding company model quite closely. At first, they purposely invested limited amounts in plant and standard equipment, produced as few components internally as they reasonably could, and leveraged their limited resources by sourcing externally.

Mr. Konosuke Matsushita simply assembled his bicycle lights and portable electric lights using standard parts made by others, but fitted into his own unique designs. Sony first rented a bombed-out corner of a department store in Tokyo. Its first permanent quarters were some old warehouses in Shinagawa, whose roofs were so leaky that experiments had to be run under umbrellas. Knowing it could not design and make all the needed parts for its miniaturized electromechanical devices, Sony outsourced major portions and taught suppliers how to produce to world quality standards. Genentech rented warehouse space in South San Francisco and bootlegged other space from its researchers' university-related laboratories. Genentech primarily performed research and coordinated the complex processes of early scale production, clinical trials, regulatory clearance, patenting, maintaining a home for advanced researchers, and networking worldwide with university researchers to stay on the frontiers of its remarkable new technology. It licensed the large-scale production, marketing and distribution of its early high-volume products to others like Eli Lilly and Kabi. And so on. Similar approaches at Nike, Apple, Honda, and Polaroid enabled their start-up.

As these and many other successful manufacturing companies grew to large sizes, they continued to focus on a selected set of intellectual or service skills and to leverage these against multiple products to develop dominating product-market positions.

Service-Based Strategies Support Broad Product Lines

The broad lines of all these companies—and some other even more remarkable examples—demonstrate that strategic focus lies not so much in narrowing or limiting one's product lines and product-market scope as in focusing strategy around a uniquely developed set of core intellectual and service capabilities important to customers. A broad or mixed product or service line may not signify a loss of focus at all. In fact a broad line may add to strategic focus—when one can coordinate the deployment of an especially potent set of service skills against numerous marketplaces.

In strategic circles it has recently become popular to seek increased focus by concentrating only on fewer and more closely related product lines. After a prolonged period in the 1960s and early 1970s when ill-conceived financial strategies drove companies to overly extend their product lines through conglomeration, a reverse fad developed. Those who had made fees from the acquisition programs of the 1960s and 1970s found that they could make further fees by "deconglomerating" and selling off divisions of companies who had followed the preceding fad too far. These narrowing (or divestiture) strategies were often justified as giving the company greater strategic focus. Unfortunately, as many have sadly learned, such strategies make the company considerably more risky because it is subject to much more violent responses when the total economy turns down, or its particular segment of the economy goes sour.

By contrast, looking beyond mere product lines to a strategy built around core intellectual or service competencies provides both a rigorously maintainable strategic focus and long-term flexibility. Once a company develops sufficient depth in a few such activities, these can become linchpins for a consistent corporate strategy and competitive edge lasting for decades. Innumerable new products or services can spring off of these core activities over the years, providing the company with constant refreshment for its line and with enough diversity to stabilize earnings and offset downturns—unlike more traditional product-focused strategies. The concept has worked well for companies as diverse as Merck, Sony,

Intel, Motorola, Pilkington Bros., Moulinex, Matsushita, Sharp, Texas Instruments, Nike (and the myriad other companies already noted) whose widely diversified product lines have been powered by a few core competencies, mostly knowledge-based service activities. 3M Corporation provides probably the classic U.S. case.

• 3M's extensive growth has been founded on its R&D skills in three critical, related technologies: abrasives, adhesives, and coating-bonding. In each of these areas, it has developed knowledge bases and skill depths exceeding those of its major competitors. To these core technologies (referred to as historic in Exhibit 1), 3M has attempted to add four other compatible sets of core technologies, at least partially from acquisitions. When combined with 3M's remarkable entrepreneurial-innovation system and with a strong broad-based distribution system, its historic technologies let 3M develop a wide variety of products internally. They sustained continuous growth for six to seven decades (through 1980) at a compounded annual growth rate of 10 percent. From time to time, 3M identified a specific application area, for example, small labels, which offered an opportunity to leverage its core technologies or distribution skills by acquisition. Sometimes it needed the complementary skills of a small manufacturer to realize strategic timing goals or to attain a full product presentation in a key area for its "wave front" of products. But, for decades, 3M's growth basically exploited its core knowledge-based and service competencies in its three or four historical technologies, its unique innovative system, and its broad-based distribution system.

However, as 3M began to see its growth rates fall in the early 1980s, it tried to acquire new core technologies well beyond its origins—that is, in imaging and instrumentation. Acquisitions to support these markets were no longer gap filling, but moved the company into new business areas with less connection to its core competencies. As 3M moved further from its well developed competencies, success became harder to achieve. Despite strong efforts to diversify further, businesses built off 3M's adhesives, coating, abrasives, and nonwoven technologies continued to generate a return on assets, on average, about 50 percent higher than the new areas.

As product cycles become shorter, technological performance or style become more important, and

product-based experience curves recede in importance, we find that many sophisticated long-term strategists no longer look primarily to market share and its associated cost reducing potentials as the keys to strategic planning.[1] Nor do they build vertically integrated empires to achieve ephemeral scale economies. Instead, they concentrate on identifying those few core service activities where their company has, or can develop, (1) a continuing strategic edge and (2) long-term streams of new products to satisfy future customer demands. They develop these competencies in greater depth than anyone else in the world. Then they seek to eliminate, minimize, or outsource activities where the company cannot be preeminent, unless those activities are essential to support or protect the chosen areas of strategic focus. To develop this kind of service-based strategy, managers concentrate their competitive analyses, not on market share, but on "activity share"—that is, the relative potency of the key knowledge-based or service activities underpinning their own and all direct and functional competitors' positions.

• Pilkington Brothers PLC—after thriving as a growing company on its process innovations (particularly in flat glass and fiberglass)—stumbled when it forgot this adage. As it became the largest flat glass producer in the world, Pilkington relied more on economies of scale and attempted to move into other areas where its skill base was not as applicable. It also maintained an integrated posture as competitors outsourced more. As demand for flat glass fell 4 percent in 1990–91, its profits plummeted 52 percent compared to European rival St. Gobain's loss of 20 percent. Although other glass companies had flattened their organizations to be more market responsive, a combination of Pilkington's conservative personnel policies and the support needed for vertical integration kept its fixed overheads high. Pilkington's 1990 sales per employee were only $83,000 compared to $171,000 at PPG and $500,000 at Nippon Sheet (*The Economist,* 10/12/91).

Services Disaggregate Production, Force Global Manufacturing

When they are most effective, disaggregating strategies extend across national borders to utilize truly best-in-world suppliers or to benchmark the company's capa-

EXHIBIT 1

3M Technology-Driven Strategy

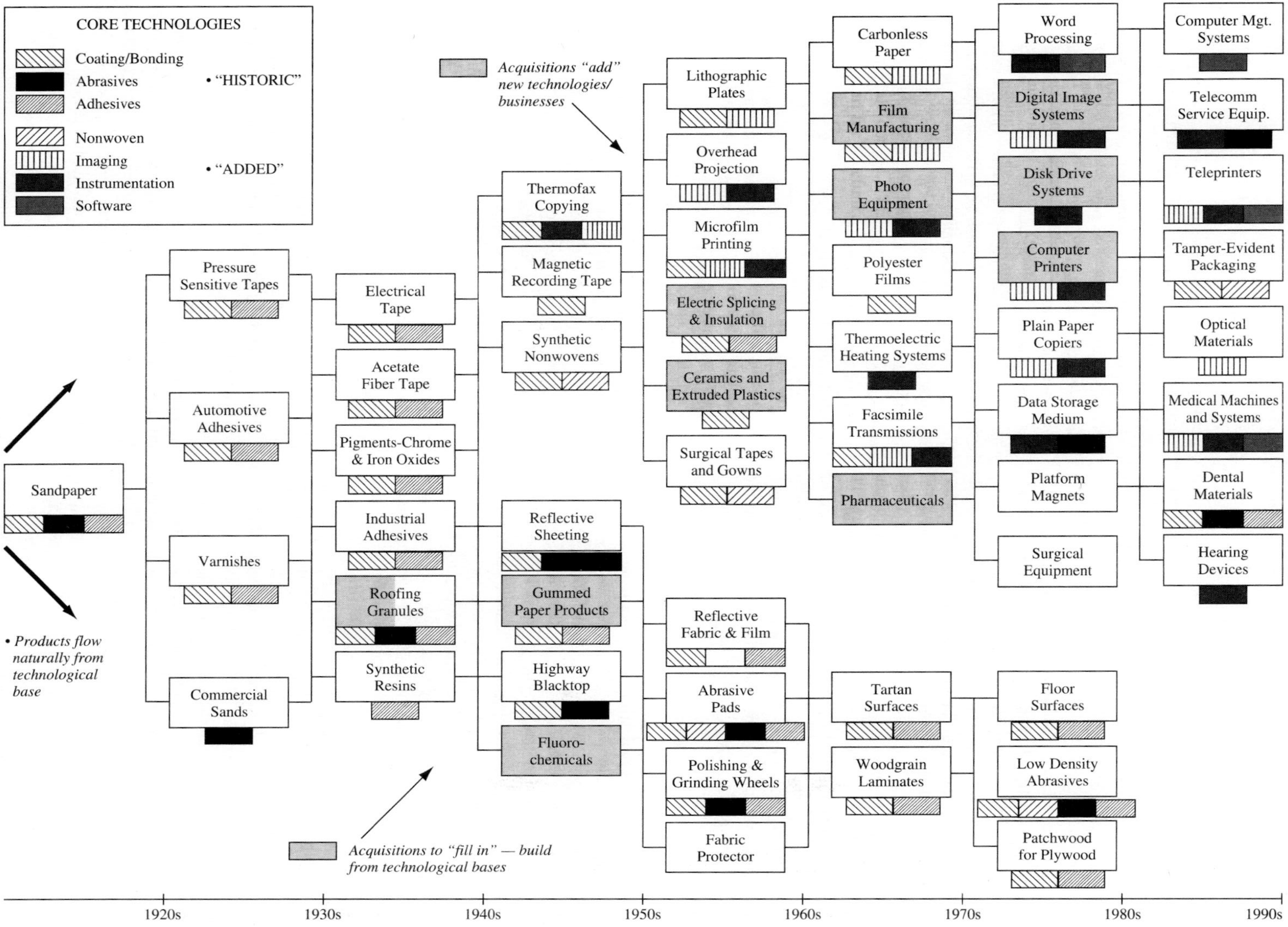

CORE TECHNOLOGIES

- Coating/Bonding
- Abrasives
- Adhesives
- Nonwoven
- Imaging
- Instrumentation
- Software

Legend bands: *"HISTORIC"*, *"ADDED"*

Acquisitions "add" new technologies/businesses

Acquisitions to "fill in" — build from technological bases

Products flow naturally from technological base

Timeline: 1920s — 1930s — 1940s — 1950s — 1960s — 1970s — 1980s — 1990s

Sandpaper

Pressure Sensitive Tapes · Automotive Adhesives · Varnishes · Commercial Sands

Electrical Tape · Acetate Fiber Tape · Pigments–Chrome & Iron Oxides · Industrial Adhesives · Roofing Granules · Synthetic Resins

Thermofax Copying · Magnetic Recording Tape · Synthetic Nonwovens · Reflective Sheeting · Gummed Paper Products · Highway Blacktop · Fluoro-chemicals

Lithographic Plates · Overhead Projection · Microfilm Printing · Electric Splicing & Insulation · Ceramics and Extruded Plastics · Surgical Tapes and Gowns · Reflective Fabric & Film · Abrasive Pads · Polishing & Grinding Wheels · Fabric Protector

Carbonless Paper · Film Manufacturing · Photo Equipment · Polyester Films · Thermoelectric Heating Systems · Facsimile Transmissions · Pharmaceuticals · Tartan Surfaces · Woodgrain Laminates

Word Processing · Digital Image Systems · Disk Drive Systems · Computer Printers · Plain Paper Copiers · Data Storage Medium · Platform Magnets · Surgical Equipment · Floor Surfaces · Low Density Abrasives · Patchwood for Plywood

Computer Mgt. Systems · Telecomm Service Equip. · Teleprinters · Tamper-Evident Packaging · Optical Materials · Medical Machines and Systems · Dental Materials · Hearing Devices

121

bilities against them. Some global sourcing or joint venturing has always been present in manufacturing. What is new is the extent to which improved knowledge bases along with service technologies now facilitate—or force—global disaggregation.

Improved telecommunications, air transport, financial services, storage, and cargo handling technologies mean that virtually all manufacturers (regardless of size) must consider supply sources, markets, and competition on a worldwide scale—or lose their competitive positions. About one-fifth of the total capital invested in U.S. manufacturing firms has now moved outside the U.S.[2] The knowledge-based activities of coordinating production, sourcing, and value-added services among these overseas investments have become critical to multinational profitability. Most value-adding economies of scale have shifted toward knowledge-based services (like R&D, marketing, design, information systems, etc.) and away from plant economies of scale. And the profits, royalties, and intracorporate sales these enterprises remit to the U.S. are among the few strongly favorable net balances of trade U.S. manufacturing has provided in the late 1980s and early 1990s. In addition to the royalty fees and profits these companies remit to the United States, they also account for a major portion of the goods shipped into the U.S. (i.e., their sales from overseas divisions to the U.S. are significant components of U.S. imports from abroad).

Through strong importers in certain sectors (like Nike, IBM, or Exxon), U.S. manufacturing companies dominate the design, specification, and location of much of the world's trade. Through its powerful wholesaler-retailer systems, however, the United States directs even more of the world's manufacturing trade. With their purchasing power and superior knowledge of markets, these service companies often now specify both what will be made and how it will be produced. In addition to the strong influence these capabilities give the U.S. in world trade, they exert other powerful economic impacts. They lower costs for U.S. consumers and increase the purchasing power of those consumers. Through their relative efficiency, these companies' networks increase U.S. workers' purchasing power, giving them higher real wages and higher living standards compared to their foreign competitors. For example, because distribution channels are so much longer and less efficient in Japan, Japanese workers must pay a multiple of the (exchange weighted) price a U.S. worker pays for the same item. U.S. manufacturers' competitiveness is further sup-

ported by America's generally superb and lower-cost communications, finance, and air transportation services.

For mass produced consumer goods, large-scale service enterprises and the power of service technologies are perhaps the key factors making worldwide coordination of integrated manufacturing, global product and process development, and functionally segmented manufacturing-distribution joint ventures effective—and indeed possible—in modern competition. Services drive globalization at many levels, but perhaps nowhere so powerfully as in the retailer–manufacturer relationships which interconnect world economies so tightly today. They extend customer demands directly into foreign producers' plants on a daily updated basis. For example:

- Virtually all retail chains—like Kmart or The Limited's group of companies with their 2,250 to 3,860 retail outlets and sales of $29.5 billion and $4.8 billion, respectively—aggregate their day's sales each night from their EPOS systems. These systems break down sales to the minimum replicable level of detail—such as type of item, cut, size, material, color, style, number sold, price, margins, and so on. Forecasting programs at corporate headquarters then convert the day's sales into a cutting order for Southeast Asian fabric suppliers on the next day. Within a few days, a wide-bodied aircraft takes off from Southeast Asia for the distribution depots of The Limited or Kmart in the United States. A few days later, the merchandise is on their shelves. Thus, stocks are aligned to current demands, markdowns are limited, and inventories are kept to a minimum. Other programs keep track of experimental sales on new items being sampled throughout the system. What is stocked is dictated by the customer and the retailer, and manufacturers are linked as directly to their order givers as possible.

For intermittently produced or specialty products, other service arrangements dominate. For example, VTI Inc. has a flexible worldwide sourcing network to obtain least-cost product design and production of its high value-added, applications-specific integrated circuits (ASICs). Through electronic interfaces, its designers can work with customers anywhere to create a new ASIC design upon request. Its software in Silicon Valley converts these designs into photo masks. The photo masks go to Japan where others etch the chip. Chips then go to Korea for dicing and mounting, and then to Malaysia for assembly. From Malaysia they are shipped directly to customers by overnight parcel delivery, if desired.

For continuous production operations, global sourcing networks have long offered advantages. Overhead and direct costs tend to drop markedly with offshore manufacturing. On the other hand, logistics costs tend to *increase* by a factor of about 20 percent and tariffs and exchange rates become increasingly significant.[3] In these circumstances, global information concerning local costs, suppliers' capabilities, transportation possibilities, en route location of materials, and financing potentials becomes a crucial competitive weapon for manufacturers—and a critical component of strategy. So important are logistics costs in worldwide manufacturing networks that before Toyota began its Nummi joint venture in the United States with GM, it set a target of having "the most cost-efficient inbound-outbound logistics system in the world." Since its own costs for production in Japan would be essentially fixed (excluding exchange rates), its capacity to control the profitability of its Nummi versus Japanese sources depended mainly on logistics. Without very sophisticated capabilities Toyota would have been largely competing with itself. Another Japanese group, Mitsubishi, has recognized that its combined financing and logistics functions will be so important to its future profitability that it is currently planning to spend multiple billions (some estimate $5 to $10 billion) on its new MIND logistics system to support worldwide manufacturing and distribution for its broad line of manufactures.

For economies of scale, multinational manufacturing operations today usually look more to knowledge-based service activities (i.e., their technology development, marketing, technology transfer, financial, and logistics functions) than to plant-scale economies.[4] With plant economies of scale constantly dropping, multinational companies' strategies increasingly seek to exploit the companies' core service activity strengths on a worldwide basis. Many of these services can flow duty free across borders, offering new strategic flexibilities when a multinational company can handle cross-border data and services flows more effectively than its competitors. Since it is the service and knowledge components of a multinational's capabilities that a host country can least easily reproduce, these become the company's bargaining points in dealing with host nations, with suppliers, and with customers in each country. As host countries increasingly see these data flows as potential tax sources and as threats to their companies' competitiveness, maintaining the freedom of data flows has become a very sensitive and critical political issue affecting the future international competitiveness of both manufacturing and service enterprises.[5]

International simultaneous development of products has become a sine qua non for most manufacturers, if they hope to develop the most competitive available products or processes. But potential suppliers and partners must be intimately and continuously coordinated throughout the design process. In fact, many companies find that they can obtain a competitive edge by using the differences in time zones between countries to obtain a 24-hour per day workday during design cycles. A design team begins working on a product in the United States in the morning, transfers its status to the Japanese team after 11 hours of coordinated work in the United States (an eight-hour day plus three time zones). Its Japanese partners then pick up the design and carry it forward through the next 8–12 hours, before it is passed along to European design teams. By the next morning, when the U.S. designers return, two full eight-hour days of further work have advanced the design. However, even without such sequenced design capabilities, many firms are coordinating worldwide development with different supplier groups to obtain "best in world" design capability as a matter of competitive necessity. Ford Taurus/Sable and Boeing have been widely cited as outstanding examples.

Whole Industries Restructure

Whole industries are restructuring to achieve global simultaneous interactions on a variety of projects. These industries are becoming merely loosely structured networks of service enterprises joining together (often temporarily) for one purpose—and being suppliers, competitors, or customers in other relationships. This phenomenon is common in the financial services world where cross-competing consortia constantly form and reform to finance different projects or to spread risks worldwide. But the same is true for enterprises in the mineral resources, construction, publishing, entertainment, or software development fields among others. Publishers, for example, outsource virtually the whole process of book creation to independent authors, copy editors, art work groups, compositors, printers, binders, advertising agencies, distributors, retailers, and so on anywhere in the world. Biotechnology provides another interesting global example. Almost all biotech products are developed through a number of different specialist teams in varying enterprises joining together temporarily for the sole purpose of creating and introducing a particular biological entity to the marketplace. Highly specialized enterprises have developed at each level of the industry to perform individual functions.

• Many biotechnology research groups—for example at universities—only seek to identify and patent active biological entities (or proteins) at the laboratory level. Others develop and license the cell lines that are used to reproduce promising entities. Having identified and cultured cells containing the genes to "express an entity" is often as important as knowing the active protein and its effects in vitro. Still others—companies like Verax and Damon—have developed pilot level processes which utilize cell lines owned by others to produce the desired entities in sufficient quantity for clinical tests and early commercialization, but not at full-scale "fermentation" or "flow process" levels. Medical centers handle the highly technical problems of actually administering and running clinical trials. Other enterprises or professional groups may oversee regulatory relationships and FDA clearances. Then other companies—usually major pharmaceutical companies—may take over the large-scale market introduction, detailing, production, and sale of the products, while still other service companies may handle their wholesale or retail distribution. Once the product is in the marketplace, another wider group of doctors prescribe and administer it to patients. And so on. In essence a unique consortium of specialists, intentionally tapping best-in-world capabilities, forms for each stage of research, development, product introduction, or full-scale production-distribution.

• The semiconductor, ASIC, and electronics industries are becoming similarly structured. Independent design, foundry, packaging, assembly, industrial distribution, kitting, configuration, systems analysis, networking, and value-added distributor groups do over $15 billion worth of customized development, generating almost $140,000 of revenue per employee.[6] Even the largest OEMs are

finding that these groups' specialized knowledge, flexible production facilities, and fast turnarounds decrease investments and increase value at all levels of the value chain.

In advanced technology fields particularly, a single company often cannot effectively span the full chain of activities needed—because of the specialized expertise, high risks, and varying time horizons required—at each level of the development process. As a result, many high tech industries—from biotech and ASICs to oil exploration, dam building, nuclear power, or commercial aircraft—are developing as multiple-level consortia, with each consortium and enterprise having its own network of contract and information relationships embracing a variety of research, development, production, finance, and marketing groups around the world. Although biotechnology and ASICs are commonly thought of as manufacturing industries, most of the units which comprise these industry consortia are essentially service centers, performing specialized activities for each other.

New Methods of Financing

These kinds of networks present some different financial opportunities than financing a single company. One can participate at any risk level desired. For example, at the university level one can sponsor research seeking individual patentable biological entities with very low probabilities of any specific project succeeding—but with generally low investments required and potentially high royalty payoffs if the project is successful. Alternately, one can invest larger amounts in companies like Genentech, Biogen, or Amgen (or a new biotech start-up) which are pursuing multiple projects at the research level. At the next stage, financing independent pilot-scale processors (like Verax) allows one to average somewhat higher investments—and their associated risks—across a number of projects, yet potentially participate in individually large upside licensing incomes if the investments pay off. Clinical limited partnerships have been developed to spread investments and risks of failure at the clinical trials stage, while sharing partially in larger benefits if successful. Full-scale production and marketing investments—usually undertaken by more integrated companies—are quite large, but their risks are much lower.

Each level has developed some creative new forms of financing. Only in rare instances has a single enterprise financed the complete development of a new biotech entity from research through volume production and marketing. The combination of risks, the huge amount of capital required, and the long time horizons makes such an integrated undertaking too risky and unwieldy. For this reason alliances are common in biotech, with more than 170 formed just between pharmaceutical manufactures and other independent biotech groups in 1990. Given the rapid technological advances throughout such industries, companies can lower their risks substantially by specializing, by *avoiding* investments in vertical integration, and by concentrating on managing highly disaggregated intellectual systems instead of workers and machines worldwide. Because of their high value-added and easy portability, the knowledge and service-based inputs to such systems can come from anywhere in the world. The core strategy of participating companies becomes: "Do only those things in-house that contribute to your competitive advantage. Try to joint venture others, or outsource them from the world's best suppliers."

Interestingly, this opens up opportunities for myriad smaller companies. By concentrating on a few selected intellectual skills and attracting best-in-world talent to the company, they can become the suppliers of larger companies for whom these are not specialties. This is the core cause of the growth of the number of smaller companies—and the changing and increasing outsourcing expenditures of large companies. Price-Waterhouse looked at 500 software start-ups with an average age of eight years. Two-thirds got some form of financial help from partners—in the form of marketing assistance, equipment support, or guarantees from customers or computer builders. Only one-fifth used venture capital. Many such companies become part of the second leaves of the "shamrock" companies or the nodes of the "spider's web" companies described in the book. If they develop their core competencies in sufficient depth, these companies' small scale, flexibility, and responsiveness make them ideal partners for intelligent enterprises with other core competencies.

Global Financing and Manufacturing Strategies

Another change in the financial realm has also been of prime importance in restructuring manufacturing strategies. The integration of world capital markets (service institutions) through electronic communications (service

technologies) has forced almost all manufacturers into some form of globalization, disaggregation, or structural shifts in their sourcing strategies. While the total of all measured goods and services sold in international trade was only $4.5 trillion in 1990, the Clearing House for International Payments (CHIPS) alone handled almost $250 trillion in international financial transactions. Euromarkets and world bond markets added more than $1,000 trillion in further transactions to this sum. Instead of following goods or trade, money now flows toward the highest available real interest rates or returns in safer, more stable, economic situations.[7] These factors are generally influenced more by government policies than trade. As money flows have sprung free of trade, exchange rates have fluctuated wildly at times—±50 percent among major trading partners within a few months in the late 1980s—principally because of fiscal or monetary, not trade or management, decisions.[8] Such fluctuations change the relative costs of production or importing from a particular location enormously in a short period of time.

Manufacturers cannot cope with changes of this magnitude by vertically integrating and rapidly adjusting their internal productivity rates—no matter how responsive they may be. A manufacturing firm now needs to manage several groups of global portfolios—consisting of its (1) financial positions, (2) market outlets, (3) assembly sites, (4) supplier sources, and (5) subassembly units in different geographical locations—among which it can switch its resources and product developments rapidly and flexibly. Given such high cost variabilities, few firms can afford to own all of their producing entities themselves. Hence the increased need to form the kind of worldwide coalitions noted above—through purchasing arrangements, long-term contracts, alliances, or joint ventures. These are inevitably linked more by information, communication, and mutual interests than by ownership (vertical or horizontal integration) ties. Because of their high value-added potentials and the ease with which their products can be transferred across borders, services activities or companies are the central features in many of these coalitions.

Services Create Disaggregation . . . and Global Networks

Services and the technologies have been the main drivers of more globalized competition and the disaggregation—or diverticalization—that has accompanied it. First, of course, new service technologies for communications, information, storage, transportation, materials handling, and so on, have made it possible for manufacturers to compete directly over wider geographic ranges. Second, the fact that more of the value-added in products comes from intellectual inputs and service outputs means that one can afford to seek out the best providers (for design, finance, etc.) wherever they exist because their services can be shipped across borders at very low cost and tariff free. Both have been major causes of the increased disaggregation and worldwide service competition that have converted certain manufacturing sectors into network industries.

Most manufactured products now function in conjunction with some other systems from which they obtain specialized inputs, components, software, distribution, or repair services. And it is frequently far more effective to obtain such capabilities by forming coalitions with exceptionally strong external units, than by developing all needed activities internally or acquiring and owning a total vertically integrated operation.

Why? Mainly because vertical integration forces companies to be expert in more areas than they can possibly sustain as best-in-class. Unless transaction costs are very high, integration is unlikely to offset the costs of having lesser expertise and a higher investment base in a highly variable marketplace.

• For example, liquid crystal displays (LCDs) are crucial to the next generation of computers and perhaps television. Color LCD sales (probably made from thin films) are expected to exceed those of memory chips by the year 2000. But exploitation requires multiple skills. One set supports the thin films themselves, another is for the special glass needed for displays, another is for the advanced testing equipment to control defects, and another is for the equipment which uses the displays. As a result, a number of consortia are forming to link crucial skills and to reduce investment risks during the expected prolonged development cycle.

• Silicon Graphics, a leading manufacturer of 3D workstations, has been one of the most rapidly growing companies ever in Silicon Valley. Its high-powered computers sell for around $200,000. Seeing the need to up volume and to lower prices for its complex technologies, it introduced a $10,000 IRIS Indigo workstation. Then it entered agreements with Compaq and Microsoft and opened its software to third party licensees. Silicon Graphics is relying on its accumulated knowledge base about 3D and an enforced fast-response culture to keep it ahead. Without such alliances, its CEO (Ed McCracken) felt others could eventually force competing technologies to become the industry's standard.

• By contrast, electronic home equipment giants Sony and Matsushita saw their basic entertainment hardware products moving toward a commodity status in a few years. Instead of entering alliances, they vertically integrated. Each purchased a major software (film and distribution) company to capture the higher margins and more stable revenues there. It remains to be seen whether their strong consensus-type core design and manufacturing cultures will be compatible with the creative, risky, egocentric world of movies, television programming, and rock concerts—or whether alliances would have lowered risks and investments.

Vertical integration exposes the company to all of the risks at each activity level in which it participates and amplifies the systematic risks of the volatility in its own industry. Whenever there is a downturn, such companies must absorb not only the losses in their own final marketplaces, but also those in each of the supplier marketplaces in which they are vertically integrated. Outsourcing lets companies spread these risks upstream to suppliers and downstream to distribution networks. Proper outsourcing and managing of supplier networks allows the company to concentrate on what it does best, surround that activity with enough value-added services to give it uniqueness and depth, avoid the investments and risks in areas where it is less expert, and tap the innovation and expertise of best-in-world suppliers in the latter areas. As the COO of a rapidly growing telecommunications company said: "You know how many advanced technology people I have working for me now? About 20,000! Less than 1,000 on my staff and over 19,000 in my suppliers' shops. And they are the best available anywhere in the world. We basically plan, design and oversee what these people can do for our customers."

This changes the entire concept of strategic focus in manufacturing, from a focus on product classes to a focus on those activities (usually services) which the company can perform and link uniquely well to customer needs. In some cases, this may mean a single-minded focus on certain aspects of manufacturing itself, as it does in SCI. More often it means surrounding the company's product skills with a complex of service activities that are so integrated as to give the company a unique ability and depth in servicing selected customers' needs.

• Despite current admonitions to "stick to one's knitting," for a Xerox to have stuck to manufacturing and selling reprographic machines or an IBM to have been only a computer manufacturer would have been a strategic disaster. Xerox became a huge success primarily because it created an invulnerable patent wall around its product, found a unique way to finance purchases by smaller customers so they could pay for their units as they used them, and coped with the product's early erratic performance with the best field service force then available. Xerox later extended broadly into support software and systems to give its customers the flexible image reproducing qualities and network interconnection capabilities they began to demand. Both before and after Xerox's products went off patent, the sum of its profit contributions from service activities were at least equal to its profits from the direct sale of equipment.

As many have noted, IBM has long received more than one-third of its gross profit from direct sales of software and services—rather than sales of its information processing equipment. When one takes into account the value of the system software and design services traditionally built into or associated with the equipment IBM sells and the value of the equipment sales it would lose without its awesome service support activities, most of IBM's profits during its long period of success were truly due to its service-based focus on its customers' needs. Each company had built up a service core that best delivered its carefully defined document handling (Xerox) or information management (IBM) capabilities as a system to its customers. Yet as large and as capable as these companies were, increasingly neither could internally create and control the full range of design, hardware, software, communications, and networking capabilities it needed. Hence, both moved steadily away from their earlier attempts to vertically integrate—and toward a wide ranging and constantly changing set of coalitions with outside service and support groups that let them compete globally against similar networks of other companies who had come together for similar

Exhibit 2

Competing Global Networks: IBM and AT&T

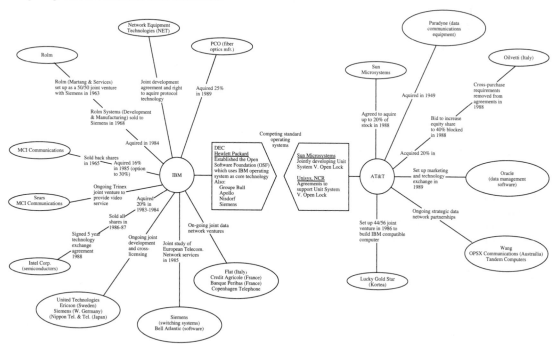

purposes. Essentially, each company now competes as a network against other networks—like those in Exhibit 2—formed to use best-in-world capabilities. Each thus forces others to either join their coalition or compete against their network's full power.[9] (See Exhibit 2.)

- Given the rapid changes in technologies and world marketplaces, IBM in the late 1980s began dismantling the insularity and self sufficiency that dominated it in the 1970s and early 80s. Even its huge multibillion R&D program—largest in the industry—needed to be leveraged externally. In addition to its partnerships with Apple on (RISC, UNIX, and Taligent) software and helping the MCT consortium to do basic computer technology research, IBM began teaming with Siemens to launch the next generation of 16 megabit DRAMS and to design the 64 meg DRAMS that will replace them. Siemens will distribute the chips in Europe. IBM is also trying to forge partnerships with Disney, MCA, Spielberg, and Warner to exploit the multimedia worlds of industrial and personal computers. Its traditionally strong skills in industrial marketing, information, and distribution should give it advantages in that market. But it will need coalitions for success in the consumer-entertainment segment of multimedia (*Business Week,* April 6, 1992).

These arrangements look much like the Japanese keiretsu structures, but with a real difference. For years, combined production–service integration (of banks, producers, and export-distribution companies) has been at the heart of Japan's keiretsu-based trading power. Although some large manufacturing groups wield enormous economic clout within the keiretsu, the Japanese generally have been wise enough to practice quasi-integration, not complete vertical integration. Keiretsus operate largely through carefully interlocked self-interest links, not central authority structures. Given the Japanese success, it is not surprising that similar coalitions—but extended to a worldwide basis—are providing an essential model for other countries' competitive postures today.

A Service or Knowledge-Based Strategy for True Focus

The key lies in maintaining strategic focus while disaggregating. This does not necessarily mean a tight focus

on a limited set of products. Products rarely provide a maintainable competitive edge today. They can be too easily back-engineered or cloned. True strategic focus means developing a selected set of knowledge factors, databases, and service skills—of particular importance to customers—in such depth that the company becomes best-in-world at providing these to customers. It then concentrates its resources on these activities, and seeks best-in-world partners (or performance parity) in other areas by careful benchmarking, process updating, and outsourcing to others when it cannot reach best-in-world status internally.

To maintain its position from a strategic viewpoint, the company's selected focus *must control some crucial aspect(s)* of the relationship between its suppliers and the marketplace. The company must block its suppliers from bypassing it to the marketplace as Giant Manufacturing of Taiwan, originally a bicycle frame subcontractor, did Schwinn. And it must defend itself from big purchasers attempting to vertically integrate into its turf. The best way to do both is to control some key knowledge-based segment(s) of the value chain. Apple, historically, has defended its position by controlling the look and feel of the personal computer's operating software and the knowledge about computer demands that it generates from its well-developed user network.

- Excel Industries of Elkhart, Indiana, for example, had developed a better method for making auto windows. When Ford tried to bring production in-house during a recent recession, it could not master Excel's complex process and ended up having to give Excel a multiyear contract as well as investing in the company. Excel's sales grew by four times, as it reinvested in a faster, more efficient process, cutting design cycles by a year. Ultimately both companies gained by the new relationships.

The company's depth in its selected core activities and their importance to the customer must be such that customers cannot destroy the company by short-circuiting the company directly to its customers, or suppliers by simply assembling components and selling clones to the market—as Dell Computers and other imitators have done in PCs.

This approach radically shifts the basis of strategic analyses in manufacturing. Strategists must analyze all present and potential (direct and cross) competitors able to perform the *service activities* on which the strategy focuses. Because there is so much cross-competition among most service activities, managers cannot simply look at the companies in their own product industry. They must also strategically analyze all those companies which cross-compete in providing the particular function(s) they have chosen as their core competencies and make sure they focus more talent on these areas than anyone else in the world, while benchmarking other crucial service activities to ensure that they maintain sufficient parity there not to be overtaken by cross-substitutions.

As companies begin to simplify internal operations and outsource nonstrategic activities—particularly overheads and peripheral activities—they often discover secondary benefits. The overhead cost leverages can be very impressive. For example, Black and Decker found out that as it eliminated steps in its own manufacturing processes, simplified its designs, and consolidated its suppliers, it decreased the service activities needed to support its production line, and obtained $3 of benefits in overhead cost reduction for each dollar of direct cost it eliminated from production activities.

A More Market Driven Strategy

For almost all firms, focusing strategy on a few core service competencies will lead to a more compact organization. The firm usually ends up with fewer hierarchical levels and a much sharper focus on recruiting, developing, and motivating the people who can create most value for the company. Knowing that it can be potentially outsourced, each activity in the company becomes more market driven to provide better and lower cost service for its internal users. In many cases, the market-driven process can be extended to providing such services directly to outside customers—for example, selling one's accounting or personnel services to outsiders. Some authorities even suggest that if an internal staff group cannot sell at least one-third of its output to outside users, this is a sure sign that the internal activity is not world competitive and ought to be outsourced. Some companies establish their overhead service units as small private business units, which must sell their services to operating groups on a continuing basis, just as component divisions must sell their products in competition with outsiders. Some companies go beyond this to link services directly to defined and prioritized customer needs in a strategic mode.

• Although it is a relatively smaller company (versus its competitors, the "Baby Bells"), United Telephone of Ohio (UTO) provides an excellent example. UTO is attempting to match up the level of services it offers to customers in a profile that is much more congruent with the pattern of its customer's true needs—first understanding in depth what customers most want and need from UTO, then allocating its internal resources and scaling its organizational units' sizes to better fit the defined service balance. UTO tries to benchmark the best available competitive sources for each service and to beat that performance. To make sure that it is best-in-class in the right places, UTO consciously patterns its organizational elements and resource commitments to be overstaffed relative to those needs its customers define as most critical and those in which it is attempting to achieve its own competitive edge. Conversely, those services which are less essential or desired from the customer's viewpoint may be consciously understaffed or eliminated to lower overall costs. All systems and organizational elements are aligned to ensure that those activities most valued by customers receive most attention.

Not only do such approaches achieve greater and more consistent strategic focus, management's attention shifts away from an internal or functional orientation—and the capacity to manage these functions' associated bureaucracies—and toward those more coordinated, strategic, and conceptual tasks that add greater value for customers. The skills needed at the top level shift strongly toward: (1) coordinative interfunctional skills, (2) logistics and contract management skills, (3) specialist skills at the forefront of their fields, and (4) leadership skills which can conceive, implant, and coordinate a broad vision across the much more geographically diffused activities of a company. With fewer bureaucracies, the company can become much more quality and customer focused.

Conclusions

True focus in strategy means the capacity to bring more power to bear on a selected sector than anyone else can. While this once meant a manufacturer owning the largest production facility, research laboratories, or distribution channels supporting a single product line, this is no longer desirable or sufficient for most companies. Physical positions like a raw material source, a plant facility, or a product line rarely constitute a maintainable competitive edge today. This is especially true of manufactured products. They can be too easily bypassed, back-engineered, cloned, or slightly surpassed in performance. A truly maintainable competitive edge usually derives from developing depth in skill sets, experience factors, innovative capacities, know-how, market understanding, databases, or information-distribution systems—all service activities—that others cannot duplicate or exceed.

This requires a redefinition of what a truly focused company really is. Competitive focus does not mean concentrating on a few product lines, sets of production facilities, or markets. Instead, strategic focus means concentrating on those particular skills, service activities, or knowledge elements in the value chain where the company is, can be, or must be best in the world in order to have a competitive advantage its customers deem to be critical. There are several imperatives for this kind of strategy. First, the company must ensure that it is and remains measurably better in its selected core service activities, developing them in greater depth than anyone else can. Then it must seek to achieve at least parity—either internally or through external arrangements—in most other key elements of its value chain. Finally, it must surround its selected core competencies with defensive positions—both upstream and downstream—that keep existing or potential competitors from taking over or eroding its selected positions.

Maintaining the Knowledge Core

Many companies fear that following this approach they may not be able to maintain the knowledge at the core to manage specialist suppliers, and this can be a real problem if not properly handled. To avoid losing control in the areas they outsource, successful companies maintain a small cadre of sufficiently specialized and talented managers at the top to oversee their outsourced relationships expertly. Many companies have found that their new activity coordinators, by riding circuit on all potentially best-in-world outside suppliers, can generate a greater knowledge of the outsourced activities than the company had when its internal bureaucracies were producing these outputs on a proprietary basis. For example, as a portion of its Taurus/Sable project, Ford installed a "must see before" contracting policy, which forced its teams into the field to investigate alternate suppliers in detail. This led to greater understanding of suppliers and design problems, new ideas for the car, and a higher level of internal understanding about possibilities than the old process allowed.

Fortunately, new knowledge-based service technologies—especially online systems for remotely monitoring research, design-logistical activities, quality, and cost relationships—can markedly reduce the transaction costs and improve the effectiveness of managing disaggregated systems. Most companies find their other internal costs and time delays drop as longstanding bureaucracies disappear or are reduced in power, and as their managements concentrate more of their time directly on more coordinative activities and the important core strategic activities of the business. None of this is easy. Implementing this kind of strategy is a complicated undertaking, and it usually must be approached incrementally. However, when successful, the changes in the company's posture can be very impressive.

End Notes

1. D. Abell and J. Hammond, "Cost Dynamics: Scale and Experience Effects," in *Strategic Market Planning: Problems and Analytical Approaches* (Englewood Cliffs, NJ: Prentice Hall, 1979).

2. P. Drucker, "From World Trade to World Investment," *The Wall Street Journal,* May 26, 1987.

3. "International Logistics Management," *Distribution,* October 1987.

4. R. Shelp, *Beyond Industrialization: Ascendancy of the Global Service Economy* (New York: Praeger, 1981).

5. K. Sauvant, *International Transactions in Services: The Politics of Transborder Data Flows* (Boulder, CO: Westview Press, 1986).

6. "Services Get the Job Done," *Electronic Business,* September 15, 1988.

7. S. Bell and B. Kettell, estimated that 95 percent of daily volume in foreign exchange markets is not connected to trade; see their *Foreign Exchange Handbook* (Westport, CT: Quorum Books, 1983).

8. J. Bleeke, and L. Bryan, "The Globalization of Financial Markets," *McKinsey Quarterly,* Winter 1988.

9. K. Ohmae, "Triad Power: The Coming Shape of Global Competition," *Harvard Business Review,* July–August 1991.

CASE 3–1
OAK RIDGE ASSOCIATED UNIVERSITIES

Robert R. Bell
Ramachandran Natarajan
Greg Butler

The telephone was ringing as Janett Trubatch walked into her office at Oak Ridge Associated Universities (ORAU) in Oak Ridge, Tennessee. She answered and found Jon Veigel, the President of ORAU on the line. "Well," she smiled as she responded to his greeting, "a voice from far away." Jon had been at a technology conference in Berlin and was calling from St. Louis, enroute back to Oak Ridge.

"Good talking to you too," Jon responded. "I'm flying in to Knoxville late tonight. I wondered if we could meet at the office tomorrow morning. I need to talk to someone about tech transfer."

"Sure, Jon. I need to work on some things anyway. I'll see you here at the office at seven o'clock."

Dr. Janett Trubatch served as Vice President for University, Industry, and Government Alliances at ORAU. Trubatch held a doctorate in physics from Brandeis University, and she later completed an MBA at the University of Miami. She had previously served as Vice President for Research at the University of Miami, and as Associate Vice President for Research at the University of Chicago. One of her responsibilities at ORAU dealt with technology transfer.[1]

* * *

It was 7:15 A.M. and the coffee pot was on at the ORAU complex. After parking his car, Jon Veigel hurried to Janett's office. "Sorry I'm late," he said as he slumped into a chair. "It must be jet lag."

"No problem, Jon." Janett looked up from her computer console. "What's up?"

Jon propped his feet up on the desk and began. "Here's the problem. Both of us have been around this business a long time. We've seen a lot. But this problem of technology transfer has taken a lot more importance lately. DOE is paying significant attention to it. President Clinton and Vice President Gore are talking about it. My question is this: What is our role at ORAU in technology transfer? We've known the problem for some time and we've studied several organizational mechanisms for dealing with tech transfer. But what is really the right structure? How do you organize to turn basic research into applied research? How do you take high technology research results and turn them into commercial applications? Can we do a better job of tech transfer at our universities? Are they doing it right here at the National Lab? How can we build a stronger technology transfer relationship between our university faculties and students and the employees and laboratories at the National Lab?"

Trubatch laughed as she pulled up a chair. "I better put a second pot of coffee on. I think this might last a while." Veigel couldn't stay seated, so he started pacing around the room as he talked. "Part of the challenge lies in the development and history of the National Lab, and part lies in our changing mission. Some of the technical staff at the laboratories are not convinced that technology transfer from federal labs is a good idea. They think there is a real conflict when basic research is sacrificed for applied research, and they see tech transfer as a strategic threat to our ability to keep the best minds focused on really solid leading-edge research."

The Oak Ridge Operation

In September 1992, Oak Ridge, Tennessee, celebrated its 50th anniversary. Although relatively young, "The Atomic City" has a history as unique as any city in the world. It all began during World War II.

---

[1]The U.S. Department of Energy (DOE) defines technology transfer as "the process by which technology . . . information developed in one organization, one area, or for one purpose is applied or used in another organization, in another area or for another purpose" U.S. Department of Energy (1990).

Source: This case was developed by Professors Robert R. Bell, R. Nat Natrajan, and Greg Butler of Tennessee Technological University. Copyright © 1994 by the National Consortium for Technology in Business, c/o Thomas Walter Center for Technology Management, Auburn University, AL.

In 1939, Albert Einstein urged that an atomic research program be started in America. In August 1942, President Roosevelt ordered the formation of the Manhattan Engineer District (organized under the Army Corps of Engineers) with a goal of producing an atomic bomb within three years.

That fall, one of the sites chosen for the "Manhattan Project" was Anderson County, Tennessee. This site would be the home of a series of plants which used electromagnetic and gaseous diffusion processes to produce the enriched uranium needed in an atomic bomb.

The city which would later become Oak Ridge formed in practically no time. The government made land acquisitions and construction soon followed. In addition to constructing three plants (X-10, K-25, and Y-12), temporary dwellings and other supporting facilities were built for the workers. At one point, a new home popped up every 30 minutes.

Oak Ridge's population boomed to an all-time high of 75,000 by 1945 as people from the area and from all over the country moved in for work. Oak Ridge became the fifth largest city in Tennessee only three years after its creation. An additional 40,000 workers commuted from nearby communities. The infrastructure for the whole area was modernized due to the increased need for better roads, railways, and electrical power.

Perhaps even more surprising than the growth rate was the tremendous ability to maintain secrecy during the war. The Oak Ridge area—tens of square miles— was contained by high fences and heavily armed guards. When people on the outside tried to contact loved ones on the inside, they were told that no such town existed. Military and intelligence officials instilled in workers the need for secrecy and threatened them with firing and federal prosecution if they talked about their work. Approximately one in four adults in the city was a government informant on the alert for any loose talk. These informants were often ordinary people such as waiters and bus drivers who had signed agreements with the government to act as informants. Also, phones were tapped, mail was inspected, and many workers were subjected to periodic lie-detector tests.[2]

Ironically, most workers did not understand what the project was making anyway. Employees were not allowed to see the big picture, and buildings, equipment, and chemicals were referred to by code number and not by name. These code references remain today in the X-10, K-25, and Y-12 plants. Many workers were not even sure that they were producing anything. Finally, when the bomb was dropped, everyone understood more about the complex project they had been involved in. When the Enola Gay made its historic flight over Hiroshima and dropped the first atomic bomb, that bomb was designed at Los Alamos, New Mexico, and fueled with enriched uranium produced at Oak Ridge. After the war, the United States entered a cold war period when the demand for nuclear weapons, and the interest in nuclear energy, remained high.

From the war years until 1983, Union Carbide Corporation managed the Oak Ridge facilities. Union Carbide decided not to renew its contract with the U.S. Department of Energy (the old Atomic Energy Commission) in 1983. Martin Marietta Corporation was awarded the contract and in 1984 formed a wholly owned subsidiary, Martin Marietta Energy Systems, to manage the facilities. This contract was renewed in 1991 for another five years.

Headquartered in Bethesda, Maryland, Martin Marietta (Martin) was incorporated in 1961. Martin is a technology-based company involved with the design, manufacture, and integration of systems and products in the fields of aerospace, defense, electronics, information management, energy, and materials.[3] Examples of the company's products and accomplishments include advanced systems used in Operation Desert Storm, the Titan series launch vehicles, the Magellan spacecraft used by NASA to orbit Venus, Space Shuttle external fuel tanks, and computerized equipment for the U.S. Postal Service.

The National Laboratory

The Oak Ridge National Laboratory (ORNL), managed by Martin Marietta Energy Systems for the U.S. Department of Energy, is a large, multidisciplinary research and development center in Oak Ridge, Tennessee. ORNL's primary mission is to carry out applied research and engineering development in energy production and conservation technologies as well as experimental and theoretical research in the physical and life sciences to

---

[2]Jay Searcy, "Top Secret Activity in the Tennessee Hills," *The Oak Ridger,* Sept. 20, 1992, '40s Special Section, p. 2.

[3]Martin Marietta Energy Systems, Inc., *Career Opportunities* (Bethesda, 1991), p. 2.

advance fundamental knowledge and to lay the foundation for technology development. A secondary mission is to address other nationally important issues, such as environmental protection and waste management and non-nuclear defense technologies, when such work is closely related to the primary mission.

ORNL also designs, builds, and operates unique research facilities for the benefit of universities, industry, other federal agency and national laboratory researchers and is the site of 11 major user facilities and other unique resources for academic and industrial research. The transfer of science and technology to U.S. industries and universities, a key factor in increasing the nation's international competitiveness, is an integral component of ORNL's R&D missions. In addition, ORNL helps to prepare the scientific and technical workforce of the future as a DOE Science Education Center, and it is one of the Southeast's major employers of technically trained graduates.

The 5,500-member staff and facilities that represent an original investment of several hundred million dollars provide a broad-based capability for programs ranging from basic, applied, and developmental research to the operation of pilot plant and small-scale demonstration facilities. These activities span the full range of short-, intermediate-, and long-term energy options, from conservation to fusion. The development of energy technologies draws on extensive research efforts in the engineering, physical, life, and social sciences. About 40 percent of the ORNL employees hold technical degrees; more than half of those have at least a master's degree.

The laboratory's major programs are concentrated in four broad, closely interrelated areas: nuclear (fission) technologies and safety research; physical sciences and advanced materials; environmental, life, and social sciences; and advanced energy systems, including fusion, fossil, conservation, and renewable energy programs. About 80 percent of the budget is provided by the U.S. Department of Energy. Work for other federal and nonfederal agencies, including the Department of Defense, the Nuclear Regulatory Commission, the Department of Health and Human Services, the National Aeronautics and Space Administration, the National Space Foundation, the Environmental Protection Agency, and the Federal Emergency Management Agency, accounts for the remaining effort.

Research roles of engineers—chemical, civil, electrical, environmental, mechanical, materials, and nuclear—range from engineering sciences research and technical support to large-scale, high-technology designated development. Basic and applied research in the physical sciences—chemistry, nuclear physics, materials, solid-state physics, and other theoretical areas—provide a reservoir of knowledge that serves as a major foundation for energy technology development. Areas of emphasis include materials research, including high-temperature materials, neutron scattering, and surface physics; chemical sciences, including analytic and separation techniques, atomic physics and high-temperature aqueous chemistry; and nuclear physics, with focus on heavy-ion reactions.

Programs in biology, ecology, and other life-science disciplines are directed toward understanding of fundamental processes as well as comprehensive assessments of the health and environmental effects of energy production and use. Emphasis in this area is on the interaction of energy-related physical and chemical agents with living organisms. Social scientists are involved in a variety of projects centering on the environmental and socioeconomic impacts of technological change.

Nuclear-related research and development is centered primarily in two areas: the fuel cycles for current and advanced reactor systems, and waste management and reactor safety research in which data are developed for licensing and regulation of commercial nuclear power facilities. A significant effort is underway to understand and develop technologies for managing nuclear and chemical waste. Two newer programs include the development of concepts for the inherently safe reactor and for space nuclear power systems.

Activities in the conservation and renewable energy program concentrate on generic research on high-temperature materials, energy storage, power systems, biomass production, and technology development for buildings and industry. Energy supply and demand analyses, as well as efficiency and end-use studies, and socioeconomic analyses are also carried out as part of the conservation program. Both fundamental and applied studies focus on energy from nonconventional sources. The fossil energy program is directed toward materials research and environmental health and safety research for coal conversion systems.

Major areas of growth for the laboratory include broad multidisciplinary programs in biotechnology, environmental protection and waste management, advanced materials development, and defense, space, and transportation technologies. The Department of Defense has become the largest non-DOE sponsor of work at ORNL and elsewhere in Energy Systems, including research relating to hazardous waste management, data systems development, and other technologies of national significance.

In support of programmatic objectives, ORNL operates diverse research facilities, including fusion devices, research reactors, particle accelerators, robotics laboratories, heavy element facilities, supercomputers, environmental research areas, and a large mouse colony used in studies of the genetic and somatic effects of chemicals and radiation. ORNL's Advanced Neutron Source, planned for construction later in this decade, will provide a new research reactor of unprecedented flux to produce intense steady-state neutron beams in support of basic and applied research on new technologies.

Each year, about 1,700 students and faculty from colleges and universities across the nation participate in research or advanced study at ORNL. Another 2,000 guest investigators from industry and other U.S. and foreign research centers also use the ORNL's facilities to conduct independent or collaborative research.

Oak Ridge Associated Universities

Oak Ridge Associated Universities is a private, not-for-profit consortium of 82 colleges and universities established in 1946 with a mission to provide and develop capabilities critical to the nation's technology infrastructure, particularly in energy, education, health, and the environment. ORAU works with and for our member institutions to help faculty and students gain access to federal research facilities; to keep members informed about opportunities for fellowship, scholarship, and research appointments; and to organize research alliances among our members in areas where their collective strengths can be focused on issues of national importance.

ORAU manages and operates the Oak Ridge Institute for Science and Education (ORISE) for the U.S. Department of Energy. ORISE is responsible for programs in national and international science and engineering education, training, medical sciences, and the environment. ORISE meets its responsibilities by carrying out basic research, applied research and analysis, and technical assistance and assessment.

As a multiuniversity consortium, ORAU's members collectively graduate 25 percent of the nation's science and engineering Ph.D.s. To support members in meet-

ing their educational and research responsibilities in science and technology, ORAU assists faculty and students in gaining access to federal research facilities. ORAU keeps its members informed about opportunities for fellowships, scholarships, and research opportunities. The organization also arranges research alliances to enable the collective strengths of its members to focus on science and technology-based issues of national importance.[4]

A single university or institution can no longer assemble the necessary critical mass of researchers, resources, or facilities to have a significant impact on major science and technology problems. An obvious response is partnerships developed among universities. In the past, such collaborative alliances have been viewed primarily as pleasant opportunities. The changing scales of science and economics increasingly make such partnerships a necessity.

ORAU is designed to foster such a partnership, with 82 doctoral degree–granting institutions and an associate class of colleges with a primary undergraduate focus. ORAU member schools stretch from New Mexico to Pennsylvania and Puerto Rico to Idaho.

In the 1991 annual report, Jon Veigel commented on the changing roles of ORAU:

> We live in an age in which our options have been dramatically increased because of science and technology while at the same time our problems have gotten bigger and more numerous—often also because of science and technology. The net result is that our expectations of science have changed. Compared to the way science was done yesterday, tomorrow will present us with both new requirements and new opportunities.
>
> For ORAU, the question of how we position ourselves in the future revolves as much around how we do our science as it does around the details of what science we do. What we do, and how we do it, resonates between our activities as a laboratory in the family of DOE laboratories and our separate activities as a multi-university consortium.
>
> We have to address questions like:
>
> • How can we assist our educational systems to produce the quality and quantity of scientists, engineers, and technologies needed by society? How can we build toward a public that is aware of the importance of science and technology to our energy future?

---

[4]*ORAU Resource Guide,* Oak Ridge Associated Universities, 1992 (L61).

- How do we reliably and effectively ensure the nation has a scientific, engineering, and technical workforce trained to meet the increasingly demanding job performance requirements of a competitive world economy?[5]

The Meeting with Bill Goodwin

A few weeks after their early-morning discussion, Trubatch and Veigel hosted another conference at the ORAU campus near the national laboratory. The conference ended about 2 P.M., and they had a chance to remain at the site to talk with Bill Goodwin, associate vice president for research at Tennessee Technological University. Goodwin had previously served as interim vice president for industry and university relations prior to Janett's appointment.

Jon began the conversation. "Bill, we've been doing some brainstorming on tech transfer. We wonder how long it will take to 'catch on,' to get to a place where we know we've done it right."

Trubatch smiled and added: "The main problem is that people don't sit around the National Lab trying to come up with commercial, end-use products. They often think they are . . . but they're not. Most products are just not yet in the form needed for industry. And research does not match industry needs. Getting the match is the difficult part.

"Let me give you an example. At the University of Chicago, a researcher came up with a new process for producing antibacterial drugs. The new process was great, but there are already many antibacterial drugs on the market. The drug companies said the process was desirable, but determined that it would not be able to capture enough of the market to justify sinking an estimated $21 million in further development. Good research, but with little commercial application.

"And I remember a second example from Chicago. A group did a lot of research a few years ago on the formation of diamonds and asteroids—they're related processes, you know. This could really affect the diamond industry. After doing years of research, the team discovered that their work was too preliminary to even get a patent. The principal researchers just weren't interested in spending the next 10 years to take it to the next step. So it stayed on the shelf."

Technology Transfer and National Competitiveness

The group spent the rest of the afternoon discussing the tech transfer problem. Goodwin noted that during the past two decades, international competitors have eroded the once commanding advantage in technology held by U.S. corporations. There is strong concern that the United States is continuing to lose its competitiveness. When it comes to advanced technology, national security is no longer purely a military issue; it also involves economic security.[6] During the 1980s, the U.S. economy lost market share in both base industries such as automobiles and in new high-technology industries such as integrated circuits.

Goodwin pointed out the seriousness of the problem by discussing the integrated circuits industry. In 1975, the U.S. produced over two-thirds of the world's integrated circuits. Today, Japan is the leader and also leads in the development of key semiconductor processing equipment. Without leadership in processing equipment, the ability to manufacture leading-edge technologies of any type is in jeopardy. Since the United States no longer holds the leadership position in integrated circuits, he argued, some people question whether leadership in any of the markets which depend on this critical technology can be retained.

Several reasons were discussed as causes of these competitive woes: heavier government regulation in the United States, the lower cost of money in foreign countries, better educational systems in other countries, poor worker–management relations in the United States, and collaborative efforts between government and industry in other countries. Trubatch noted that some people feel that much of the problem is due to the way the United States has managed new technology in the entire process of technology transfer (the transfer of ideas from the research lab to the delivery of products to customers).[7]

Jon Veigel added information on tech transfer from NASA. He noted that the space program produced over

---

[5]Oak Ridge Associated Universities, *Annual Report,* FY 1990.

[6]B. R. Inman and Daniel F. Burton, Jr., "Technology and Competitiveness: The New Policy Frontier," *Foreign Affairs,* Spring 1990, p. 116.

[7]William J. Spencer, "Research to Product: A Major U.S. Challenge," *California Management Review,* Winter 1990, pp. 45–47.

30,000 spin-off products, including such familiar items as smoke detectors and automatic teller machines.[8]

Goodwin noted that there are almost 726 federal research labs in the United States, with combined federal funding of $40 billion. These labs offer a tremendous source of untapped knowledge and technology. Although most of the research is available to industry, only a small percentage of the technologies developed in federal labs have resulted in commercial products.

In contrast, 85 percent of the research performed by Japan's public labs in 1991 was aimed at commercial applications.[9] Most of Japan's research is privately funded with the government acting as an organizer and coordinator. Since Japanese industry supplies the funding, Japanese companies have a major say in policy decisions. Whether publicly or privately funded, the results are the same. Federal research in other countries is geared toward commercialization and, critics charge, research in U.S. federal laboratories is not aimed at commercial applications. Government agencies and professional societies in other countries (notably Japan) take a more active role in technology transfer than do their American counterparts.[10]

Trubatch led the discussion back to some key questions: "Is there much on any of the lab campuses worth transferring? How can the nature of the labs be changed—both in their mission and in their vision? More importantly, should the mission of the labs be changed? How can we develop pull mechanisms so that the labs do the type of work that industry wants? I'm not sure the federal labs want to set themselves up this way . . . but perhaps parts of some labs may be willing and able to do it." She added: "To improve the global competitiveness of U.S. industry, technology transfer, along with total quality management practices, must receive priority attention. However, since one of our country's greatest competitive strengths is the research capabilities in our universities and our national labs, we certainly need to give serious consideration as to how we take appropriate parts of these organizations and help align their interests with industries."

---

[8]John Christie, "Let's Improve Technology Transfer," *Machine Design* 7 (Nov. 1991), p. 191.
[9]Ibid.
[10]Robert S. Cutler, "A Survey of High-Technology Transfer Practices in Japan and in the United States," *Interfaces,* November–December 1989, pp. 76–77.

Janett ended the day's discussion by describing the ORAU funding summary (Exhibit 1). She noted that governmental funding priorities were changing. "Since 70–80 percent of our funding remains tied to the U.S. Department of Energy, we've really got to be concerned with shifts in federal priorities. Obviously, the cold war is becoming less of a national issue, and defense-related nuclear research will probably continue to decline. Yet the national labs will still have a mission, and energy-related nuclear research and research funds for nuclear medicine may actually increase. Clearly, the pressures on national economic competitiveness will increase. So what is our role? What should ORAU be doing to facilitate technology transfer? We're basically a small staff with a vast array of university faculty and laboratory resources, connected to another vast array of facilities and personnel here in Oak Ridge. How do we posture ourselves for the turn of the century?"

The December Meeting

Trubatch, Veigel, and Goodwin held a series of meetings dealing with technology transfer. In December 1993, they met at a conference room at the ORAU site. Janett began the discussion: "We've had a good set of meetings, and we've covered a lot of ground these last few weeks. Let me see if I can summarize: the picture is becoming clearer as to how the major players at Oak Ridge might fit together for tech transfer. DOE, like the rest of the federal government, is becoming more concerned with technology transfer. Accordingly, Energy Systems shares this concern because their job is to satisfy DOE. The changing mission for Energy Systems seems to fit well with Martin Marietta's need to expand its nondefense business base. The end result is a lot of people working toward the same goal. Combined effort is exactly what this country's technology transfer efforts need. And, from our side, how can ORAU and its member universities work together with ORNL and Martin Marietta to improve the process of technology transfer from the research labs at universities and at the National Laboratory to U.S. industry? And what about the scientists at the National Lab? They're trained for and focused on heavy, basic research. Are they really geared up to work in commercial tech transfer projects? How can we get our best and brightest to benefit themselves and benefit U.S. industry?"

Goodwin pointed out that ORAU is not unique. Several other types of university consortia exist across

EXHIBIT 1

Funding for Oak Ridge Associated Universities

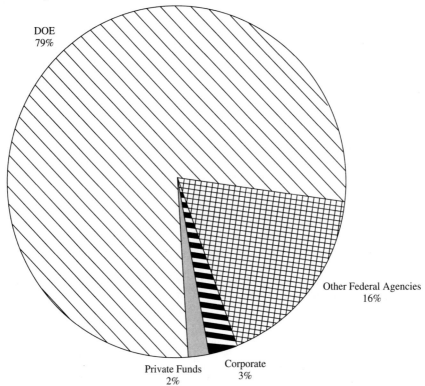

Source	1990	1989
DOE	$38,070.10	$31,115.60
Other federal agencies	7,616.70	9,550.00
Private sector	1,081.00	835.70
Corporate	1,454.70	1,397.50
Total funding	$48,222.50	$42,898.80

Source: Oak Ridge Associated Universities Annual Report–1991.

the United States and in several foreign countries. Historically, the ORAU facilities were located in Oak Ridge so that faculty members from member universities could get access to the research facilities at the national laboratory and other nuclear sites in Oak Ridge. But, Bill pointed out, today the ORAU complex could work just as easily in Atlanta or Chicago as in Oak

Ridge. "We don't have to be physically present in Oak Ridge to serve our liaison role and coordinator role," he said.

The technology transfer problem is a bit different from that found in federal agencies. "While ORAU does not play a major role in *generating* or *creating* new technologies, we obviously have created some," he said.

"Our main role is to *uncover* technology—to help others discover it."

Goodwin suggested that ORAU is in a unique position to enable a form of reverse technology transfer. "Rather than focusing on tech transfer *from* the federal labs, the biggest contribution we can make is to get the technologies currently existing on university campuses out into the public domain, at the national labs and in other settings. All universities have faculty and graduate students (many at the masters level, a lesser but still significant number at the doctoral level). These faculty and students, especially in the engineering, science, and medical fields, create many inventions and new research contributions each year. But the universities don't have a mechanism by which these research results move into the hands of people doing applications work. A second problem, then, is how to move the research into commercial settings. These are the really significant tech transfer issues for ORAU."

"Well, Bill, that's a different perspective," Janett said. "But you're right. We must consider the universities as a vital customer—and a vital resource. This adds an entirely new flavor to our technology transfer problem. One set of our clients—the universities—is spread all over the United States and in other countries. The other set is concentrated in the federal facilities here in Oak Ridge. My problem is that I want to help facilitate ORAU's move into a significant leadership role in the technology transfer process. What do you recommend that we do?"

CASE 3–2
OAK RIDGE NATIONAL LABORATORY AND FLUID TECHNOLOGY INC.

Robert R. Bell
R. Nat Natarajan
David W. Yarbrough

Jim Miller stepped into his office after lunch. He noticed that somebody had left a message on his answering machine. As the tape started to roll he heard the voice of vice president of engineering of Fluid Technnology (FT) say: "Congratulations Jim, it is now official, you will be the project manager for the air dryer project. You will be responsible for making the initial recommendation to the engineering and marketing committee concerning FT's entrance into the air dryer market. In addition, if the recommendation is in favor of the product and the company approves the decision, you will oversee the project development. Now let us get on with it. I am leaving town this afternoon to visit our unit in Australia. I will talk to you later."

Jim Miller received a bachelor's degree in mechanical engineering from the University of Tennessee in 1964. After graduation, he worked for Pratt and Whitney Aircraft Company for two years and Lockheed Aircraft Company for three years. He joined FT in 1969 as a product development engineer and has remained in product development. He was promoted to product development manager in 1976, manager design and development in 1985, manager application engineering in 1987, manager corporate advanced engineering in 1990, and technical products manager in 1992.

Jim reflected on his new assignment and why he believed he was chosen project manager:

> I've been with the company 23 years and my responsibilities have always been in engineering roles. With the emphasis on customers, however, the company wanted to get more employees involved with end-users. The company is in transition. Traditionally, when a project would come along and it looked like top management wanted to do it, we would go directly to the development stage and design a prototype. After that, we would do a study to determine if

we actually wanted to manufacture and market the product. More than ever, the company is trying to be market driven, even in state-of-the-art technology. We are trying to get customer input and put our financial plan together before we spend lots of time and money on a new project.

Jim felt he should begin by preparing a feasibility report for presentation to the engineering and marketing cross-functional committee of FT. He knew he wanted to include in his report the possibility of a cooperative research and development agreement (CRADA) with Oak Ridge National Laboratory (ORNL). He started looking for his notes on CRADAs.

Company History

Fluid Technology, Inc., manufactures and markets filtration systems for the trucking, chemical, medical, military, and aerospace industries. The company has marketing offices in the United States, Australia, Belgium, Canada, England, France, Greece, and Singapore. Fluid Technology owns three manufacturing facilities, two in the United States and one in France, and has licensing agreements with three joint venture companies located in Mexico, India, and South Korea (Exhibit 1). In addition, the company owns five distribution centers worldwide.

Fluid Technology's Evolution.   Fluid Technology began as a division of Advanced Technology Engine Company in 1958. Advanced Technology, Inc., headquartered in a midwestern state, produces engines for heavy-duty trucks and equipment. Throughout the 1950s, Advanced Technology management became increasingly displeased with the cost and quality of filters available for heavy-duty engines. In 1958, the company started an in-house product improvement program to develop a high-quality, low-cost filter. In 1963, the company began selling filters to other engine manufacturers. At this time, the company's name was changed to

Source: This case was developed by Professors Robert R. Bell, R. Nat Natarajan, and David W. Yarbrough of Tennessee Technological University. Copyright © 1994 by the National Consortium for Technology in Business, c/o the Thomas Walter Center for Technology Management, Auburn University, AL.

EXHIBIT 1

Worldwide Locations of Fluid Technology

Fluid Technology, and the company's filters were marketed under that name. The company's reputation for producing high-quality, low-cost filters grew rapidly, and by 1965 Fluid Technology became the main filter supplier to major companies, including Cummins, Deere, International Harvester, White Motor Company, and Clark Equipment. Due to its rapid growth, Fluid Technology began searching for a location to build a new manufacturing and distribution facility. In early 1966, after a year-long search, the company built a 137,000 square-foot facility in a southeastern state and produced its first filter on April 10, 1967. The facility started with 20 employees but quickly grew to 200.

Management wanted to expand into new markets with deeper penetration into its current markets and wanted to develop new types of filter products. The company then set a goal to enter the replacement parts market. The company reached sales of approximately $7 million by 1970 and grew to employ over 400 people. Fluid Technology had also established over 120 distributors throughout the United States and had added Ford, Kenworth, and Peterbilt to its growing customer list.

Engineering and Product Development.   Throughout its history, Fluid Technology's technological advances had allowed the company to better meet the normal application needs of its customers and design products for customers that had special filtration requirements, helping the company's rapid growth. Due to its expanded product line and larger customer base, Fluid Technology outgrew its capacity and in late 1973 again the company expanded its facility. The $9 million addition increased manufacturing space to approximately 400,000 square feet and added 300 more employees. Production in the new facility began in early 1974.

On January 1, 1974, Fluid Technology's status changed from that of a division of Advanced Technology, Inc., to a wholly owned and incorporated subsidiary. Fluid Technology was to operate autonomously. Strategic decisions were now the responsibility of Fluid Technology's management.

International Expansion.   By the early 1980s Fluid technology products were carried by more than 1,000 distributors and the company was serving more than 100 OEMs worldwide. Total sales for the company were over $50 million.

Diversification.   Throughout the 1980s the number of customers grew, as did the company's sales and profits. Management felt that it was time to expand into other markets. Due to its expertise, however, Fluid Technology wanted to stay in the area of filtration. Therefore, the company looked for opportunities to diversify in the filter industry. Fluid Technology acquired companies involved with fluid processing, biomedical research, aerospace, and other industries with filtration requirements. By 1992, the company sold products to over 3,500 customers in 87 countries. Consolidated sales topped $300 million. Exhibit 2 shows Fluid Technology's current organizational structure.

Company Culture.   Fluid Technology had a strong commitment to product quality and to customer satisfaction. This commitment led the company to become the filter industry's innovative leader. Joe Adams, senior vice president, worldwide operations support, described the company's total quality philosophy:

> Customers select whom they deal with every day, and at Fluid Technology we want the customer so convinced of our excellence that it might be frightening for them to consider leaving Fluid Technology as their supplier of quality filtration products and services.

Development of New Product Lines

After reviewing several new product lines in the filtration industry, the decision was made to study the feasibility of developing and marketing air dryers which are installed in the air systems used in heavy trucks. FT and its parent company, Advanced Technology, were well known in the trucking industry and enjoyed a reputation as producers of quality heavy engines and filters.

Air Dryer Product Offering.   Air dryers are part of the air system used in trucks. The air system takes in air, compresses it, and stores it in reservoirs for later use. Air provides power for several systems on a truck, most importantly, the braking system.

Fuel Economy.   Fuel economy is a major concern for trucking companies. The air system is powered by the truck engine, requiring fuel consumption and diverting power from pulling the load. OEMs are continually looking for products to offer fleet managers that will increase fuel economy. A small increase in fuel economy can significantly reduce costs for a fleet. For example, a 1 percent increase in fuel economy will reduce annual fuel expenses by $100 to $200 per truck.

Air Dryers.   The air system is sensitive to moisture, oil, and other contaminants found in air. These contaminants, when combined with water vapor from compressed air, produce sludge that corrodes the air system. Eventually, corrosion leads to repairs or replacement of the air system and can cause brake failure. Air dryers remove the moisture and contaminants from compressed air prior to the air's storage. The most popular air dryer is the desiccant-type. Desiccant air dryers have a cartridge filled with desiccant beads that chemically hold moisture and contaminants. The spin-on cartridge is attached to a base with several valve functions. Air from the compressor passes over the desiccant material which dries the air by removing moisture and other contaminants. When the beads are full, the cartridge must be cleaned. As system demand for air is satisfied, the contaminants are isolated from the compressor and the valves call for a purge cycle. To purge the dryer, air is routed from a holding tank back through the desiccant blowing the contaminants out to the atmosphere. The desiccant is thereby regenerated and the cycle is repeated as the vehicle travels.

Pressure System Air Dryers.   In mid-1992, FT was approached by JBM Engineering, a truck accessories designer, to cooperate in developing technology for a new generation air dryer. The new air dryer, called the pressure system (P-system) dryer, would include ceramic filter and dryer elements and operate with lower engine power requirements. Since less power is required to operate the air system, less fuel is consumed by the engine. P-system technology operates by preventing a

EXHIBIT 2

Organization Chart of Fluid Technology Inc.

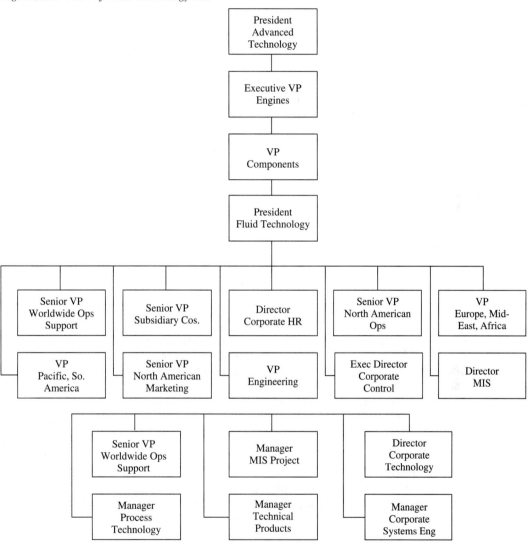

pressure loss when the compressor is not running. Therefore, overall power requirements for the compressor are reduced, resulting in better fuel economy. Fuel savings estimated for trucks using the P-system average approximately 3 percent annually.

Project Development

JBM Engineering discussed three issues with FT before the project started: product release dates, patents, and individual company responsibilities.

Release Dates. FT indicated that it wanted the air dryers available to OEMs for the 1995 new engine production runs. Therefore, the product would have to be released for manufacturing in the third quarter of 1994. To meet this requirement, FT would have to start prototyping as soon as possible. A key issue was the possibility of using a collector medium (to go with the desiccant) that would trap the contaminants. The collector would be a ceramic element that would serve as the particle separator, capable of extremely fine particle separation, on the order of one or two microns. Such a collector would greatly extend the desiccant life and filtering efficiency.

Patents. JBM applied for and received a patent for its P-system technology. JBM left the component design open to the component manufacturer. Therefore, a specific component design patent using the technology had not been applied for.

Project Responsibilities. JBM's responsibility was to deliver the P-system technology to FT. FT was responsible for designing, manufacturing, marketing, and distributing the air dryers. In addition, profits or losses from sales would fall to FT. In essence, if it chose to produce air dryers, FT would have total responsibility for the product.

Cooperative Research and Development Agreements (CRADAs). It was late in the afternoon that Jim was able to go through his notes on CRADAs. CRADAs are the direct consequence of the Technology Transfer Act of 1986, which permitted the federal laboratories to enter into agreement with the private sector or other entities for technology development and transfer. A CRADA is an agreement between one or more federal labs and one or more nonfederal parties. The lab provides personnel, facilities, equipment, or other resources with or without reimbursement. The nonfederal party provides funds, personnel, facilities, equipment, services, or other resources to conduct specified research.

CRADA partners can be industries, universities, nonprofit organizations, or local governments. A requirement for participation in a CRADA is that the client company has to be a U.S. company and that the technology will be used on products "substantially manufactured in the United States."

A concern about all companies was whether they could fully exploit the technology and be successful with the CRADA technology. The same laws also require that the client company use the technology generated by the CRADA to manufacture substantially in the United States.

The CRADA can result in several benefits. It acts as a mechanism with which the private firm can leverage scarce R&D resources. The laboratory and the client company stand to complement one another's capabilities. Technology is transferred during the R&D phase rather than after it is already completed. This means of transfer allows the client to have input on developing the technology to suit its needs. Inventions produced by the CRADA belong to the inventor's company and do not go to the government by default. The contributions made by the government and the client company respectively should be relatively equal, although contributions may take different forms. CRADAs require that no funds leave the laboratory. For example, the client company may make a contribution that is half direct funding to the laboratory and half labor. Since the laboratory cannot allow funding to flow from the lab to the client company, its contribution must be in a different form such as labor, equipment, services, and the like.

If technology generated under the CRADA is made public immediately, no competitive advantage is gained by the client company or by U.S. industry in general. Therefore, intellectual property rights are an important concern with CRADAs. The provisions regarding intellectual property rights must be worked out during the contract negotiation process, but some data may be protected as proprietary information for up to five years.

The typical length of CRADA agreements was anywhere between two to three years.

If the company brings sensitive information as a resource contribution to the CRADA, that information can be designated "proprietary." The company declares at the outset what information it considers to be proprietary, and that information either does not become part of the CRADA documentation or measures are taken to ensure its security.

Definition of what information is proprietary and what can be released as public domain must be spelled out in the negotiation process. Generally, the agreement includes a statement that the industrial partner will have the right to review anything before it is released. Having that understanding from the beginning is an important element of the agreement.

According to the federal legislation under which CRADAs are formed, information generated by CRADAs can be protected as proprietary information for up to five years. During this time, the client company can exploit the information and technology as much as possible. After five years, the information or technology becomes public under the Freedom of Information Act.

The Negotiations Process.   If a company approaches the federally funded lab requesting assistance in a specific research area, the negotiation process involves simply deciding the effort level to be assigned to the task and the contribution to be made by each party. If the lab has a technology it feels can be commercialized, representatives search for a private sector partner. Once this partner is found, a preliminary presentation about the laboratory's capabilities is made. If a potential industry partner expresses an interest, a statement of work (SOW) is completed, which includes what the objective is going to be.

Resource Allocations.   Part of the SOW, or a document closely related to it, identifies the resources to be contributed by each party as part of the cooperative effort. In this case, resources mean money, labor, facilities, services, and knowledge.

According to a DOE orientation handbook on technology transfer, the federal party can provide "personnel, facilities, equipment, or other resources with or without reimbursement (but not funds to nonfederal parties). The nonfederal parties provide funds, personnel, services, facilities, equipment, or other resources to conduct specified research or development efforts that are consistent with the laboratory's mission."[1] An important fact to note is that no funding flows from the lab to the nonfederal party. Any exchange of funds must go from the client company to the laboratory.

Only a very small fraction of the resources exchanged are monetary. Typically, in a CRADA that's worth a million dollars the company might put up a half a million dollars in terms of time. The government very likely puts up a half a million dollars in terms of time. There may be no cash that changes hands at all. But they're both benefiting from this concentrated effort of more people and more laboratories examining the problem. In cases where there is little exchange of funding, the resources consumed by the joint effort are mainly labor, plant and equipment, and information. On the government side, someone has to pay for these resources. Most of the money comes from program funding.

To get the program funding, the laboratory must go to its financial sponsor in Washington and convince that person that the proposed research is worthwhile. Although Oak Ridge National Laboratory is a Department of Energy facility, this does not limit ORNL to soliciting funds from DOE. In the case of ceramic parts, ORNL might go to DOE citing benefits in energy conservation. But another possibility might be the Department of Commerce, which would be interested in the applications of ceramic elements in the U.S. industry.

Once the laboratory convinces a sponsor that the project is worthwhile, the program manager from the government agency will authorize a given amount of money as the government's contribution to that CRADA. The money stays in the laboratory; it does not get paid to the client company at any time.

The negotiation process for a CRADA can take anywhere from three months to two years. One of the factors that can cause delays is funding considerations. If industry is putting up a sum of money, the company wants to make sure the technology in question will yield a good return. If the company is willing to "ante up," it is a sign that the agreement looks like a good investment. If a company is not serious enough about CRADA involvement to make the financial commitment, this step in the process will screen it out.

Another screening process takes place on the government funding side. If a technology does not look promising to any financial sponsors in Washington, the project will not receive any funding. In this way, the project is screened out rather than the company.

Jim's notes on the research activities at Oak Ridge National Laboratory (ORNL) indicated that one of the areas in which ORNL conducts a great deal of research is advanced materials, including ceramics and ceramic composites. Much of this research was conducted at the High Temperature Materials Laboratory (HTML). Jim also had notes on the capabilities of the Y-12 manufacturing facility. He had noted that, once the construction site for bomb parts, Y-12 would soon be home for the Precision Manufacturing Technology Center. Included in the notes was a press clipping about a CRADA with Lanxide Corporation that combined the research capabilities of ORNL with the manufacturing capabilities of Y-12.[2] There was another press clipping about the work

---

[1]U.S. Department of Energy, *Technology Transfer: A DOE and Industry Partnership for the Future,* January 1991, p. 3-2.

[2]Hayden Evans, "First Cooperative Project Signed by Y-12 Plant/ORNL," *Roane County News,* Kingston, TN, September 28, 1992, p. 5.

EXHIBIT 3

CRADA News Story

First Cooperative Project Signed by Y-12 Plant/ORNL

The first cooperative research project involving U.S. Department of Energy's Y-12 Plant and Oak Ridge National Laboratory together with private industry kicked off Friday during a ceremony at the laboratory.

A $2.4 million cooperative research and development agreement (CRADA) was signed last Friday by officials of Martin Marietta Energy Systems Inc. and Lanxide Corp. in a ceremony in front of ORNL's High Temperature Materials Laboratory (HTML).

Energy Systems manages Y-12, ORNL, and three other energy-related facilities for DOE.

Lanxide Corp. of Newark, Delaware, represents the world's largest development and commercialization effort dedicated to ceramic and metallic composites.

The collaborative research effort between Energy Systems and Lanxide is based on Y-12's machining capability honed in manufacturing nuclear weapons and ORNL's experience with advanced materials. The collaboration will help Lanxide develop new, more efficient, more cost-effective means of manufacturing composites for automotive use.

"This project is a perfect marriage between Y-12 and HTML," said ORNL Physical Sciences Division Associate Director Bill Appleton. "There's been a lot of talk about combining capabilities and this the first time the two facilities have worked together on a project such as this to assist private industry," he continued.

Appleton explained that the intent was to merge the expertise of the two facilities, Y-12's machining and HTML's ceramics, to solve problems in the ceramics industry.

"We are excited about working on this project with Lanxide," said Director of Y-12 Technology Transfer D. H. Johnson. "It has been less than three months since we announced a new technology transfer mission for Y-12, and agreements such as this one prove what we already knew—that we have valuable technology and expertise to share with industry."

Y-12 Assistant Plant Manager Mike Cuddy said the transition from the cold war truly was testing the nation and that the collaborative agreement ceremony being witnessed represented an opportunity to provide a return on investments to taxpayers.

Lanxide Corp. Senior Vice President Andrew Urquhart said, "We are very pleased to initiate this cooperative effort with the Y-12 Plant and ORNL. We hope it will provide important benefits to us in reducing future manufacturing costs and increase our competitiveness both domestically and internationally."

"This is the first CRADA Lanxide has entered into and we're not just testing the water here, we're going 'whole hog' with you."

The collaborative effort is intended to develop cost-effective machining techniques for the composites. In addition, work also will be done on establishing process control and material characterization techniques.

The CRADA will be funded through the Conservation and Renewable Energy Program Office and DOE's Defense Programs Office in Washington.

Initial project work will be conducted at Y-12 during establishment of the Ceramic Manufacturability Center in the High Temperature Materials Laboratory.

The high cost of machining is considered to be a principal barrier to the use of ceramic-containing composites in the automotive industry.

The project's objectives include improving the accuracy and consistency of critical workpiece dimensions generated by processes such as threading, drilling, grinding, honing, cutting, broaching, turning, and milling. The initial focus will be in developing techniques and tooling for the cost-effective machining of metal matrix composite connecting rods and brake calipers and rotors.

Source: Hayden Evans, *Roanne County News,* September 28, 1992. Reprinted with permission.

done at ORNL on easier and more economical production of complex ceramic forms.[3] (See Exhibits 3 and 4.)

Jim looked outside through his office window after he finished reading his notes. He got up, stretched, walked around, and sat down. He spent the next few minutes thinking about what he had read. He went back to his notes and began jotting down the strategic objectives of Fluid Technologies to be achieved through a CRADA. Jim listed the following.

- To gain a greater competitive advantage through ceramic filtration element.

---

[3]Paul Kemezis, "Ceramic Parts: Quick and Easy," *Chemical Week,* August 30, 1989, p. 13.

EXHIBIT 4

Ceramics Production News Story

Ceramic Parts: Quick and Easy?

Ceramic engines run hotter longer and are more efficient and more environmentally appealing than those made with metal parts. But until recently it has been difficult to create the intricate parts that go into engines such as turbine blades entirely out of ceramics. Now a new method that allows easier and more economical production of these complex ceramic forms is close to commercialization, thanks to research at the Department of Energy's Oak Ridge National Laboratory (Oak Ridge, Tennessee).

The new process, which uses a water-based vehicle instead of wax or solvents to set the ceramics in the mold, has attracted the interest of leading specialty ceramics maker Coors Ceramics (Golden, Colorado). Earlier this month the company licensed the process from lab operator Martin Marietta Energy Systems. Coors plans to build a $2 million plant at Oak Ridge to produce parts using the new process. It expects the plant to be open within a year.

Until now, ceramic powders have been held in molds with 100% paraffin or polymer-based substances. Once the part is formed, heat is applied to remove the binder. That process is slow, causes imperfections in the material, and limits the size of the parts to an inch or two in thickness.

The new process, on the other hand, involves a vinyl monomer solution that can be polymerized into a cross-linked gel. This is done once the suspension has already been set in the mold, which makes it easier to work with than previous systems that gel while they are being put into the mold. The part that results is stiffer and can be machined before sintering.

Chemical companies have been working on similar techniques. Allied-Signal has patented a process that uses the seaweed derivative agar, a common food thickener, to turn ceramic powder into a gel. And Dow Chemical has developed another water-based molding process, based on its Methocel family of polymers.

Source: Paul Kemezis, *Chemical Week,* August 30, 1989. Reprinted with permission.

- To redirect the R&D resources made available at FT due to CRADA to other projects.
- To gain new knowledge from ORNL for future but not necessarily immediate use.
- To gain access to the research capabilities at ORNL and use it as an outsourcing alternative for doing R&D in ceramics.
- To protect proprietary information from within the company from competitors and potential competitors.

Jim thought that there were other issues that should be considered. What about JBM and its possible involvement in a CRADA with FT? Jim had always felt that JBM offered opportunities for a strategic alliance for technology development, particularly in the ceramics field. As a small business JBM qualified for special grants under Department of Energy's 1993 Small Business Innovative Research (SBIR) solicitation[4] (see the AIA Newsletter in the appendix), but it lacked the legal resources that a firm like FT would be able to command

in negotiations involving intellectual property. Further, JBM lacked the resources to make significant manufacturing investments to capitalize on CRADA output. In the event of a three-way CRADA partnership, releasing the details of the technology to the ORNL scientists and to each other was going to be a necessary step if significant advances were going to be made in the CRADA. Then there were other concerns: Would FT, being a global business operation, even qualify as a "U.S." company in order to become a CRADA partner? Jim did not want FT to get involved in a very lengthy negotiations process since the design has to be released for manufacturing within a year. Jim wanted to know if there was any off-the-shelf technology that was readily available at ORNL. How does technology transfer from direct licensing differ from a CRADA? How would FT and ORNL measure the effectiveness of technology transfer through a CRADA? The list of questions kept growing.

Next morning, Jim called one of his classmates from University of Tennessee days who worked as an engineer at ORNL. He began by saying, "Tom, I have here a press clipping about the work you guys are doing at ORNL in ceramics. Could you please arrange for me a meeting with someone from ORNL who can talk to me about CRADA or other modes of technology transfer from ORNL involving ceramic elements? . . ."

[4]Barry M. Daniel, "Technology Transfer—A National Energy Imperative," *Aerospace Industries Association Newsletter* 5, no. 6 (December 1992).

APPENDIX A
TECHNOLOGY TRANSFER—A NATIONAL ENERGY IMPERATIVE

Barry M. Daniel
Director of Public Affairs
U.S. Department of Energy

Many policy changes will occur with the new administration in January, but one area—the emphasis on government-to-industry technology transfer programs—should continue to develop and may even accelerate.

Along with the Departments of Commerce and Transportation, NASA, and several other agencies, the Department of Energy (DOE) has enthusiastically embraced both the Federal Technology Transfer Act of 1986 and the National Competitiveness Technology Transfer Act of 1989, which grant authority to federal laboratories to expand their use of cooperative research and development agreements, also known as CRADAs. To date, DOE has signed more than 250 government/industry CRADAs worth more than $300 million, and the process has just begun.

At 15 National Technology Initiative (NTI) conferences across the United States this year, more than 5,000 business leaders have shared industry's experiences in technology transfer, while working together with government to tap the intellectual wealth of more than 700 national scientific laboratories. The purpose of the NTI is simple: to promote U.S. industry's use of technology to strengthen the domestic economy and to compete in global markets.

DOE research and development (R&D) facilities focus on energy technology, aerospace, pollution minimization and remediation, materials, biotechnology, manufacturing, information and communications, and transportation. The United States has invested money, manpower, and intellectual effort in its science laboratories for 50 years; they helped win the cold war. Now they should be considered more national rather than national security assets. The American people should be able to draw on the scientific and technological assets we've created to help the United States win in economic competition.

With CRADA and other partnership arrangements, companies can engage in a wide variety of cooperation,

ranging from developing joint research projects to obtaining licenses for a wide variety of patented and copyrighted technologies from DOE and its laboratories. Perhaps most important to technology transfer, the federal government is willing to work with large and small companies to protect R&D information produced as part of a joint activity and industry-produced proprietary information. It can transfer intellectual property rights to industry when products and processes are developed with the assistance of federal laboratories.

One of the administration's primary economic goals with the NTI has been to bring government partnerships into the modern age. DOE's practical goal for technology transfer is to provide money from R&D to put a commercial product on the shelf. With government's notorious reputation for, shall we say, studying issues, however, industry at first was reluctant to believe DOE could act in a timely fashion.

Due to a concerted effort to address this issue, DOE R&D agreements are now on a fast track. CRADAs can be signed and projects begun within weeks of the initial approach to DOE by an interested company. Our record, in fact, has been a CRADA signed in 15 days. DOE has created a flexible, responsive process for government/industry partnerships, focusing on projects providing dual-use benefits to scientific research and commercial development.

One of the best known of these government/business alliances has been the Advanced Battery Consortium, or USABC. This $260 million research project brought the "Big Three" U.S. automakers—Ford, Chrysler, and General Motors—and a number of small, specialized firms, such as Johnson Controls, together with government for the first time. The goal, to develop a practical, lightweight battery system that would make electric vehicles widely available by the year 2000, was hailed by President Bush in a Rose Garden ceremony. "The development of a competitive electronic auto industry," the president said, "will do more to reduce oil imports than rigid fuel efficiency standards that risk jobs and public safety."

Source: Reprinted from *Aerospace Industries Association Newsletter* 5, no. 6 (December 1992), pp. 8–9.

Just a month and a half ago, W. R. Grace and Co. and SAFT America Inc. received a $41.6 million contract under the USABC to develop a lithium polymer and a lithium disulfide battery, working with DOE's national laboratories.

The Department of Energy is actively seeking industry partners to utilize national laboratory technology to develop other competitive U.S. advanced technologies. In addition to industry consortia and CRADAs, access mechanisms for DOE technologies include user facilities, reimbursable work, consulting, personnel exchange, and contracts with businesses that agree to bear part of the cost of a specific research project.

Three important resources have been established to offer U.S. industry access to the array of federal scientific expertise. The National Technology Transfer Center, Regional Technology Transfer Centers, and the Federal Laboratory Consortium Locator Network provide valuable resources to locate research, technical information, or staff expertise from federal sources. DOE's Enhanced Technology Transfer Program, headquartered in the Office of Technology Utilization in Washington, D.C., handles contacts with industry interested in exploring these exciting new alliances.

In addition, DOE recently issued its fiscal year 1993 Small Business Innovative Research (SBIR) solicitation, open to firms with 500 employees or fewer. Grants, which are intended to strengthen the role of small, innovative firms in R&D as well as to support the use of federal R&D as a basis for technological innovation, will be awarded in amounts up to $75,000 to explore the feasibility of companies' ideas. Up to $500,000 is available in the second phase for those ideas with the highest potential to meet SBIR program objectives. The closing date for applications is March 8, 1993; inquiries should be directed to the SBIR Program Manager in Washington, D.C.

With the end of the cold war has come a renewed national purpose to transfer America's undisputed scientific and technical superiority from military to commercial use. The Department of Energy invites industries eager to compete in the global economy to come to the table and share in America's new commitment to be the world's technological marketplace, second to none.

Appendix B

Oak Ridge National Laboratory and Fluid Technology Inc.

ORNL is located on a 2,900 acre site 10 miles south of the city of Oak Ridge. ORNL was constructed in 1943 and was originally known as Clinton Laboratories. Its mission during World War II was to produce and separate the first gram quantities of plutonium for the Manhattan Project.[1]

In modern times the lab's mission includes basic and applied research in energy production and conservation, environmental studies, education, and technology transfer. ORNL also performs research for non-DOE sponsors if the research complements the lab's overall mission.[2]

The population of the laboratory includes over 1,500 scientists and engineers, 482 managerial and administrative personnel, 504 technicians, and 1,936 crafts and other support personnel for a total of close to 4,500 workers. The laboratory hosts approximately 3,700 guest researchers annually, including about one-third from industry. The laboratory has a relatively fixed budget each fiscal year with which to do both basic and applied research. According to the fiscal year 1991 budget, operations consumed $443 million, and capital equipment and construction consumed $34 million.[3]

Martin Marietta Energy Systems (MMES) is a subsidiary of Martin Marietta Corporation. Starting in the mid-1980s under government contract, MMES began operating a number of plants for the Department of Energy (DOE), including the K-25 Site, the Y-12 manufacturing facility, and ORNL, also known as X-10. The three plants at Oak Ridge were an integral part of the historic Manhattan Project that produced the first atomic bomb during World War II. Following the war, the facilities continued to play an important role in the nuclear arms race: K-25 produced enriched uranium, Y-12 manufactured weapons parts, and X-10 conducted applied research in a variety of areas.

With the end of the cold war, attention focused on ways to convert the plants' capabilities from defense functions to commercial applications. Gaseous diffusion of uranium, the primary function of K-25, was discontinued, and that plant underwent the first wave of drastic downsizing. Y-12 also felt the effects of the new era after the cold war with cutbacks in workforce of its own. Oak Ridge National Laboratory was perhaps the best able of the three facilities to adapt to the new conditions.

Competitiveness Issues

Technology transfer can be defined generally as technology or knowledge developed in one place by one group for a purpose that is applied in (or transferred to) another place, by another organization, or for another purpose. When applied to the Department of Energy's purposes, technology transfer is "the process of making federally funded science and technology responsive to the needs of the marketplace and users in industry, academia, or state and local government. These users will then develop the technology further, into new products, processes, materials, or services."[4]

The primary reason technology transfer is at the forefront at ORNL and other national laboratories is simple—to help the United States improve its competitive position as an economic power in the world marketplace. Labs like ORNL are warehouses of scientific and technological knowledge largely untapped by the private sector. Some labs like ORNL, historically, have focused much of their efforts toward defense programs. With the end of the cold war, the federal government recognized the need to convert the labs' missions to more commercial applications.

Japan, a major U.S. competitor, uses the partnerlike relationship between government and industry for gaining strategic competitive advantages. In Japan the research efforts in the private sector are coordinated through the Ministry of Finance (MOF) and Ministry of

---

[1]Fact sheet provided by Martin Marietta Energy Systems, Inc., Oak Ridge National Laboratory, Oak Ridge, TN.
[2]Fact sheet provided by Martin Marietta Energy Systems, Inc., Oak Ridge National Laboratory, Oak Ridge, TN.
[3]Fact sheet provided by Martin Marietta Energy Systems, Inc., Oak Ridge National Laboratory, Oak Ridge, TN.

---

[4]U.S. Department of Energy, *Technology Transfer: A DOE and Industry Partnership for the Future,* January 1991, p. 1-1.

International Trade and Industry (MITI). Government pays for some research and development, but only about 20 percent of the total versus 80 percent by industry.[5] Government labs perform some limited, well-targeted basic research and new product development. The idea is to limit the risk of development to Japanese companies.[6]

During the days of the cold war the U.S. government had funded, in considerable amounts, defense-oriented R&D conducted in private firms like Martin Marietta and in universities. It also funded mission-oriented research administered by agencies such as NASA. Traditionally in the U.S., the R&D for commercial purposes has been conducted in the laboratories of private firms. U.S. companies often are forbidden by antitrust laws to enter into agreements to work together on R&D and new product development, the result being increased R&D costs and less-efficient research overall. The constraints placed on American business by these laws place the country at a disadvantage in the international arena since Japan and several European nations not only allow such collaboration but encourage and facilitate it.[7]

In recent years, however, the United States has begun to refocus on issues like quality, efficiency, and its competitive position in the world market. We are looking for ways to use our resources more efficiently, including the storehouses of knowledge that are our federally funded laboratories. This new focus has resulted in a debate on technology transfer and new legislation resulting in mechanisms such as cooperative research and development agreements (CRADAs).

Changing Methods.   The traditional mode of technology transfer from the federal laboratories like ORNL has been direct licensing of technologies that have been developed by the labs. This approach to technology transfer can be described as the technology push approach. Technologies were developed first and then applications were sought in the private sector. Such technologies may have no application in industry; and even if they had application potential, they might not be commercially viable.

The new approach to technology transfer, that is, through CRADAs, will involve companies in the technology transfer process at an earlier stage in the pipeline. Inputs and resources can be obtained from industry during the early development stages, and the technology development will be oriented toward satisfying the needs of the industry. In this case the development and transfer of technology is based on demand pull. In this mode of transfer, the likelihood that the technology will be usable once it leaves the lab increases.

Notes on Technology Transfer Enabling Legislation

Federal Technology Transfer Act of 1986.   This section is a summary and translation into layman's terms of Public Law 99–502 of the United States Statutes at Large. This act, also known as the Federal Technology Transfer Act of 1986, amends the Stevenson-Wydler Technology Innovation Act of 1980. The amendment authorizes government-operated laboratories to enter into cooperative research agreements with outside entities. The act also establishes a Federal Laboratory Consortium for Technology Transfer within the National Institute for Standards and Technology (NIST).

Section 1. Cooperative Research and Development Agreements.

General Authority.   Some federal agencies, such as the Department of Energy or Department of Defense, have federal labs under their departmental authority. According to the act, these agencies may permit the directors of these labs to enter into cooperative research and development agreements (CRADAs) with the following entities:

1. Other federal agencies.
2. Units of state and local governments.
3. Industrial organizations.
4. Public and private foundations.
5. Nonprofit organizations, including universities.
6. Other persons, including licensees of inventions owned by the federal agency.

These laboratory directors also may be authorized to negotiate licensing agreements for government-owned inventions or other inventions by federal employees that may be voluntarily assigned to the government.

---

[5]"Japanese Technology Survey: Back to the Drawing Board," *The Economist,* December 2, 1989, p. 4.
[6]Hamid Noori and Russell W. Radford, *Readings and Cases in the Management of New Technology* (Englewood Cliffs, NJ: Prentice-Hall, 1990), p. 444.
[7]Ibid., p. 441.

Enumerated Authority. When a federal laboratory enters into a CRADA, the act allows the lab to share personnel, services, funding, and other resources with the other members of the agreement, subject to certain contract considerations. The lab is also permitted to grant the CRADA partner patent licenses or assignments on inventions where a federal employee has taken part. Subject to government approval, the agency can waive any rights of ownership by the federal government to inventions covered under the CRADA. A potentially very important part of this section is that lab employees are permitted to help commercialize the subject inventions.

Contract Considerations. Along with certain technical stipulations the lab must follow in establishing CRADAs, two points in this section could help U.S. businesses specifically. Special consideration is to be given to small businesses or consortia involving small businesses. The act also gives preference to firms located in the United States that agree to manufacture goods using that CRADA's technology in the United States.

Section 3. Establishment of Federal Laboratory Consortium for Technology Transfer. This section establishes the Federal Laboratory Consortium for Technology Transfer. The consortium's purposes are:

1. To make federal lab employees more aware of the commercial potential of lab technology and innovations.
2. To assist and advise federal agencies in their technology transfer programs.
3. To provide a clearinghouse for requests for technical assistance received at the laboratory level.
4. To assist in coordinating the efforts of different federal agencies and offices.
5. To assist technology transfer clients such as universities, governmental units, and businesses.

The representatives comprising the consortium include a senior staff member from each federal lab and an appointee from each federal agency with one or more of these labs. Section 3 goes on to discuss the administrative and funding procedures for the consortium.

Section 4. Utilization of Federal Technology.

Responsibility for Technology Transfer. The act says that technology transfer is a responsibility of each lab engineer and scientist. This responsibility should be considered in job descriptions, promotion policies, and evaluations of job performance.

Section 5. Functions of the Secretary of Commerce.

Functions of the Secretary. Working with the federal agencies, the Secretary of Commerce may provide expertise from Commerce regarding the commercial potential of and commercialization opportunities for certain technologies. The Secretary and Commerce Department may also furnish advice and assistance on CRADAs on request.

Section 6. Rewards for Scientific, Engineering, and Technical Personnel or Federal Agencies. If a federal agency spends more than $50 million on research and development in its laboratories, the agency head is authorized to establish cash awards for:

1. Inventions, innovations, or other scientific contributions of value to the United States because of commercial application or benefit to the agency in carrying out its mission.
2. Exemplary activities furthering domestic technology transfer efforts by the federal government.

Section 7. Distribution of Royalties Received by Federal Agencies. Generally, this section provides that employees responsible for the invention or development of new technology for which the agency receives royalties are entitled to at least 15 percent of what the agency receives. These payments are to be made in addition to the employees' regular pay.

Section 8. Employee Activities. If the agency does not exercise its right to a patent or license on a particular technology, the agency must allow the government employee(s) who developed the technology during their employment to retain title to it.

C ASE 3–3
TEMIC TELEFUNKEN: A PARTNER, NOT A VENDOR (A)

Timothy W. Edlund
Gee-In Goo

The Black & Decker Company (B&D) was developing a new coffeemaker, to fit under kitchen cabinets. This drip coffeemaker would come in three models; two would use sophisticated electronic controls; a third would use a simpler manual control. TEMIC Telefunken (hereafter TEMIC, short for TElefunken MICroprocessor), of Ingolstadt, Bavaria, Germany, received B&D's letter of intent (LOI), contracting for designing and making the electronic control module for these two products. 400,000 of each model (and 400,000 of the simpler coffeemaker) were scheduled for 1994; mass assembly of the complete coffeemaker was scheduled to begin in February 1994, 13 months away, in Asheboro, North Carolina. By then a great deal had to happen. In early 1993 Johannes Werther and Michael Zirngibl discussed how to organize the project team and make other arrangements to ensure that TEMIC completed its commitments to B&D on time, with desired quality, function, and cost.

The shape of the coffeemaker was a rectangular block, with the carafe and the filter funnel on the left; the control panel was to the lower right, below the water supply. Therefore, the face of the electronic control panel had to completely seal off electronic components to protect them from water spills and vapor. The controls also would be miniaturized state-of-the-art controls. See Exhibits 1 and 2 for preliminary sketches of the coffeemaker.

TEMIC Telefunken

Eight years earlier, in 1985, the present firm was in the "board stuffing" business. This meant that they operated

The authors thank TEMIC Telefunken and the Black & Decker Company for their enthusiastic cooperation. These cases are intended for class discussion only, and are not intended to illustrate effective or ineffective handling of administrative situations.

Source: This case was developed by Professors Timothy W. Edlund and Gee-In Goo of Morgan State University. Copyright © 1994 by the National Consortium for Technology in Business, c/o the Thomas Walter Center for Technology Management, Auburn University, Alabama.

as a subcontractor, assembling parts onto printed circuit boards (PCBs) in accordance with customer designs and specifications. This business was essentially a commodity business. Competition was on price alone; the firm added no design value. What became TEMIC was a typical German-oriented company, focused on manufacturing, quality, and with little focus upon marketing or volume production. There was little awareness of the needs of consumer products manufacturers, no orientation to US companies, which was also true for their parent firm, AEG. TEMIC's exports were in the range of 10 to 15 percent, all to other European countries; the balance of their business was done with German firms.

In 1987 there was a change in management. Mr. Klaver, previously with the Dutch firm Philips, was appointed director. He had been in Brussels about 8 years, and previously had spent 10 years in the Far East. A Netherlander, Mr. Klaver was used to thinking in terms of global business. Appointed by Telefunken to take charge of the business unit in Ingolstadt, he began the process of creating the present business unit. Essentially a subassembly firm then, now it's a microsystems development and manufacturing organization. Because of the International environment, he saw that it was necessary to obtain business from America. Business in Germany was declining. Germany had very high labor rates, so it became necessary to build a manufacturing organization outside of Europe, to permit manufacturing in the Far East or in Latin America.

Also in 1987, Rosemary Smith, a representative of AEG in the U.S., contacted B&D to solicit business. She talked to Bob Wall, manager of corporate commodities purchasing, at B&D's Towson, Maryland, corporate headquarters. She communicated directly with TEMIC regarding several possible programs at B&D, which eventually resulted in the program described in this case.

In 1993, total turnover (revenues) of the Telefunken semiconductor businesses was about DM 1.1 billion (deutsche marks). Total Telefunken revenues were about DM 3.1 billion. For about two years, Telefunken results

EXHIBIT 1

External View, under-the-Counter Coffeemaker

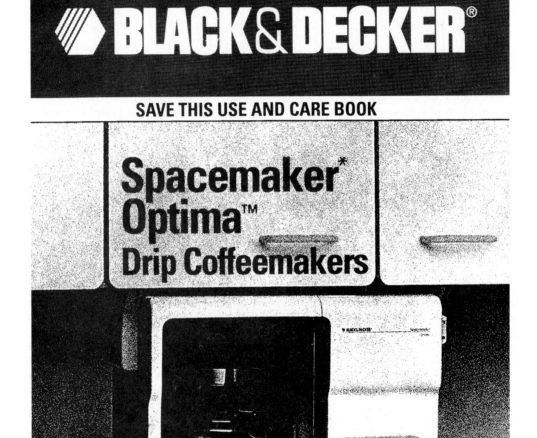

Source: Black & Decker Preliminary Owners' Manual for SDC series Spacemaker Optima® Coffeemaker. Spacemaker is a trademark of General Electric Company (USA).

EXHIBIT 2

View of Controls and Internal Arrangement, under-the-Counter Coffeemaker

Model ODC 350 Shown

1. "Keeps Hot" Plate
2. Carafe with Cup Marks (12 Cups)
3. Flip-Up, Removable Carafe Lid
4. Sneak-A-Cup™ Interrupt Drip Stop (Under Basket)
5. Filter Basket
6. Water Reservoir with Water Level Markings
7. Reservoir Cover with Thumb Latch
8. On/Off Button/Light
9. Activate Auto Button/Light
10. Cup Select Dial
11. Adjustable Auto Off Program Button
12. Auto On Program Button
13. Time Program Button
14. Up and Down Set Button
15. Digital Clock Display Window
16. Mounting Template
17. 2 Mounting Brackets with Tabs
18. 4 Screws
19. 4 Nuts
20. Set of Spacers/4 Washers
21. Cord Hook

Items 17-21 are packed in the Water Reservoir. Be sure to remove them before mounting or operating the unit.

Source: Black & Decker Preliminary Owners' Manual for SDC series Spacemaker Optima® Coffeemaker. Spacemaker is a trademark of General Electric Company (USA).

had been fully integrated into their parent firm, Daimler-Benz, whose turnover (revenues) were DM 98.5 billion in 1992. Organization and ownership changes affecting TEMIC are described in succeeding sections of this case.

Black & Decker[1]

Founded in 1910, Black & Decker (B&D) manufactured a wide range of corded and cordless portable power tools, small household appliances, other household products, and other products. In 1992, household products accounted for 14% of B&D's $4.8 billion sales revenue. B&D was the world's largest and oldest power tool maker; and its "Household Products business [was] a major global competitor and North American market leader in the small appliance industry." B&D complemented its power tool business by purchasing General Electric's small appliance division in 1984. This provided a wide range of small appliance products (irons, mixers, etc.) to which was added B&D's popular line of Dustbuster® vacuums and other battery-driven appliances.

In 1985 Nolan Archibald, formerly a marketing and operations specialist with Beatrice Foods, was elected president and began reorganizing B&D. He organized plants around motor sizes and reduced product variations and streamlined manufacturing processes. B&D's restructuring drew attention. They developed an approach to simultaneous engineering, in which manufacturing engineering meets regularly with product engineering, an approach aimed at reducing lead times and costs. B&D's factory in Spennymoor, County Durham, England, was called one of six superplants in the United Kingdom. Archibald's cut-and-build concept drew compliments as an effective approach to cost cutting and firm rebuilding.

Major Changes in Product Requirements

Before the redesigned coffeemaker, the normal B&D household product used electronics built around stuffed PCBs, which took considerable space, considering what

---

[1]Adapted and updated from "The Black & Decker Corporation (A) & (B)," by Timothy W. Edlund and Sandra J. Lewis. Copyright © 1991 by Timothy W. Edlund. Used and adapted with permission. See that case for sources.

functions were accomplished. Almost any subcontractor could build these, and there was substantial pressure on price. Use of microprocessors and miniaturization promised to change all that, providing both enhanced function and reduced size and cost. Not every firm could design and build these, nor was every customer ready to utilize such capabilities.

Klaver believed it necessary to completely redesign the business to be competitive and profitable in the new markets. Together with improved products, including design capabilities to create them, production capabilities in the Far East had to be started to be competitive, to first provide for European business. Subsequent moves into the Americas would be possible, for both sales and production. TEMIC's business was 85–90 percent in the German market. There were very few people who were able to speak English or other languages.

Seizing on the opportunity reported by Rosemary Smith, Klaver joined her in a 1987 call on Bob Wall at B&D. Serious discussions resulted about providing TEMIC's developing technology and engineering capabilities to B&D, which Klaver saw as a useful way to enter the strategic U.S. market much earlier than might have otherwise been practical. As these discussions developed, both firms slowly came to realize that they could enter into a strategic partnership, from which both might benefit.

Changes in the German Firm

In 1988, Johannes Werther was hired to direct the sales and marketing effort for this new business. Previously he had been employed by Westinghouse Electric Co. & General Signal, and had wide experience in European business. About this same time Michael Zirngibl was engaged as manager of engineering.

Determined to change the culture at the Ingolstadt business unit headquarters, TEMIC started emphasizing the need to know the English language. Special English lesson programs were provided. English became the official language of the firm, although German was still used for traditional German customers. New employees either knew English, learned it, or found other employment. New, younger, bilingual design engineers were hired for Ingolstadt, and similar industrial and production engineering capabilities were also added.

Also in 1988, TEMIC obtained their first piece of business from B&D. They contracted to produce the electronic module for a new electric iron, of rather basic design. TEMIC already had a semiconductor factory in Manila. Alongside this a new plant was erected to produce the new product line. It was air conditioned and contained subassembly facilities and other necessary equipment. An initial workforce of 200 people was hired, which swelled to 1,500 by mid-1993. Although the module for the iron was a board stuffing project, TEMIC considered this project the first step in training their people to learn how to do subcontracting well.

It represented a way to get started in consumer-type business; including delivery on tight timetables, testing, signoff of the product, and the like. Up to then nearly all TEMIC's business had been industrial. Time pressure became much more important. It was absolutely necessary to learn to figure in parts of a cent, not parts of a deutsche mark.[2] They entered intense negotiations on pricing, the consumer product kind of tough pricing, with their purchasing people to show them how important it was to be accurate in pricing in this kind of business, considering that 1 or 2 million pieces would be delivered. They transmitted this kind of price consciousness to the factory. Managing material pricing was crucial. It was very important whether cost was 36 cents or 36.1 cents per piece. A change in the mentality of the structure was necessary to depart from what was considered to be high volume for European products, in which it was not necessary to worry about parts of a cent. The transfer to the Far East, under absolute price consciousness, with more engineering, higher technology, and Far East suppliers, provided a focus on these three positive attributes. These were also important in the developing partnership with Black & Decker.

TEMIC considered that they "bought" the B&D program then. There were lots of programs in production, including two with B&D: first the iron and then a new toaster, which was also a relatively simple project, having no part of the electronic module visible on the outside of the toaster. For a while there were no profits. Delivery of the first parts from the new factory was made at the end of 1988; it was believed that two years were needed to learn how to do this business.

As a simple example for their personnel, they made the comparison, of how important 10,000 pieces of an industrial product having one dollar unit profit were, compared to a 1-million-piece consumer product run,

yielding a dime profit for each. This was a simple calculation, and was considered to demonstrate the value of consumer-type products.

New Ownership

In 1993, Daimler-Benz acquired the organization. When the reorganization was complete, Telefunken was now owned 50 percent by AEG and 50 percent by Deutsche Aerospace, which were in turn both owned by Daimler-Benz. Major decisions had to go up through all these levels. Moreover, under German law each organization had two boards; a managing board and a supervisory board, both of which had to consider and approve such decisions. By law, labor was represented, and could delay any project labor felt was against their interests.

Moreover, Mr. Klaver left the organization in 1991. As a replacement, TEMIC got what seemed to be a typical Daimler–Benz–oriented management, including their new director. "They couldn't understand what we [TEMIC] were doing with Black & Decker, doing low-unit-profit, high-volume business." In Europe, and particularly in Germany, B&D did not have a high-quality, high-reputation status. B&D was selling drills[3] and consumer products of perceived lower quality, at lower prices, and management was not particularly interested in doing business with firms like B&D.

Werther set about to convince the new director, Mr. Keller, of the value of this type of business. Together with Mr. Kohl, the new manager in Manila, he showed that consumer business was a stable business, which permitted training people to handle increasingly complex work, both in design and in production. The plan was to keep both types of work, using the same plants and design staff. Very sophisticated industrial/military and consumer products should be in the same plants. It was absolutely necessary to keep this type (volume consumer products) of production in the plant to train people in the program, so they would learn how to do more sophisticated manufacturing. Werther stated that it was strategically important to keep this business, because it would teach how to do profitable business,

---

[2]In 1993, conversion ratios were approximately $ 1.00 = DM 1.65 and DM 1.0 = $ 0.60.

[3]AEG Telefunken also made a line of power tools, although this line was considered to have higher quality and competed more in the professional market, composed of construction workers and others who depended on their tools for their living.

which in turn would provide substantial competitive advantage for industrial and military contracting.

Consumer business would always be important, adding to total volume. Rosemary Smith, resident in Towson, Maryland, was now concentrating solely on B&D business. B&D was increasingly interested in developing new programs with TEMIC. Because of the economic slowdown in Germany and Europe, in 1991 people were very open to going into new programs. Although the B&D name had not earned much credence in Germany yet, they argued that B&D could be a very strategic customer. They showed information and independent articles about B&D, to provide awareness of the U.S. market size and B&D's share of the U.S. market. They emphasized the high volume, the stable business, the acceptable level of profits, and the restructuring going on at B&D.

Mr. Keller set up meetings between TEMIC and B&D. He prepared a strategic analysis, showing the actions of B&D; its future in high-quality, high-volume, high-design products; its careful selection and qualifying all important suppliers; its efforts to be at the very high end of technology. It was pointed out that U.S. technology was the best on circuit boards and other electronic components. Senior management began to accept the strategy after a series of meetings, both internal and with B&D. The message became clear that B&D tries to be in strategic partnership relationships with crucial manufacturer/suppliers with intent to share all pertinent technologies. Mr. Keller accepted that these ideas were valid and correct. It was projected that $30 to $40 million in business would develop in the future for TEMIC.

TEMIC planned to start operations in Mexico. They already had contracts with Volkswagen Brasil, providing them with ignition and motor management systems for vehicles assembled there. A Mexican plant, eliminating many subcontractors, serving VW operations in Brazil and Mexico, combined with B&D work, was proposed and endorsed by Mr. Keller. He agreed that it made sense to start up production on consumer products with high technology in Mexico, taking a year or so, starting the same way as in Manila. They would have training products in consumer electronics first, particularly the existing B&D products, then automotive, then others.

They proposed spending $10,000,000 to start a Mexican operation, relying on only two customers: VW and B&D. It took about 10 months to get approval from Daimler-Benz. A new building was started, about 60 kilometers from Mexico City, to house this production. Legally, ownership was vested in AEG Mexico, which was already licensed to do business in Mexico. Under construction before NAFTA legislation passed, the plant was expected to start at the beginning of 1994 and would train on the older products before beginning assembly of the coffeemaker module.

The Letter of Intent (LOI) for the Coffeemaker

Michael Zirngibl visited B&D in December 1992 and discussed requirements for the new coffeemaker, concentrating on requirements for the electronic control. He showed a product TEMIC was building for Carrier Corporation USA: a remote control for air conditioning units. It was a two-way infrared communication and control system for major units, permitting no displays at the air conditioning unit. He contrasted this with products made in 1985, the board stuffing technology used in the two products being made for B&D, and compared those with the next generation technology product, having chips on silicon, using 85 to 90 percent full automatic insertion of components, full quality control, and closer mechanical relationships. The control for Carrier also had rubber buttons, backed with carbon to complete circuits when pressed, with backlighting provided by LCDs (liquid crystal displays) showing through clear inserts in the control panel. B&D expressed great interest, indicating that the Carrier remote control incorporated about 80 percent of the features they wanted in the new coffeemaker. Most of the technical problems in the coffeemaker control had already been solved in other programs; it was the combination that would be different.

B&D was in a hurry. Zirngibl was asked how the product should be designed and built, and what the cost would be. He borrowed a desk at B&D's Towson headquarters, sketched out his ideas and developed costs, taking two days. His proposal was presented on 15 December 1992; TEMIC received the letter of intent on 7 January 1993.

Crucial Considerations

As Werther and Zirngibl conferred, they knew several things that served to complicate their planning. So far, most negotiations had occurred at B&D's headquarters in Towson, Maryland. But the Household Products group was based in Shelton, Connecticut, five hours drive north. Black & Decker would assemble the electronic module into the coffeemakers at Asheboro, North Carolina, a day's drive south of Towson. Both locations were remnants from the time that General Electric (USA) owned the household products business. Design and marketing would be done at Shelton, as would major initial purchasing; some purchasing, including purchase of plastic mold tooling, would be done at Asheboro. This was critical because the front panel designed and made by TEMIC must seal perfectly into B&D-designed and -specified housings, permitting no leaks of water, whether liquid or vapor. Moreover, much of the production engineering would be done at Asheboro; this was important because assembly tooling would have to be fully compatible with the electronic module, both for quality and for cost.

TEMIC would be communicating over long distances with others beside B&D; the module would be made in Mexico, in a still inexperienced plant. TEMIC's own supplier network stretched around the world; important components would probably be made far from Germany, Manila, or Mexico. They reviewed TEMIC's own quality assurance program to determine whether it would fit the needs of this crucial program.

B&D had scheduled initial shipments of the new coffeemaker for June 1994, the month necessary to stock merchants and fill distribution pipelines for the Christmas 1994 major selling season. TEMIC had to be sure it did not cause its partner to miss that crucial selling season.

CASE 3–4
BLACK & DECKER'S NEW COFFEEMAKER—PROCURING THE ELECTRONIC MODULE (A)

Timothy W. Edlund
Gee-In Goo

Black & Decker's (B&D) Housewares Division was developing a new coffeemaker designed to fit under kitchen cabinets; thus the name, Spacemaker. This drip coffeemaker would be made in three models. One model would use relatively simple controls; two models would use sophisticated electronic controls. The outside shape of the coffeemaker was a rectangular block, with the carafe and the filter funnel on the left; the controls were to the lower right, right below the water supply. It was crucial that the face of the electronic control panel completely seal off all electronic components to protect them from water spills and vapor. The controls also required miniaturization and state-of-the-art microprocessor controls. Final assembly of the first units was scheduled for February 1994.

The electronic module was to be designed and built by TEMIC Telefunken (TEMIC hereafter), a German firm, based in Ingolstadt, Bavaria. TEMIC was a second-level subsidiary of Daimler-Benz, best known for its Mercedes-Benz automobiles and trucks. On July 13, 1993, after a joint meeting of B&D and TEMIC personnel at B&D's Household Products Headquarters in Shelton, Connecticut, Esko J. Nopanen, of B&D's Sourced Products Engineering and B&D's program manager for this project, commented:

> For almost 25 years, I've been involved in buying products from Far East suppliers, first with GE, and then with B&D, since they bought us. I've been involved in specifying and

The authors thank TEMIC Telefunken and the Black & Decker Company for their enthusiastic cooperation. These cases are intended for class discussion only, and are not intended to illustrate effective or ineffective handling of administrative situations. Spacemaker is a trademark of General Electric Company. Optima is a trademark of Black & Decker Company.

Source: This case was developed by Professors Timothy W. Edlund and Gee-In Goo of Morgan State University. Copyright © 1994 by the National Consortium for Technology in Business, c/o the Thomas Walter Center for Technology Management, Auburn University, Alabama.

identifying what the product should be and which suppliers will make it, private label it, and send to us. I've got experience working with outside suppliers and with the communications needed to make it work for a long time.

> For this project TEMIC is a supplier in a way, but not the traditional kind of supplier. They were selected to be a partner rather than a supplier, which puts a somewhat different perspective into the communications that go out. In a lot of ways a partnership evolves after having a supplier–customer relationship. It matures into a partnership. You already know each other very well. You may change attitudes a little because now you're partners; there may less checking up on each other, accepting just the word of each other. With TEMIC it was a little different; we didn't have a supplier–customer relationship first. At the very first we agreed that this will be a partnership, and then we went into working in that partnership. It's taken both of us a little while to say, what does that really mean? It would have been easier in several respects to have a customer–supplier relationship first.

Deidre Elloian, director of electronics engineering, had other concerns about the partnership. She said:

> I'm puzzled why TEMIC is putting so much effort into this project. We only do a few hundred million [dollars] here; they're a multibillion dollar outfit; and most of our products won't need this degree of electronic sophistication. Of course, there's more volume in our power tools division, but I'm not sure about the application there. What's in it for TEMIC?

> Also, to some extent, we're giving up the ability to do our own electronic work. About all we'll be doing is second-guessing their work; and, if the partnership works out, we shouldn't have to do much of that. Of course, trying to build the capability they already have would be very difficult; there's not enough of that kind of work to attract and keep such an engineering team together.

They both agreed that the meeting went well and that difficulties were being resolved on a timely basis. At this point, the focus was upon completing the project successfully. That involved the electronic module, the

Exhibit 1

1992 Revenues by Product Group within Business Segments

(Millions of Dollars)	Year Ended December 31, 1992	
	Amount	%
Consumer and Home Improvement Products:		
Power tools	$1,175	25%
Household products	674	14
Accessories	341	7
Security hardware	515	11
Outdoor products	312	6
Plumbing products	173	4
Product service	189	4
Total consumer and home improvement products	$3,379	71%
Commercial and industrial products:		
Fastening systems	$ 384	8%
Other commercial and industrial products	283	6
Total commercial and industrial products	$ 667	14%
Information systems and services	$ 734	15%
Total consolidated revenue	$4,780	100%

Narrative description of the business (partial): Household products include a variety of both corded and cordless cleaning and lighting products, and a full line of small home appliances, including irons, mixers, food processors and choppers, can openers, blenders, coffeemakers, kettles, toasters, toaster ovens, waffle bakers, knives, and smoke alarms.

Source: Form 10-K for the fiscal year ended December 31, 1992, pp. 4–5.

mechanical parts, the various connections, and how well everything fit together. The first volume production was scheduled for February 1994.

Black & Decker's History[1]

The Black & Decker Manufacturing Company was incorporated in 1910 by S. Duncan Black and Alonzo Decker in Baltimore, Maryland. The first product was milk bottle capping machines. In 1916 the first product of their own, a portable electric drill, was produced and sold under the Black & Decker trademark. Subsidiaries were established in Canada in 1922, England in 1925, and Australia in 1929.

Black & Decker manufactured a wide range of electric and cordless portable power tools, small household appliances, and other household products and also had a diversified information technology subsidiary. Household Products accounted for 14 percent of the company's overall sales (see Exhibit 1). Corporate annual growth goals had been reported to be 15 percent in sales and earnings per share.

The company was the world's largest and oldest power tool manufacturer, and its "Household Products business [was] a major global competitor and the North American market leader in the small appliance industry."[2] Black & Decker's distribution channels included: national merchandisers (Wal Mart, Kmart, Sears, etc.), department stores (Hechts, Macy's, etc.), hardware stores, home centers (Hechingers, 84 Lumber, etc.), and government contracts (Army & Air Force Exchange Stores). Black & Decker was an international company with over 100,000 distribution outlets worldwide and

---

[1]This section and the next three sections are adapted and updated from "The Black & Decker Corporation (A) & (B)," by Timothy W. Edlund and Sandra J. Lewis. Copyright © 1991 by Timothy W. Edlund. Used and adapted with permission. For additional detail and sources see those cases. Additional material is taken from Black & Decker 1992 Form 10-K.

[2]1992 annual report, p. 6.

236 centers service centers around the world, of which 115 were in the United States.

Recent Developments

Black & Decker experienced a downturn in the early 1980s, when it still was primarily a maker of power tools and accessories. Management was complacent, manufacturing costs were too high, marketing efforts were loose, and product quality was poor. The dollar was overvalued, and competitors, such as Makita Electric of Japan and Robert Bosch of Germany, the second- and third-ranked companies in the world tool market, were quickly taking over much of B&D's market share in the United States and elsewhere. In 1981, the recession decreased sales of B&D's most important line, power tools. By 1985, the business had deteriorated to the point that the company posted a loss of $158 million on sales of $1.7 billion, although this loss was due to a $215 million write-off for plant shutdowns and other cost-saving measures.

Black & Decker fought back, complementing its power tool business by purchasing General Electric's small appliance division in April 1984. In addition, B&D also purchased Rank Electric's housewares operations in Australia and New Zealand. These purchases increased B&D's access to European markets, by providing both access to their distribution channels and a wide range of small appliance products (irons, mixers, etc.) to which was added B&D's popular line of Dustbuster® vacuums and other battery-driven appliances. The company dropped "Manufacturing" from the corporate name in February 1985.

In 1985 Nolan Archibald, formerly a marketing and operations specialist with Beatrice Foods, began reorganizing Black & Decker, having been elected president. He described B&D as a number of "little geographical fiefdoms" around the world, each with its own product-design center and marketing team. Under that old organization, the company had over 100 different motor sizes. Furthermore, it split consumer and professional tools into two separate groups that seldom communicated with each other.

Archibald organized plants around motor sizes and reduced product variations and streamlined manufacturing processes. In 1985, the company closed five plants, a process which continued. By 1987, B&D had 19 plants, 5 of which were inherited from General Electric, a substantial reduction from 25 plants in 1984. In this

reorganization over 2,000 workers, including many highly paid managers, were let go. Resulting savings were used for new product development, quality control, and advertising. These recovery actions paid off; in 1988 the company earned nearly $100 million on sales of $2.3 billion. In March 1986 Archibald was elected CEO.

Black & Decker's restructuring drew attention. The firm developed an approach to simultaneous engineering, in which manufacturing engineering meets regularly with product engineering, an approach aimed at reducing lead times and costs. B&D's factory in Spennymoor, County Durham, England, was cited as one of six superplants in the United Kingdom. Archibald's cut-and-build concept drew compliments as an effective approach to cost cutting.

Other Company Information

See Exhibit 2 for a five-year summary of operations, and Exhibit 3 for details by Business Segments.[3] Prominently displayed near the entrance of the Shelton facility were four framed sheets, describing B&D's quality policy. Exhibit 4 represents the text and graphics of these posters.[4]

Critical Unit Functions

The new coffeemaker was designed to fit under kitchen cabinets and was a replacement for an earlier highly successful design. Black & Decker gave a letter of intent (LOI), dated January 7, 1993, to design and build the electronic control module for the two new models that would require electronic microprocessor controls.

The outside of the coffeemaker was a rectangular block, with the carafe and the filter funnel on the left; the control panel was to the lower right, below the water supply. See Exhibits 1 and 2 of Case 3–3.

In the unit, the water reservoir was removable for filling, and would plug into the heating system. There was a valve to let the water into the heating mechanism when the reservoir was inserted. The whole assembly was designed to be mounted under kitchen cabinets on special brackets. It was required that there be no gap

---

[3]Black & Decker Form 10-K for the fiscal year ended December 31, 1992.

[4]Copied and reproduced by the first author, who is responsible for any errors.

Exhibit 2

Business Segments

	Consumer and Home Improvement Products	Commercial and Industrial Products	Information Systems and Services	Corporate and Eliminations	Consolidated
1992					
Sales to unaffiliated customers	$3,379.0	$ 666.7	$733.9	$ -	$4,779.6
Operating income	218.4	(44.7)	18.6	6.9	199.2
Operating income excluding restructuring costs and goodwill amortization	307.5	80.4	21.7	6.9	416.5
Identifiable assets	4,753.7	1,390.6	426.1	(1,178.5)	5,391.9
Capital expenditures	152.3	9.3	16.3	6.1	184.0
Depreciation	93.8	15.7	12.7	3.6	125.8
1991					
Sales to unaffiliated customers	$3,224.4	$ 728.2	$684.4	$ -	$4,637.0
Operating income	254.1	95.6	32.3	19.4	401.4
Operating income excluding goodwill amortization	307.2	113.3	35.4	19.4	475.3
Identifiable assets	4,605.9	1,574.1	380.6	(1,027.9)	5,532.7
Capital expenditures	80.1	12.8	12.7	2.0	107.6
Depreciation	92.6	16.1	12.1	4.2	125.0
1990					
Sales to unaffiliated customers	$3,425.7	$ 887.5	$519.1	$ -	$4,832.3
Operating income	306.6	126.4	25.9	27.5	486.4
Operating income excluding goodwill amortization	355.5	143.4	28.3	27.5	554.7
Identifiable assets	4,792.1	1,532.3	327.8	(762.7)	5,889.5
Capital expenditures	85.5	16.4	9.9	1.2	113.0
Depreciation	102.1	22.0	9.9	4.0	138.0

around the control panel or through any of the joints between the panel and control buttons or past the clear plastic inserts which let the LEDs (light emitting diodes) shine through. A tactile feel to the buttons was required; that is, the user must know that activation had happened.

The Meeting of July 13, 1993

Convened promptly at 10:00 A.M., the meeting quickly progressed to discussing a number of technical details. Among the Black & Decker personnel present were Nopanen, Elloian, Duc Tran (senior electronic design engineer), Paul Donoski (manager, Beverage Products Development), Julian Watt (senior electrical engineer), and Jon Rayner (director, Corporate Purchasing).

TEMIC was represented by Werther, Zirngibl, Smith, and Blank (an engineer and the project manager for the B&D project). (See the TEMIC case for positions of the first three.)

One intense discussion focused on the sample panel brought here to show what the current design was like. B&D expressed concern about included angles on the edges of the clear plastic insert to ensure that there was sufficient light transmission. It was pointed out that the lights had to be visible not only in the dark, but also in a fully lighted kitchen.

TEMIC submitted a proposed schedule for completion of various milestones in the program. This was compared to B&D's desired schedule. B&D asked that two dates be improved by seven days. TEMIC would

Exhibit 3

Five-Year Summary in Millions of Dollars except per Share Data

	1992	1991	1990	Transition Period	1989	1988
Total revenues	$4,779.6	$4,637.0	$4,832.3	$1,111.3	$3,172.5	$2,280.9
Net earnings (loss)	(333.6)	53.0	51.1	(3.2)	30.0	97.1
Net Earnings (loss) per common share	(4.52)	.81	.84	(.05)	.51	1.65
Total assets	5,391.9	5,532.7	5,889.5	6,175.9	6,258.1	1,825.1
Long-term debt	2,108.5	2,625.8	2,755.6	2,786.4	2,629.7	277.1
Cash dividends per common share	.40	.40	.40	.10	.40	.40

meet those requests, Werther replied without hesitation, as Zirngibl smiled.

Following several technical discussions, Nopanen inquired about TEMIC milestone release points. Werther described these as follows: QB (an abbreviation of the German words for quality control) was the general descriptive term, resulting in the following checkpoints:

QB 1: release indicated that the concept is good, design could proceed.

QB 2: release for engineering builds.

QB 3: release for preseries production (trial/pilot lots).

QB 4: released for series production.

Approval was required from purchasing, sales, and production engineering at every step, including everyone concerned. The QB 4 release required approval by every department, certifying that all work had been done; it was designed to generate cooperation to solve problems and to complete the project under the responsibility of the project manager, who also is responsible to see that everyone has done their job.

Nopanen responded that it was very similar to the B&D procedure, except that different names were used. He added that B&D would now be able to understand these terms when used in TEMIC releases. But Werther responded that all communication to B&D would use the B&D terms, to avoid any possible confusion. Moreover, these would be used internally at TEMIC along with the QB designations, so that all project personnel would be fully familiar with them.

After resolution of all pending technical problems, the next item of business was a slide show presented by Werther explaining TEMIC's relationship to its parent organizations, its own internal organization, and the various types of work they were qualified to do. (Also scheduled for the same day were sessions with the B&D project teams for the iron and the toaster, attended by different B&D personnel.)

After the meeting, the comment was made to Elloian that it was interesting to see that TEMIC and B&D personnel were intermingled around the conference table. She responded with a chuckle: "That didn't just happen; we made sure it would."

EXHIBIT 4

Black & Decker Quality Posters

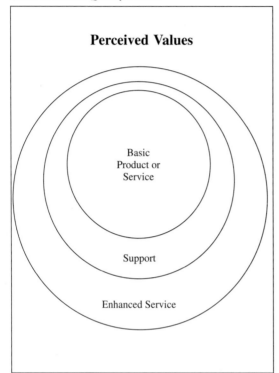

Perceived Values

Basic
Product or
Service

Support

Enhanced Service

Quality: The Basic Principles

1. Focus on the work process, issue, or behavior, not the person.

2. Maintain the self-confidence and self-esteem of others.

3. Maintain strong partnerships with your internal and external customers and suppliers.

4. Take initiative to improve work processes and partnerships.

5. Lead by example.

QUALITY POLICY

WE are dedicated to exceeding the
expectations of our internal
and external customers with
uncompromising integrity.

In a participative environment of
continuous improvement, our
commitment is to satisfy our
customers by providing error-free
products and services every time.

QUALITY is the most important
element of our business.

CORE VALUES

• INTEGRITY means we have complete and uncompromising honesty in the conduct of our business. Individually and collectively we do what we say. We make appropriate commitments and we honor them.

• INNOVATION means we will strive to delight our customers by maintaining an environment which stimulates new and creative approaches to all aspects of our business.

• EXCELLENCE means we will excel in all areas of our business by setting goals and standards which foster continuous improvement in our people, products, and services.

• TEAMWORK means we will create a participative environment in which each employee is valued as an important contributor, as an asset or resource of the business. We will have an atmosphere that attracts, retains, and develops excellent and committed people who want to share in the success of the company.

CASE 3–5
TEMIC TELEFUNKEN (B)

Timothy W. Edlund
Gee-In Goo

On 9 July 1993 Johannes Werther described some of the internal workings of TEMIC, including its quality system. The following material is condensed from that conversation.

Given the changes in the product and quality focus at Black & Decker, we saw ourselves becoming the supplier of microprocessor-based electronics for their high-end products. We are a qualified supplier for General Motors. We furnish 1.5 million assemblies per year of their ABS (anti-lock brake system) systems, at $100 each priced from Manila. When we make them in Mexico, we'll be at or close to that price. Our production technology and engineering capability are oriented to production line requirements. We build to automotive rules, using the same equipment and quality. Even for consumer products we produce with very low ppm (parts per million) defects, and guarantee very fine quality in all our products.

Temic Program for the B&D Coffeemaker

You may remember that, before Bob Wall (of B&D) started the program with us, the usual B&D electronic product was a stuffed pcb (printed circuit board). It was bulky and relatively crude.

Our design was done by Michael Zirngibl's staff. We developed the program plan, then did the engineering work, and did our part of the hardware design. We established our milestones, built them into the program

The authors thank TEMIC Telefunken and the Black & Decker Company for their enthusiastic cooperation. These cases are intended for class discussion only, and are not intended to illustrate effective or ineffective handling of administrative situations.

Source: This case was developed by Professors Timothy W. Edlund and Gee-In Goo of Morgan State University. Copyright © 1994 by the National Consortium for Technology in Business, c/o the Thomas Walter Center for Technology Management, Auburn University, Alabama.

plans. Normally our scheduled completion dates were two weeks earlier than we told B&D they would be.

We intensified our English language training program; all of our people have to speak English. By the way, we found that helps us in France, too. You can't get business in France speaking German; no one can speak French well enough to please a Frenchman, but it's okay to speak English there!

The design was finalized; we built our first prototypes on pcb boards (showing how they would function), prepared an overview discussing whether the concept and program were working, and put together the breadboard (an early type of prototype model to demonstrate function) by late April or May (1993). They visited us in May. The basic concept was released for further development. This was very fast work; we Germans take a lot of holidays, but we work very hard, too.

There have been some small bumps so far. We're in daily communication with Rosemary Smith, and with the local TEMIC engineer in Shelton. The plan is, we send an engineer over there for six weeks. He has an office at B&D, Shelton, works with their design staff, and communicates with us. He will return for two weeks to confer with the rest of the engineering staff here in Ingolstadt; then another engineer goes to Shelton for six weeks, returns for two, and is followed by a third, after which the cycle starts over again. The aim is to have essentially interchangeable people, who have knowledge of the department *and* specific knowledge of the program. Each engineer spends about one-quarter of his time in the States. We have an apartment; he can take his family. Last week Mr. Blank, one of our younger guys, went over and will be there until September.

As soon as this partnership idea arose, as we discussed it with Mr. Keller, our director, we decided it was vital to get into a very close relationship with B&D. In the beginning, we decided that if we would do this at all, we want to do it right. From a business point of view, a partnership was necessary. That was our position from the beginning. It may also have helped convince B&D that we were serious about building a partnership.

After prototypes and the engineering build, the electronic module is tested in the finished product; we do this together; we did it some weeks ago for the toaster, using the international B&D Procedure. The engineering build 1 and 2 for the coffeemaker module are planned; if necessary, number 3, 4, and so on, will be scheduled. We go to preseries production next, first 1,000 pieces, then 2,000. February 1994 is scheduled for mass production: 400,000 per year [those coffeemakers having the electronic control]. We have 10 months to make sure everything is working; their procedures and ours are reasonably congruent.

[Next was described the QB, or quality control program, discussed in the meeting of July 13, 1993.] We are now between stages QB 2 & QB 3. Our internal releases dates are two weeks ahead of B&D. We always schedule earlier than our customer's wanted dates.

Mr. Blank, one of Michael's engineers, is responsible for our B&D programs. He is the engineer now in the States. Also on the project business team are Mr. Bartoff (one of my sales engineers), Michael, and myself. The marketing and engineering group people are the business team. We share the technology; it is a part-time assignment for everyone.

Our business team involves engineering and production, quality and logistics (components availability after purchasing), purchasing, Mexico production, and project responsibility. The QB procedure is totally separated from customers' outside information. Logistics ensures that everything is shipped in time. We have our plan and then we provide the customer with a plan. We meet our standards, qualify under our standards, under our automotive standards, which are tougher than customers' standards. We prequalify everything to our standards. We do live tests and mechanical tests, even if the customer doesn't want to have that. We do it because we have to sign that the product is acceptable to us, even though those requirements may be 20 percent higher than the customer's requirements. It doesn't matter whether the customer specifies this; we produce according to this rule. This is clearly supported by all of us, from our top management down.

Again, it doesn't matter whether the customer wants that quality standard; we produce according to our requirements. Therefore, if in six months the customer has a problem in the field, we can show that we have tested it 100 percent according to our rules, even though he hasn't seen those tests. [This is 100 percent testing in planning and in qualification, not 100 percent testing of all series production parts.] We include drop testing, shock testing, durability testing, whatever is necessary according to design and intended use, we do all this even though not asked. We follow the Ford standard; that's what Ford specifies for all their products, even those produced in the United States. It has higher standards than the ISO 9000 standard. [That's the international standard that's been getting so much publicity and which a number of U.S. firms are adopting.]

We communicate to the customer that we should be more involved in the customer's activities. Communication does not always happen. Our people are busy doing what they have to do, the B&D engineers get worried, they haven't heard anything for two or three weeks; it's in between milestone times. The residential engineer is stationed in Shelton to solve those concerns, so that B&D can know "the Germans are working on it." They will come to know him and believe they can trust him. There are regular conference calls within the TEMIC engineering group so that the residential engineer and the sales engineer (Rosemary Smith) can be fully informed about what's going on.

We also have ongoing communication with our management, up to the boards of directors every two or three months, much more frequently to our own top management, and also to the B&D board. We provide communication lines from engineers and the sales group up to our vice president. Moreover, everyone is talking to his equivalent in B&D. Engineer to engineer, production to production, sales to purchasing, to and from our purchasing director in Mexico. That director knows B&D; he set up our quality procedure while here in Ingolstadt. He wrote the rules; he knows how to follow them.

CASE 3–6
BLACK & DECKER'S NEW COFFEEMAKER—PROCURING THE ELECTRONIC MODULE (B)

Timothy W. Edlund
Gee-In Goo

It was February 28, 1994. Esko J. Nopanen, B&D program manager for the new coffeemaker project, described the current status of this project and the developing partnership with TEMIC. The following material is condensed from that conversation.

As you know, this partnership was started without first having a supplier–customer relationship. Although I've had over 20 years experience dealing with sourcing our products from many vendors, this has been different. It was already understood that TEMIC would provide the electronics and the control panel; they [management] said TEMIC will be the expert; we won't specify our requirements very closely to them. We told them in general what the control module has to do and they'll tell us how it's going to work and exactly what the customer interface will be. We relied on TEMIC to provide a design that will satisfy our customers.

We encountered difficulties in that we tended to sit back too much and kind of let things happen. We should have had more involvement to specify what was needed more fully in the beginning. Yes, we did the iron and toaster with TEMIC earlier, but those involved internal parts only. Those controls were not visible to the customer. On the coffeemaker, the panel and the buttons, the parts the customer touches, are TEMIC supplied. They showed us a remote control they did for

The authors thank TEMIC Telefunken and the Black & Decker Company for their enthusiastic cooperation. These cases are intended for class discussion only, and are not intended to illustrate effective or ineffective handling of administrative situations. Spacemaker is a trademark of General Electric Company. Optima is a trademark of Black & Decker Company. Copyright © 1994 by National Consortium for Technology in Business.

Source: This case was developed by Professors Timothy W. Edlund and Gee-In Goo of Morgan State University. Copyright © 1994 by the National Consortium for Technology in Business, c/o the Thomas Walter Center for Technology Management, Auburn University, Alabama.

Carrier; that background said they're capable of doing the whole design. [They did the whole remote control; it didn't have to fit into anything else.] With both sides learning what the strengths and weaknesses of each firm were, in November [1993] we had the first engineering build of what it was that would fit into our coffeemaker. In a lot of respects it was a very complete product already at that time.

But some difficulties usually are found, and some *were* present that needed to be addressed. We eliminated those in later sample runs, before actual production started.

Were these problems of function, fit, or cosmetics? All three! There was some testing of the electronic circuitry to be sure it will have reliability for use in the home. Some problems showed up in the customer interface, involving what does it feel like pushing the buttons? What is the feedback received that initiation of brewing has actually taken place? There were some cosmetic problems in getting exact color matches on the external parts.

You remember the discussion last July, about our concern about just how the lights would shine through the backlighted display. We were concerned about lighting efficiency, just how much light would come out. Could it be seen under all lighting conditions? If not adequate, the display would be too dark; the customer would have to get right up close to see it.

The environment is severe. There is both heat and steam. We put one of the first sample coffeemakers in the engineering area. Just a week or two ago, reliability problems started showing up in the electronics. Water was getting where it's not supposed to be. The display window was fogging up, just where we didn't want water to be. As you know, the controls are below the water area.

This is one of our early units; as you see, the water reservoir plugs into the heating system. There is a valve at the back bottom of the reservoir that lets the water out when plugged in. From the reservoir as it engages the pipe, there was some leakage, which ran out that compartment and down into the control panel. In that panel there are two hard plastic materials. There was enough gap to allow water to get in. We had to improve the valve. TEMIC has been working on the panel; later production may have that problem fixed.

As he tested Duc Tran found some problems, in that the noise of the solenoid we furnished engaging the heater would sometimes cause a reset of the clock timer back to 12:00. Since the clock controls the timed start of the brewing cycle, modifications were needed. He (Duc Tran) came up with a solution; TEMIC didn't agree with his solution; together we worked out something else that addresses that problem.

We felt we needed better tactile feedback from pushing the buttons. We said, TEMIC is the expert in these things, why don't you work with your manufacturer in Taiwan who is a specialist in them? Why don't the two of you propose a way of improving the tactile feel? There was too much interfacing to be sure that the size of the buttons was compatible with the bezel [the control panel], that the openings through which the buttons protruded were exactly the right size.

The bezel is made in Spain; both the tooling and the plastic molding are done in Spain. The rubber parts come from Taiwan. All these parts are assembled into their product at their plant in Mexico. They have a very long supply line; many of their components are sourced worldwide. That provided problems getting everything to the final assembly point in Mexico on a timely basis.

So the need for interfacing is not just between B&D and TEMIC. They design in Ingolstadt. Much of the integration of the parts was done in Shelton [Connecticut] at Black & Decker. One interface that had to be done by B&D was how well the panel fit into our product. That interface had to be defined very closely. At first we said we don't care very much about this; we said it should be TEMIC's concern. But we had to develop that fit. The panel is a snap fit into our housing from the back, which is then covered by the back panel.

We have Underwriters Laboratory testing of all our products, which includes testing for structural integrity. They have a metal ball on a string, which they let crash into various parts of the coffeemaker. When directed at the panel, the holding latches weren't strong enough to keep the panel in place. They had to be strengthened.

When it came to the heater, the one that boils the water, the more heat, the quicker the boiling, the quicker the pot of coffee is delivered. The industry standard has been one minute per [5-ounce] cup. We wanted to do better than that. We specified a heater with higher watt density to heat faster. In our first design, we found that the heater would not survive. After just a few brewing cycles, it burned out, just like a light bulb. We had to downgrade the watt density [to the industry standard]. There was not enough room to put in a larger heating element. We had to lower the watt density, so the heater would survive. Even though the goal was to shorten the brewing cycle, we had to relax that objective and build in reliability.

We also source from a wide area; for example, B&D buys the heater in Taiwan. Tooling procurement has been a real challenge, presenting coordination problems for Asheboro to get everything in time. Projected volume is over half a million coffeemakers in the first year [including the simple electric control not made by TEMIC]. First shipments will be in June, at the rate of almost a million per year. There are twenty different thermoplastic plastic parts, all injection molded, and one phenolic part. Engineering is all done in Shelton; Asheboro orders tooling and plans work for parts made at Asheboro. Purchasing for parts is done at both Shelton and Asheboro. The Shelton person has the early involvement in purchasing. Corporate purchasing [Towson] was involved in making corporate-type agreements with some of our suppliers, such as TEMIC, to be sure we get the best total volume pricing.

The original TEMIC pricing was done in Towson. We know and agree that, as the design evolves, cost changes, and so should price. We kept asking TEMIC, what is your cost estimate now? They kept replying, no change. Very late in the game, our marketing department set the actual market price for the product. Then TEMIC came back and says, now we really know what the cost is. We responded, it's a little late. We were asking for this kind of update earlier. So TEMIC said they'd stay with their earlier estimates.

This puts engineering under pressure. Almost always, actual costs tend to be higher than first estimates. The pressure on TEMIC is showing up. They're finding quite a few alternate suppliers for components. In the early stages, the samples had a certain supplier network already in place which provided components, and as time has gone on they would like to use alternate components instead. This has placed pressure on B&D, because component qualification cycles are long. If suppliers for key components are changed, we have to requalify them, because B&D is concerned with the entire product. Minor components (like screws) are not important; but if TEMIC wants to use a different relay from a different maker, from what we know about relays, each specific relay has to be evaluated. We would have to insist on the original relay until qualification is completed, and then make a running change. If we qualify a second relay, it would have to be substitutable for the original one [if it is to be replaceable as a separate component].

Asheboro is responsible for making the product. Although separated from design, our CAD/CAM system assures the parts should fit together. This is particularly a concern with polypropylene (plastic) parts; it's kind of a flimsy structural material which doesn't hold a specific shape. Even though the tool is built to provide the exact shape of the product, as the plastic comes off the tool it may sag a little bit, so the proof of how well it assembles is done in the preproduction builds that may identify assembly problems. There is lots of review before actual parts are built; there is advanced manufacturing input before actual parts and tools are built. They work with and look at the concept before details are firmed up.

The coffee carafe sits on a black phenolic[1] part, which also keeps the coffee warm. We had a problem in assembling it into the housing. It has to mate with the housing all around its perimeter. People got blisters trying to force fit the two together. We had to take a heat gun and soften the (white polypropylene) plastic parts; we had to make modifications to make fit easier, but it still has to have a solid fit all around, to resist water penetration. Polypropylene is a good material to be impervious to steam and water. It has high temperature-stability. Despite the phenolic base, there still is quite a bit of heat that it [the polypropylene] has to handle.

The panel is polycarbonate; there is some insert molding in which the clear panels are molded into the grey polycarbonate material. We need to get a hermetic seal between the two parts, and not just to keep water

---

[1]Phenolic is a thermosetting plastic having high heat resistance. Used for applications involving high heat, it is relatively expensive to make and is permanently cured under pressure in heated molds. Polypropylene is one kind of thermoplastic plastic. Thermoplastics are relatively inexpensive, are reusable, and melt under sufficient heat. One process for making parts uses cooled molds, into which the melted plastic is injected.

out. There are electrostatic concerns; in winter when it's very dry, an electrostatic charge would tend to force its way through any cracks. Special attention is given to all junctions, and also to the clear parts where the two lights show through. There is a recess to ensure a seal. It's also important to have good visibility of the red and green lights. The physical configuration is such that a bubble tends to form in the clear part. Last Friday we were on the phone to TEMIC; they have to find a solution to eliminate the bubble.

Concerning our delivery schedule, through last May the expectation was that introduction would be earlier than June, that we would be in production in February. Last Summer, we realized that was overoptimistic. The introduction points for these products are twice yearly, January for Spring/Summer, June for the Christmas sales period.

There is competition in this business, but B&D has a very strong position in Spacemakers. This is the next generation of the Spacemaker. We've already established a presence and it is the strongest offering even before this redesign. B&D dominates the under-cabinet market.

Many of us have become the first home testers of our products. We check the mounting instructions completely; for each new Spacemaker product, the mounting instructions are different. We tend to be very critical. We may not be unbiased, but we tend to be biased in the severe direction. Perhaps we feel, "You gave my product a hard time, I'll give yours a hard time too."

The first production lot is scheduled for the end of March. The TEMIC [revised] schedule said they would provide control modules to support that date. There are some problems in meeting that, but there is one thing that still allows us to keep the Asheboro start date. There is one model that is not associated with TEMIC, the one with the manual controls only. We can start on that, and fit the other models in as the electronics arrive. The only difference is the control module; mechanically the rest of the three models are identical. It's still marginal; TEMIC may be able to meet the start date. The latest indication is no. Although there was some slack built in, it wasn't enough.

One thing that got in the way was time differences. Ingolstadt is six hours ahead of us, and seven or eight ahead of Mexico. We're not working at the same time, so we tend to lose a day or two on every communication. Now they're starting an engineering center, somewhere in Texas. We'll be able to communicate better, just because of the time. They've added a salesman in New Jersey, who handles Shelton. Rosemary Smith is still in Towson, concentrating on the rest of the B&D account.

Yes, the marketeers will want the sophisticated coffeemaker out at the same time as the simpler unit. But it's not a problem yet. Our deliveries to our customers start taking place in the June time period. So if we start by the first of April, we build up some stock before we start making deliveries; we will have built up stock of all three models by June, for the Christmas time period. Most of our products are sold [to the consumer] in the fourth-quarter time period; most of these products are gift related.

4 RESEARCH & DEVELOPMENT AND COMMERCIALIZATIONS OF TECHNOLOGY

READING 4–1
IMPROVING R&D DECISIONS AND EXECUTION

Michael M. Menke

Productive R&D requires capable people doing the right things right. Doing the right things requires an understanding of which R&D activities have the greatest potential to create value for the organization, as well as the time, cost, and difficulty of achieving them. This understanding generates sound priorities supporting a productive allocation of resources across businesses, technologies, projects, and programs.

Doing the R&D right means clarifying the project definition and goals, understanding customer needs, identifying the sources of value, and organizing tasks to work on the most valuable project attributes and to tackle technical hurdles in the most timely and cost-effective way. This requires sound prioritization of tasks and personnel within R&D projects.

Both objectives are strongly aided by a comprehensive, high-quality project evaluation and decision process. This process includes a common set of project and portfolio evaluation quality tools—strategy tables, influence diagrams, sensitivity analysis, decision trees, and expected value—that help improve R&D quality at the levels of R&D strategy, project selection, and project management and execution.

This article shows how the process adds value by developing sound priorities for allocating R&D resources and supporting smart execution of R&D projects. Throughout, I use R&D, applied research, new product development, new process development, and technology development somewhat interchangeably to describe a purposeful, planned set of activities designed to exploit science and technology to achieve a commer-

cially attractive objective. None of this discussion is intended to apply to (or constrain) basic, knowledge-building research.

R&D management encompasses strategic management (allocating resources—doing the right R&D), operational management (execution of projects—doing the R&D right), and, possibly the most important, people management (leadership, organization, motivation, teamwork). All these management roles must be performed at a high level of quality for an organization to achieve its full potential.

Strategic and Operational Management

Highly productive R&D requires a quality organization dedicated to doing the right R&D and doing the R&D right. A study by the Industrial Research Institute found that 9 of the 12 most important actions R&D organizations can take to improve productivity involve strategic management of R&D [1]. Strategic management of R&D asks some very important questions, namely:

- Do we have the *right* total R&D budget?
- Are we allocating it to the *right* business and technology areas?
- De we have the *right* balance of risk and return, of long-term and short-term R&D, of research versus development, of innovation versus incremental improvement?
- Are we working on the *right* projects and programs with the *right* levels of effort?

These questions all address the *allocation of R&D resources*. As any R&D executive will attest, these are difficult questions to answer at all, let alone with confidence. Answering them well results in quality strategic management of R&D.

Strategic R&D management and operational (or project) R&D management are coupled by project evaluation and project decisions. The highest level project decisions are of the go/no-go variety—project selection, continuation, modification, and termination.

Michael Menke is a principal of Strategic Decisions Group in Menlo Park, California, where he consults on strategic management, business portfolio planning, and R&D resource allocation. He has introduced decision analysis to the chemical, pharmaceutical, office products, and telecommunications industries, and has structured R&D and strategic plans for many European and U.S. firms. He holds a Ph.D. in physics from Stanford University.

Source: Reprinted with permission from *Research Technology Management,* September–October 1994, pp. 25–32.

Many important project strategy decisions are also involved in defining the project and its goals.

The fundamental basis of R&D productivity is an effective organization. I concur with many others that one of the keys to productivity and effectiveness in modern R&D organizations is executing R&D projects through *functionally complete teams* that are *highly empowered* by senior management to get the job done. Organizationally, this means the teams must have the authority and the resources to get the job done; the traditional scientific and engineering functional departments become reservoirs of competence, but they do not call the shots.

High-Quality Project Evaluation and Decisions

Decisions to initiate, continue, modify, and terminate R&D projects are the key to doing the right R&D. Such decisions require careful consideration of the R&D cost and time; the probabilities of technical, implementation, and commercial success; and the potential value, given success. Although these factors have traditionally been assessed qualitatively, it is increasingly common today to assess them quantitatively for applied R&D. In fact, the goal of a high-quality project evaluation process is to provide sound, comprehensive, and reliable quantitative assessments of the key project results to support high-quality R&D decisions. The tools discussed here help eliminate the "garbage in/garbage out" experience that many companies have had in the past.

Our research has identified six dimensions along which to measure and improve the quality of R&D decisions.

1. Is your R&D project appropriately framed; that is, does the project have a strategic fit, a clear definition, and goals mutually agreed on by all functions?

2. Does a range of creative and feasible alternatives support pursuit of project goals?

3. Do you have (or can you get) reliable information—including the appropriate range of uncertainty—on customers, markets, competitors, technologies, and the like.

4. Are your organization's values, such as time preference (e.g., cost of capital), risk preference, nonfinancial objectives, and so forth, clear?

5. Can you logically combine all the information to reliably evaluate the project results, including time, cost, probability, and value?

6. Can you do these five things in a way that generates organizational credibility, acceptance of the results, and a commitment to action?

We have found that several of the tools and techniques most powerful for improving quality in the R&D project evaluation and decision processes are equally powerful for improving the quality of R&D project management and execution. For many R&D managers, this will not only be unexpected, but even counterintuitive. Yet this is completely in keeping with the quality movement, which teaches us that to improve any process—including the R&D process—clear definition and measurements are essential.

Five Project Evaluation Tools

High-quality assessments of the time and cost to completion, the probability of success, and the potential value of an R&D project provide the basis for high-quality R&D project decisions and strategic R&D management. Moreover, several specific methodologies developed initially to build quality into project decisions also support high-quality project management and execution. Five powerful management tools that support R&D project evaluation, project decisions, project execution, and strategic management are: (1) strategy tables, (2) influence diagrams, (3) sensitivity analysis, (4) decision trees, and (5) expected value. These tools help not only to do the right R&D, but also to do the R&D right [2].

1. *Strategy Tables.*—These are used to clarify a project team's vision of a new product, such as a new medical diagnostic system (Figure 1), by helping to surface differences of opinion, clarify project goals, and generate alternative product concepts. The first step in using this tool is to include every major project design decision as a column and to list under the columns a wide range of design options. This can be an excellent aid to creativity. Another even more important use is to map alternative product concepts and reveal possible differences of opinion, such as the substantial difference between the R&D manager's vision of the product and the marketing manager's vision. Failure to build a shared vision of a potential new product from the start is

FIGURE 1

Strategy tables like this one for a medical diagnostic system help project teams develop project alternatives, as well as capture and harmonize diverse points of view

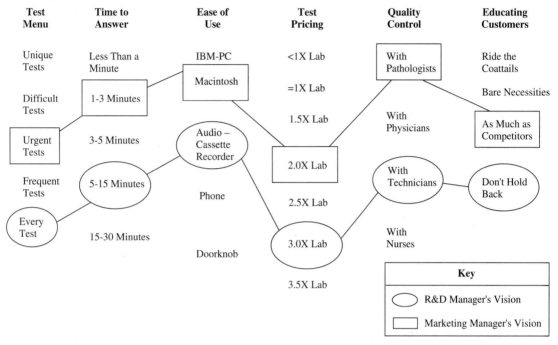

Test Menu	Time to Answer	Ease of Use	Test Pricing	Quality Control	Educating Customers
Unique Tests	Less Than a Minute	IBM-PC	<1X Lab	With Pathologists	Ride the Coattails
Difficult Tests	1-3 Minutes	Macintosh	=1X Lab		Bare Necessities
Urgent Tests	3-5 Minutes	Audio – Cassette Recorder	1.5X Lab	With Physicians	As Much as Competitors
Frequent Tests	5-15 Minutes	Phone	2.0X Lab	With Technicians	Don't Hold Back
Every Test	15-30 Minutes	Doorknob	2.5X Lab	With Nurses	
			3.0X Lab		
			3.5X Lab		

Key

⬭ R&D Manager's Vision

▭ Marketing Manager's Vision

one of the most common and most destructive failure modes, leading to enormous rework and wasted time in many industries. Senior management should require the team to present an explicit, accepted, and shared vision before funding a major new product development project. Similar tables can be used to develop technical and market alternatives for the new product.

2. *Influence Diagrams.*—An influence diagram identifies the sources of commercial value for a new product (Figure 2). In developing this diagram, the project team identifies and prioritizes all the possible drivers of commercial value. The influence diagram is a group product that should identify all important factors, or variables, that create uncertainty in assessing the value of the project if it is commercialized. Market, competition, manufacturing, and technical issues should always be considered; in some problems, regulatory, environmental, or financial issues can also emerge. From the influence diagram, issues can be qualitatively prioritized; moreover, it provides a blueprint for design-

ing a business model to evaluate potential commercial value. Management should not fund an R&D project if the team cannot clearly explain how its efforts can be expected to generate value.

Another very productive use of influence diagrams is clearly defining and subsequently quantifying the probability of introduction success—the probability that the project will be technically successful, be commercialized, and reach some (specified) level of profitability. Typically, overall success breaks down into research success, development success, implementation success, and commercial success. (The definition of these categories is flexible.) Creating this diagram assists the team in early identification of all the technical hurdles that could block success. The influence diagram is a framework to highlight the toughest hurdles (Figure 3), which can be identified qualitatively or more accurately by assigning probabilities of overcoming them. Working systematically on the toughest hurdles first, especially very early in the project, can greatly improve productivity. The

FIGURE 2

Commercial influence diagrams help identify sources of risk and opportunity as well as provide a blueprint for valuing projects

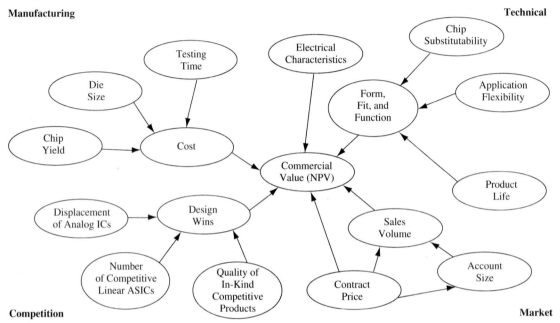

organization weeds out losers early, avoiding large expenditures on projects doomed to failure, and keeps salvageable projects on track by identifying and correcting problems at the earliest possible time.

3. *Sensitivity Analysis.*—In the display of the results of a sensitivity analysis (Figure 4), the bars show the impact on the commercial value of a project (i.e., project net present value if successful) as a function of low, median, and high values for each influential variable. By low, we typically mean the 10th percentile value; by high, the 90th. The median, of course, is the 50/50 value of the variable. This analysis requires team members to quantify their uncertainty about each variable and then shows which variables have the greatest impact on commercial value. From a decision-making viewpoint, this analysis indicates risks, whereas from a project management viewpoint, this diagram identifies opportunities. In many cases, product features can be improved by the addition of technical resources, so this tool helps the team allocate incremental effort to the most important features, those that can add the most value to the product.

4/5. *Decision Trees and Expected Value.*—Using strategy tables, influence diagrams, sensitivity analysis, and its experience and judgment, the project team can provide credible and reliable assessments of time and cost to completion, probability of success, and potential commercial value of R&D projects. These assessments not only are critical for quality project decision-making, but can also be used in many frameworks to improve R&D strategic management, as explained in the next section.

Three of these parameters—R&D cost, probability of success, and potential commercial value—can be used in a *decision tree* format to improve project decisions and measure the productivity (or return) of each project. The potential commercial value is the expected net present value *if successful* (i.e., averaged over the various market uncertainties but assuming technical and introduction success).

Taking the ultimate goal of industrial R&D as creating shareholder value, a reasonable decision rule for R&D projects is to fund those that are expected to create positive shareholder value; that is, those whose

FIGURE 3

Technical influence diagrams help define and quantify the technical hurdles that determine the probability of technical success

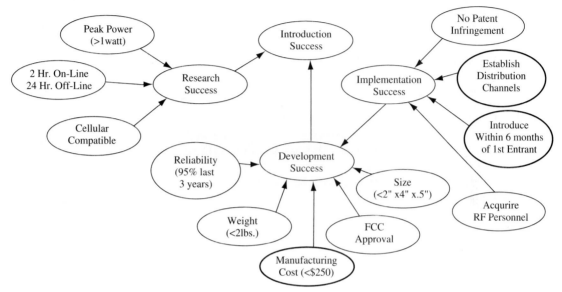

potential commercial value multiplied by their probability of success exceeds their R&D cost. (We measure shareholder value by the incremental expected NPV of the project minus the expected R&D cost to completion.) This calculation is illustrated in the box in the upper left of Figure 5.

In an organization with unlimited resources, all projects with a positive expected value would be funded. In the more realistic situation of constrained resources, the expected return (or productivity index) shown in Figure 5 can be a useful guideline for setting sound priorities. The expected return is simply the potential commercial value times the probability of success divided by the R&D cost; it measures how efficiently this project uses R&D resources to create shareholder value.

Improving Strategic R&D Management

Strategic R&D management involves the total R&D budget, its allocation to business areas and technology categories, the balance of risk and return (and other strategic attributes), and the selection and termination of projects. In the previous section, I discussed how reliable evaluation of R&D projects support the selection/continuation/termination decision, as well as how they support project management and execution. In this section, I show how various displays of the results of the analysis support strategic R&D management decisions and productive resource allocation [2].

1. *R&D Portfolio Grid.*—One of the most challenging strategic questions is whether the whole R&D program is balanced. One of the most useful frameworks to explore balance is shown in Figure 6. We see immediately many projects in the high-probability/low-value ("bread and butter") area and in the low-probability/low-value ("white elephant") area, as well as a dearth of projects in the low-probability/high-value ("oyster") area. This organization is very imbalanced in the distribution of low-probability projects. It should have few projects of low potential value and many of high potential value. Clearly, management needs to investigate why the reverse is true in this situation. On the other hand, we see an exceptional number of high-probability/high-value projects ("pearls"). Since

The sensitivity "tornado chart" identifies the biggest generators of uncertainty in commercial value and allows the project team to focus their efforts where they will add the most value

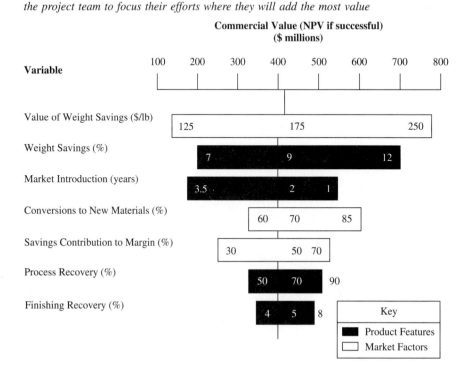

low-probability projects are usually several years from commercialization, the head of this R&D organization will appear to be successful for the next several years, but his successor may be in for trouble. Monitoring and improving the balance of the R&D portfolio is one of R&D management's prime responsibilities.

2. *R&D Productivity Curve.*—Actual R&D projects in most organizations cover a broad range of expected return, at least an order of magnitude (Figure 7). By *return* we mean expected value divided by expected cost, calculated exactly as shown in Figure 5. The expected returns for each project plotted against the cumulative R&D cost to completion nearly always show this characteristic shape. On the left are R&D projects with little R&D cost required for completion and showing very high returns. In the middle ($5 million to $20 million) are projects typical of this organization in this industry, covering their costs and generating a modest "excess" return. The last 25 percent of the cumulative

cost in this laboratory, however, is allocated to projects whose expected return is less than one (i.e., their expected value does not even cover their development cost). Management must ask why. Many of these projects can and should be improved, but some should be terminated. Instead of cutting all projects uniformly when budgets get tight, it is probably better to completely eliminate some of the weakest projects if they cannot be dramatically improved. Yet this is not the most common organizational response, partly because management rarely has credible assessments on which to base the decision to terminate projects.

3. *Portfolio Segment Return Analysis.*—In a similar type of analysis, all the R&D projects in various categories are aggregated to show the potential and expected return and success rate for the entire portfolio, for business areas, and for other categories of interest (Figure 8). This dollar-on-dollar return comparison across businesses and technologies frequently yields

FIGURE 5

Decision trees can be used to evaluate complex R&D projects and then display key decision criteria in a simple format

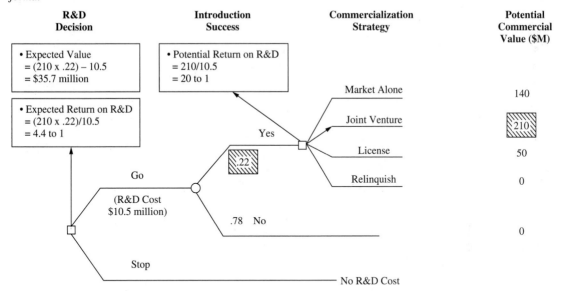

FIGURE 6

R&D portfolio grids can be used to balance R&D effort across many interesting tradeoffs, such as risk versus return

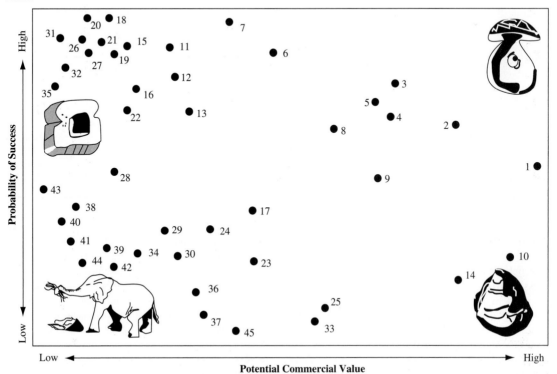

FIGURE 7

An R&D productivity curve helps identify superior, typical, and less-attractive projects in terms of efficiently using R&D resources to create business value

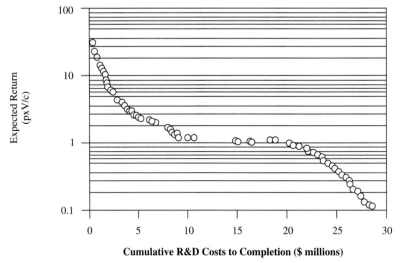

FIGURE 8

A portfolio segment return analysis identifies areas of greater and lesser expected return and provides insights on how to improve technical and business strategies

	R&D Portfolio	Core Business	New Business	New Technology for Existing Markets	Existing Technology for New Markets
Return if successful	8 to 1	4 to 1	4 to 1	6 to 1	24 to 1
Rate of success	50%	75%	25%	35%	50%
Expected return	4 to 1	3 to 1	1 to 1	2 to 1	12 to 1
Percentage of R&D budget	100%	45%	30%	49%	5%

insights not only about R&D effectiveness but also about R&D/business communication and the value of the opportunities R&D is targeting (or that the businesses are requesting). Our experience suggests this type of analysis is a rich source of ideas for redeploying resources to improve R&D productivity. This analysis suggested the need to reexamine the new business category and to explore increasing extensions of existing technologies to new markets (see shaded blocks).

4. *New Product Revenue Forecast.*—A final, very useful, analysis is to see whether the overall R&D

pipeline can deliver the type of revenue and profit growth that top management and business management are expecting. This is especially important for companies like H-P and 3M that have set explicit goals for continually generating new product revenues to fuel growth. By combining the estimates of time to completion and probability of success with the peak sales revenue and information used to assess the product life cycle, a reliable assessment of potential and expected new product revenue can be made (Figure 9).

FIGURE 9

A probabilistic new product revenue forecast helps business managers understand whether the R&D pipeline will allow them to meet business and personal goals

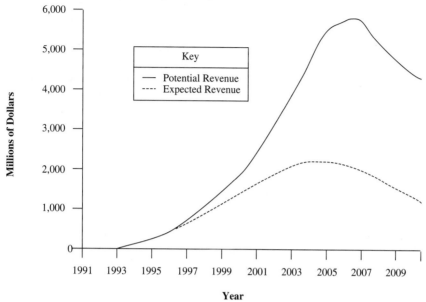

Potential revenue assumes that all projects will be technically successful and be commercialized. Although this is clearly unrealistic, we have seen well-managed R&D organizations present the potential revenue as their forecast, only to lose significant credibility a few years later. The expected revenue, which takes into account the probabilities of success, is the more meaningful estimate. If the R&D pipeline is not expected to deliver the results needed, management can explore a range of options: increase R&D funding, increase R&D productivity, acquire new technology, acquire existing products or businesses, or improve the productivity of the existing businesses. With the type of analysis depicted in Figure 9, deviations from the long-term goals and plans can be spotted early enough to take corrective action.

Both project and portfolio strategy are designed to maximize shareholder value, and we have recommended expected value of new and improved products and processes under development as a measure to guide us in the right direction. This measure has been extremely effective at Eastman Chemical Company, for example. After establishing new/improved product and process concepts as the "main output" of research and then

focusing their efforts on how to increase estimated value of these, they indeed saw the estimated value of their research nearly triple in two years (over the average of the previous ten years)! This achievement "is worth tens of millions of dollars" to them and "is a critical element to achieving [their] strategic vision and plans" [3]. A recent follow-up indicates they are maintaining the increased level of value [4].

In Conclusion

This set of R&D process quality tools can improve the quality of R&D project evaluation, project management, project execution, and project decisions, as well as strategic R&D management and resource allocation. These tools are designed to help project teams do collaborative work more efficiently and effectively by aiding in structuring thinking, in communication, and in quantification. They help achieve R&D evaluations possessing quality, integrity, and credibility. These tools are simple to understand and appreciate but are nontrivial to apply. We believe the effort required to apply them and make them a way of life is worthwhile.

Acknowledgments

The methods, findings, and experience on which this paper is based reflect learning from hundreds of projects conducted for dozens of companies over the past quarter-century. Among the contributors to the development of our R&D management approach and tools are members of Strategic Decisions Group's (SDG's) R&D team: Terry J. Braunstein, Patricia A. Evans, James E. Matheson, Donald W. Mules, and Nezam Tooloee. Companies from which we have learned include Alcoa, AT&T, Boeing, CIBA-GEIGY, Du Pont, Exxon, Eastman Chemical, Ford, General Electric, Hewlett-Packard, Hoffmann-La Roche, Johnson & Johnson, Kodak, Lilly, Merck, Mitsubishi Kasei, Pitney Bowes, Procter & Gamble, Sandoz, Shell Oil, Sumitomo Electric, 3M, and Xerox; their experience has helped demonstrate and validate the conclusions presented in this paper. In addition, a comprehensive research effort undertaken by the IRI Quality Directors Network, the R&D Decision Quality Association, and SDG to benchmark R&D decision quality practices among leading R&D organizations reveals widespread use of these tools [5].

References

1. R. N. Foster, L. H. Linden, R. L. Whiteley, and A. M. Kantrow, "Improving the Return on Research and Development: A Stimulus for Thought and Action," Industrial Research Institute, Inc., 1984.
2. J. E. Matheson, M. M. Menke, and S. L. Derby, "Managing R&D Portfolios for Improved Profitability and Productivity," *Journal of Science Policy and Research Management* 4, no. 4 (1989), pp. 400–412.
3. J. D. Holmes and D. J. McClaskey, "Improving Research Using Total Quality Management," Juran R&D Quality Symposium Conference Proceedings, 1992.
4. J. D. Holmes and G. E. McGraw, "White Water Ahead: Eastman Proposes for Turbulent Times," *Research Technology Management,* September–October 1994.
5. D. Matheson, J. E. Matheson, and M. M. Menke, *R&D Decision Quality Association Benchmarking Study,* Strategic Decisions Group, Menlo Park, 1993.

CASE 4–1
MOUNTAINEER

The 21st Century Incubator Project

Afzel Noore
Ann Pushkin
Bonnie Morris
Michael Lawson

Background

Sales for the 220 incubator continue to be disappointing. The second quarter sales report for the 220 model reflects only 25 incubators per month, far below sales for the long-standing model 120 incubator that it was designed to replace. At the beginning of the 220 project, the design team envisioned that this incubator would take Mountaineer into the 21st century. However, there appear to be operational and product design problems with the 220 incubator.

The older 120 cell culture incubator is a family (series) of models designed to meet the needs of different users in various countries. For example, many foreign countries require electrical wiring different from the standards used in the United States. Consequently, each time a production order is initiated for a different 120 model, manufacturing setup time is necessary to switch from manufacturing one model to another model. Additionally, it is necessary to maintain inventory stocks for many different 120 models.

The model 120 incubator is holding its own in the marketplace even though its design does not make use of the most current technology. Just how long the demand for the 120 model will continue is a matter of concern. In an attempt to upgrade to digital technology, to add new technical and operational features for the 21st century, and at the same time to reduce manufacturing and storage costs, Mountaineer designed and developed the 220 model. This model is a basic cell incubator with add-on features dependent upon the customer's need. The objective was to replace a family of nine models with a single model that could be

Developed by Afzel Noore, Ann Pushkin, Bonnie Morris, and Michael Lawson, *West Virginia University.* Copyright © 1994 by the National Consortium for Technology in Business, c/o the Thomas Walter Center for Technology Management, Auburn University, Auburn, AL.

adapted at the end of production to accommodate the customer requirements. Also, if a single model was used, the number of spare parts, number of models in finished goods, time to train sales representative and repair personnel would all decrease.

However, the manufacturing costs of the 220 are quite high compared with the 120 models. Some managers of Mountaineer believe that the high manufacturing costs of the 220 are a result of low volume. Other managers assert that the high manufacturing costs are the consequence of the cost allocation system.

Mountaineer recently assembled a multidisciplinary team to make recommendations to solve the problems associated with the 220 and the 120 models. The incubator team is wrestling with the following key questions about the design, marketing, manufacturing, and accounting of the 220 and the 120.

- Specifically, what features do customers want?
- What changes should be made to the incubators given our limited development resources?
- What price should be set for each product?
- Should changes be made to the current cost accounting system?
- What is the impact of the team's recommended changes in design, pricing, and costing on the company's profitability?

Mountaineer History

Mountaineer is an international manufacturer of precision scientific and laboratory equipment. Today Mountaineer designs, engineers, and manufactures over 300 products for use in biomedical, pharmaceutical, clinical, and industrial laboratories throughout the United States, Canada, Puerto Rico, and almost every country around the world. Mountaineer has grown from a 600-sq.-ft. establishment to a 234,000-sq.-ft. industrial complex in

37 years. More than 420 people are employed at the company's sole manufacturing facility, where they are engaged in one phase or another of research and development, engineering, production, quality control, management, service, sales, or marketing (for organization, see Exhibit 1).

Mountaineer is among the world leaders in cell culture incubators. These incubators are extensively used for in vitro cell growth, bacterial diagnostic culturing, large-scale environmental control, and storage. They are precision engineered to meet the stringent demands of microbiological and cell culture research.

The Incubator Industry

Incubators are used extensively throughout the health care industry, primarily as a means to promote growth of organisms in a simulated human biological environment. Incubator uses range from research applications, such as in vitro cell growth, to clinical applications, such as bacterial diagnostic culturing, to simple instrument warming. Mountaineer's products are targeted at the tissue/cell culture segment of the market where price, reliability, service/support, and features (condensation/humidity control, temperature control, CO_2 control) are the determining factors in the purchase of an incubator. Mountaineer's main customers are pharmaceutical, industrial, and biotechnology companies, clinics, and hospitals.

The cell culture incubator market is comprised of many small manufacturers, with Mountaineer leading slightly in worldwide market share (see Exhibit 2). Mountaineer's closest competitor, Norden, has been steadily losing share to low-cost manufacturers such as Perkin. Mountaineer's market share has been increasing,

although not as fast as the low-cost manufacturers. Mountaineer's model 120 has been positioned in the mid to high range of the price/performance curve (see Exhibit 3). Total world market for incubators was estimated at $60 million.

Reliability is of paramount concern to customers. Reliability is a function of the manufacturer's reputation as well as the stated warranty coverage. Mountaineer has an excellent reputation in the incubator market. However, that has possibly worked to the detriment of the 220, as customers are reluctant to move away from what has been called the workhorse of the industry, the model 120.

Service/support issues are also considered in the buying decision. Mountaineer employs a direct sales force to serve its customers domestically (internationally they have a network of dealers and distributors). Similarly, Mountaineer employs a dedicated service force to maintain and repair the Mountaineer equipment. Mountaineer believes that its direct sales and service department provide it with a competitive advantage. Most of Mountaineer's competitors sell their cell culture incubators through sales representatives. Sales representatives are nonemployees of the manufacturer who may sell different noncompeting product lines. For instance, a sales representatives might sell one manufacturer's incubator line and another manufacturer's freezer line. The use of sales representatives is less costly than employing a dedicated full time sales force. Of course, the manufacturer has no direct control over the sales representatives, and ancillary tasks such as collection of marketing data and in-depth product training normally are not asked of the sales representative force.

Although there still exists brand loyalty for the Mountaineer name, incubator customers are becoming

Organization Structure

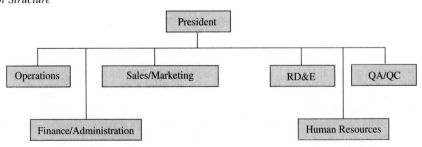

EXHIBIT 2

1992 Market Share Worldwide Cell Culture Incubators

Market	Company	Market Share Units (%)	Price ($)	Performance Rank
High:	Mountaineer 220	8	3400	910
6000 units	Newton	30	3500	1120
$22.45M	Baxter	30	3800	1190
	Herfields	32	4000	1260
Medium:	Mountaineer 120	33	2300	750
11000 units	Sanyo	17	2120	620
$20.55M	Norden	29	2300	730
	Bard	21	2370	700
Low:	Perkins	46	1900	580
9000 units	LINE	54	1550	535
$15.41M				

more and more price sensitive. Increased regulatory scrutiny of the health care industry is expected to make price a larger factor in incubator purchasing decisions. Currently, however, Mountaineer's primary strategy remains feature differentiation.

The primary functions of a cell culture incubator are temperature, humidity, and CO_2 control. Temperature is regulated to provide an ideal environment in which to grow organisms independent of the ambient laboratory environment. Incubators provide the capability to regulate the temperature of the chamber, however most of the time the incubator is run at 37°C, body temperature. Temperature control has not posed a significant challenge to the industry. Humidity is regulated to simulate the moist environment of the human biological system and to encourage rapid growth of the organism under study; the primary role of humidity, however, is to keep the growth media from drying out. The desire is to maintain the chamber at as high an RH (relative humidity) as possible; however, the development of water droplets through condensation must be avoided. Water droplets can be the cause for contamination by carrying unwanted bacteria. Since some of these tests can go on for six to eight months, contamination in the latter stages of a test would cause significant costs to the testing lab. Finally, CO_2 is used to control the PH of the media as well as the growth rate of the media. Incubator operators depend on the color of the media as an indication of the PH.

Mountaineer's Incubator Product Line

The 120 Incubator. Mountaineer's automatic CO_2 incubators have set the standard for reliability in the laboratory. Considered the flagship of the industry, these incubators are available in different configurations to meet the individual laboratory space requirements. Reverse door swing on single and dual chamber units allow side-by-side arrangement. Engineered to prevent contamination, the stainless steel interior is smooth seam–welded to provide a crevice-free chamber.

Mountaineer manufactures several units in single- and dual-chamber designs and allows CO_2 and/or O_2 control. Fiberglass insulation is combined with the water jacket to form triple-wall protection of the chamber temperature. Single- and dual-chamber units feature triple-wall construction for unmatched temperature uniformity and stability. Chamber temperature is controlled at a fixed +37°C (+98.6°F) or adjustable from +5°C above ambient to +60°C (+140°F). The water reservoir elevates internal relative humidity conditions up to 96 percent ±2 percent at +37°C and prevents desiccation. Mountaineer water jacketed incubators feature a smooth-seam-welded stainless steel interior to provide a crevice-free chamber. Many competitors' units utilize folded seams, which harbor contamination. An external blower motor provides gentle air flow and prevents stratification of gas and temperature. Ultra-flat, electropolished shelves are perforated for uniform air movement.

Exhibit 3

Incubator Price versus Performance

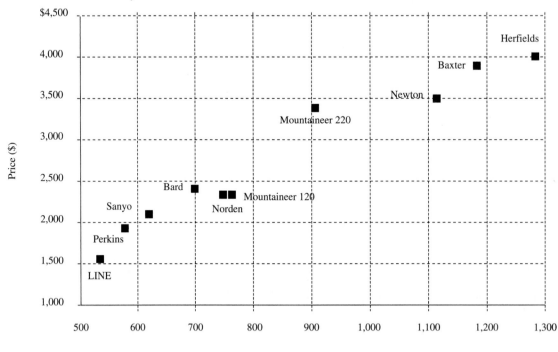

Shelves and ductwork are easily removable, thus providing free access to the chamber for cleaning. A low-watt heater in the outer door minimizes condensation on the inner glass door to maximize chamber visibility. Incubators include independent temperature, overtemperature, and gas control systems.

The self-diagnostic electronics module monitors and controls CO_2 across the full 0–20 percent range. Digital setpoint can be adjusted to within 0.1 percent and easily checked. The module also displays gas percentage on LCD readout. A self-diagnostic control system monitors chamber temperature, which is constantly displayed in easy-to-read digital form. Overtemperature safety system is independent of temperature controller, adjustable in 0.1°C (1°C on constant flow) increments, with audio/visual alarms. Tamper-resistant controls prevent accidental alteration of gas setpoints, and overtemperature safety settings. Audio/visual alarms indicate CO_2/O_2 deviations 1 percent above or below setpoint. Standard alarm delay avoids nuisance alarms during door openings. An audio/visual add-water alarm warns of low water in the water jacket. Tamper-resistant controls prevent alteration of temperature and CO_2 setpoint and overtemperature safety. Mountaineer's CO_2 sensor is a dependable, time-proven, solid-state thermal conductivity type, which features sintered filter and dual-glass-bead, matched thermistors. CO_2 passes through an in-line microbiological filter. If power fails, CO_2 is automatically cut off. Through-wall access port allows access to the accessory outlet located on the rear utility panel. The sample port is easily accessible for checking gas concentration. Most models feature a recorder jack for programmable digital recorder and dry contacts for connection to a remote temperature alarm system. Nonmarring leveling feet protect floor and/or tabletop.

The 220 Incubator. Mountaineer's model 220 automatic CO_2 water jacketed incubator incorporates a microcomputer for controlling temperature and CO_2, time-proven thermal conductivity CO_2 sensor, HEPA filters and a more aseptic culturing chamber, to provide the ultimate environment for cell growth. An easy-to-read control panel features a vacuum fluorescent display for alphanumeric viewing of all incubator performance parameters. The functional design of the model 220 incubator is truly a global incubator and provides the flexibility to address any lab configuration. One model will accommodate virtually all world electrical voltages. The Mountaineer model 220 incorporates a microcomputer control/data system providing ultimate temperature and CO_2 parameters. The unit combines proportional and integral (PI) algorithms with fuzzy logic to yield consistent/repeatable performance. Fuzzy logic characteristics automatically compensate for fluctuations in lab ambient conditions, thus providing a stable culturing environment. A patented interactive dual temperature probe system enhances the fuzzy logic techniques by precisely balancing the chamber air for ultimate temperature control and uniformity. Better than +0.1°C temperature control is maintained.

The microcomputer control system incorporates a tracking alarm for overtemperature and undertemperature conditions. Additionally, an independent, electronic overtemperature safety-alarm system ensures product protection as the heaters are shut down if temperature deviates beyond overtemperature setpoint. An audible alert and a message display are provided for both alarm modes. A thermal conductivity CO_2 sensor with sintered diffusion filter has been refined through use on thousands of Mountaineer cell culture incubators. Value-proven year after year, this control method continues to provide precise CO_2 measurement. To maintain accurate CO_2 control, fuzzy logic techniques enhance the proportional and integral (PI) algorithms. Audible alert and message displays warn of CO_2 deviations 1 percent above or below setpoint. Built-in 15-minute delay avoids "nuisance alarms." CO_2 audible alert can be silenced after the time delay period. In addition, it will ring back in 15 minutes as a reminder to reset CO_2.

The door-mounted control panel features a microcomputer system which conveys performance data through a 20-character, two-line, vacuum fluorescent alphanumeric dialog screen. The ergonomic design of this control panel permits wide-angle viewing at all light levels. The vacuum fluorescent display eliminates UV (ultraviolet) washout associated with liquid crystal displays. Clear, self-prompting messages allow the technician to program the desired temperature and CO_2 parameters with ease. In case of power failure, setpoints and calibration values are retained in nonvolatile continuous memory. No battery backup is required. Built-in self-diagnostics feature automatic and manual test functions.

The percentage door-heat-setting determines the amount of time that the door heater will be on relative to the main heater. A value from 0–100 percent can be selected. If water needs to be added to the jacket, this message will appear on the dialog screen. When the jacket is full, a visual message is momentarily displayed and the audible alert switches off.

When the door is opened, the CO_2 supply is automatically cut off and the blower stops to minimize CO_2 usage and prevent contaminants from being drawn into the chamber interior. When CO_2 deviates 1 percent above or below setpoint, warning messages will be displayed. For unmatched temperature uniformity and stability, the model 220 incubator features triple-wall construction. A welded, crevice-free, stainless steel chamber with mirrored finish features 100 percent, 1/2-in.-radius (1.27 cm) coved corners. Fifty percent improvement in surface smoothness over units using 2B finish is achieved by utilizing an RMS 2-3m inch finish. Superior cleanability is ensured as the entire interior is comprised of three components, easily removable without the use of tools. Construction of the new chamber promotes aseptic culturing conditions. An easily removable stainless steel humidity pan is provided standard to prevent desiccation and facilitate cleaning.

An external blower motor provides gentle airflow to prevent stratification of gas and temperature. Disposable blower wheel snaps out for complete decontamination. A HEPA filter (99.97 percent efficient at 0.2 microns) on the CO_2 supply assists in preventing contamination. A CO_2 sample port for checking gas concentration also includes a HEPA filter. Key components and HEPA filters are accessible from the front of the unit. To minimize CO_2 usage and prevent contaminants from being drawn into the chamber interior during door openings, a door switch has been incorporated to shut off the CO_2 supply and stop the blower.

Ultraflat electropolished shelves are square for convenience and perforated for uniform air movement. The ideal size of the shelves allows for easy removal and manipulation of cultures in a biological safety cabinet or clean air bench. Shelves are interchangeable with other styles of Mountaineer water jacketed incubators. A low-watt heater in the outer door minimizes condensation on the inner glass door and optimizes chamber uniformity and visibility. As an added convenience, the nonsiphon drain system is located on the front of the cabinet for draining the water jacket chamber. Through-wall port allows access to the chamber. Front-entry drawer houses primary electronic components. For durability and a high-quality appearance, the exterior of the incubator is powder coated. Salt spray test exceeds 1,000 hours per ASTM Standard B117-85.

One model can accommodate the lab requirements. It can be set on a counter top with backsplash as small as 24 in. (60.96 cm) deep, or as the research needs grow, they can be stacked for maximum utilization of space. Nonmarring leveling feet protect floor and/or tabletop. For side-by-side operation or changing lab layouts, the inner and outer doors are field reversible in a matter of minutes (left-hand door standard). If one would like the door reversed prior to shipment, it may be specified when ordering.

Truly a global incubator, the model 220 will accommodate virtually all world electrical voltages. The incubator has been designed to operate on 90–125 volts, 50/60 Hz, or 180–250 volts, 50/60 Hz. A selector switch allows choice of desired incubator voltage. Built-in surge suppressors protect incubator against most power transients. Internal fuses are provided to protect against incorrect voltage selection. Universal plug-in connector allows the flexibility to match main power line cord to appropriate electrical supply.

The 220 incubator is C.S.A. certified and U.L. listed. It is designed and manufactured to the strict requirements of these independent testing facilities.

Cost Accounting at Mountaineer

Joe Craig reports to Ed Harris, the senior vice president of Finance and Administration (see Exhibit 4 for an organization chart for Finance and Administration). Among Craig's responsibilities is the construction of the labor and overhead rates for Mountaineer's cost accounting system. Mountaineer uses a full absorption costing system. Each year, as part of the budget process, Joe Craig constructs the cost rates for each work center using the direct labor charges, work center direct overhead and indirect overhead. Direct labor charges represent the average wages paid to employees in the work center. Work center direct overhead consists of overhead items that can be traced specifically to a work center. Examples are: indirect work center labor; fringe benefits such as, hospitalization; FICA, federal, and state unemployment taxes; vacation pay; workmen's compensation premiums; and direct operating supplies and depreciation for the work center equipment.

Indirect overhead consists of items that are not directly traceable to a particular process or product. Examples include: plant management (VP operations, plant manager, plant maintenance and safety department expenses), human resources, purchasing, inventory control, production control, plant occupancy (utilities and property taxes), quality assurance/quality control (QA/QC), and the stockroom and warehouse. These expenses

EXHIBIT 4

Finance Organization Structure

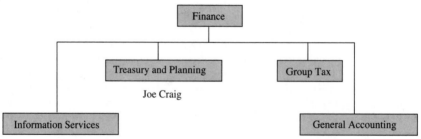

are not directly traceable to a work center. Craig allocates these expenses to the work centers as follows:

Human relations	Number of budgeted direct labor hours in the work center
Plant management	Number of budgeted direct labor hours in the work center
Plant maintenance and safety	Number of budgeted direct labor hours in the work center
Purchasing	Total expense ÷ the number of work centers
Inventory control	Total expense ÷ the number of work centers
Warehouse	Total expense ÷ the number of work centers
Stockroom	Total expense ÷ the number of work centers
Plant occupancy	Square footage of plant space occupied by the work center

The total product cost for each of the 120 and 220 incubators must be calculated in a series of steps as discussed below. First, the factory overhead (FOH) rate for each work center (WC) is calculated as follows. Please refer to Table 1 for specific numbers. The indirect overhead expenses for plant occupancy, warehouse, purchasing, inventory control, plant manager, plant safety, and maintenance are added to provide a total allocated overhead (OH) per WC. The total allocated OH is divided by the budgeted direct labor hours to obtain the factory OH rate per WC.

The factory OH rate is now added to the direct labor (DL) rate and the direct OH rate (Table 2) to obtain the direct labor OH (DLOH) rate.

The DLOH rate is multiplied by the number of direct labor hours (DLH) to obtain the DLOH$ per WC (Table 3). Please note that the DLOH$ per WC are calculated for both the 120 and 220 models.

Then, for each model the direct material costs from Table 4 must be added to the DLOH$ from Table 3 to obtain the total product cost.

TABLE 1   Allocation of Factory Overhead to the Work Centers

Work Center	Floor Space %	Plant Occupancy*	Warehouse, Purchasing, Inventory Control†	VP Operation, Plant Manager, Plant Safety, Maintenance and Human Resources‡	Total Allocated Overhead	Total Budgeted DLH	OH Rate per Work Center
Assembly	18%	442304	354623	228338	1025265	48575	21.11
Welding	10	245725	354623	381441	981789	81145	12.10
Paint room	21	516021	354623	69190	939834	14719	63.85
Grinding	4	98290	354623	47407	500320	10085	49.61
Mechanical	7	172007	354623	89300	615930	18997	32.42
Press brakes	9	221152	354623	216126	791901	45977	17.22
Electrical	11	270297	354623	285673	910593	60772	14.99
Integration	9	221152	354623	148092	723867	31504	22.98
Testing	11	270297	354623	88773	713693	18885	37.79
Total	100	2457245	3191610	1554341	7203196	330659	

*Plant occupancy includes utilities and property taxes. It is allocated to the work centers based on the area (in square feet) occupied by the work center.
†Allocated to the work centers equally (i.e., one-ninth for each work center).
‡Allocated to the work centers on the basis of budgeted direct labor hours.

TABLE 2   **Work Center Direct Labor and Overhead Rate**

Work Center	DL Rate	WC OH Rate*	Total Plant OH Rate†	DLOH Rate
Assembly	11.89	13.49	21.11	46.49
Welding	13.42	12.43	12.10	37.95
Paint room	10.05	17.12	63.85	91.02
Grinding	12.47	6.49	49.61	68.57
Mechanical	11.95	11.47	32.42	55.84
Press brakes	11.95	9.52	17.22	38.69
Electrical	12.27	8.79	14.99	36.05
Integration	12.06	14.23	22.98	49.27
Testing	15.05	15.67	37.79	68.51

*Includes nonproductive labor in the work center, work center supplies.
†Includes plant occupancy, materials overhead (warehouse, purchasing, inventory control), human resources, VP of operations, plant manager, plant safety and maintenance, (see Table 1 for calculation).

TABLE 3   **Estimated Direct Labor Hours (DLH) and Direct Labor and Overhead Dollars (DLOH$) for the 120 and 220 Incubators**

Work Center	DLOH Rate	120 DLH	120 DLOH$	220 DLH	220 DLOH$
Assembly	46.49	3.72	172.94	8.71	404.93
Welding	37.95	3.93	149.14	7.00	265.65
Paint room	91.02	1.54	140.17	2.98	271.24
Grinding	68.57	0.93	63.77	1.81	124.11
Mechanical	55.84	2.11	117.82	3.29	183.71
Press brakes	38.69	1.98	76.61	2.61	100.98
Electrical	36.05	1.96	70.66	1.97	71.02
Integration	49.27	0.16	7.88	0.00	0.00
Testing	68.51	1.90	130.17	1.78	121.95
Total		18.23	929.17	30.15	1543.59

Product Development at Mountaineer

Mountaineer Inc. continues to strive to produce the highest-quality equipment at a reasonable price. The management and staff believe that aggressive research and development and carefully coordinated manufacturing and sales/marketing efforts will lead Mountaineer into the 21st century with the introduction of many new products. New products are the key to a company's sales growth. This attitude is becoming more prevalent among global manufacturers. According to a Booz Allen & Hamilton survey: "About 75 percent of the nation's growth in sales volume can be expected to come from new products, including new brands." According to a 1980 report from the Conference Board, of the 148 companies surveyed, 15 percent of their current sales volume is attributable to the sale of major new products introduced by them during the past five years. Looking to the future, two-thirds of the reporting executives expect their companies to have an even greater dependence on new products over the next five years. Mike Geer, Mountaineer's senior vice president of Research, Development, and Engineering, views new products as being essential for viability. Mountaineer must continu-

TABLE 4   **Raw Material Cost ($) Comparisons**

	Model 120	Model 220	Difference	Major Source of Differences	
Mechanical:					
Exterior door	49.42	98.47	−49.05	Stamping	41.03
				hinges	6.35
					47.38
Chamber	129.48	175.92	−46.44	Sheet metal	39.06
Exterior	66.77	96.78	−30.01	Gaskets	5.85
				Sheet metal	10.55
				Collar heater	12.03
					28.43
Miscellaneous parts (inner door, heater assembly, drain parts)	117.59	133.54	−15.95	Filter	8.72
				Motor	3.68
					12.40
Ductwork and shelves	149.49	147.52	1.97		
Humidity pan	0.00	25.79	−25.79		
Packaging	28.85	43.34	−14.49		
Total mechanical	541.60	721.36	−179.76		
Electrical:					
Sensors	40.42	43.60	−3.18		
Probes	48.67	55.60	−6.93		
Display	24.57	108.09	−83.52		
Controls (w/o display)	101.19	93.18	8.01		
Control Panel	0.00	58.89	−58.89		
Miscellaneous	87.23	102.24	−15.01		
Total electrical	302.08	461.60	−159.52		
Total material cost	843.68	1182.96	−339.28		

ously adapt to the changes in technology if it has to sustain its leadership role in the competitive growing world market.

Mountaineer has recently instituted a structured process for their product development programs. The process is based on the concept of product development process "funnels" which "gate" the progress of a development program by requiring certain information to be gathered and certain questions to be answered before subsequent phases of the development can begin.[1]

The level of detail and analysis for each gate is significant. For example, Gate 1 addresses the following issues:

- Is feasibility study acceptable?
- Does product require new core technology?
- Have we identified major customer?
- What are the effects to the overall product lines?
- What is market introduction window?
- Has the resource allocation committee signed off?
- Have resource requirements been identified?
- Is it possible to design this idea into a product which meets quality standards?

[1] K. B. Clark and S. C. Wheelwright, *Managing New Product and Process Development: Text & Cases* (New York: Free Press, 1993).

- What is return on investment?
- Is financial analysis complete?
- What are the critical product specifications?
- Is customer/sales force/marketing input obtained?
- Is preliminary marketing plan complete?
- Does product general looks and concept fit company looks?
- Has the completion been fully evaluated?
- What is market introduction strategy?
- Does the product fit Mountaineer's mission/vision?
- What are performance and reliability expectations?
- Is there a market need?
- Has cross-functional involvement agreed to proceed?
- What is the make/buy decision?
- Is the marketing and engineering preliminary study finalized and approved?

Mountaineer has also committed to the concept of team-based design. Team-based design is accomplished by assigning to the design team members from the different functional groups (engineering, marketing, manufacturing, quality assurance, finance, reliability, etc.), empowering them to make critical product design decision, and fostering a culture which emphasizes team performance as opposed to individual or functional group accomplishments. This is a precursor to concurrent engineering (Noore and Lawson), or integrated product development (IPD), which incorporates multifunctional teams and strives to reduce product development time by doing the individual design tasks in parallel, thereby reducing total cycle time.

With this new interdisciplinary team, product planning is not viewed as merely a corporate function. In the development of the 220 incubator, R&D, marketing, finance, accounting, manufacturing all work closely as a team for the common benefit of the company rather than competing against each other. No department alone has all the skills required to undertake the manufacture of world-class incubators, and Mountaineer will not readily get a "buy-in" from the functional groups unless that group was a part of the planning effort. Overall, this process does save a considerable amount of time and the entire process is well understood by various disciplines.

It also makes the problem-solving and decision-making ability better.

The interdisciplinary team at Mountaineer analyzes the current technology, and the projection of where technology is heading. Marketing provides the analysis of the current incubator market and market trends. They share information on the current and potential markets, analyze trends, and project direction. The team:

- Discusses information on the competition.
- Understands the market need and size.
- Determines the unique incubator features/capabilities.
- Devises a marketing strategy.
- Assesses the available technology.
- Estimates development and manufacturing costs, estimates resource requirements.
- Constructs the proposed product schedule.

Product Management Team

The incubator product line is in its most turbulent time in recent Mountaineer history. While the sales projections look stable for the 120 line, they cannot be expected to continue indefinitely, and if a competitor introduces a strong product, they could decline very quickly. The 220 was designed to be the replacement for the 120, but because of a lack of features and/or a high price, it has not demonstrated the sales volume that Mountaineer needs.

Product Management Team—R&D. The R&D organization (Exhibit 5) is responsible for the design and development of all Mountaineer products. The disciplines represented in this group include electrical engineering, mechanical engineering, cryogenics, manufacturing engineering, and quality. Don Howard, Product Engineering Manager, describes the present situation:

> I think we may have missed some features that the customers expected at the price that we have set for the 220. We have just completed a product improvement project which will add some features to the 220 as well as fix some problems in the design. I think it will still be necessary to add another set of upgrades to the 220 to position it as our flagship incubator.
>
> We plan to do this next upgrade project differently, however. We are using a new tool called quality function

Exhibit 5

RD&E Organization Structure

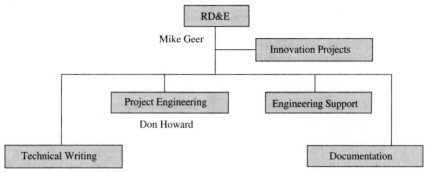

deployment (QFD), which provides an analysis methodology to trade off product features versus customers needs. I'm hoping that it will help us improve our ability to select upgrades as well as provide traceability back to customer requirements if we ever get into a situation in the design phase where we need to relax some specifications.

While all of our focus is on the 220, we can't forget the 120. It is our most profitable line, and PROFIT is the #1 item here. There will have to be some funds spent to sustain the 120 as well as add some features. Otherwise we risk losing market share to competitors' products.

A list of potential project upgrades, along with their estimated manufacturing costs, for the 120 and the 220 are included in Appendix A.

With all this going on, I think our biggest problem is going to be staffing the projects. We have limited engineering resources and we won't be able to do it all. I hope this QFD tool allows us to prioritize and make the best use of our resources. Of course, even if we prioritized correctly we still have to be concerned about inaccurate estimates and project slipups. In the past we have missed, both on the good side and bad, schedules and cost by as much as 30 percent. It seems we do better when we take the time to think through the issues upfront. When we do a poor analysis of our options we tend to stray more from our estimates. I think the QFD tool could be of benefit here, too. If we do need to replan because of problems, we can easily go back to our QFD analysis to remind us what the top priority projects are.

Table 5 lists the resources available to the engineering group for the next year.

Table 5   Headcount per Quarter

	3rd Quarter 1993	4th Quarter 1993	1st Quarter 1994
Electrical	7	7	7
Mechanical	8	8	8
QA	4	4	4
Manufacturing	5	5	5

How are we approaching the problem of the incubator market? Well, first we are re-looking at what we believe to be our customer requirements. This is the foundation of any good design project. We are prioritizing these requirements based on surveys we have conducted with customers. We have identified engineering projects, both feature upgrades and cost reduction projects, for each incubator. Using the QFD tool, we intend to determine the impact each project has on the customer requirements. This will allow us to prioritize the projects, since we do not have enough resources to do it all. We will come up with potential product configurations and then, in cooperation with the marketing and accounting departments, we will determine the cost and tradeoff pricing points to find the best total profitability. Of course, this is based on where we think our competitors will position their products and how fast we think they can bring them to market. Once that's all done, we go to the executive committee for approval.

Exhibit 6

Sales/Marketing Organization Structure

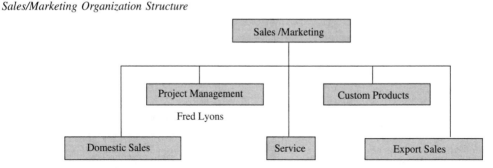

Product Management Team—Marketing. The marketing organization (Exhibit 6) in Mountaineer is responsible for determining the long-range direction of their product lines. They, in cooperation with the direct sales force, project the future needs of the customer base and specify overall functional needs of the product. This group also sets the selling price of each product and therefore is held responsible for the profit margin of the product line. They are an integral part of the product development team, making sure that the "voice of the customer" remains the ultimate decision-making criteria for the team.

The Incubator Market. "The incubator market has become extremely competitive. We have more competitors, as well as the size of our competitors is increasing through market consolidation. At the same time, the customer is becoming smarter and more cost conscious," stated Fred Lyons, product manager for incubators.

There was a time where a sale was made on the relationship between the buyer and the salesperson. Those days are fairly well gone, most of our customers' buyers are required now to seek competitive bids and they are pressured to justify any decision made on other than low cost. I have a chart which shows the price/performance behavior in the market [Exhibit 3]. As you can see, there are three prominent segments, the low end at $1,500–$2,000, the medium range of $2,100–$3,000, and the high end range at $3,100 and above. This price behavior is pretty standard in this market. There are certain customers that have built-in price ceilings, and they will not consider buying outside of these ranges. Over the years the segment ranges have drifted higher, but that's only a function of inflation. Unit sales have remained fairly constant in each market segment, and we expect this to continue.

Lyons continued:

You will also notice that there is a ranking of the product performance or features for each product as represented by the horizontal axis of the graph. The performance scale is somewhat subjective. I used the QFD tools to look at what the customers need, assigned a weight to those needs, and then the engineers looked at our own and our competitor's products to see how well they met those needs. Finally we used the technical importance rank from the QFD as our performance ranking for each product. As you can see, the low-end market generally has products with performance rankings of between 350 and 700, the medium has between 600 and 950, and the high end between 800 and 1,200.

This is the start of how we estimate how many units we will sell within a given price segment. We know that from year to year each segment's unit sales are fairly constant. The big issue is how your product compares to the competition's in that segment. What I do is sum the performance rankings for each product within that segment. I divide our product's performance ranking by the sum, and that percentage is my initial estimate of the percent of that market's unit volume we will sell. Next I have to adjust the estimate for the effect of price. I compare the percent difference of my product's price and performance ranking with the competitor's products. I then look at the difference of my product's price and performance ranking with the competitor's products. I then look at the difference between these two numbers and adjust the market share based on this number. The system works well because I know that some of the customers actually make these types of tradeoffs to make their purchasing decisions. It isn't a fancy algorithm, but I believe it gives me a reasonable estimate of demand.

This time, we think we have a good feel for our customer needs. We did a marketing survey recently [Exhibit 7] which looked at what things our customers thought were important—I don't think there were any surprises. We also did a survey of what they thought about our potential

Exhibit 7

Customer Requirements Ranking

Product Features	CUSTOMER									
	1	*2*	*3*	*4*	*5*	*6*	*7*	*8*	*9*	*10*
Temperature control	7	9	9	5	3	3	7	6	4	8
Humidity control	7	4	4	8	8	9	9	5	8	8
CO_2 control	9	7	4	4	8	8	3	1	8	7
Physical accommodation	3	4	4	2	5	2	4	1	2	2
Contamination	9	9	8	7	9	6	9	9	9	9
Ease of use	6	7	7	5	6	8	8	7	7	7
Display	4	3	6	5	5	4	4	3	3	5
Data	7	8	7	4	4	3	5	6	6	3
Miscellaneous	8	2	4	3	3	2	5	3	2	1

improvements to the 120 and/or the 220 [Appendix B]. On the second survey we specifically asked whether they thought the product improvement would help them slightly, moderately, or significantly.

Even though our customers exhibit a high degree of reluctance to switch products, they will switch if the competition presents a product clearly superior to ours. And once the customer switches, it will be difficult for us to bring them back. Because of this, we have to put a high priority to getting to the market first with new features. I think if we are late by one month, we might see sales erode by 5 percent; if we are late by two to four months, it could mean sales down by 10 percent. After four months, we could lose 20 percent of the sales we projected to the competitor first to market. This doesn't apply to all upgrade features, only the ones which, in the eyes of the customer, present a dramatic improvement in product performance. Of our current upgrade projects, I'd put the Dual-Chamber design and the new Airflow system projects in this category.[2]

The 120 is the product that won't die. The 220 is a better product but priced more than the 120. Our customers won't give the 120 up. The Mountaineer reputation is built on reliability and I guess most of our clients are reluctant to bet on something that's new and unproven. The problem is, the 120 will not be competitive in the long run and we have to either get the 220 sales up or do major upgrades to the 120. The sales projections for the 120 look fairly good. Of course, if a better competitive product comes along that

could go south quickly. Even if we decide to go totally with the 220, we'll have to spend some engineering resources on the 120 just to sustain it.

The 220 came along because we wanted to change things . . .

The marketing department was the primary champion of such product changes as the new fluorescent displays, the aesthetically appealing door, and the curved interior chamber.

If we could get the 220 volume up, then it would start showing better profit margins and people will have a lot more confidence in it. We are driven, I guess like most organizations, on profit. We make decisions based on what product line makes the most profit. That's why I think the 220 is getting the short end of the stick with regard to these overhead rates. The 220 is a more producible product; it shouldn't cost what the numbers says it does to produce it. In the long run the 220 will be our flagship product; we just need to stick with it.

The Product Marketing Team—Finance. The accounting department was not involved in the early stages of the development of the 220 incubator model. Prior to the adoption of the project management team (PMT) approach to new product development, RD&E relied on the published cost rates, established annually by Joe Craig, when making cost-based design decisions for new products or for engineering changes to existing products.

Recently, Mountaineer decided to include an accounting or finance representative on their project

---

[2] For further detail on the importance of time to market, see G. Stalk, Jr., "Time—The Next Source of Competitive Advantage" *Harvard Business Review,* July–August, 1988, pp. 41–51.

management teams PMTs. The role of accounting in the PMT is to act as a consultant or facilitator to assist the team in interpreting cost data and to ensure that there is consistency in the use of cost data across projects. The risk of not including an accounting or finance representative on the PMT is that cost data will be used incorrectly. For example, the accountant should recognize situations where contribution margin should be used instead of full standard cost. Accountants can facilitate what-if analyses by determining the appropriate cost measures for the alternative scenarios.

In discussing the 220, Craig noted that the product did not meet its cost objectives. RD&E had targeted a lower cost than manufacturing experienced. According to Craig, this was due to lower than anticipated sales volume for the product. Because there was no accounting department involvement in the early stages of development of the 220, Craig was unable to identify any cost issues that were considered during the product development cycle.

A number of questions have been raised regarding the cost accounting methods used by Mountaineer. A key motivation in designing Model 220 was to reduce costs by replacing a family of nine models with one single model that could be adapted at the end of the production to accommodate the customer requirements. By having a single model, the number of spare parts, number of models in finished goods, and time to train sales reps and repair personnel would all decrease. In fact the cost of the 220 is quite high compared with the 120 family of incubators. This has caused some people to question whether the cost accounting system is distorting the cost of the 220. It is not clear to the RD&E and manufacturing personnel how savings from reduc-

tions in the warehousing of raw materials, spare parts, and finished goods will ever be recognized using the current cost accounting system.

Joe Craig noted that these types of costs are related to materials used in production. He has accumulated some data about the materials used for Mountaineer's different product lines (see Table 6) that could be used to calculate a material overhead rate. The warehouse, as well as purchasing and inventory control, could handle increased volume of 3,000 units of model 220 with only modest increases in labor costs (about 7 percent of the current budget for those departments). Because the company strategy is to increase the number of product lines as well as to increase the volume of current product sales, the company would not consider moving the warehouse to a smaller building or decreasing the warehouse staff in the near future. These are considered by management to be fixed costs for the purposes of making decisions about the incubator lines.

Marketing is especially concerned about the cost of the 220. Marketing department product line managers are responsible for achieving adequate profit margins. The 220 is priced higher than the 120 series, but its margin is still much lower. The sales staff would be more enthusiastic about selling the 220 if its costs were lower.

Both the raw material costs and the direct labor hours are higher for the 220 (see Tables 3 and 4). One reason why direct labor for the 220 is higher than the 120 family is that the shiny interior of the 220's water jacket requires more manual handling of the material in order to prevent scratching by the metal wheels on the automated equipment. Also, more of the quality control inspecting is being done at the work centers before they release units of the 220 model to the next stage of production. The direct labor hours that are spent for

---

TABLE 6 Number of Parts and Material Costs by Product Line

	220	*120*	*Other*
Material per unit	$1,182.96	$843.68	$1425.38*
Budgeted number of units	300	3600	11000
Number of unique parts for each product line	53	162	873

Note: Five parts are common to all products made by Mountaineer. An additional 10 parts are common to both the 220 and the 120. Assume that all the remaining parts are used by only one product line in the ratio of one raw material part per finished unit.

*This represents an average cost of all other product lines. Because the volumes for nonincubator lines are not affected by any decisions that are made for the incubators, all other products can be treated as one group.

these tasks are very expensive because of the overhead loading.

A specific cost accounting issue that has been raised concerns the product testing. The 120 family of model sits in the quality assurance (QA, or testing) area for 48 hours for testing prior to shipping. Much of the testing of the model 220 is done at the work centers before the product moves to the next stage of production. As a result, model 220 sits in the QA area for only four hours, yet both products are assigned the same cost for that work center because they both require about one hour of direct labor. One alternative that has been suggested is to treat the entire testing work center as overhead and to distribute its costs to all the products on the basis of the other work centers' budgeted direct labor hours.

To manufacture the 220, Mountaineer invested in a special piece of equipment to do some of the spot welding. This machine is used only for the 220. It cost $205,000 and has no salvage value and a seven-year estimated life. Currently, this equipment is included in the welding work center along with other equipment that is used both for the 220 and a variety of other products. Because it is not used for other product lines, its inclusion in the welding area that services all other products may not be appropriate. If a separate work center were established for this activity, the present cost accounting method would allocate one-tenth (because there would be 10 work centers) of the warehouse, purchasing, and inventory control overhead to that center.

Another area of concern is the paint room. It has the highest DLOH rate of all work centers ($91.02 per direct labor hour). Some have suggested that the paint room DLOH rate is so high that it would be cheaper to contract out the painting (see Project 10 description in Appendix A). The paint department is highly automated, requiring very little direct labor. The paint room also occupies a very large percentage of the plant space. This is due the way many parts are "painted." First the parts are mounted on a conveyor which runs them through a wash and dry station. Then the parts are sprayed with a paint powder, which is then heated. The process requires a clean area away from the high-traffic areas of the plant. Most of the direct labor in the paint room consists of mounting the parts on the conveyor and taking them off at the end of the paint line. The 220 incurs extra DL hours in the paint room because there are several threaded parts that must be covered with masking tape prior to painting in order to prevent the paint from clogging the threads. The tape must be removed before the parts are transferred to the assembly area.

The plant manager is very much opposed to using a subcontractor, however, because Mountaineer has excess capacity (see Table 7) and doing it in-house allows for better quality control. He stated that the DLOH rate for the paint room will decrease as soon as the volume increases. In his opinion, management should not worry about the high paint room charges.

Mountaineer's management was aware that the new state-of-the-art paint room exceeded the company's

TABLE 7   Total Budgeted Direct Labor Hours (DLH) and Capacity Utilization (based on two shifts)

Work Center	Budgeted DLH	Capacity DLH %
Assembly	48575	58%
Welding	81145	56
Paint room	14719	53
Grinding	10085	54
Mechanical	18997	63
Press brakes	45977	61
Electrical	60772	59
Integration	31504	59
Testing	18885	57
Total	330659	57.78

TABLE 8   Estimated Manufacturing Times (hrs.) and Raw Material Costs by Project

Project No.	Model*	Work Center 1	Work Center 2	Work Center 3	Work Center 4	Work Center 5	Work Center 6	Work Center 7	Work Center 8	Work Center 9	Cost†
1	120	0	0	0	0	1	0.5	1	0	1	$23.10
2	120	0	0	0	0	3	2	0.5	0	1	35.40
3	Both	0	1	1	0.5	0.5	1	0.5	0	0.5	28.95
4	Both	2	2	1	1	1	0.5	0	1	0.5	45.23
5	Both	0	0	0	0	0.5	0	0	0	0.5	5.10
6	220	0.5	0.5	0	0	0.5	1	0.5	0	0.5	48.00
7	Both	0.5	0.5	0	0	0.5	0.5	0.5	0	0.5	5.12
8	220	0	−1	−0.5	−0.5	−0.5	0	0	0	0	83.52
9	Both	0.5	0.5	0	0	0	0	0	1	0	48.00
10	220	−0.5	−0.5	−1	−0.5	0	0.5	0	−0.5	0	75.00
11	Both	0	0	0	0	1	0	0.5	0	0.5	20.21
12	Both	0	0	0	0	1	1	0	0	0	15.13
13	220	−0.5	−0.5	−0.5	−0.5	0	0	0	0	0	0.00
14	220	0.5	0.5	0	0	0.5	0.5	0	1	0	5.12
15	220	−1	−1	0	0	0	0	0	−0.5	0	49.05
16	Both	0.5	0.5	0	0	0.5	0	0	0	0.5	6.38
17	Both	0.5	0	0.5	0.5	0	0.5	0	0.5	0	85.00

*Model affected by the project.

†Raw material cost.

current needs at the time they decided to invest in it. They chose to buy extra capacity because they expected the volume to increase both through additional sales of current products and through the addition of new product lines. Furthermore, the old paint room equip-ment was outdated and inefficient, and it was becoming very expensive to maintain.

Changes in cost related to proposed alternative engineering projects are provided in Table 8.

APPENDIX A
POSSIBLE PROJECTS LIST

List of Possible Projects That May Be Included to Enhance the Product Features and Marketability of the Incubators:

- Project 1: Digital Temperature Control
- Project 2: Microcomputer-Based Controller
- Project 3: Humidity Measurement
- Project 4: Dual-Chamber Incubator Design
- Project 5: Time-Tagging Incubator Performance Parameters
- Project 6: Standby Power for Uninterrupted Operation
- Project 7: Interface for Remote Diagnostics
- Project 8: Redesign Display Panel (220 Only)
- Project 9: Redesign for ISO 9000 Standards
- Project 10: Prepainted Surface Material
- Project 11: Improved CO_2 Sensor Technologies
- Project 12: Improved O_2 Fuel Cell
- Project 13: Customize Product Modularity and Flexibility
- Project 14: Upgrade Airflow System
- Project 15: Stamped Door Replacement (220 Only)
- Project 16: Digital Printer Interface
- Project 17: Multiple Glass Inner Doors

Project 1: Digital Temperature Control

Description.   The 120 incubator currently uses analog circuitry to control the chamber temperature at a fixed +37°C or adjustable from +5°C above ambient to +60°C. The temperature is set using a front-mounted variable potentiometer. The setpoint adjustment is also performed using analog techniques. This project will focus on using easy-to-use digital control techniques to set the temperature of the chamber within a resolution of 0.1°C using a thermistor temperature sensor.

Engineer's Comments.   "This project would allow us to significantly improve our temperature control capabilities. Additionally, we would make moderate improvements in our ability to rapidly configure a product for a customer and the ease of use of the product. I see a minor benefit in our ability to provide a computer interface to the sensor. This project is fairly straightforward, I am sure we can do it on time and budget."

Project 2: Microcomputer-Based CO_2 Controller

Description.   The 120 incubator currently uses digital circuits to control the CO_2 gas. The desired CO_2 level is set using tamper-resistant screwdriver adjust. The 220 uses a microcomputer to control the CO_2 solenoid for maintaining accurate CO_2 control. The desired values are set digitally using a membrane keypad. In addition, the microcomputer controls and monitors the incubator temperature, incubator water level, the blower motor for the chamber and the door heater. It provides the flexibility to add new features or modify the present design and supports the message display driver board. The microcomputer reduces the electronic component parts significantly by replacing a number of discrete digital integrated circuits.

Engineer's Comments.   "The addition of a microcomputer to control the operating parameters would have a moderate improvement in our ability to control them. And I suppose it might create a little improvement in our ability to rapidly configure products, as well as ease of use. It would surely improve our ability to interface a computer to the system. Our ability to interface the entire unit to a computer would be greatly enhanced. The problem is we don't have much experience with microprocessor design. I'm sure it's not going to be that difficult, but you never know. As far as the other sensors being controlled by the microprocessor—it's not that much more risky. If you can figure it out for one, doing the rest is no big deal."

Project 3: Humidity Measurement

Description. Presently CO_2 levels within the incubator are measured using the thermal conductivity method. The thermal conductivity within the incubator depends on the amount of water vapor (humidity) present in the incubator chamber and the amount of CO_2 present. In order to monitor the CO_2 levels accurately within ±0.1 percent, the humidity of the incubator chamber must be held constant by incorporating a control mechanism to precisely regulate the humidity. Such a mechanism entails higher cost. The 120 and 220 incubators use a relatively simple approach of regulating humidity using a humidity pan and maintaining the water level in it. This technique does not always guarantee a constant humidity level and therefore would affect the CO_2 measurements. One way of compensating for this is to precisely measure the change in humidity level and then use this information to control the amount of CO_2. This project focuses on developing a simple, economical, and accurate method of calibrating the CO_2 levels by measuring the changes in humidity with the following specifications:

Measuring range:	10% to 95% RH
Accuracy:	±2.0% RH
Resolution:	0.1% RH

As an alternate design solution, the humidity measurement can be combined with temperature measurement using an integrated RH/temperature sensor.

Engineer's Comments. "I see this as a real winner for improving the humidity control. It's also going to help us somewhat on rapid configuration and ease of use. An integrated RH/temperature sensor design would put us in the forefront of temperature and humidity control. The problem is, it's not a sure thing. I see this as very risky; I'm not sure we'll end up with what we are shooting for."

Project 4: Dual-Chamber Incubator Design

Description. At the present time, the temperature of the entire incubator chamber can be controlled and monitored precisely as per the specifications of the 120

and 220. If there is a need to provide an environment for cell culture research experiments that require different chamber temperatures, the only solution is to complete the first experiment before the next experiment can be scheduled or to use two separate incubators. This project focuses on the physical design modification that allows two separate temperature control and monitoring capabilities within a single incubator for effective usage of the resources. The internal chamber is partitioned and thermally isolated so that the temperature in each chamber can be independently controlled and monitored according to the following Chamber 1 and Chamber 2 specifications:

Temperature	Specifications
Control	±0.1°C
Range	+5°C above ambient to +50°C
Sensor	Precision thermistor
Controller	Microprocessor controlled
Setpoint	Digital
Uniformity	±0.2°C @+37°C
Tracking alarm	+2.0°C over temperature, −2.0°C
Differential/delay	Under temperature for longer than 15 minutes

Engineer's Comments. "The dual-chamber design would moderately impact our ability to control temperature, humidity, and CO_2. It would hurt our ability to configure products for customers. It's not an easy project, but I think the risks of not completing it are reasonable."

Project 5: Time-Tagging Incubator Performance Parameters

Description. The incubators currently display temperature and CO_2 levels on an LCD readout for the 120 and on vacuum fluorescent display for the 220, respectively. This project will focus on tagging the time associated with each of the measurements taken and sending it to a recorder or a printer or downloading it to a computer via an RS232 Serial Communication Interface. Thus by tagging time with each measurement, it is possible to detect when a power failure occurred, identify how long it took for the power to be restored. This data will also help in determining if an experiment has to be aborted or if it is okay to continue with the experiment after a power failure. It also provides a better perspective on the entire experiment.

Engineer's Comments. "The time-tagging will improve the ease of use as well as the data collection features of our product, but only a small amount. From an engineering standpoint, it's a fairly simple project."

Project 6: Standby Power for Uninterrupted Operation

Description. Certain biological research experiments depend on continuous operation of the incubator. In the 220 incubator, when a power failure occurs, all programmed setpoints and calibration values are saved in an EEPROM. This data is loaded and the experiment resumes once the power is restored. In order to ensure continuity of critical experiments performed, a redundant standby power supply is designed to switch over in case the main power supply fails.

Engineer's Comments. "I think this is a feature the customers really want. You know, it will also improve our ability to control temperature, CO_2, and humidity, in that the operators won't have to check their experiments after each power outage—at least it's a small selling point. The only problem I see is the cost of the unit; it's not a very risky project."

Project 7: Interface for Remote Diagnostics

Description. The 120 and 220 incubators have the ability to perform self-diagnosis to detect:

- Any fault in the sensors.
- Low or high CO_2 levels.
- Low or high temperature levels.
- Low water level in the jacket.
- If the incubator door is open.
- If the incubator temperature exceeded the overtemperature setpoint.

These diagnostics can be performed automatically when the power is turned ON or at any time when needed. When an abnormal condition is detected, alarms are activated and an appropriate message is displayed. These features are very helpful to the users of the incubators. For service technicians to troubleshoot the incubator, it would be economical and convenient if an interface for remote diagnostics can be built into the system. With an RJ-11 modular jack included at the rear of the incubator, the telephone lines can be used for two-way data communication.

Engineer's Comments. "This we should have done years ago. This really improves our ability to service the equipment in the field. It's not an easy project, however. I think it's going to be a moderately difficult project."

Project 8: Redesign Display Panel (220)

Description. Presently the 120 uses liquid crystal displays (LCDs) to display the incubator's numerical performance parameters such as temperature in degrees C and CO_2 level in percents. The LCDs are not used to display messages. Light Emitting Diodes (LEDs) are used to indicate an overtemperature condition or if the water level is low. The contrast of an LCD degrades noticeably as the viewing angle changes from the optimum angle. Also, the contrast is affected with changes in the ambient light conditions. The only benefit is the low cost associated for these generic LCDs.

The 220 incubator, on the other hand, uses a 20×2 vacuum fluorescent alpha-numeric display. This display can accommodate 20 characters per line and can display a maximum of 2 lines. The display serves as a dialog screen, for displaying the incubator parameters and also prompting users with messages and easy directions. It does not have the disadvantages associated with the LCDs but it does add to the final cost of the product.

There are however some disadvantages besides cost. For instance, when an abnormal condition is detected, alarms are activated and appropriate messages are displayed in sequence because of the two-line limit. This project will focus on a display panel design that can display all incubator parameters and conditions simultaneously. The following are some options:

1. Design an alpha-numeric display panel that uses a 20×4 LCD module for the 220.

Engineer's Comments. "This all comes down to economics and aesthetics. Except for the optional interface part, all the projects are easily doable, and even the optional interface is only moderately risky. The LCD display would be sufficient for the customer, although I think the vacuum fluorescent would be more attractive. The linear bar graph would moderately enhance the product."

Project 9: Redesign for ISO 9000 Standards

Description.   Currently the 120 and the 220 incubators are C.S.A certified (Standard C22.2 #151) and U.L. Certified (U.L. 1262). Over 19 percent of our incubators are sold in Europe and we expect that market to grow significantly. To continue to sell in Europe, we must comply with the ISO standards. ISO 9000 is a set of standards for quality assurance administrated by the International Organization of Standards (ISO), in Geneva. Manufacturers and distributors in the European Community are demanding suppliers be accredited according to these standards. These standards are expected to gain worldwide acceptance. Therefore, it is important to redesign these incubators to meet the ISO 9000 Standards.

Engineer's Comments.   "There are no technical hurdles in doing the re-designs, it's just a matter of how much manpower you throw at it. It's (ISO 9000) a requirement to doing business now in Europe."

Project 10: Prepainted Surfaces

Description.   This project involves the selection of vendors who can provide prepainted incubator enclosures. This will result in a significant savings in the number of labor hours in the paint room, but will increase the material costs.

Engineer's Comments.   "This is a fairly straightforward project, requiring manufacturing engineering and mechanical engineering input, primarily. It's a very low-risk cost reduction project."

Project 11: Improved CO_2 Sensor Technologies

Description.   Currently, the 120 and the 220 incubators make use of thermal conductivity sensors to measure CO_2 levels within a range of 0–20 percent. The goal of this project is to enhance the sensor reliability by using better sensors and eliminating moving parts. A heterogeneous combination of infrared, ultrasonic, or

humidity-compensated thermal conductivity sensor design is undertaken to accurately monitor and control the CO_2 level independent of temperature and humidity within a range of 0–15 percent.

Engineer's Comments.   "This would be a major enhancement to our ability to control CO_2. The problem is, it's not a well-developed sensor technology and it's pretty risky. This would also improve slightly our product configuration needs as well as ease of use."

Project 12: Improved O_2 Fuel Cell

Description.   For cytogenetic research and superior culturing needs, O_2 levels are electronically controlled within ±0.1 percent in the range of 2–20 percent. The O_2 sensor is an accurate direct set/read fuel cell. Current O_2 cell life is three to five months. In this project, the design will focus on enhancing the cell life to support easy O_2 control for in vitro modeling of any in vivo environment.

Engineer's Comments.   "This is another project that, if successful, would be a major accomplishment for the engineering group. The O_2 fuel cell project will be very risky, but when its over, we'll have something to be proud of."

Project 13: Customize Product Modularity and Flexibility

Description.   Currently, the 220 incubator is designed to be versatile. This model can accommodate several lab layouts by having the flexibility of configuring the incubator with a left-hand hinged door or a right-hand hinged door, or as an independent unit that can be set on a countertop or as a unit that can be stacked on top of other units. The 220 is a truly a global incubator since it is also designed to accommodate virtually all world electrical voltages. The incubator has been designed to operate on 90–125 volts, 50–60 Hz, or 180–250 volts, 50/60 Hz. The modularity and flexibility is further enhanced by allowing the user to choose the sensor technologies as well.

Engineer's Comments.   "This would have a big impact in our desire to put out configurable products as well as being inexpensive to repair. It's moderately risky, though—it's just difficult to say what problems you'll encounter when you try to minimize product differences."

Project 14: Upgraded Airflow System

Description.   At present the 220 incubator has a sterile HEPA filter (99.97 percent efficient at 0.2 microns) which continually returns contaminant-free air to the chamber atmosphere, thus protecting the chamber contents. This airflow process eliminates the need for unproven methods of heat disinfection which are time-consuming and ineffective. An improved airflow system will further increase the resistance to contamination. This entails optimizing the airflow patterns and velocities to control unavoidable airborne contamination and provide ideal cell temperature, CO_2 and humidity conditions to enhance cell growth.

Engineer's Comments.   "This is something we need to do to reduce the potential contamination significantly. This is a moderately risky project, in that when you redesign the airflow, you don't know what set of problems you'll run into."

Project 15: Stamped Door Replacement (220 Only)

Description.   The 220 has a very aesthetic, yet costly, stamped door. This project will redesign the door for in-house production capability. It is estimated that the customer technical ranking for the stamped door was 45.

Engineer's Comments.   "A fairly straightforward project once again. Low risk."

Project 16: Digital Printer Interface

Description.   In this project a small programmable digital printer interface is designed to record the temperature in Fahrenheit or Celsius, percent CO_2, percent relative humidity, and percent O_2, at any given time of the experiment. The printer interface will be able to send data to the printer even when the power fails. In addition, diagnostic messages can be sent to the printer when the main display fails.

Engineer's Comments.   "I think this will have a moderate impact in our customers' data needs as well as the ease-of-repair issue. It's a pretty easy project, too."

Project 17: Multiple Glass Inner Doors

Description.   In this project the front door of the 120 and 220 incubators will be redesigned with the objective of viewing the interior of the chamber without opening the door. The new see-through door will be manufactured using a transparent material for improved visibility. Also, in order to reduce the CO_2 consumption and leakage, the large door will be replaced by multiple smaller doors.

Engineer's Comments.   "This should have a small effect on temperature, CO_2, and humidity control, but a bigger impact on chamber visibility and overall appearance. You know, it may seem like an easy project, but a lot of things could go wrong to delay it. It's so-so in risk."

APPENDIX B
CUSTOMER SURVEY ON THE PROPOSED PROJECTS

Ten customers were surveyed concerning the proposed projects. The comments of the customers indicate the extent to which they believe each project will meet the needs for the stated features.

Project 1: Digital Temperature Control.

- **Customer 1:** "This would be a moderate improvement to our ability to manage the temperature of the environment. I think it might also help a little with the ease of use and our ability to collect data on the experiments."
- **Customer 2:** "This would help moderately. Mostly in temperature control. I don't see any benefits elsewhere."
- **Customer 3:** "That's a big help to me. We need better temperature control."
- **Customer 4:** "I'd say it was a moderate improvement in temperature control. A slight improvement in data acquisition."
- **Customer 5:** "Good improvement. Moderate impact to temperature control and ease of use. Slight improvement in data acquisition."
- **Customer 6:** "Moderate improvement in temperature control."
- **Customer 7:** "Slight improvement in temperature control and data acquisition."
- **Customer 8:** "Moderate improvement in temperature control."
- **Customer 9:** "That's a good change. I think it would be a big improvement in temperature control and moderate improvement in ease of use of the incubator."
- **Customer 10:** "Moderate improvement in temperature control."

Project 2: Microprocessor-Based Control.

- **Customer 1:** "As far as the operating parameters (CO_2, humidity, temperature) are concerned, I see this as a moderate improvement. I also see ease of use and data acquisition impacted slightly."
- **Customer 2:** "Yeah, this would be a moderate improvement for us."
- **Customer 3:** "We could use better control of the operating parameters. A moderate improvement, I'd say. Also helps make the incubator easier to use."
- **Customer 4:** "Moderate improvement."
- **Customer 5:** "Well, it would make the incubator easier to use for sure. I'd say that was a moderate improvement. I don't need tighter temperature or other control, so that's a slight improvement, I'd say, in the operating parameters. A slight improvement in data handling, too."
- **Customer 6:** "Good feature. I'd say a big improvement in operating parameters."
- **Customer 7:** "Moderate improvement in temperature, CO_2, and humidity control."
- **Customer 8:** "Slight improvement in operating parameters, ease of use, and data acquisition."
- **Customer 9:** "Moderate improvement."
- **Customer 10:** "Moderate improvement in temperature, CO_2, and humidity control."

Project 3: Humidity Measurement.

- **Customer 1:** "I see this as a big improvement in humidity control and a moderate improvement in contamination control."
- **Customer 2:** "Moderate improvement in contamination and humidity control. Slight impact to ease of use and data acquisition."
- **Customer 3:** "Big improvement in humidity control. Moderate improvement in contamination control. Slight improvements in ease of use and temperature control."
- **Customer 4:** "Good idea. I see it as a moderate improvement in humidity and

contamination control as well as an improvement in data acquisition."

- **Customer 5:** "I see this as a big help in humidity control. Also a help in contamination control."
- **Customer 6:** "Moderate improvement in humidity and contamination control."
- **Customer 7:** "Boy, that would be a big improvement in humidity control, which would probably lead to an improvement in contamination control. I also see some improvement in ease of use as well as data acquisition."
- **Customer 8:** "Moderate improvement in contamination control. Big improvement in humidity control."
- **Customer 9:** "Moderate improvement."
- **Customer 10:** "Big improvement in humidity and contamination control. Moderate improvement in data acquisition. Slight improvement in ease of use."

Project 4: Dual-Chamber Incubator Design.

- **Customer 1:** "This is a real benefit in my opinion. Primarily, I see it reducing my risk of contamination. It also helps with controlling the operating parameters better."
- **Customer 2:** "This would help moderately. I don't do many experiments that would run in just one chamber dimension as you have spec'd it. It helps with contamination control, but I don't see that big of a deal with other parameters (CO_2, temp, RH)."
- **Customer 3:** "Yeah, I like it. It would be a big help with contamination problems. I see it helping somewhat with controlling temp, RH, and CO_2."
- **Customer 4:** "I don't need it."
- **Customer 5:** "I've been suggesting you guys do this for years. It helps me out by controlling the operating parameters. It makes a big difference."
- **Customer 6:** "Sure that sounds like an improvement that would help me with contamination issues moderately. I don't see that much impact for operating parameters."

- **Customer 7:** "The chambers aren't big enough already—now you're going to cram two chambers in the space of one. No thanks."
- **Customer 8:** "I'd consider it, but I don't see it as that much of an improvement in any area. Maybe a little in contamination control."
- **Customer 9:** "Yeah, I think it needs to be done. It would speed my test along because I wouldn't have to use the temperature control so much."
- **Customer 10:** "I'd buy it. I need the extra flexibility of running small tests. From a temp and RH standpoint it would be a big benefit. A little impact on contamination and CO_2 control, too."

Project 5: Time-Tagging Incubator Performance Parameters.

- **Customer 1:** "I'd like to see a feature where we could download data to the computer. I think it would moderately help our testing analysis."
- **Customer 2:** "That's a good idea. It would help us somewhat in problem detection."
- **Customer 3:** "It would assist us a little. Not that much though."
- **Customer 4:** "I don't need that."
- **Customer 5:** "I could use it. Sometimes we're not sure exactly what caused a problem. It's not a major benefit to what we do, but it would help somewhat."
- **Customer 6:** "I think we need that. We need to do more quantitative analysis of problems. It would be a big help."
- **Customer 7:** "That's good. It would help us. It's not something I would pay a lot for, but it could save us some time."
- **Customer 8:** "Sure, it would help. I think it could save us maybe four to five hours each time we have to diagnose a problem. It's not a great help, I'd call it an average benefit."
- **Customer 9:** "It wouldn't help me that much."
- **Customer 10:** "I would use it. I could do a better job of pinpointing problems. I think it a very good idea."

Project 6: Standby Power for Uninterrupted Operation.

- **Customer 1:** "We don't have many power problems. I don't see a big need for it."
- **Customer 2:** "I guess some people could use it but not us."
- **Customer 3:** "I'd like to see it as an option. I would consider it."
- **Customer 4:** "I don't need it."
- **Customer 5:** "Our power is pretty reliable. I wouldn't need it."
- **Customer 6:** "No."
- **Customer 7:** "We have a central backup power unit. I don't need one for each incubator."
- **Customer 8:** "I'd look into it. Sometimes we have power problems. I guess it all depends on what it costs."
- **Customer 9:** "No need."
- **Customer 10:** "I don't think so."

Project 7: Interface for Remote Diagnostics.

- **Customer 1:** "Whatever you can do to get us up and running is fine by me. It would be a big help, but you know your units don't go down that often."
- **Customer 2:** "If it would get us back online quickly, that's a big help."
- **Customer 3:** "It's good to have, but I don't know that I would pay a lot for it. The incubators are pretty reliable so I'm not sure that I would be using that feature that often."
- **Customer 4:** "Good idea. I like the idea of getting the incubator back online quickly. It's a big deal."
- **Customer 5:** "No. I like to have the service tech out here so I can get some other things checked out without the cost of a service charge."
- **Customer 6:** "Yeah, that's a good idea. If you could save me from downtime, I'd pay for it. It's a big help."
- **Customer 7:** "Faster service, that's fine with me. As long as the job gets done. It would be a big advantage to us to get the unit up and running faster."

- **Customer 8:** "The units don't go down that often that I would consider remote diagnostics to be that important."
- **Customer 9:** "That's what we are looking for. Better service. I think I'd pick any model that had that type of feature."
- **Customer 10:** "Good idea, but the units aren't down that much. When you're down, it would be a big help, but we are not down that often."

Project 8: Redesign Display Panel (220).
No customer survey was requested on this.

Project 9: Redesign for ISO 9000 Standards.

- **Customer 1:** "That's not important to me."
- **Customer 2:** "I don't need that."
- **Customer 3:** "We aren't European, but I guess it's important for your export business."
- **Customer 4:** "No."
- **Customer 5:** "Don't need it."
- **Customer 6:** "It's a requirement with us."
- **Customer 7:** "We are also going to ISO 9000 certification. I think the push will be for vendors, like you, next."
- **Customer 8:** "It's required from our suppliers."
- **Customer 9:** "No."
- **Customer 10:** "I don't need it."

Project 10: Prepainted Surfaces.
No customer survey was requested on this.

Project 11: Improved CO_2 Sensor Technologies.

- **Customer 1:** "I don't need it."
- **Customer 2:** "That would be a moderate improvement to CO_2 control."
- **Customer 3:** "Slight improvement to CO_2 control."
- **Customer 4:** "No need."
- **Customer 5:** "I think it might help a little with CO_2 control. Nothing else."
- **Customer 6:** "Slight improvement in CO_2 control."
- **Customer 7:** "Slight improvement in CO_2 control. Maybe contamination, too."

- **Customer 8:** "Moderate improvement in contamination control."
- **Customer 9:** "Moderate improvement."
- **Customer 10:** "Slight improvement in CO_2 control."

Project 12: Improved O_2 Fuel Cell.

- **Customer 1:** "We would like a longer fuel cell life. I'd call it a big improvement."
- **Customer 2:** "That's a real improvement. Do it."
- **Customer 3:** "We don't do that type of work. No need for it."
- **Customer 4:** "I'd like to see that. It would be a real improvement."
- **Customer 5:** "We need improvements in this area. If you can achieve what you say you can it would be a significant improvement."
- **Customer 6:** "Good idea. How soon can you get it done? It would be a big help for us."
- **Customer 7:** "No need."
- **Customer 8:** "That's a good idea. I think we would be very interested because it would improve our productivity greatly."
- **Customer 9:** "I'd buy it. We do a lot of cytogenetic research. It would help us a lot."
- **Customer 10:** "I like the idea. We need better performance from the fuel cell. Could be a big improvement."

Project 13: Customize Product Modularity and Flexibility.

- **Customer 1:** "I like the idea of having better customization options. I think in terms of physical accomodation it's a moderate improvement. It also lets me tailor the operating parameter control better to what I need. I'd say a slight improvement there. Also helps in the display selection area."
- **Customer 2:** "Slight improvement in physical accommodation."
- **Customer 3:** "Moderate improvement in physical accommodation. Slight improvement in operating parameters."

- **Customer 4:** "Good idea. I think it would be a big improvement in picking what I need—I guess you call that physical accommodation."
- **Customer 5:** "Slight improvement in physical accommodation."
- **Customer 6:** "Moderate improvement in physical accommodation. Slight improvement in operating parmaeter control."
- **Customer 7:** "I don't see a need for all these options."
- **Customer 8:** "I think it would be a moderate improvement in physical accommodation as well as operating parameter control."
- **Customer 9:** "A moderate improvement in physical accommodation. Slight improvement in temperature, CO_2, and humidity control and displays."
- **Customer 10:** "Slight improvements in operating parameter control and physical accommodation."

Project 14: Upgrade Airflow.

- **Customer 1:** "This could be a big impact to contamination control."
- **Customer 2:** "I think it would be a moderate improvement to operating parameter control, as well as contamination control."
- **Customer 3:** "Contamination control, contamination control, contamination control. That's the issue and this would be a big help."
- **Customer 4:** "I see a big impact in contamination control. Slight impact in operating parameter control."
- **Customer 5:** "Moderate impact to operating parameter control. Big impact to contamination control."
- **Customer 6:** "Significant impact to contamination control."
- **Customer 7:** "Big benefit to contamination control. Slight benefit to operating parameters and physical accommodation."
- **Customer 8:** "Contamination control improvement would help us significantly. Small impact to operating parameters and physical accommodation."

- **Customer 9:** "Big improvement in contamination control. Small improvement in operating parameters."
- **Customer 10:** "Significant improvement in contamination control. Slight improvement in physical accommodation as well as operating parameter control."

Project 15: Stamped Door Replacement (220 Only).

No customer survey was requested on this.

Project 16: Digital Printer Interface.

- **Customer 1:** "I wouldn't use it."
- **Customer 2:** "I'd like to see it, but I don't think I'd pay much for that feature."
- **Customer 3:** "I don't need it."
- **Customer 4:** "No."
- **Customer 5:** "I like it. I think it would be a moderate improvement."
- **Customer 6:** "I don't see a need for that."
- **Customer 7:** "I don't want it."
- **Customer 8:** "Good idea. A slight improvement."
- **Customer 9:** "Slight improvement."
- **Customer 10:** "No."

Project 17: Multiple Glass Inner Doors.

- **Customer 1:** "The smaller doors would be a nice feature. I'd say it was a big improvement."
- **Customer 2:** "I like the idea. Moderate improvement in contamination control."
- **Customer 3:** "That's a good idea. I think it would help us with control of all operating parameters, as well as contamination control."
- **Customer 4:** "Good idea. I think it would be a big improvement."
- **Customer 5:** "I don't think so."
- **Customer 6:** "Sounds interesting. Probably only a slight improvement."
- **Customer 7:** "Big improvement. When could you have something available?"
- **Customer 8:** "I'd like to see multiple doors. It would help us a lot, if it's done right."
- **Customer 9:** "I think that's a moderate improvement."
- **Customer 10:** "I would look hard at something like that. If it would help us with contamination control, it could be a big help."

CASE 4–2
BROOKTROUT TECHNOLOGY, INC.: THE COMMERCIALIZATION PROCESS

Raymond M. Kinnunen
Thomas E. Hulbert

Brooktrout Technology, Inc., had gone public in October of 1992. Eric Giler, president and one of the founders of Brooktrout, reflected on the decision-making process that top management went through in order to go public:

> One aspect was that the public offering market was pretty hot. But the way that we came into the process was that we were at the next stage asking ourselves—what is the next thing that we do?
>
> The first goal of the company was to make a prototype and once we did that then let's see if anyone wants to buy it, sell some. Then we raised some money and each one of those was just a different challenge. Somewhere along the line we turned profitable. Actually it was the 3rd quarter of 1990.
>
> Once you do that you try to grow it faster, so what's the next thing you do?—go public.

The date of the prospectus was October 20, 1992, and the Underwriters offered 1,600,000 shares of Brooktrout at $10 per share to the public. The offering was successful and all shares were sold. The common stock was offered through the National Association of Securities Dealers Automated Quotation (NASDAQ) National Market System under the symbol BRKT. During the remainder of 1992 the stock traded in the range of $12 to $18.

The Company[1]

Brooktrout Technology, Inc., was founded on 1984 by Eric Giler, David Duehren, and Patrick Hynes; all had worked together previously at Teradyne, Inc. (see Exhibits 1–2 for financial statements). Eric Giler had

received an undergraduate degree in management science from Carnegie-Mellon and an M.B.A. from Harvard (in 1982). Pat Hynes (vice president of engineering) and Dave Duehren (vice president of R&D) were electrical engineers. Both had bachelor's degrees from MIT; Duehren's M.S. was also from MIT while Hynes's was from Columbia. Hynes, an avid trout fisherman, chose the name for the new company. (See Exhibit 3 for company management profiles.) Brooktrout designed, manufactured, and marketed computer hardware and software products for use in facsimile (fax) and voice messaging applications in telecommunications and networking environments. The company's products helped direct the flow of electronic information efficiently and addressed the growing use of fax in business communications. Brooktrout sold its products to original equipment manufacturers (OEMs), value-added resellers (VARs), and system integrators, including American Telephone and Telegraph, MCI International, Inc., Octel Communications Corporation, and Sharp Electronics Corporation.

The company's first products were voice processing boards and voice mail systems based on those boards. The company became a significant supplier of small-business-oriented, personal computer–based voice mail systems for OEMs. Since 1990, the company has been AT&T's sole supplier of Merlin Mail, a voice messaging/automated attendant system for the Merlin and Merlin Legend telephone systems, which the company believed to be the sales leaders in the market for small business telephone systems.

Brooktrout had been particularly active in the development of products for enhanced fax applications, which integrated the processing power of computers with the information transmission capabilities of fax. Enhanced fax applications provided communications management and specialized service support capabilities that were not available with ordinary fax machines. An example of an enhanced fax automated information retrieval and delivery application using Brooktrout's Flash-Fax system could be accessed by dialing 1-800-7-BROOKT (1-800-727-6658). The Flashfax system

---

[1] A major portion of this section on the company was taken directly from the prospectus dated October 20, 1992.
Raymond M. Kinnunen and Thomas E. Hulbert, *Northeastern University* Management, cooperated in the field research for this case, which was written by them solely for the purpose of stimulating student discussion. All events and incidents are real. Copyright © 1993 by the National Consortium for Technology in Business, c/o the Thomas Walter Center for Technology Management, Auburn University, Auburn, Alabama.

Exhibit 1

BROOKTROUT TECHNOLOGY, INC.
Statements of Operations
(in thousands, except share data)

	Year Ended December 31,			Nine Months Ended September 30,	
	1989	1990	1991	1991	1992
				(Unaudited)	
Revenue (includes sales to a stockholder of $1,120, $581, $326 and $309 for 1989, 1990, 1991 and the nine months ended September 30, 1991, respectively)	$2,856	$5,662	$ 8,040	$ 5,476	$ 8,682
Cost and expenses:					
Cost of product sold	1,267	3,600	4,025	2,896	4,138
Research and development	571	1,055	1,182	808	1,310
Selling, general and administrative................	1,112	1,738	1,998	1,427	2,003
Total cost and expenses.......................	2,950	6,393	7,205	5,131	7,451
Income (loss) from operations	(94)	(731)	835	345	1,231
Other income (expense):					
Interest income	6	42	45	33	49
Interest expense..............................	(142)	(86)	(36)	(36)	(19)
Total other income (expense)	(136)	(44)	9	(3)	30
Income (loss) before income tax provision (benefit) and extraordinary items	(230)	(775)	844	342	1,261
Income tax provision (benefit)	—	(122)	340	137	505
Income (loss) before extraordinary items..............	(230)	(653)	504	205	756
Extraordinary gains on extinguishment of debt (net of income taxes of $122, $53 and $7 in 1990, 1991 and the nine months ended September 30, 1991, respectively)....................................	—	184	79	11	—
Extraordinary item—Reduction of income taxes due to carryforward of prior years' operating losses..........	—	—	323	119	316
Net income (loss)	$ (230)	$ (469)	$ 906	$ 335	$ 1,072
Pro forma income per common share:................					
Before extraordinary items			$.17	$.07	$.29
Extraordinary items.............................			.13	.04	.11
Net.......................................			$.30	$.11	$.40
Pro forma weighted average number of common and common equivalent shares			2,987,851	2,987,851	2,650,924

provided callers the opportunity to select or request, through use of a telephone Touch-Tone keypad, information for transmission by fax to a predetermined fax number.

During the 1980s and early 1990s the use of fax transmission had increased greatly to assume a role of major importance in business communications. The widespread acceptance in fax had led to increasing interest in enhanced fax applications, which started with the basic elements of fax transmission and added further value through the ability to manage fax communication electronically. Enhanced fax applications integrated the processing power of computers with the information transmission capabilities of fax. The integration was

EXHIBIT 2

BROOKTROUT TECHNOLOGY, INC.
Balance Sheets
(in thousands, except share data)

	December 31,		September 30, 1992	Pro Forma September 30, 1992 (Note 1)
	1990	*1991*		
			(unaudited)	*(unaudited)*
Assets				
Current assets:				
Cash and equivalents......................................	$ 455	$ 1,700	$ 2,036	$ 2,036
Accounts receivable (less allowance for doubtful accounts of				
$13, $75 and $131 in 1990, 1991 and 1992, respectively).......	1,162	1,333	1,302	1,302
Inventory	789	419	860	860
Prepaid royalties and other	114	95	131	131
Total current assets	2,520	3,547	4,329	4,329
Equipment and furniture:				
Computer equipment.............................	257	257	427	427
Furniture and office equipment.........................	102	114	152	152
Total...	359	371	579	579
Less accumulated depreciation and amortization.............	(195)	(235)	(291)	(291)
Equipment and furniture—net.........................	164	136	288	288
Long-term portion of prepaid royalties	51	—	—	—
Deposits and other......................................	41	10	90	90
Total..	$ 2,776	$ 3,693	$ 4,707	$ 4,707
Liabilities and Stockholders' Equity (Deficiency)				
Current liabilities:				
Demand notes payable to banks..........................	$ 366	$ —	$ —	$ —
Current portion of long-term debt	121	89	21	21
Accounts payable.....................................	1,146	880	941	941
Customer deposits....................................	—	449	347	347
Accrued warranty costs................................	30	54	73	73
Accrued compensation and commission....................	89	234	220	220
Other accrued expenses................................	192	266	554	554
Accrued income taxes.................................	—	68	14	14
Total current liabilities	1,944	2,040	2,170	2,170
Deferred rent	143	146	82	82
Long-term debt	88	—	55	55
Commitments...				
Redeemable convertible preferred stock at redemption value; 1,066,667 shares issued and outstanding in 1990, 1991 and 1992 (none outstanding pro forma in 1992) (aggregate liquidation preference, $1,937 in 1992)	1,713	1,841	1,937	—
Stockholders' equity (deficiency):				
Common stock, $.01 par value, authorized, 7,500,000 shares; issued and outstanding, 2,116,507 shares in 1990 and 1991, 1,704,655 shares in 1992 (2,447,031 shares pro forma in 1992)	21	21	17	24
Additional paid-in capital	2,119	1,991	1,720	3,650
Deficit...	(3,252)	(2,346)	(1,274)	(1,274)
Stockholders' equity (deficiency)	(1,112)	(334)	463	2,400
Total..	$ 2,776	$ 3,693	$ 4,707	$ 4,707

Exhibit 3

Company Management

Eric Giler has been president of Brooktrout since its inception in 1984 and is a company founder. He has considerable experience in technical marketing and sales. Prior to that he was a product manager with Teradyne, Inc., a leader in automatic test equipment (ATE). He began his career as applications engineering manager for Intec Corp. in Europe. Intec is a U.S.-based maker of laser inspection systems for process control applications.

Mr. Giler is a cofounder and officer of the International Computer Facsimile Association and represents Brooktrout as a member of the American Electronics Association and Massachusetts Computer Software Council. A frequent speaker at industry events, he has a B.S. degree in Management Science from Carnegie-Mellon University and an M.B.A. from the Harvard Business School.

David Duehren, another Brooktrout founder, is vice president of research and development. His experience includes work in digital signal processing, speech processing, and analog circuit design. Duehren was a design engineer at Teradyne, Motorola, and Codex. He received his bachelor and master of Science degrees in electrical engineering from Massachusetts Institute of Technology.

Patrick Hynes, vice president of engineering, is the third Brooktrout founder. He has worked in the areas of digital circuit design, digital speech technology, and software development. He held the position of design engineer at Teradyne and at IBM's Watson Research Laboratory. Hynes has a B.S. degree in electrical engineering from Massachusetts Institute of Technology and a master's degree in electrical engineering from Columbia University. Hynes, an avid trout fisherman, chose the name of the company.

Steve Ide, vice president of sales and marketing, is a 20-year veteran of the communications industry. Prior to joining Brooktrout he was president and founder of Computer Telephone Corp., a publicly held regional interconnect company, and a vice president of operations for Rolm of New England Corp.

Robert Leahy, vice president of finance and operations, has a diverse background in high technology finance. Prior to joining Brooktrout, he was corporate controller and treasurer for Cambridge Robotics Systems. Mr. Leahy has worked in corporate finance at Data General Corp. and in manufacturing finance with the Foxboro Company. He received a B.S. degree in accounting and holds an M.B.A. from Bentley College.

---

achieved through digital signal processing (DSP), a technology which permitted the complex signals transmitted through the telecommunications network to be interpreted and rapidly processed in much the same manner as basic numerical data. Since its organization in 1984, Brooktrout had developed considerable expertise in DSP as used in fax and voice messaging applications, and had created a strong foundation of DSP-related technology for its products.

Throughout its history, Brooktrout had sought to complement its strength in DSP technology with an applications focus. The company had emphasized the development of firmware and programming interface software tools that support the rapid and flexible development of effective electronic messaging applications. At an early stage in the marketing of its fax products, the company began making drivers (a part of the programming interface software) available for use under a number of popular operating systems. In 1991 Broooktrout introduced its Applications Programming Interface (API) for use by software developers. The API provided a development environment which not only afforded convenient access to the functionality of Brooktrout's TR Series but also supported portability of applications between different major operating systems and expedited adaptation of existing applications to function with Brooktrout's advanced fax and voice products.

Giler commented on the early days of the company:

> We started out proving to ourselves that we could digitize a voice and put it on a disk. We were amazed. It was really neat and nobody had heard of it, but why are people going to pay you money for that? So we raised our first capital.
>
> What actually happened was that Dave saw a presentation in 1982 on digital signal processing and its use over dedicated hardware approaches to the same problems. You could in fact use these newer digital signal processor chips, program them with software so that you could make it speak or modulate data. We said that seems like a very interesting business to be in and so we said how about the convergence of voice, data, and image communications. The thing is that we didn't know that in time image was going to be facsimile.

Eric and his partners decided to seek money privately, and in several private placements in the first two years raised $1.5 million from approximately 50 investors. In 1987 a major telephone equipment manufacturer injected $1 million in cash for a minority equity position. By 1989 Brooktrout had raised a total of $2.5 million to finance its growth. The founders, equal owners from the beginning, still retained approximately a 17 percent ownership stake in Brooktrout after the public offering. Giler commented:

> Actually, we went out and raised capital for seven years funding our losses because there were not enough people to buy our products to fund it versus what we were spending. When we first developed FlashFax we actually put it back on the shelf because there was no marketplace.
>
> The first $200,000 we raised, we blew it all developing our first product. My wife built the first 10 circuit boards on our dining room table. My father showed her how to do it. They were hand soldered. We really didn't have very many resources. Dave wanted to invent a microprocessor on the first board and I was against that because I said how could we afford that and could we really do it.
>
> We pulled out our original business plan recently and we are actually doing what we said we were going to do, which is amazing to me. The thing is, we really didn't know exactly what we were going to be doing, but what is amazing to me is how close we picked it.
>
> In 1985 Dave started developing the first fax board for personal computers. But we took the thing and stuck it back on the shelf because nobody had any fax machines. We figured that nobody would want to buy it. So we continued perfecting the voice technology. Then we resurrected it a year later when we saw a company in California called Gammalink come out with a PC fax board; we dusted it off and made it work. We sold thousands of those and determined that we were not going to be a retail player and would be best served by the OEM market.

In July of 1992, Brooktrout introduced the TR-114 "universal port" product, which was designed to meet the needs of the still evolving electronic messaging market. Unlike other products on the market which were capable of handling only one signal type, the TR-114 processed both fax and voice signals under software control. The product became commercially available in September of 1992 (Exhibit 4 outlines the development history of the company's principal products). Giler commented on the universal port technology:

> We recently came up with a thing called the universal board and that is a bit of a technology leap. That is the biggest development project we have had to date. Instead of doing things with dedicated voice boards and dedicated fax boards, we are doing things with universal boards where software determines what its functionality is going to be.
>
> My contention would be, if we are right then we win everything. If we are wrong we have a really nice business. It's a very low downside risk business. We chose, however, to take a risky technological alternative by using National Semiconductor as the digital signal processing supplier as opposed to a more staid solution like Rockwell that makes most of the fax chips that people use today or Texas Instruments that makes most of the voice chips. We chose to take the more radical approach.
>
> We have done it well in advance of other people and should this universal concept take off, first of all, can we deliver on it and second will people buy into it? If they do, we will win the horse race—we will win the war. We may lose a battle or two along the way but we will win everything.
>
> Intellectually it seems correct but the question is, how quickly is the technology adapted? So we embarked on a rather ambitious project to develop the universal port technology and had a lot of risk involved. We had to do our own custom chips, we had to use uncertain software from National Semiconductor, and we had to bet on what the semiconductor supplier was doing—and sometimes they weren't delivering.
>
> If you look at the stock market, they are betting on the company that this project is going to be successful—the TR 114. And if it hits, the company may grow more than 50 percent next year—it may double.

Brooktrout's strategy was to strengthen its position as a leading supplier of software and hardware for electronic messaging systems manufacturers through technological innovation, applications focus, and strong product development and support. Brooktrout intended to increase the value it brought to its customers through continued development of applications software for full-feathered fax and voice systems. Giler commented:

> The way we sell our circuit boards and software is, we tell the customer here is the capability and you figure out how to use it, so they write the applications software. But technical support becomes a major issue. Our technical support department [people] are all trained engineers who can answer software programming questions, and that is one of the reasons people buy from us—because we have excellent technical support

Dave Duehren, vice president of research and development, commented on the technical support aspect of the Brooktrout strategy:

EXHIBIT 4

History of Brooktrout's Principal Products

First Year Shipped	Product	Description
1992	TR-114	Four-channel universal port product providing integrated processing of various signal types under software control
1991	API	Applications programming interface simplifying the task of writing applications software and supporting portability between widely used operating systems
1990	TR-112 T1	Version of TR-112 permitting connection of multichannel fax systems to T1 high speed digital telephone lines
1990	TR-112	Dual-channel fax product with optional speech playback, DTMF interpretation, and DID capability
1990	Merlin Mail	Voice messaging/automated attendant system for AT&T's Merlin small business telephone system (based on TR-200)
1990	Flash Fax	Self-contained fax-on-demand system (based on TR-111 MC)
1989	TR-200	Dual-channel voice product
1988	TR-111MC	Single-channel fax product designed to provide multiple-channel fax processing on a single computer platform
1987	Fax-Mail 96	Single-channel fax system, including fax transmission, reception, display, and printing capability (based on TR-110)
1987	TR-110	Single-channel fax product
1985	V-Mail 470	Small business voice mail system with up to six channels (based on TR-100)
1984	TR-100	Single channel voice product (sold together with voice mail applications software)

We have people in technical support who have histories of information of what has been passed to the board and what interrupts have come in. We can analyze their software and help them debug it. We have been working with this one division of AT&T where we have debugged half their code.

Typically, what happens is that the people in technical support have their own list of common suggestions and things to try. If that doesn't work then I or somebody else gets called in and we talk about what else we can do. As time goes on it gets higher and higher attention.

We have been in several situations with our fax cards, particularly where we've gotten people to switch from one vendor to us. One of the reasons they always talk about is that we are very good with our technical support.

Brooktrout's technology was embodied in its TR series of products, which provided high-quality processing of fax and voice signals. The TR series products were sold to OEMs VARs, and system integrators who designed those products into their own systems. Brooktrout added value to the TR series for applications software developers and encouraged "design in" selection of its products by offering an advanced Applica-

tions Programming Interface (API) which permitted the developer to make full use of the features of the TR series products with a minimum of programming effort and with full portability across major computer operating systems. Examples of customers for TR Series products included AT&T, Octel Communications Corporation, Centigram Communications Corporation, and Hong Kong Telecommunications Limited. Giler commented on the company strategy:

The issue we deal with competitively is that you go for the design win. That is what you want. You go in for the next thing, whatever that may be. You don't want the customer to have to re-create software because that opens it up to competition again. So when you get the design win it is hard for anyone else to get in and it is hard for you to lose it. I like to call it getting your product designed in. That becomes a barrier to entry.

Brooktrout also designed, manufactured, and marketed complete fax and voice messaging systems and subsystems by incorporating its TR series products with proprietary applications software on a standard micro-computer platform. The system level products were sold primarily to OEMs who incorporated them into product lines sold under the OEMs' names. Brooktrout supplied fax systems to AT&T, Sharp, and Ricoh Electronics, Inc. They also supplied the Merlin Mail voice messaging system to AT&T, which incorporated it into its Merlin and Merlin Legend small business telephone systems.

The Commercialization Process: Some Viewpoints

Bringing a new technology or concept to market was a difficult task for any company. In the 1980s and 90s it seemed that U.S. companies in general were not doing as good a job as some of their foreign competitors. The remainder of this case focuses on some of the problems and issues that a company confronts when attempting to commercialize a technological idea. Giler commented on bringing an idea to the marketplace:

> It was never a question of, could we make it work? It was always a question of, once we made it work, did any one want to buy it? Now we have plenty of people that want to buy the stuff and we find ourselves in a position where we have to make it on schedule and all those other sorts of things.
>
> In the early days of our business the technology was not our biggest problem. Now, what is interesting about it is that the technology tends to become more of a problem. But it is more of the management of the technology and the whole process.
>
> Everything is uncertain, and engineers like to say it will be done when it is done. But you have to live by a schedule and Pat's [Pat Hynes] biggest problem is managing all the people, getting them to commit, because he commits all the time. I will have it done on such and such a date. His ability to hit that or not is based on the whether the people doing the work actually deliver on what they say they are going to do and it gets harder and harder to manage that process.

Duehren commented on the role of the market as opposed to developing technology:

> So far in our history we've had two product ideas—technologies if you will—that we have brought to the market and the success of them has been different in both cases. That had less to do with the actual technology itself, but how we went after the marketplace.
>
> It is easy to get enamored with a technology or an idea, but your success is a commercial venture. It's completely dependent on how you view the market and how you decide to go after it. We were inexperienced both in the sense of

how to go about marketing things, as well as our own design skills, as I look back.

Giler commented on the role of one of his partners and chief scientist, Dave Duehren:

> Dave is the chief scientist and thinks stuff up before anyone else. He is the main strategic technology thinker. He architects it and makes sure it makes sense. He does it with some market input but less than he would like to have.
>
> Then we have this handoff process after he does some amount of creating; it gets handed off to the people that actually do all the implementation. It is very hard to execute the implementation, and you hope he did the right thinking up front because if you do something that's wrong you can spend a lot of money.
>
> It's like the flames get bigger. Jump out of the pan into the fire. It was kind of nice being in the frying pan, at least things were under control.

After obtaining his bachelor's and master's degrees from MIT, Duehren had worked for a couple of years, mostly in research areas trying to apply digital signal processing to speech recognition and designing chips at Motorola, or testing circuits at Teradyne where both applications were at the cutting edge of technology at the time. At those jobs cost was not important and it was more of an experimental environment than production. Duehren commented:

> Moving from that to starting a company and trying to develop a product that you eventually want to produce was a complete shift and something that I had no experience in. When I look back, we made a lot of mistakes and had to go through several revisions before we found the end result.

Commenting further on the early days of developing the technology into a product, Duehren noted:

> We had some idea of the technology but very little idea on how to implement it and very little idea about how it was going to be sold. One thing that we did do right away was to figure out ways to demonstrate it, especially to lawyers and accountants and other people we wanted to take notice of us. So being able to demonstrate some prototype was very important all along, especially trying to raise money and hire professionals.

Pat Hynes, vice president of engineering, commented on the handoff process that Giler had referred to earlier:

> What will happen in the process is that we will first get an agreement that someone will buy it. Then, sometimes Dave will do the early development work, and I will get into it in a slightly later stage and manage to bring it to the market.

That is a handoff that we are still working on. How do we perfect it? How do we do it? In the case of the TR-114, we may have done it a little later than we should have. The question becomes, once you have done a design test, when should you be designing something new?

In the early days the company tried to maintain market focus. Within the first three or four months the founders sat down and wrote down all the applications they could think of where a board was required to digitize voice into Touch-Tones. Voice mail was one they identified and audio-dispersed information was another (a way to retrieve information like a bank account). They identified at least 10 different applications. At that point Duehren remembered them saying, "We have to pick one of them and go after it." Duehren said: "That was our idea of focus so we circled voice mail."

Brooktrout had some successful competitors that took a different approach. Duehren commented:

It isn't that they bet on more things; they had a different market and their concept of focus was different than ours. Our concept was a product focus and theirs was a technology focus. They said, "I've got this technology, what are all the different places I can get into?" As opposed to, "I have this technology and it's really well suited for this particular application."

Hynes commented on the difficulty of a young technology-oriented company keeping focused:

It almost seems that at any point in time there is this infinite number of ways that we can diverge. It's like this constant process of trying to keep ourselves on a sensible path. You know you have to keep things moving technically or you are going to fall behind. On the other hand you can diffuse yourself working with 30 or 40 new products at the same time and getting nothing done. That to me is one of the biggest challenges.

Duehren spent countless hours and months in the lab designing the first boards. There were times when he questioned whether the company had the time to do something over or run another test. He noted:

I think you can make a good argument from a success point of view—whether the company is going to survive—that you always can't design it right the first time because you just don't have the time to do it. It takes a balancing act driven by when your next paycheck is coming, when you have to demonstrate something, and that tends to drive your process a little different than if you are in a purely research environment.

Duehren felt that the most cost-effective marketing of a new product was to have a prototype and demonstrate it to people and get their reactions and see if they will buy one. Recently they had been focusing on product enhancements and building more powerful versions of the basic technology that the company started with. In the beginning it was different, however.

In both cases, the fax and the voice, they were not popular things to do when we started out. Nobody really understood what was going to be good about the technology or why it would be used and if big companies could do market studies to find out. Therefore, big market studies and that kind of approach doesn't work when you talk about new technology, in my opinion. You need to build it and demonstrate it.

Duehren went on, commenting on getting a new product to a beta site:

First of all, getting a beta site is a whole sales process in itself. Getting a beta site for our four-channel fax card is no problem because we have all these people out there that have already taken our two-channel card. We have an established customer base that we are selling into, but when you have a new product, you don't have an established customer base.

When Brooktrout developed their fax board technology, for the first two years they were debugging it using their customers. They were unable to buy the 3,000 different brands of fax machines that were in the world to make sure they could send and receive to everyone of them. The customers became the beta sites and they found that they were fairly tolerable about problems as long as they tried to fix them in a certain amount of time. After that they began selling into industrial applications because they were confident that the performance and compatibility were there. Duehren tied the support aspect of Brooktrout's strategy to getting the customers to become the beta sites.

That gets back to the whole issue of beta sites and throwing things out in the field. If you are going to just dump it on someone and not support it, it better work.

But if you are going to be able to spend the energy and try to work with it and try to find out about it, then it's a little more forgiving of an environment. That is true especially if you are up front with them and tell them that it is new and you are expected to have problems. But that takes good technical support.

Steven Ide was vice president of sales and marketing and a 20 year veteran of the communications industry (see Exhibit 3 for company management profiles). He commented on the commercialization process from a marketing perspective.

> What the job of sales and marketing really has been is to get stuff out of the back room and into the hands of customers and generate a revenue stream. Regardless of how many brilliant engineering people you have, the most difficult thing to do is to respond to the market. That probably is the most difficult challenge facing a high-tech company.

Ide commented on the approach Brooktrout had taken bringing their family of products to the marketplace:

> The path that Brooktrout has taken is such that the products have pyramided in terms of technology. We started with some very simple approaches, single-channel voice cards, single-channel, almost consumer level fax card, but always with a view towards the future. What we did not want to be, however, was a company that sold commodity products to the end user. We wanted to build very high-performance, industrial strength, integrated messaging systems.

Being at the forefront of messaging technology, Brooktrout's major marketing question was how to create awareness of their capabilities in that area and how to get OEMs interested in purchasing from them. In most cases what they did was set up a small dealer network. Ide explained:

> What we would do is go out and set up a few dealers, particularly dealers that carried the current product line, and present them the opportunity to sell all of our products direct and create some pull through the channel. That approach eventually got us OEM contracts with Sharp, Ricoh, and AT&T for those products that we had to create a market awareness for.

Ide summed up his view of the requirements for commercializing a technology:

> The first thing you absolutely have to do is understand what is needed out there, not what you think is needed but what the customer wants. Then you build it and hopefully exceed the requirements.
>
> Sometimes the customer does not know that there is a problem and what you have to do is point it out to them. In that sense, the technologist has to figure out the application or take the technology and figure out what problem it is going to solve. It becomes a different challenge when the customer does not know that there is a problem.

The Engineering Organization

Pay Hynes and Dave Duehren had met each other as freshman in college and had belonged to the same fraternity. Pat reflected on that relationship and how it related to the organization at Brooktrout.

> It may be unusual in business, but we have a level of trust which I think has been useful. We both have interests in researchy things, doing something new in the area, and getting them to the market. The roles that have evolved over the years is that Dave is basically the great idea guy, and Eric too actually. I have thought of lots of ideas, but they tend to nail them pretty quickly. Dave is wonderful at doing the correct solution at the risk of overstating the right way to do it.
>
> I am working at the other end. I am very pragmatic and sometimes too pragmatic to risk taking shortcuts. I spend a lot of time talking to customers, mainly AT&T, so I tend to be very schedule conscious. We tend to temper each other and offset each other's weaknesses. I draw on Dave a lot in terms of, What's the best way to solve this problem? Who should do this? What would you do in this situation? He draws on me in terms of, How do I get this done? How do I get equipment quickly? What do we do here? How do we organize this? Who should be working on it? Dave characterizes it as the producer-director scenario and I think that is a good way to describe it.

In the fall of 1992 Brooktrout had changed the structure of the engineering department. Previously it was Duehren and Hynes with 18 or 19 people reporting to Hynes. They observed that there were people in the organization with experience and natural leadership abilities. They decided to formalize that. Hynes commented:

> We formed three groups trying to recognize the kinds of things that we build and sell. One group is the Hardware Group, which is basically whatever we design at the board level and system level hardware.
>
> The second group is the Core Technology Group, which is basically all of the firmware and the software tool kits that support our fax and voice products—tools that would be sold to other people who would be building our fax and voice products.
>
> The third group we call our OEM Systems Group, which is our voice mail and fax systems. They help the customer with the coreware and the tools they develop and hardware from the hardware group and package it into outgoing systems.
>
> We hold regular engineering meetings for the whole department every two weeks. I have a meeting with the

three group leaders on a weekly basis with the idea of just trying to make sure that everyone knows, what did you do last week and what are you going to do in the next week? It is just a way of exchanging information so that I know what is going on especially in terms of problems or changes that someone has made so I am fully informed when talking to our customers.

One of the things that I want to make sure continues is that we get more engineers who are people that understand that we look seriously at different source code and hardware and software for the system because we don't want to waste money. If you go and spend six months designing something that has no price or competitive advantage over something else, you just wasted a lot of money. You need to design things that have a reason why yours is better.

Continuing on the people aspect of the organization, Hynes commented:

One of the other challenges we have right now is hiring people that we can learn from. We have been fortunate in the last couple of years to bring in some people that have tremendous knowledge in the hardware and software area. They are much better hardware and software designers than I am. I learn quite a bit from them. What we are trying to do is let them have their head, but at the same time understand what they are doing in the process.

The future looked bright for Brooktrout. In early 1993 the stock continued to trade in the $15 range. The market was huge, but continuing to develop new products and enhance existing products, and following through to commercialization was a never-ending challenge. Ide commented on the Brooktrout approach:

Our choice is that we want to be where the high margins are and where it is very difficult to copy us. We want to create big barriers to entry and software is an enormous barrier because of the time it takes to develop it. In order to do that you need good people and our people are wizards.

5   INNOVATIONS IN MANUFACTURING

READING 5–1
MAKING SENSE OUT OF MANUFACTURING INNOVATIONS*

Paul M. Swamidass
Auburn University

Traditionally, when people speak of design, they are referring to a front-end activity that precedes a sequence of activities such as tooling and manufacturing. In reality, design has become more and more integrated with these activities, whose effects can be seen on the output side of the firm. This changing reality is addressed in this article.

We recently completed a study which investigated two kinds of technologies in U.S. manufacturing plants: soft and hard.[1] In manufacturing, the conversion process that takes raw materials, equipment, labor, and the like, and turns them into finished products uses both hard technologies (which consist of a combination of hardware, equipment, computers, and software) as well as soft technologies (which are know-how, manufacturing techniques, and procedures). Our study focused on six soft and nine hard technologies. From that study, we will abstract a brief explanation oriented for designers. Among the questions we will address are the following:

- How do the various technologies fit together?
- How do they complement each other?
- Are there any notable benefits associated with manufacturing technology use?
- What are the implications of these manufacturing technologies for designers?

In recent years, the range of manufacturing technologies available to manufacturers has grown substantially. Manufacturers often view the hard and soft technologies seen in Figure 1 as different entities. This paper encourages them to view soft and hard technologies as a single entity, as a first step towards bringing greater integration in their use.

But the average manufacturer may find the task of selecting the appropriate soft and hard technologies challenging because, with so many different ones now available for their use, it can be quite confusing as to how the various technologies work together meaningfully.

Figure 2 shows how various hard and soft technologies can be pieced together into an effective and efficient whole: some call it *integration*. Improved plant performance will result when the collection of hard and soft technologies in the nucleus and the shells surrounding the nucleus in the figure are assembled by a manufacturer to complement each other. Even this figure does not include the hard technologies which are less frequently used, such as AGV, but which are useful in integrating technologies within a cell. Nor does it include MRP, MRP II, LAN, or CIM, which are useful for integrating the hard technologies of the nucleus with the soft technologies in the surrounding shells, and with the rest of the organization. Several benefits await the manufacturer who can integrate them into a meaningful whole as visualized in Figure 2.

In the study recently completed by the author,[2] which involved 1,042 manufacturing plants in the United States, we found that, among plants employing 100 or more people, at least three-fourths of the plants use CAD, TQM, JIT, CNC, SQC, CAM, and manufacturing cells. It should not come as a surprise to designers that nearly all larger manufacturing plants (those with 100 or more employees) in the United States use computer aided design (CAD). However it may be

---

[1] Paul M. Swamidass, *Technology on the Factory Floor II: Benchmarking Manufacturing Technology Use in the US,* Manufacturing Institute, National Association of Manufacturers, Washington, D.C., 1994.
*This paper is based on a study of manufacturing technology use in the United States partially funded by the National Science Foundation and conducted jointly with the Manufacturing Institute of the National Association of Manufacturers, Washington, D.C., January 1995. Data entry and analyses reported in this paper were conducted by Mike Hickman and Hubert Jerome, Graduate Research Assistants, Thomas Walter Center for Technology Management, Auburn University. Reprinted with permission from *Design Management Journal*, Spring 1995.

---

[2] Ibid.

FIGURE 1

Glossary of Manufacturing Technology Terms

Hard Technologies	*Soft Technologies*

Hard Technologies

1. Automated Guided Vehicles (AGV): AGVs are unmanned carriers or platforms controlled by a central computer that dispatches, tracks, and governs their movements on guided loops. AGVs are primarily useful for materials handling, particularly between workstations as replacements for conventional forklifts and transfer lines.

2. Automated Inspection (AI): Automation of one or more steps involved in the inspection procedure.

3. Computer-Aided Design (CAD): CAD is computer graphics software used in conjunction with hardware that allows engineers and designers to create, draft, manipulate, and change designs on a computer. CAD output is often handed off to CAM.

4. Computer-Aided Manufacturing (CAM): CAM uses computers to control and monitor various manufacturing elements such as robots, CNC machines, and automated guided vehicles.

5. Computer-Integrated Manufacturing (CIM): CIM involves the total integration of all computer systems in a manufacturing facility: accounting, engineering, production, etc. This integration may extend beyond one factory into multiple manufacturing facilities in one or more countries and even, sometimes, into the facilities of vendors and customers.

6. Computer Numerical Control (CNC) Machines: CNC machines are locally programmable, with dedicated micro- or mini-computers. CNC provides great flexibility by allowing the machine to be controlled and programmed on the floor.

7. Flexible Manufacturing Systems (FMS): A flexible manufacturing system is a group of reprogrammable machines linked by an automated material-handling system and a central computer. The intent of such a system is to produce a variety of parts that have similar processing requirements with low setup costs.

8. Local Area Networks (LAN): Local area networks are the backbone of communication systems that connect various devices in a factory to a central control center. The LAN, through the control center, allows the various devices connected to the network to communicate with each other.

9. Robots: The Robotics Institute of America defines an industrial robot as: "A programmable, multifunctional manipulator designed to move material, parts, tools, or specialized devices through various programmed motions for the performance of a variety of tasks." The basic purpose of the industrial robot is to replace human labor under certain conditions, usually dangerous or boring.

10. Just-In-Time (JIT) Manufacturing: The concept of just-in-time manufacturing requires materials and goods to arrive on the shop floor, or to be delivered, "just in time" to be used in production or by the customer. The philosophy of JIT has embedded in it a "continuous habit of improving" and the "elimination of wasteful practices."

Soft Technologies

11. Manufacturing Cells (MC): A manufacturing cell is composed of a small group of workers and machines in a production flow layout—frequently a U-shaped configuration—producing a group of similar items called part families. Proponents of cellular manufacturing have claimed several benefits for this type of dedicated production system, including less inventory, less material handling, improved productivity and quality, improved worker job satisfaction, smoother flow, and improved scheduling and control.

12. Materials Requirements Planning (MRP or MRP I): MRP I is primarily a scheduling technique: it is a method for establishing and maintaining valid due dates or priorities for orders using bills of material, inventory and order data, and master production schedule information as inputs.

13. Manufacturing Resource Planning (MRP II): Manufacturing resource planning is a direct outgrowth and extension of closed-loop materials requirements planning (MRP) through the integration of the business plan, purchase commitment reports, sales objectives, manufacturing capabilities and cash flow constraints.

14. Statistical Quality/Process Control (SQC/SPC): SQC/SPC apply the laws of probability and statistical techniques for monitoring and controlling the quality of a process and its output. SQC/SPC can be used to reduce variability in the process and the quality of output.

15. Total Quality Management (TQM): TQM is built on the principle of continuous quality improvement in manufacturing, as well as the entire organization. It works through frequent feedback of performance measures to various system elements empowered to make changes in their operations so that the system moves closer and closer to its stated goals.

Note: Certain soft technologies such as MRP and MRP II use computers for developing schedules, plans and for maintaining databases. Further, SQC is sometimes implemented on shop floors using ordinary PCs. Some manufacturing cells are very machine intensive, yet it is the *shop-floor's layout, and the nature of the work flow* which create the cell. The point is, when computers are often used to do very mundane activities, the mere use of a generic computer in the implementation of a technology does not make it a hard technology.

Source: Adapted from P. M. Swamidass, *Technology on the Factory Floor II: Benchmarking Manufacturing Technology Use in the U.S.,* Manufacturing Institute, National Association of Manufacturers, Washington, D.C., 1994.

FIGURE 2

How Various Manufacturing Technologies Fit Together

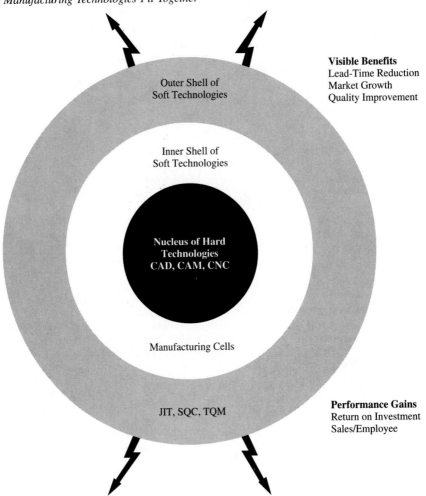

surprising to learn that CAD is the first manufacturing innovation or technology to reach such a level of penetration in manufacturing plants. Given the benefits associated with technology use, and the better performance of larger plants which use more technologies than smaller plants, manufacturers must take seriously the use of manufacturing technologies in their operations.

Benefits

Indeed, manufacturing technologies are associated with notable benefits. We find the most commonly experienced direct benefits from technology use are reduced manufacturing lead time, market-share growth, and improved quality, in that order. Lead-time reduction was mentioned as a direct benefit of technology use by two-thirds of the respondents, market-share growth by 41 percent of the respondents, and progress toward zero defects by 40 percent of the respondents. Lead-time reduction was mentioned far more frequently as a direct benefit of technology use than any other benefit.

One could infer from this finding that investments in manufacturing technologies are frequently directed toward reducing lead time. Designers should relate easily to this finding if they consider how CAD systems actually help them reduce the time for developing better designs, and how more time is therefore available for designing more models and options. Further, when CAD systems are used in conjunction with CNC and CAM, the handoff time between design and manufacturing is substantially reduced.

An excellent example of this is the way the time to develop and introduce new products is being reduced by most manufacturers to keep up with their competition or to stay ahead of competition. The successful efforts of Chrysler Corporation to drastically cut new-car development and introduction time are now well known; Viper, one of Chrysler's sportier introductions, is said to have been accomplished in about 3 years, while it has been customary for United States automakers to take from 8 to 10 years to introduce a new car.

Case Studies in Technology Use: The Use of Manufacturing Cells

The study found that the use of manufacturing cells provided more direct benefits to manufacturers than the use of any other technology. In large plants, nearly three-fourths use manufacturing cells. Considering the fact that manufacturing cells began to get attention in the United States only about 15 years ago, their use has grown faster than most new technologies. Perhaps the well-known benefits of cell manufacturing are attracting more and more use of this technology. According to a report in *The Economist*,[3] manufacturers such as Compaq intend to replace conventional production lines and to invest heavily in manufacturing cells in order to increase the number of models they offer from around 23 to about 100. This is intended to help Compaq compete in more markets, and to take on more competi-

tors; Compaq's thinking may explain why many manufacturers reported market growth as one of the benefits of technology use. A report in *The Wall Street Journal*[4] describes how a similar shift to cellular manufacturing from conventional manufacturing is occurring in plants owned by other well-known Japanese manufacturers. For example, the *Journal* mentions NEC's cellular and cordless phone manufacture as a good candidate for cell manufacturing because, in order to be competitive, the number of models NEC makes has increased from three to nineteen, and the product life cycle has shrunk from three years to one.

Cells are designed to focus on the production of a family of products. In rapidly changing product markets, cells enable frequent changes in the products/models to suit changes in customer tastes; the benefits include the ability to hold on to one's customers as well as the ability to gain new customers. But cells can be very useful even if the products do not undergo changes very frequently. One excellent example of this is the case of the Falk Corporation plant at Auburn, Alabama. This plant makes industrial couplings of various sizes and shapes, but the product undergoes relatively few fundamental design changes; that is, the product design is very stable. Rather, the market for these products is price, delivery, and quality sensitive.

This Falk plant is in the midst of a $10 million modernization project over a period of two to three years. At the end of the modernization project, the plant will be transformed to 100 percent cellular production employing some of the older machines and about 80 percent new equipment. The Falk cells are composed of CNC equipment, which is linked to their CAD systems for smooth transfer of information between the cells and the design office. This plant stands out as an example of how cellular production is not just for manufacturers competing in a rapidly changing product market. According to Don Large, the plant manager, "The desired results of the Falk cellular system will be reduced machine setups, faster throughput of parts, less work-in-process, more just-in-time manufacturing, and increased productivity." He predicts that "the Auburn facility will, after cellular implementation, have a state-of-the-art

---

[3] "The Celling Out of America," *The Economist*, December 17, 1994, pp. 63–64.

[4] See M. Williams, "Some Plants Tear Out Long Assembly Lines, Switch to Craft Work," *The Wall Street Journal*, October 24, 1994, p. A1

coupling manufacturing that will enable Falk to remain a world leader in the coupling market well into the twenty-first century." Falk's action is an example of the strategic use of manufacturing technology to attain the long-term goals of a manufacturer. The advantages of the new technology are that it permits the plant to (1) manufacture couplings in smaller lots without penalty, (2) accommodate changes to the design more efficiently, (3) ship more customer orders on a timely basis, and (4) produce a larger variety of products to attract sales.

Switching to cell production is relatively easy in these assembly operations, which are labor-intensive, without the use of heavy machinery. If expensive machinery is called for in a cell, a plant may be slowed in its progress toward cell manufacturing by the size of the needed investment in new equipment. In such instances, plants may go cellular when older equipment is due for replacement, as in the case of Falk, Auburn. This approach to the timing of the introduction of cells may be attractive in stable product environments typified by the Falk plant—in rapidly changing product environments, the need for product variety and the need to change more rapidly with the needs of the customer may dictate the timing of the introduction of cell manufacturing.

Two Clusters of Technologies

In our study mentioned above, extremely skilled users of JIT reported outstanding performance on a number of measures: return on investment at 17.6 percent as opposed to 12.99 percent for the average plant, rejection and rework at only 2.9 percent as opposed to 4 percent for the average plant, and inventory turns at 9.8 as opposed to 8.04 for the average plant. The study also found that JIT appeared frequently in a cluster of technologies, which included SQC, cells, and TQM. These technologies are mutually complementary in the sense that SQC and cells are useful in the implementation of both JIT and TQM, and that JIT is an excellent vehicle for implementing TQM in manufacturing settings.

Other technologies appear in clusters also. For example, CAD, CAM, and CNC appear together in a cluster in most plants. These technologies, which are used by more than 80 percent of U.S. plants, together form the nucleus of hard technologies used in manufacturing firms. These technologies are mutually complementary: that is, the output of one is the input to the next. This improves the efficiency as well as the effectiveness of the handoff between design and manufactur-

ing. As the handoff is done electronically, it can be almost instantaneous, and so results in a paperless manufacturing environment.

CAD, CAM, and CNC appear together frequently as a cluster of hard technologies because these three are relatively easy to integrate. Therefore the acquisition of one technology builds on one or more existing technologies in this cluster. The resulting synergy multiplies the benefits accrued by any one technology alone. CAD is reported as the most widely used technology in this cluster: therefore it appears that CAD paves the way for the implementation of CNC and CAM. When these three technologies are used in concert, the distance between the designer and the shop floor is drastically reduced, *and the designer becomes a more involved member of the manufacturing system.*

The clusters indicate that there is a pattern to the use of the various hard and soft technologies. For example, manufacturing cells can be assembled from a nucleus of hard technologies (CAD, CAM, and CNC) devoted to the manufacture of a family of components or finished products. At a higher level of aggregation, a cluster of technologies made up of JIT production, SQC, and TQM can use cells as an effective tool to attain the goals of lead-time reduction, low inventory, smooth flow, and improved efficiency and profitability.

Plant Performance

The use of technologies varies with plant size. Small plants (less than 100 employees) tend to use fewer technologies than larger plants (5.4 used by an average small plant versus 9.03 used by an average larger plant). Small plants are extremely skilled users of fewer technologies (1.23 technologies); more so than larger plants (2.57 technologies). This comparison of small and large plants on technology use may explain the statistically significant advantages of larger plants over small plants. For example, larger plants report much higher return on investment (14.7 percent) than small plants (11.5 percent). Larger plants are also more efficient: $144,000 in sales per employee in larger plants versus $114,000 per employee in small plants.

Conclusion

There are some unique characteristics associated with these technologies. Soft technologies such as TQM tend to become popular sooner, since often the sizable capital investment needed for introducing hard technologies slows down their introduction. But manufacturers report that a greater proportion of hard technology users are "extremely skilled users" when compared to soft technology users because it is more difficult to become extremely skilled in the use of soft technologies. Hard technologies, being more narrowly focused than soft technologies (e.g., JIT, TQM), are easier to learn, and once learned, to use with greater dexterity. Because of the broad-based effects of soft technologies, their use is associated with more benefits than hard technologies, which are more narrowly focused.

Most of the technologies described here are used to help manufacturers succeed in competitive environments, where product life-cycles are shrinking, product variety is increasing, typical lot sizes are shrinking, and manufacturability imposes restrictions on the designer. In this environment, the designer must develop newer, highly manufacturable models more frequently. The market demands newer models with greater frequency and the manufacturing technology is geared to handle the increased frequency of new model introductions. Can designers meet this challenge? These technologies can make it a lot easier.

Suggested Reading

Paul M. Swamidass, *Technology on the Factory Floor II: Benchmarking Manufacturing Technology Use in the US.* Washington, DC: The Manufacturing Institute, National Association of Manufacturers, 1994.

READING 5–2
THE CELLING OUT OF AMERICA

Blame the Honourable Evelyn Ellis. In 1894 he commissioned France's Panhard et Levassor to build a car to his own exacting specifications, and became the first man to drive on British soil. Early this century, however, the art of "building to order" was all but killed off by Henry Ford's moving assembly line. Until now, that is. After 80 years of me-too mass production, consumers are once again demanding infinite variety. To meet such demands, firms are adopting "cell manufacturing"—a technique in which small teams of workers make entire products. Can a descendant of the "craft" production that spawned Ellis's boneshaker really rival the economies of scale of mass production?

A study of manufacturing technology in 1,042 American factories, published by the National Association of Manufacturers on December 15th, shows that 56 percent of them are now trying it out to some extent. According to Paul Swamidass of Alabama's Auburn University, who wrote the report, the keenest users are big firms, rather than cottage industries. The survey found that three-quarters of factories with 100 or more employees use cells, compared with 40 percent of smaller plants. That would not surprise Japanese giants such as Mazda, Toyota, and Sony, which have been toying with cells for years. But it is new in America.

In cell manufacturing, workers are divided into teams—usually of between two and 50 employees—grouped around the manufacturing equipment that each needs. A single cell makes, checks, and even packages an entire product or component. Each worker performs several tasks, and every cell is responsible for the quality of its products. As such, cell manufacturing is the ultimate factory-floor refinement of other team-management techniques that western companies have embraced in recent years. But so far, team-based practices have usually focused on bringing together people from different departments, such as design, production, marketing, and sales. Cell manufacturing is a narrower process, concentrated purely on the factory floor.

More important, it directly challenges mass production. Cellists—as they might wish to be known—

concede that long assembly lines of semiskilled workers make sense if you want to churn out large volumes of standardized goods. But introducing variety, or changing the product being made, means stopping the whole assembly line. Breakdowns and shortages are costly for mass-producers, so they have to carry large stocks of parts and spares. And stocks of partly finished products also tend to be high; those that have undergone part of the production process sit idle, waiting for the next stage. Big warehouses and mass production go hand in hand.

By contrast, introducing variety in a cell-based factory is simple: each cell can make a different product. A breakdown or product-change will stop only the cell involved; a slow worker will hinder only his own cell, rather than the entire line. And because products are made in one burst, cells do away with stocks of partly finished goods. Mr. Swamidass notes that, of all the technologies covered in his survey, cells produced the biggest benefits, the most notable of these being speed, productivity, flexibility, and higher quality.

For example, before Harley-Davidson, a motorcycle maker, introduced cells at its engine-and-gearbox plant, components were machined and stored repeatedly by the firm's 900-strong workforce. The parts meandered along the assembly line, often corroding while they sat idle. A cylinder-head took a week to make. Now, manufactured by a two-man cell, the process takes less than three hours. That means that the firm no longer has to carry big stocks so as to be ready if demand suddenly jumps. The upshot, according to Gary Kirkham, a manufacturing manager at the plant, is that the floor space occupied by the factory has fallen by a third. It now turns over its stock 40 times a year, compared with just 4½ times in 1981.

W. L. Gore & Associates, based in Newark, Delaware, tells a similar tale. A privately owned firm with 5,700 employees and annual sales of about $900 million, Gore makes everything from high-tech cables to Gore-Tex fabric. It is adopting cell manufacturing at several of its 46 plants. The effect, says Paul Phillips, an associate at one of the firm's factories (employees at Gore have no job titles), has been to cut the time taken to make its silver-based computer cables by half, to reduce stocks by a third, and to shrink the space taken up by the plant by a quarter. In the past only 75 percent of the products from Mr. Phillips's factory were delivered on time. Now, 97 percent are.

The effect of cells on productivity seems to be equally encouraging. Compaq, a big Texas-based personal-computer maker, has replaced three of its 16 Houston assembly lines with 21 cells; four more will be converted early next year. So far, says Brij Kathuria, manager of product integrity, productivity has risen by between 20 percent and 25 percent. The cost of converting to cells will, he says, "pay back in six months." Lexmark, a manufacturer of computer printers based in Greenwich, Connecticut, has also converted 80 percent of its 2,700-employee factory in Lexington, Kentucky, to cells—and productivity has soared by 25 percent.

Increased flexibility is another gain. Compaq's long-term goal is to build all its computers to the specifications laid down by customers or retailers. With its planned 100 or so cells in Houston, the company will be able to build a wide variety of different models—and to increase or decrease production of individual models in line with demand. With 16 production lines, such adaptability would not be cost-effective. Harley-Davidson's Mr. Kirkham says that cell manufacturing has given the company "huge flexibility" to adjust to short-term fluctuations in demand for its products.

Mine, All Mine

Ask Mr. Kathuria the secret of cells, and he will reply in two words: employee satisfaction. Stuck on an assembly line, each worker may spend just a few seconds on each product before it passes on. Few see the finished widget. Worse, notes Marshall Fisher of Wharton business school, on an assembly line "the first worker never meets the 60th worker." In cells employees see their product through from start to finish: in Mr. Kathuria's words, "They own the serial number." Problems are tackled as they arise, rather than uncovered down the line.

As a result, cell manufacturing leads to big improvements in product quality. At Harley-Davidson's cell-based plants, the number of quality inspectors has been cut significantly, Bill Ramsey, head of operations at Compaq, believes that "a very minimal quality audit" of cells will eventually be needed. Lexmark not only gets better quality, it gets it faster. With its old assembly lines, it used to take several months to raise quality to

acceptable levels when a new product was introduced. Now, this process takes days—and is driven by workers, not managers. As a result, Lexmark's cell-based factories have raised the number of employees per manager from fewer than 20 to around 100.

Cells are not, however, without drawbacks. They work most effectively with products (such as PCs) that rely on a relatively labor-intensive use of flexible machinery for their manufacture, and which share some common "building blocks." Mr. Kirkham notes that the heat-treatment of some motorcycle components can at present be carried out only in large centralized ovens, making those parts unsuitable for cell manufacturing. The company is, however, thinking of investing in smaller, cheaper ovens that could be incorporated into each cell.

There can also be resistance to the self-reliance and broader responsibilities of cell-based work, especially from employees used to the "command and control" of assembly lines. Most of the companies that have introduced cells have found themselves spending more time and money on training: Compaq reckons its cell-based workers spend 6 percent of their time being trained, compared with 4 percent for assembly-line workers. It believes, however, that the results more than recoup the cost of extra education.

If there is still a niggling problem, it lies in ensuring that the level of expertise in each cell is evenly matched: failure to do so would mean varying output and quality. And as Mr. Phillips of Gore points out, although rivalry between cells can boost quality, it can also be counterproductive. There is a danger that the cells become too autonomous: "You can get a little too focused on your own team and forget the good of the whole company." To avoid that, Gore and other devotees of cell manufacturing periodically move employees from one cell to another.

Such challenges seem not to deter those companies that believe in cells. All say they aim to scrap more assembly lines in favor of cell manufacturing; Compaq hopes eventually to use cells to make all of its products. And in an era when shrinking product life cycles and widening product variety mean that traditional economies of scale are less easily exploited, more firms will follow suit. No longer can manufacturers simply sell what they produce; these days, they must produce what sells. That spells cells.

READING 5–3
MANAGING INNOVATION ON THE FACTORY FLOOR

Marcie J. Tyre*

In December 1982, a factory in Alton, Pennsylvania, installed a new high-precision machining line that promised to move the plant into the modern age of metalworking. Managers hoped eventually to convert all of the plant's production lines to similar technology.

In December 1986, I walked through the line with a plant engineer who had spent the last four years trying to debug it. Although the line was operating, he explained that it seldom ran reliably at full capacity. And because engineers on the project had never found time to install and learn to use new measuring equipment, no one was sure whether quality had improved appreciably. Despairing, company managers decided to ship the production line off to a sister plant overseas. Soon after, they closed the Alton factory.

While somewhat extreme, this case illustrates a serious failing of industry: U.S. companies—and many of their counterparts worldwide—still have not learned how to introduce and exploit advanced production technologies to become competitive in global markets. Manufacturing managers often buy the most advanced equipment and systems but then fail to integrate them fully into production. Unsolved problems can persist for years, hindering quality improvement, product delivery, and factory efficiency.

The main reason for such difficulties is that managers do not fully understand the tasks involved in bringing new technology into the plant. Introducing new manufacturing technology is not simply a question of implementing well-developed solutions. Once new equipment

*Marcie J. Tyre is an assistant professor in the Management of Technology group at MIT's Sloan School of Management. She has also taught production and operations management at Harvard Business School and at the Indonesian Institute of Management. Her most recent research on the problems of introducing new technologies has been published in a variety of journals and will soon appear in the forthcoming conference collection *Transforming Organizations* (Oxford University Press).

Source: Reprinted with permission from *Technology Review,* October 1991, pp. 59–65.

has been installed, continuing efforts are needed to identify, diagnose, and address problems—and opportunities—that emerge only once the technology is online. Companies must invariably modify both their existing systems and the new technology to integrate the advanced equipment, define its role, and exploit its novel capabilities. The problems they encounter are often unfamiliar, requiring users to develop new methods of investigation or to rely on untried sources of expertise. In the process, many existing routines must be unlearned.

To integrate new technology into day-to-day operations, an organization must respond to two conflicting sets of demands. Solving problems that arise from a new process frequently requires assumptions and behavior that differ radically from traditional approaches to managing production: a company needs to invest time and money in developing, trying, and evaluating alternative solutions. Yet ongoing operations require applying routines predictably, efficiently, and accurately. Too often, routine wins the battle. Managers insist that the advanced manufacturing lab or the equipment vendor take responsibility for ensuring that new machinery lives up to expectations.

Unfortunately, manufacturing issues cannot be resolved independently of production. In a recent study of automated assembly robots, fellow Sloan School professor Eric von Hippel and I found that some 80 percent of the changes made after a plant installed a new system proved necessary because the developers could not foresee all the realities of the factory environment. Likewise, in *The Sources of Innovation* (1982), von Hippel showed that in industries as diverse as scientific instruments and strip-steel production, the parties best positioned to identify and solve problems with new technologies are the users themselves.

To implement new technology successfully, plants need to schedule time for testing and experimentation just as diligently as they would schedule time for production. They need to create what I call forums for change—to set aside times and places in which users and experts can gather and reflect on data, formulate new questions, and develop new solutions without disrupting normal production.

I base this conclusion on a field study I conducted at eight plants and four development labs in the United States, West Germany, and Italy, all operated by a major global producer of precision metal components. The corporation is one of Europe's most consistently successful manufacturers: in the last 10 years, it has decisively bested a Japanese challenge in Europe and the United States, expanded operations in Asia and Eastern Europe, and maintained worldwide dominance in both market share and reputation for quality.

I examined 48 projects where the plants installed new processes, ranging from minor changes (such as a molding machine similar to equipment already in place) to radical departures from existing manufacturing processes (such as a microprocessor-controlled integrated assembly line). What I discovered was that where managers set up forums for change, they saved months of start-up time—and the resulting processes were both more reliable and more efficient.

Time and Space

While forums for change vary in kind, they all tend to provide four key conditions:

- Enough physical or cognitive distance from normal operations to offer a temporary haven from their most restrictive influences.
- Enough proximity to production operations to allow participants to probe a machine's unique requirements and to observe how it will work in its intended context.
- Enough new people and new perspectives to provoke a fresh way of viewing the technology.
- Enough continuity among people to link problem solving and production.

A particularly successful forum for change was devised at an Italian plant that introduced programmable robots into its traditional finishing and assembly line. The robotics equipment was set up close to where it would later be installed, but for two months it was separated from the line by half-height plywood partitions. This space, which plant personnel called the development box, sheltered the project team from normal production pressures while the team ran trials, examined mistakes, and conceived new solutions. One of the innovative ideas that emerged from the development box was a new group called pronto intervento.

This was a small team of technicians who would be stationed on the plant floor, ready to respond immediately to problems spotted by operators on the line.

A long-term "resident" of the development box was the project leader, an expert operator and machine setter who had been trained in robot technology and who had helped design and select the system. Inside the development box, the project leader studied and adapted the equipment and software as the robot ran a simulated production sequence. At first, he collaborated with technicians from the equipment vendors to work out bugs in the hardware and configuration of the robot as they emerged. Then he enlisted the help of specialists in the plant technical office and the production supervisor on the line to develop new ideas or test new sequences.

In working with production and maintenance personnel, the project leader realized that the robot cell, the company's first experiment with flexible production, would require "a whole new philosophy, or new mentality, of production." To encourage this realization among prospective users, he brought them into the development box to watch and experiment with the machine themselves.

The development box offered several benefits. First, the project team could formulate solutions in close proximity to production. This was important because it enabled team members to test their ideas with production personnel. People and information could move freely between the production line, the development box, and the engineering office. Also, because the robot cell was brought into the plant two months before it was to be installed on the production line, project members had a chance to modify both the new technology and the existing production system without the pressures of daily quotas. They could try out ideas without disrupting production and thus could repeat experiments rapidly and relatively cheaply.

Indeed, project members explicitly tried to ferret out problems—something that would not have been in their interests if they were subject to normal production targets. They attempted complicated routines as soon as possible, for instance, and ran the robot cell at high speeds for long periods to investigate possible failure patterns.

The development box was also a place where outside experts and plant personnel could collaborate on the difficult job of adapting the equipment to the plant. Often, this proved invaluable to both parties. At one point, for example, a manufacturing engineer noticed that the robot was placing parts into feeder trays at an angle. Puzzled, she asked the robot vendor's engineer why this might be happening. At first, he said such an occurrence was impossible. But when the two engineers got together in the development box, they traced the problem to an unusual part configuration and the robot programmer's way of dealing with it. Finding the solution required at least two crucial ingredients: the shared perspective of the vendor and the user, and the opportunity to experiment.

Finally, the development box was a powerful asset because it brought together both technical and operating personnel from within the plant. This not only enabled those most closely involved in day-to-day functioning of the equipment to participate in technical decision making but also forced technical personnel to consider the actual needs and constraints of the production line.

Once the robot went online, the start-up time was one of the shortest recorded: it took only 2 months to reach full production, versus an average of over 14 months. Further, the technology's performance was outstanding. "Once we put the new cell into regular operation," said the department manager, "we discovered lots of ways to improve the process. But because of what we had learned already, putting improvements in place did not require any major changes." New operating and maintenance procedures were already in place. When operators needed help, they knew whom to call and how to describe their problems. And technicians already had a clear sense of operating requirements on the plant floor. These things did not have to be worked out in real time.

Ingredients of Success

Erecting plywood partitions is not the only way to create temporary forums for learning about new process technologies. Other successful teams in the study established forums that, like the development box, were both closely linked to the production process and sufficiently separated from it to escape the rigors of production. These forums altered the conditions of business as usual by focusing attention on problem solving, by lowering the costs of trying new ideas, and by decreasing the uncertainty associated with solving problems.

Most of the forums for change I observed were less tangible than the robot cell's development box. Instead they consisted of three organizational ingredients that I call preparatory search, joint search, and functional overlap.

In preparatory search, a plant invests in problem solving before it installs equipment. Project personnel might negotiate technical specifications with equipment suppliers, work with suppliers on developing and testing concepts and techniques, and create systems and components to support the new technology.

When an Italian factory was planning to introduce a sophisticated drill press, for example, project participants knew they could not foresee all the implications of the change. But they drew on their experience with other presses to identify the key challenges. They determined that their most critical task was to create new high-precision tooling systems. Accordingly, a small group of tooling engineers and technicians started designing new tools even before the equipment was ordered. While the machine itself was being built, the equipment vendor advised the group on what sort of interface they needed to construct between his computer controls and the tools they were developing. The tool study took over a year to complete, but it was not subject to normal time pressures because the equipment itself was still being developed. And the results benefited not only the new press but existing machines as well.

The second ingredient, joint search, involves using outside technical experts to help solve problems during the actual start-up of a process. Because outsiders are available only temporarily, their participation signals a change from business as usual. At a plant in Germany, an advanced robot cell built overseas was failing to perform reliably or precisely. The developer set aside a week to visit the plant on condition that the plant schedule no production on the cell during that time. "Finding a way to free up the cell for a week was a real burden," said the plant technician in charge of the cell. "But we learned an enormous amount, and the robot cell is now one of the most reliable machines in the plant."

Because production pressures were lifted for a short time, plant engineers had a chance to discuss the whys underlying the machine's routines and the changes that the developer made to it. Plant engineers reported that they learned not just how to keep the machine running but also how to improve it further.

A special location for joint activities can also underline the break from routine. In an Italian plant that was installing a high-precision grinding line, one of the chief designers of the equipment insisted before visiting the factory that the project group set up a small offline facility for team meetings to review production data and test results. In other successful cases, plant personnel visited outside labs or production facilities to discuss problems.

Like preparatory searches, these working partnerships provide opportunities for trying new ideas in a protected, low-risk environment. In many cases, relationships with outsiders give plant personnel access to pilot lines or specialized testing facilities that could not be replicated in the plant. Links to outside experts enabled users to try out ideas through discussion and "mental simulation" before investing time and resources in actual changes.

Functional overlap, the third ingredient of successful forums, entails merging the roles of a plant's technical and production personnel. In one major project, an Italian plant pioneered a new metal-forming technology, the "United" process. For this factory, which had relied on traditional metal-*removal* processes, the United Process was a fundamentally new approach to producing precision metal components. Accordingly, plant management emphasized the need to build technical skills through hands-on experience and to create closer links between technical personnel and plant operations. On each shift, a process engineer, a maintenance engineer, and an experienced senior operator formed a crew that shared responsibility for production. As the department manager explained, "The graduate engineers wore the overalls and ran the parts."

Thus, production personnel had ready access to technical input, while process engineers were never far removed from production realities. "It was important to get the opinion of each person in the group," said the project manager. "Each had an input into the final decision, but the final decision could not have come from any one person."

Besides breaking down barriers between traditional roles, arrangements like this one enable people to step back from the new production line and examine their experience. Each member of the production crew, for example, kept a daily log of irregularities. Once a week the entire project group—including the department manager, technical specialists, and production team members—met to investigate problems. "We used the logs to look back over days or weeks of production," explained one project engineer. "When we noticed a specific pattern of events, that's how we traced a lot of problems to their source."

Finally, bringing together multiple perspectives within a plant can spawn new ways of looking at problems. This occurred at a U.S. plant that introduced a novel integrated thermal treatment process. "On day one," said a project participant, "each person on this project brought a specific area of expertise. But there was a lot of cross-training and cross-learning. On day 100, every person was an expert in the system."

All three approaches help create forums for change by making it possible to explore technology in many small, reversible steps instead of a few giant blind leaps. A member of a U.S. team that had collaborated with the vendor in introducing a milling center commented, "Working together, we were able to do a great deal of mental testing of the ideas from both sides." With technical experts working close to the line, project managers are less fearful of trying new routines or running experimental tooling. Operators are reassured that small errors are not likely to destroy complex machinery, and production managers are less apt to assume that online testing will hamper their ability to deliver parts at the end of the day.

The Payoff

Forums for change do more than ease fears among those introducing manufacturing technologies. They also produce tangible benefits. For each project, I measured the elapsed time from installing new equipment to completing the introduction process. I also gauged the improvements achieved with the new technology in reliability, efficiency, and other areas. Finally, I asked project leaders and participants to rate the amount of preparatory search, joint search, and functional overlap they had used in each project.

I discovered that each of these three ingredients contributed greatly to a project's success. First, they significantly shortened start-up times. Start-ups at plants that relied heavily on preparatory search, for instance, were almost four months shorter than at plants that did not. Doing a great deal of joint search saved two months. In fact, projects that used all three approaches extensively saved an average of seven months in start-up time.

The three approaches also boosted performance improvement. Projects that aggressively employed preparatory search, joint search, and functional overlap together reaped performance improvements 70 percent greater than the average for all projects. Indeed, heavy use of preparatory search alone accounted for a 35 percent increase, and high use of joint search led to a 20 percent increase.

The evidence even suggests that a failure to create forums for change may contribute to the relatively poor performance of some U.S. plants in introducing technology. MIT economist Lester Thurow and others have noted that American manufacturers are slower than European and Japanese ones in adopting processes that can make better products more cheaply. On average, the three U.S. plants in this study took almost 40 percent longer to introduce a process than the five European plants. And performance improvements were almost 50 percent greater in Europe than in the United States.

These differences turned out to be more than vague national tendencies. They depended largely on how vigorously project groups in each country pursued forums for change. If the European and the U.S. plants had used identical levels of preparatory search, joint search, and functional overlap, the gap in start-up time would have been only about 10 percent; the gap in performance improvement would have been halved, to just 25 percent.

Establishing forums for change is not always easy. Preparatory search, joint search, and functional overlap all entail costs in the short term and concerted managerial guidance in the long run. This is because they require the time and attention of both operators and technical support staff. They also demand cooperation across traditional organizational boundaries— boundaries that can be broken down only through long-term changes in career paths, training, reward systems, and organizational structures.

Most managers I have talked to readily agree that they need to work on developing both better skills throughout their plants and greater willingness to share those skills. But they are often surprised to hear that even a highly skilled and motivated workforce cannot guarantee that advanced manufacturing technologies will be introduced smoothly. While it has become fashionable to acknowledge the need for constant learning or "continuous improvement," my findings suggest that learning does not occur naturally on the factory floor, even in a well-run plant. Engaging production personnel in genuine problem solving means allowing them to step back temporarily from the pressures of regular production. In the future, success in using advanced technologies will go to those companies that vigorously pursue the approaches outlined here and also devise their own ways of building forums for change.

CASE 5-1
DURIRON COMPANY INC., COOKEVILLE VALVE DIVISION (A)

John M. Burnham
David Lambert
Charles W. Smith, Jr.
John A. Welch
Dale A. Wilson

Yes, that's true. When you read the original Arthur Andersen "game plan" you note that we should have become all-cellular by the end of 1992. But there are many factors that explain why our *real* progress has been good, but our cell implementation is still not complete. People resources, people's attitudes about change, and a two-year recession all play a role. I know you'll want to look into all this, so why don't we get started?

Rob Adams, Operations Manager
Duriron Valve Division
November 1992

Overview

Beginning in 1988, the Duriron Company (DURCO) committed to becoming a world-class valve and pump supplier to the worldwide process industries. Chemical, petroleum, and other processors of corrosive or exotic fluids had long been using DURCO products of high-silicon iron and other alloy materials, but the global market had brought global competition and a need to stay competitive. Since the WCM (world-class manufacturer) decision, the company has taken many steps to become more customer responsive. DURCO, as a mature organization, required significant changes. A series of substantial consulting assignments beginning in 1989 led to the strong recommendation to DURCO that the divisions move toward cell manufacturing rather than the traditional batch-job shop environment. This case follows the progress at the Cookeville Valve Division (CVD), located in Cookeville, Tennessee.

This case was developed by John M. Burnham, David Lambert, Charles W. Smith Jr., John A. Welch, and Dale A. Wilson, of Tennessee Technological University, Cookville, TN. Copyright © 1994 by the National Consortium for Technology in Business, c/o the Thomas Walter Center for Technology Management, Auburn University, Auburn, AL.

Background Information

The Duriron Company was founded in 1912 in Dayton, Ohio, by John R. Pitman, a former DuPont acid plant manager; William E. Hall, a lawyer and financier; and Pierce D. Schenck, an electrical engineer. The group of men sought to utilize the capabilities of a new corrosion resistant metal they had invented.

Demand for the company's products skyrocketed with the beginning of World War I. Its corrosion resistant metal was essential for munitions production. As a result it was identified as an "essential industry" and almost nationalized. After the war, the company produced its first pipes and fittings, high-silicon iron pumps, and valves to handle chemical solutions.

The main product lines after World War II were pumps, valves, and heat exchangers sold under the DURCO brand name. The next major development was a Teflon-lined valve, first produced in 1965, to handle severely corrosive materials. The Teflon lining was a much cheaper alternative to the expensive alloys previously required to handle such materials.

In 1978 DURCO began a change in strategy with the shift from a centralized to a decentralized structure. They began to sense a change in how their customers evaluated suppliers. The trend was for a customer to purchase valves from a primary group of suppliers. In the selection process, these companies were looking for a commitment to quality and forming a partnership with these suppliers. Therefore, it was critical for DURCO to show buyers what it was doing for continual improvement into the next century. Also, the company felt that it was behind some competitors in keeping pace with technological changes. In response, top management chose the strategy of becoming a world-class manufacturer (WCM) and directed the divisions to take steps toward reaching this goal.

Today's corporate mission is to serve the needs of the worldwide process industries for fluid handling products, systems, and services. Current product lines include valves and automatic equipment, pumps, filtration devices, and chemical waste systems. DURCO's stated goals for continued growth are to expand into international markets, implement the latest manufacturing technologies, develop new products, and continue acquiring and divesting businesses.

The company is organized by product lines and the individual international subsidiaries. These decentralized divisions operate with relatively little detailed direction from corporate and are responsible for their own marketing and sales functions, and for profit. The company has shown steady growth over the years and has been identified as a solid investment by many analysts.

Valve Division

Due to divisionalization in the late 1970s, the Valve Division (CVD) was moved from Dayton, Ohio, to Cookeville, Tennessee. The 160,000-square-foot facility houses all valve activities from preliminary design to sales/marketing and has some 300 direct employees. From 1978 to 1988, production was departmentalized and was characterized by high inventories, long lead times, large lot sizes, and high product costs. Despite these traditional manufacturing characteristics, the division was profitable.

CVD produces a wide variety of valves and accessories to fit almost any customer need. A complete line of butterfly, ball, and plug valves are made in a variety of sizes and alloys.

Even before the corporate WCM decision was made, CVD had noted the market changes, that its customers were beginning to redirect purchasing procedures toward those suppliers with a commitment to customer service. In addition, the division's president had recently toured some Japanese production facilities and decided to reevaluate CVD's production processes.

Industry Customers and Competitors

DURCO serves the chemical process industry. Its customers include Dow, DuPont, Eastman Chemical, oil refineries, and food and beverage manufacturers. These companies are now expanding internationally, so CVD has made efforts to meet their changing needs by designing with metric measurements and the European and Asian standards for valves. CVD has augmented its design and production processes to meet these needs.

Another factor in the move toward WCM has been the increased competition, both domestic and foreign. From the 1960s to late 1970s, DURCO was the leader in the valve market. DURCO's designs were superior, and the company met the customers' basic needs. Service, including lead time, breadth of product line, and quality levels, became the main differentiator. The competitive pressures made Duriron realize the need for comprehensive manufacturing and product design strategies.

Industry demands will continue to change in the future. A large market already exists in high-temperature (over 1000° F) and high-pressure steam applications. The development of synthetic fuels and biochemical industries will create new challenges. Perhaps the biggest shifts will come in the form of increased environmental regulation. New regulation could create stricter requirements on chemical process equipment.

Targeting World-Class Manufacturing

Since corporate's directive to strive to WCM, CVD has taken steps to implement the philosophies of total quality, people involvement, and just-in-time manufacturing. The approach has been to focus on manufacturing cells as a means to incorporate these philosophies into the company. The process has been difficult, and there is still a long way to go.

Andersen Consulting

The first step in 1990 was to develop an action plan to improve operations at the plant. To provide an outside perspective, the corporation had earlier hired Andersen Consulting to develop plantwide project plans to determine what changes to make and when to make them. When Andersen carried out an assignment at the Valve Division, the objective was to design the cells around a product line, including layout and machine requirements; to create a scheduling system to provide the shortest possible lead times, to level the daily cell production, and to handle emergency orders; and to produce timetables for implementation of the cells.

The CVD plan called for eight cells of varying sizes. There were to be two T-Line plug valve cells, one for 0.5″ to 2″ valves and another for 3″ to 8″ valves. One cell would make all BTV butterfly valves, and another would produce BX butterfly valves. The remaining four cells would manufacture various sizes of the G4 Plug valve. See Figure 1 for catalog cuts of typical products.

FIGURE 1

Typical CVD Products

The BTV-2000

The Atomac Lined Ball Valve

The T-Line Plug Lined Plug Valve

In addition to the standard plans, the Andersen material called for pay for performance for the workers. The pay-for-performance concept was to be used instead of the seniority process currently used. Also, the material contained statistical process control (SPC) information, business goals, and management guidelines for the cell implementation.

The Andersen implementation plan called for a complete change to focused factories (cells) by October 1, 1992. Expected benefits were reduced lead times from six to eight weeks to one to two weeks, floor space reduction of 37 percent, increased inventory turnover from 2 to 12 times per year, improved quality through smaller lot sizes and operator knowledge, and increased capacity and flexibility as a result of the dedicated equipment. In addition, each cell was expected to pay for itself in approximately one year.

CVD has not met the Andersen implementation schedule. In mid-1993 there were five cells in operation and another coming online soon.

Implementing Manufacturing Cells

CVD's goals for the cellular manufacturing project were to eliminate work-in-process, reduce finished goods inventory, reduce set-up times, achieve 100 percent on-time delivery, and reduce required floor space and product costs while maintaining required quality levels. To accomplish the goals, manufacturing cells were to be implemented throughout the plant. Steering and implementation committees were formed to get the ball rolling. The steering committee had to choose an initial product on which to test the cellular concepts and as a demonstration project to show success.

The committee chose the 0.5- to 1.0-inch G4 plug valves for cellular productions, the reason being that this investment casting contained less variation than other valves. This valve required the fewest number of setup changes, and it was a large-volume valve. The line was not very profitable. In fact, some other manufacturers took a loss on this line to provide full customer service. Therefore, improvements coming from the cell could help the company as well as show the potential improvements from cellular manufacturing.

Each cell was to be a totally separate operation. The cell team would schedule the work, do its own purchasing, manufacture the products entirely, perform SPC and quality inspections, and track its own profits, lead times, scrap rates, inventory turns, and backlog. In addition, the cell would radically reduce the distance that a valve had to travel inside the plant from over one mile from receiving to shipping to only 80 feet. Substantially all of the cell equipment was to be added to the plant machinery, since ongoing "traditional" manufacturing required the same process steps and equipment capabilities, and could not be dedicated to serve the cell alone. New or used numerically controlled (NC) multifunction machinery made up most of the cell outfit.

A drawing of the original "traditional" plant, and of the new G4 cell, appear as Figures 2 and 3.

Empowerment

The move to WCM was more than simply implementing manufacturing cells—the cells were only a tool in the process of achieving the company's goals. It meant a change in entire corporate philosophy. The most difficult change was to give hourly employees more control over their working environment. On the production side, workers were given the power to change floor layouts, schedule work, perform inspection and SPC, and improve the process.

Employees previously concerned with running only one machine in the traditional manufacturing environment now had to learn all operations in the cell and work in a team environment. New NC machines required the workers to learn new processes. The change was just as difficult for management to accept as it was for the workers, and engineers and managers had new responsibilities as well. When these facts were combined with the knowledge that the old methods were profitable, there was the potential for organizational resistance to such changes.

Employee empowerment also made the cell team involved in hiring, skill level certification, and promotion. This required a lot of teamwork and shared responsibilities. Coincidentally, foremen under the old methods were not guaranteed positions as cell team leaders. In essence, CVD found resistance at all levels of the organization. Workers were uneasy about the new conditions, and management did not want its powers passed to the hourly employees. Also, managers were no longer controllers. They became facilitators, operations "coordinators," for employees in the performance of their work.

FIGURE 2

Traditional Layout

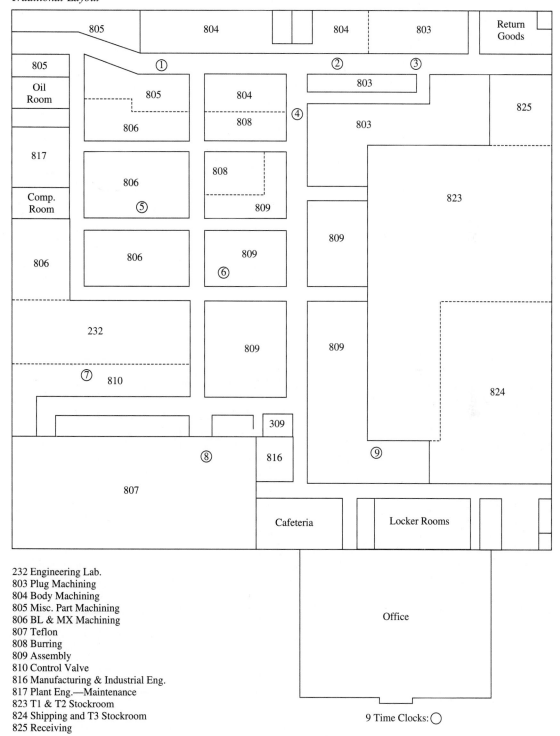

232 Engineering Lab.
803 Plug Machining
804 Body Machining
805 Misc. Part Machining
806 BL & MX Machining
807 Teflon
808 Burring
809 Assembly
810 Control Valve
816 Manufacturing & Industrial Eng.
817 Plant Eng.—Maintenance
823 T1 & T2 Stockroom
824 Shipping and T3 Stockroom
825 Receiving

9 Time Clocks: ○

FIGURE 3

G4 Cell Layout

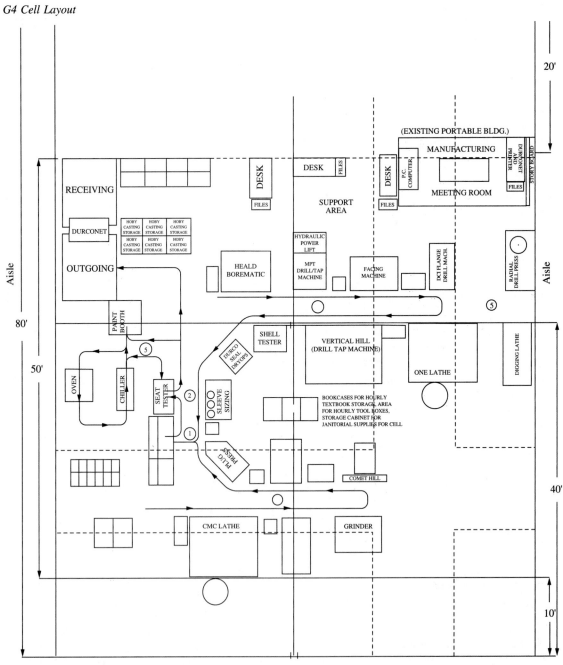

BTV-2000: The New Butterfly Valve Design

During most of 1990, one cell was operating with another in the prototyping stage. In late 1990 the additional cell (for the redesigned 3″ to 12″ Butterfly valve) was created by a concurrent engineering project team made up of representatives from sales, marketing, engineering, quality, manufacturing engineering, foremen, hourly workers, and accounting. With the goal of making the next generation (BTV-2000) valve, the team worked together to create the design and work on marketing, tooling, cell layout, and inspection techniques at the same time. After production began, many team members stayed with the product as cell support.

As before, CVD used the latest manufacturing technologies, so numerically controlled machines were chosen wherever possible. To make things more challenging, the development and capital budgets were tight, and the product was pushed toward production to generate revenues as soon as possible.

Financial Considerations

Cellular manufacturing has also had implications for the accounting and finance function. It is much easier to capture real product costs in cells. At the start of cellularization, 50 percent of costs were being allocated. Currently, this figure is at 28 percent and may reach 10 percent as CVD becomes fully cellular.

The department attempted to trace all costs to specific cells. Quality control, manufacturing, management, and shipping and receiving are still allocated. The 8 cells in the original plan plus 2 cells for new products totals 10 planned cells. CVD has allocated fixed costs by assigning one-tenth of the total fixed costs to each of the four active cells and the remaining 60 percent to traditional manufacturing areas.

Each cell has its own profits and loss (P&L) statement. CVD's controller did include important nonfinancial measures such as inventory turns and throughput on the P&Ls. Corporate requested changes in the P&Ls to reflect burden absorption. These external reports became less meaningful to the cell team members. The controller now utilizes two sets of reports to satisfy both the needs of the cell and corporate requirements. The BTV cell income statement for 1991 and an aggregated income statement for all cells appear as Figures 4 and 5.

Corporate also uses sales margins to evaluate product performance. Margins fluctuate, however, depending on any discounts given by the marketing department. Several groups in the organization feel it is too difficult to sell management on intangible costs, such as the cost of poor quality or failing to meet delivery schedules. Graphs depicting cost of goods sold and gross margin appear as Figures 6 and 7.

Conclusions

The Valve Division of Duriron Company, Inc., is in a transition from traditional to cellular manufacturing. Progress has been hindered by a slowing economy. Valve orders in some segments are down considerably. In order to avoid layoffs, inventories have been built in some areas. These increased inventories have prevented CVD from seeing the results originally projected.

Resistance to change has hampered progress. However, one staffer states, "Traditional rules are more of a barrier than the people themselves."

Pressures to remain profitable have slowed the cellular implementation. As a public company, Duriron must keep an eye on the interests of its stockholders.

CVD management stresses that the original Andersen Consulting plan was idealistic. In addition, the plan did not account for any new product additions or revisions.

New products have slowed the process considerably. CVD has designed and introduced a second generation of the BTV-lined butterfly valves, with apparent success. The BX valve has been redesigned for cost competitiveness and stands ready for production. Finally, CVD is in the early stages of designing a market replacement for its aging G4 series.

Some Case Issues

The early 1990s offer an object lesson to consultants and planners, especially those moving toward WCM status. The worldwide recession had great impact on capital expenditures, especially in process industries, and their suppliers were over capacity. Other Duriron divisions were heavily impacted, and corporate profits depended in large part on CVD.

Management tasks were much more complex with cell manufacturing and empowerment responsibilities. But bottom-line considerations led to staff reductions, and 15 percent fewer personnel were available to respond to shop floor needs. Engineers and managers were expected to "do whatever it took," and 60-hour weeks

FIGURE 4

Cellular Manufacturing

Cellular Manufacturing: Total All Cells Income Statement, 1991	Jan.	Feb.	Mar.	Apr.	May	June	July	Aug.	Sept.	Oct.	Nov.	Dec.	YTD
Sales	236,847	257,746	190,363	190,593	311,283	339,360	327,652	352,491	409,760	587,315	487,991	659,951	4,351,353
Cost of sales:													
Standard materials	60,583	67,162	57,266	72,267	101,204	101,563	92,068	97,718	169,291	193,247	137,403	195,939	1,345,712
Standard direct labor	6,675	6,027	5,661	5,614	9,700	9,423	8,400	9,484	8,090	18,910	17,073	19,163	124,220
Labor variance	3,095	6,226	6,927	6,791	16,648	12,717	15,953	15,643	15,260	14,327	11,778	8,652	134,018
Department cost	25,233	23,878	30,565	26,987	62,146	63,408	63,189	72,941	57,898	83,110	75,643	73,460	658,458
Total cost	95,586	103,293	100,419	111,659	189,698	187,111	179,610	195,786	250,540	309,594	241,898	297,213	2,262,407
Cell operating profit	141,261	154,453	89,944	78,934	121,585	152,249	148,041	156,705	159,220	277,721	246,094	362,738	2,088,946
Allocated manufacturing costs	17,039	17,039	17,039	17,039	21,903	22,876	22,388	23,170	22,473	25,508	23,962	24,722	255,157
SG&A and other expenses	45,001	48,972	36,169	36,213	59,144	64,478	62,254	66,973	77,854	111,590	92,718	125,391	826,757
Pretax profit	79,222	88,442	36,736	25,682	40,538	64,895	63,400	66,562	58,893	140,623	129,414	212,625	1,007,031
Federal income tax	30,500	34,050	14,143	9,887	15,607	24,985	24,409	25,626	22,674	54,140	49,824	81,861	387,708
Net profit	48,721	54,392	22,593	15,974	24,931	39,910	38,991	40,936	36,219	86,483	79,590	130,764	619,323
Ratios to sales:													
Material cost	25.6%	26.1%	30.1%	37.9%	32.5%	29.9%	28.1%	27.7%	41.3%	32.9%	28.2%	29.7%	30.9%
Standard labor	2.8%	2.3%	3.0%	2.0%	3.1%	2.8%	2.6%	2.7%	2.0%	3.2%	3.5%	2.9%	2.9%
Labor variance	1.3%	2.4%	3.6%	3.6%	5.3%	3.7%	4.9%	4.4%	3.7%	2.4%	2.4%	1.3%	3.1%
Department cost	10.7%	9.3%	16.1%	14.2%	20.0%	18.7%	19.3%	20.7%	14.1%	14.2%	15.5%	11.1%	15.1%
Total cost of sales	40.4%	40.1%	52.8%	58.6%	60.9%	55.1%	54.8%	55.5%	61.1%	52.7%	49.6%	45.0%	52.0%
Operating profit	59.6%	59.9%	47.2%	41.4%	39.1%	44.9%	45.2%	44.5%	38.9%	47.3%	50.4%	55.0%	48.0%
Allocated cost	7.2%	6.6%	9.0%	8.9%	7.0%	6.7%	6.8%	6.6%	5.5%	4.3%	4.9%	3.7%	5.9%
Pretax profit	33.4%	34.3%	19.3%	13.5%	13.0%	19.1%	19.3%	18.9%	14.4%	23.9%	26.5%	32.2%	23.1%
Net profit	20.6%	21.1%	11.9%	8.3%	8.0%	11.8%	11.9%	11.6%	8.8%	14.7%	16.3%	19.8%	14.2%

Note: Figure 4 provides representative data so that readers can follow detailed development of the reports. It is not an actual report of the Duriron Company, Cookeville Valve Division, nor should it be used for analytic purposes.

FIGURE 5

Cell 802

BTV Cell Income Statement, 1993	Jan.	Feb.	Mar.	Apr.	May	June	July	Aug.	Sept.	Oct.	Nov.	Dec.	YTD
Sales	173,730	108,786	101,749	188,020	148,550	208,921							929,756
Cost of sales:													
Standard materials	47,837	30,753	29,709	53,664	44,288	51,061							257,312
Direct labor	5,872	3,504	3,629	6,604	5,984	6,964							32,557
Applied burden	38,169	22,778	23,587	42,926	38,896	45,268							211,623
CGS @ standard	91,878	57,035	56,925	103,194	89,168	103,293							501,492
Gross profit at standard	81,852	51,751	44,824	84,826	59,382	105,628							428,264
Over-(under) applied burden	4,397	(15,995)	(15,291)	5,896	296	8,737							(11,961)
Gross profit at actual	86,249	35,756	29,533	90,722	59,678	114,365							416,303
SG&A and other expenses	33,009	20,670	19,332	35,724	28,225	39,695							176,654
Pretax profit	53,240	15,086	10,201	54,998	31,453	74,670							239,649
Federal income tax	20,497	5,808	3,928	21,174	12,110	28,748							92,264
Net profit	32,743	9,278	6,273	33,824	19,343	45,922							
Ratios to sales:													
Material cost	27.5%	28.3%	29.2%	28.5%	29.8%	24.4%							27.7%
Standard labor	3.4%	3.2%	3.6%	3.5%	4.0%	3.3%							3.5%
Standard applied burden	22.0%	20.9%	23.2%	22.8%	26.2%	21.7%							22.8%
CGS @ standard	52.9%	52.4%	55.9%	54.9%	60.0%	49.4%							53.9%
Gross profit at actual	49.6%	32.9%	29.0%	48.3%	40.2%	54.7%							44.8%
Pretax profit	30.6%	13.9%	10.0%	29.3%	21.2%	35.7%							25.8%
Net profit	18.8%	8.5%	6.2%	18.0%	13.0%	22.0%							15.9%

Cell Performance Measurements, 1993	Goal	Jan.	Feb.	Mar.	Apr.	May	June	July	Aug.	Sept.	Oct.	Nov.	Dec.	Ytd Avg
A. Inventory turns		4.8	2.9	3.1	5.9	5.3	6.0							4.6
B. On-time perf.		97%	92%	93%	95%	97%	100%							95.7%
C. Lead time (days)		9	10	10	14	18	12							12
D. Units/man hour		0.21	0.14	0.20	0.27	0.26	0.24							0.22
E. Sales $'s/man hour		$106	$76	$86	$128	$103	$111							$102
F. Scrap/10,000 pieces		98	141	45	46	86	72							85
G. Continuous improvement														$0
H. Backlog														
Beginning back log		76	35	14	85	147	131							
Incoming units		101	84	204	250	145	120							
Units shipped (transferred)		142	105	133	188	161	197							
Ending back log		35	14	85	147	131	54							

Note: Figure 5 provides representative data so that readers can follow detailed development of the reports. It is not an actual report of the Duriron Company, Cookeville Valve Division, nor should it be used for analytic purposes.

FIGURE 6

Cost of Goods Sold at Standard

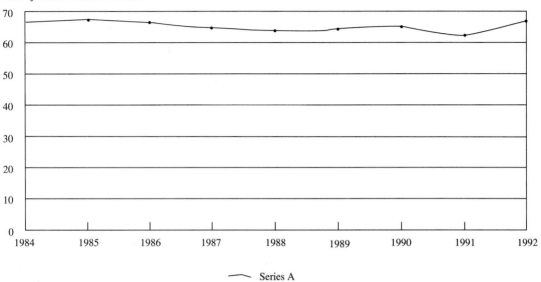

FIGURE 7

Gross Profit Percentage

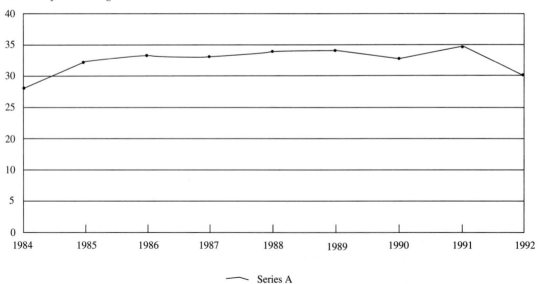

were not unusual. A contested union election in 1989 was resolved in favor of collective bargaining representation by a Federal Appeals Court decision in November 1992. Two small direct workforce voluntary layoffs also took place during the moves from traditional to cell manufacturing.

Cell implementation, exciting and challenging as it appeared, drew 40 workforce volunteers when the initial (G4 valve) cell was announced. The second cell announcement drew almost twice that many. But successive cells showed considerable foot-dragging as the tales of extra effort and unfamiliar tasks and equipment became more prevalent, along with tighter staffing than that in the traditional work settings.

These are issues currently affecting CVD. Despite its progress, there is still a long way to go.

CASE 5–2
DURIRON COMPANY, INC., COOKEVILLE VALVE DIVISION (B)

John M. Burnham
David Lambert
Charles W. Smith, Jr.
John A. Welch
Dale A. Wilson

Overview

Beginning in 1988, the Duriron Company (DURCO) committed to becoming a world-class valve, pump, and fittings supplier to the worldwide process industries. Chemical, petroleum, and other processors of corrosive or exotic fluids had long been using DURCO products of ductile iron and other alloy materials, but the global market had brought global competition and a need to stay competitive. Since the WCM (world-class manufacturing) decision, the company has taken many steps to become more customer responsive. DURCO, as a mature organization, required significant changes. A series of substantial consulting assignments beginning in 1989 led to the strong recommendation to DURCO that the divisions move toward cell manufacturing rather than the traditional batch-job shop environment. This case follows the effects of these changes on human resources at the Cookeville Valve Division (CVD) located at Cookeville, Tennessee.

Background

Since corporate's directive to strive for WCM, CVD has taken steps to implement the philosophies of total quality, people involvement, and just-in-time manufacturing. Its approach has been to focus on manufacturing cells as a means to incorporate these philosophies into the company. The process has been difficult, and there is a long way to go.

An action plan was developed in 1990 through a corporate agreement with Andersen Consulting. The plan called for a complete change to focused factories (cells) by October 1, 1992. CVD has not met the implementation schedule. In mid-1993, there were five cells in operation and another coming online soon.

This case was developed by John M. Burnham, David Lambert, Charles W. Smith Jr., John A. Welch, and Dale A. Wilson of *Tennessee Technological University,* Cookeville, TN. Copyright © by the National Consortium for Technology in Business, c/o the Thomas Walter Center for Technology Management, Auburn University, Auburn, AL.

CVD has brought two mature product lines into cells—first, smaller sizes of the G4 plug valve, followed by the T-Line valve. The Atomac ball valve, acquired from a German valve producer, is being produced in a focused factory as well. In addition, CVD developed a second-generation lined butterfly valve (BTV-2000) using concurrent engineering principles. All but the largest sizes of the BTV are produced in one cell. Recently, the BX butterfly valve was redesigned in order to improve cost through design for manufacturability. The BX is the most recent cell to be brought on line.

The cells operate as true focused factories. All inventory is maintained within the cell. Cell team members are responsible for each facet of production, including scheduling and performance evaluation. All raw material and work-in-process inventories are maintained within the boundaries of each cell. The processes use a great deal of numerically controlled equipment and are designed for flexibility.

Human Resources

WCM has had a major effect on the human resources function within the plant. A natural resistance to change has played a significant role in slowing CVD's progress.

WCM and Human Resources. From a human relations standpoint, the cells are completely different from traditional manufacturing. The responsibility of the hourly worker has increased dramatically as cell members are responsible for every facet of production. The workers must interact with each other and suppliers, as well as perform SPC analysis, preventive maintenance, and performance evaluation. In addition, hourly workers were involved in the design of the BTV and its cell from the beginning.

Hourly workers must bid to move to a new cell. The first cell had 40 bids. The second cell had 80 bids. Competitive feelings between the cells have emerged.

Individual performance evaluations are done by the cell members' teammates. Advancement within a cell is achieved by progressing through a series of five skill blocks. A person who has achieved the final skill rating can operate every machine in the cell, use SPC tools, perform preventative maintenance, and work effectively as a team player. Staff persons sit in on skill block reviews to assure that evaluations are done consistently.

Performance evaluation of each cell is maintained on a bulletin board within the cell. Included on the story-board are on-time delivery, schedule adherence, scrap rate, inventory levels, and problem notes.

Training.   As the workers gained more responsibility, advanced training was necessary. Team members are able to ask for specific training in areas where they feel it is needed. Currently, CVD is training cell members to act effectively as members of a team. A lack of resources has slowed the training pace. SPC training has been given plantwide. Workers in the traditional areas have failed to use this training, however, due to a lack of motivation.

Union.   A major human resource issue that has developed along with the WCM plan is the presence of a union interest at CVD. An election concerning represen-tation by the Steel Workers Union was held in 1989. At that time, the complaint of union advocates was that they did not have a voice in the company.

The vote was essentially a tie. The decision was taken to the Sixth Circuit Court of Appeals where the recog-nition election for union representation was found to be valid. This decision came during the plant visitation por-tion of the case development. In November 1992 CVD notified the union that it would not appeal and was ready to begin negotiations. The union representatives and di-vision negotiators have been meeting since that time.

CVD management feels that the cellular manufacturing program gives employees a significant voice in determin-ing their own future. It is generally felt that if there were to be another vote, the company would be favored.

Despite the uncertainties that arose from the disputed 1989 election results, it was decided to get on with the job of transforming the plant. Animosities between union people and company people have been surprisingly small. Some differences do arise during team meetings. Managers have tried not to let the union issue stand in the way of change. However, they do realize the issue has slowed progress toward complete cellularization.

Staff.   Demands on staff persons during the conver-sion to WCM have been enormous. The division has grown 60–70 percent in sales but has 15 percent fewer salaried people. Senior staff members consistently work 11–12 hours a day over five or even six days per week. The staff group defined these challenges for themselves.

Management is forced to wear two hats in managing a plant that operates partly under cellular manufacturing techniques and partly by traditional methods. As pointed out by members of engineering, we have had to learn to have confidence in the other areas of the organization.

Members of the staff are also involved as cell spon-sors. The sponsors are assigned to a particular cell team. They serve as a resource when needed by the team. As the cell progresses past the implementation phase, the team requires less and less of the staff resource.

Reaction to WCM.   Initially, there was considerable disbelief in the cell concept. The methods went against traditional manufacturing practices that had been fol-lowed for years. Some of this sentiment remains within the traditional areas of the plant. There is a lack of knowledge within the traditional areas of the plant concerning cellular manufacturing.

Some misdirection of cellular concepts exists among the cells. As an example, if a valve is going to be late, workers will sometimes set it aside because they know it is already late.

Some negative comments were heard by the case writ-ers referring to the team training. The human resources manager reasoned that such comments came from people who had not been through the program, as most appeared to enjoy the training. One staff member commented that the training should be more technical. Another staff mem-ber suggested that the staff receive cross-training.

To this point, those who have been moved to the cells have asked for the opportunity. There are still a lot of workers in the traditional areas of the plant who are opposed to or uncertain of the change. Many workers have been with CVD since its move to Cookeville 15 years ago. Some workers see cellular manufacturing as a way for the company to get more work for the same pay.

There is concern over reaching the point where people will have to be forced into cells. Human re-sources managers hope that people in earlier cells can be moved into the new cells so that the holdouts can be placed in existing cells.

CASE 5–3
DURIRON COMPANY, INC., COOKEVILLE VALVE DIVISION (C)

John M. Burnham
David Lambert
Charles W. Smith, Jr.
John A. Welch
Dale A. Wilson

Overview

Beginning in 1988, the Duriron Company (DURCO) committed to becoming a world-class valve, pump, and fittings supplier (a WCM, or world-class manufacturer) to the worldwide process industries. Chemical, petroleum, and other processors of corrosive or exotic fluids had long been using DURCO products of ductile iron and other alloy materials, but the global market had brought global competition and a need to stay competitive. Since the WCM decision, the company has taken many steps to become more customer responsive. DURCO, as a mature organization, required significant changes. A series of substantial consulting assignments beginning in 1989 led to the strong recommendation to DURCO that the divisions move toward cell manufacturing rather than the traditional batch-job shop environment. This case follows the progress at the Cookeville Valve Division (CVD) located at Cookeville, Tennessee.

Background

Since corporate's directive to strive to WCM, CVD has taken steps to implement the philosophies of total quality, people involvement, and just-in-time manufacturing. Its approach has been to focus on manufacturing cells as a means to incorporate these philosophies into the company. The process has been difficult, and there is a long way to go.

An action plan was developed in 1990 through a corporate agreement with Andersen Consulting. The plan called for a complete change to focused factories (cells) by October 1, 1992. CVD has not met the

---

This case was developed by John M. Burnham, David Lambert, Charles W. Smith Jr., John A. Welch, and Dale A. Wilson *Tennessee Technological University,* Cookeville, TN. Copyright © 1994 by the National Consortium for Technology in Business, c/o the Thomas Walter Center for Technology Management, Auburn University, Auburn, AL.

implementation schedule. In mid-1993, there were five cells in operation and another coming online soon.

CVD has brought two mature product lines into cells—first, smaller sizes of the G4 plug valve followed by the T-Line valve. The Atomac ball valve, acquired from a German valve producer, is being produced in a focused factory as well. In addition, CVD developed a second-generation lined butterfly valve (BTV-2000) using concurrent engineering principles. All but the largest sizes of the BTV are produced in one cell. Recently, the BX butterfly valve was redesigned to improve cost through design for manufacturability. The BX is the most recent cell to be brought on line.

The cells operate as true focused factories. All inventory is maintained within the cell. Cell team members are responsible for each facet of production, including scheduling and performance evaluation. All raw material and work-in-process inventories are maintained within the boundaries of each cell. The processes use a great deal of numerically controlled equipment and are designed for flexibility.

Operations

Despite obstacles, CVD has made considerable progress toward implementing cellular manufacturing. Five cells are fully operational while two more are near implementation.

Progress. Initially, a steering committee was formed to coordinate the efforts. The steering committee chose the 1/2″ to 1″ G4 valve plug valve as its first cellular product. The initial cell was to include only 1/2″ to 3/4″ G4 valves with 1″ G4 valves to be added to the cell later. The small G4 valve was chosen because it was produced from a high-quality casting process with little casting variation, it requires the fewest setup changes, and it was a high-volume, low-profit product. The 1/2″ to 3″ G4 line accounted for 65 percent of total unit volume and 33 percent of total sales dollars. The steering committee felt the small G4 valve had the highest chance of being successfully produced in a cellular environment.

The G4 project was approved in May 1989. The cell was to serve as a means to evaluate the effectiveness of the cellular concepts. As stated in the proposal, the project had the following objectives:

1. To completely manufacture the 1/2″ to 3/4″ G4 valve, including purchasing, scheduling, inventory control, machining, painting, assembly and shipment of the valve direct to the customer.

2. To manufacture valves based on actual customer orders, rather than forecasted inventory made for finished goods stock.

3. To create a manufacturing environment conducive to meeting the customer's needs in a global marketplace.

4. To improve overall customer service by shortening lead time and improving customer delivery time.

5. To reduce inventory levels.

6. To implement a just-in-time (JIT) manufacturing operation.

The 1/2″ to 3/4″ G4 cell became fully operational in April 1990. In 1991 the 1″ G4 was added to the cell. The cell reduced its lead time from 10 weeks to 1–2 weeks. Material handling distances have been reduced from over a full mile to only 80 feet. Layouts contrasting traditional flow and cellular flow are presented as Figures 1 and 2, respectively. The cell is responsible for scheduling, complete manufacturing, inspection, and performance evaluation.

Since this first cell, three others have become operational: the 1/2″ to 2″ T-Line valve, the Atomac lined ball valve (a valve design obtained by acquiring a German firm), the BTV lined butterfly valve, and the BX. A progress report for each of the four cells was completed for a corporate Audit/Finance Committee meeting in July 1992. A summary of the progress report is included as Appendix A.

WCM and Operations.   As part of its cellular manufacturing efforts, CVD has attempted to develop close relationships with its suppliers. This was done in an effort to reduce inventory levels and improve quality. Vendors must hold one month of inventory and promise to take up to three months. The quality of suppliers is evaluated quarterly.

Inventory levels must be maintained on castings because of resupply intervals and lead times. Order quantities on castings are fixed for two months with changes allowed on the third month. All inventory is maintained within the cell boundary—a true focused plant.

Inventory levels have grown during the recent economic downturn. Inventory was built as an alternative to laying workers off. Figure 3 shows changes in inventory turns.

The layout of each cell was designed to facilitate material flow. A drawing of the original CVD layout (prior to cellular manufacturing), the proposed CVD layout, as well as a detailed drawing of the BTV cell are included as Figures 4, 5, and 6.

ISO 9000.   During the course of plant visits by the case writers, CVD underwent an ISO 9000 audit. ISO is an international quality standards organization. ISO certification may help companies enter new markets faster. ISO was also seen by CVD as a way of gauging success and guiding continuous improvement. The division was ISO certified in December 1992.

Documentation systems are presently being developed for engineering. The paper trails required by ISO 9000 will make it much easier to review the design history of a valve.

BTV 2000.   As it became obvious that CVD would have to redesign its lined butterfly valve, the division had begun to buy into the cellular manufacturing concepts. It should be noted that the BTV was not included in the Andersen Consulting plan.

Prior to the development of the BTV, the engineering department was somewhat removed from the rest of the organization. New design ideas under the previous method usually started with the engineering department and were developed when operations support demands permitted. Some development times were in excess of five years. This traditional approach did not allow other departments to have much input into design development, nor was there much support by upper management until well into the design process. It was not unusual to have an

FIGURE 1

Present Flow (Traditional)

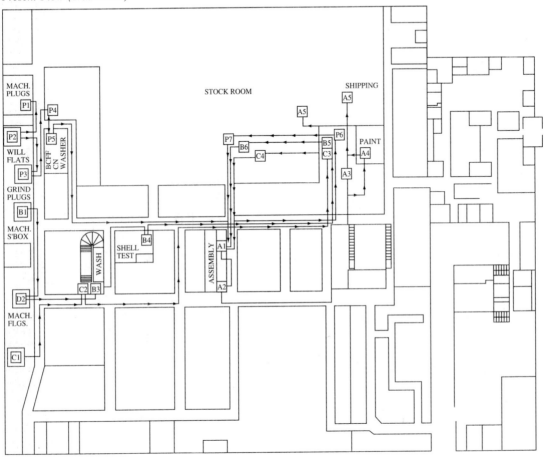

unmanufacturable design reach the manufacturing engineering department that could not be "built-per-print." In turn, this led to some cumbersome design changes.

BTV was to be the pilot program for concurrent engineering. Concurrent engineering allows for input from all parts of the organization at the earliest stages of development. Development times are reduced and designs come to the manufacturing floor in a form that can be produced with few design changes. The cell is designed along with the product. This tends to ensure that the best available manufacturing methods are used where possible.

The first step in the development process was team selection. The team comprised handpicked members of sales, marketing, engineering, quality engineering, manufacturing engineering, as well as accounting, supervisors, and hourly personnel. The team was urged by corporate to bring the product online quickly, to meet market and capital plans.

A primary goal of the design team was to design a product that facilitated manufacturability. As an example of this approach, consecutive valve sizes use identical shaft diameters, bearings, and seals. This reduces setup time, tooling costs, and bearing and seal inventories.

FIGURE 2

Cellular Flow

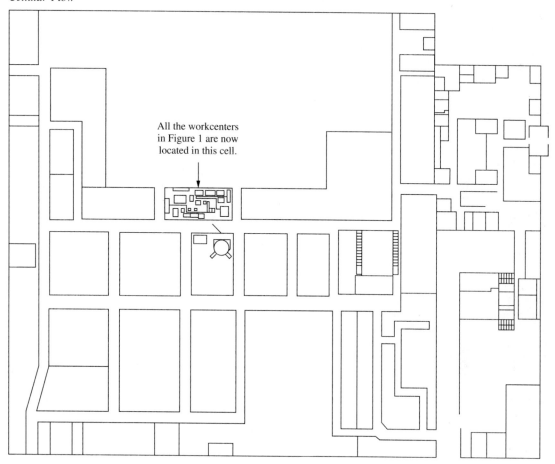

All the workcenters in Figure 1 are now located in this cell.

Only one piece of equipment was transferred from the traditional manufacturing area to the BTV cell; the remainder was bought new and used. The focus was placed on more flexible machinery. Also, much of the new equipment was considerably smaller than that in the traditional areas, to suit just the 3″–12″ valves.

The BTV has needed several significant design changes since its introduction. With market pressure to get the product online fast, there are those who feel product engineering was not looked at closely enough.

BX. The BX valve became a mature product in the late 1970s and early 1980s. The valve had matured to the point where it was no longer cost competitive. CVD had to decide whether to redesign the product or exit the market. Data showed the BX to be in a growing segment of the market. Duriron would also manufacture the redesigned BX for its recent acquisition—Valtek.

Redesign of the BX focused on design for manufacturability. The only person from the BTV design team on the BX team was team leader Gerry McDermott.

FIGURE 3

Inventory Turns

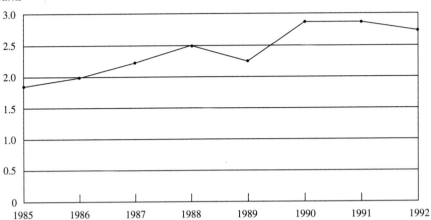

An implementation team was formed at the end of the BTV design project. The team was to use lessons learned in the BTV project to facilitate future projects. Most of the problems were personality conflicts. As a result, some mistakes were made twice, both on the BTV and BX projects.

The BX was in the testing stages when the case writers attended a team meeting in early 1993. A summary of the team meeting is attached as Appendix B.

Original Layout

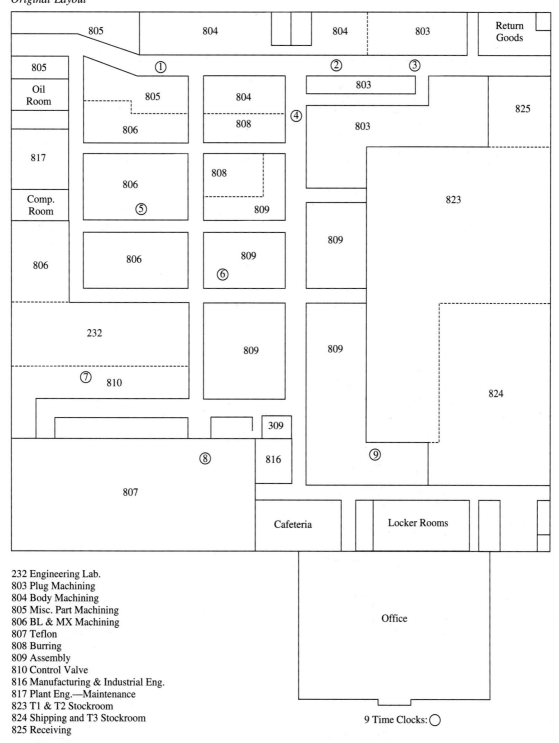

232 Engineering Lab.
803 Plug Machining
804 Body Machining
805 Misc. Part Machining
806 BL & MX Machining
807 Teflon
808 Burring
809 Assembly
810 Control Valve
816 Manufacturing & Industrial Eng.
817 Plant Eng.—Maintenance
823 T1 & T2 Stockroom
824 Shipping and T3 Stockroom
825 Receiving

9 Time Clocks: ◯

FIGURE 5

Proposed Cellular Layout

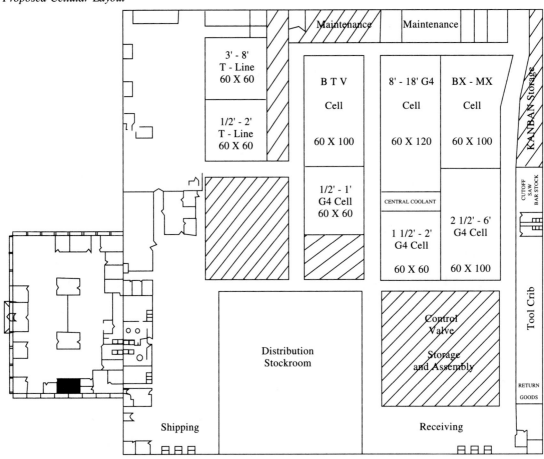

FIGURE 6

BTV Cell Layout

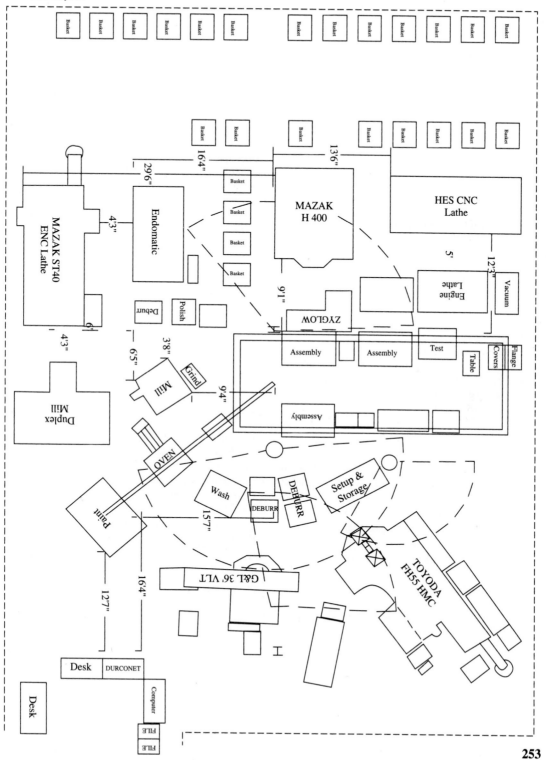

APPENDIX A
STATUS REPORT SUMMARIES

Status reports for the various cells were prepared for the corporate Audit/Finance Committee Meeting on July 20, 1992. The status reports reviewed the scope of the project then reported on capital expenditures, financial justification, and current status. The following are summaries of these reports.

Half-Inch to Three-Quarter-Inch

The project was approved in May of 1989 to convert the manufacture of small G4 valves from traditional to cellular techniques.

The project has spent 5.8 percent more than the goal of $295,000. On-time delivery is averaging 95 percent. Lead times have been reduced from 10 weeks to 1–2 weeks. The projected ROI has not been achieved due to unreached inventory goals.

The cell became fully operational in April 1990. As the first cell, it served as a test of the cellular manufacturing concepts. In 1991 the 1″ G4 was added to this cell. Currently, the cell contains 13 hourly employees.

BTV-2000 Cell

This project sought to develop a totally new product to replace the existing BL valve, which had lost its market leadership. Capital expenditures for the project have been exactly the goal amount of $3.2 million. Sales results have been significantly higher than expected. In addition, cost of sales has been slightly lower than expected and on-time delivery is 96 percent.

Half-Inch to Two-Inch

This project was to change the manufacture of the small T-Line valves to a cellular operation.

At $447,000, capital expenditures for the project are 12 percent lower than the goal. Inventory reduction goals have not quite been reached. The goal was to reduce production costs by 6 percent, while actual reductions have been 7 percent. The cell is averaging 97 percent on time delivery. Lead time has been reduced from 10 weeks to 1–2 weeks. Finally, ROI is 34.2 percent, which is 2.3 percent higher than the goal.

The T-Line cell became fully operational in November 1991, and currently has a total of 15 employees.

One-Inch G4 Valve

This project sought to add the 1″ G4 to the existing small G4 cell. Capital expenditures have been 48 percent less than expected. Inventory reduction goals have been reached. Cost reduction audit results are inconclusive. ROI, on-time delivery, and current status are the same as for the 1/2″–3/4″ G4 cell.

Atomac Cell

This project sought to transfer the manufacturing and technology of lined ball valves from Atomac in Germany. All 1″–3″ lined ball valves to be sold in the United States were to be produced at CVD.

Capital expenditures have been slightly less than expected at $1.6 million. Sales are well below goal. Cost of sales is 6 percent lower than goal. ROI figures are well below goal due to a low level of incoming business. On-time delivery is currently at 100 percent. Currently the cell staffs 17 hourly and salaried employees.

APPENDIX B
BX TEAM MEETING

1/21/93

Gerry McDermott began by addressing the current situation with the conditional release of the BX product. He mentioned that they are putting the new product in ahead of schedule.

Mike Welch (product manager for manual valves) addressed the quality issue and stated that if any problems arise, the program will be halted. He discussed what was meant by the conditional release. There is a big backlog in the traditional BX area. During the conditional release, each order will be looked at individually to mix and match with traditional and new BX cell valves. Mike discussed the good field reports that have been received on the new valves.

Gerry discussed what must happen to meet the goal. More support is going to have to come into the cell.

Hourly cell members asked if there are any particular valve sizes that the shortages involve. The answer was yes and was provided by Mike Welch.

Bill Sapp (process engineer) discussed progress on the items covered in the minutes of the previous team meeting.

Rick Sullins (manufacturing engineer) addressed problems with lug bodies from Texas Foundry along with other smaller problems.

Don Falconer (quality assurance) discussed what will be done with scrap. He also said M. Smith is still developing quality program materials for the cell. He further discussed the problems with Texas foundry and discussed the extra steps that must be taken until their quality problem is resolved. Receiving inspection will not be brought to the cell until this problem is resolved. He discussed the need to color code both incoming and WIP materials.

Bill and Rick interjected to state that they were told production would not start until they were ready.

Don Falconer continued by emphasizing that things must be looked at closely under the conditional release. He stressed the need to get the ISO program in order.

Harold Gentry (product designer) discussed the progress of the part design drawings. He got clarification on the priority of completing the drawings.

David Hart (engineer) discussed progress of fugitive emissions tests on the new BX valve.

Gerry McDermott went around the room asking for any questions. Several people, including the hourly people present, asked for clarification concerning priorities. Most of the questions are scheduling questions. The hourly people are asked for input on the problems in the cell. One hourly person asked a question concerning the organization of the cell with the new people coming into it. Gerry addressed the lack of cross-training that will be done due to the tight schedule. Due to this, there is a lot of concern from the hourly people over the skill block progression. Gerry does not have a clear-cut answer on how things will be handled. He insists that nobody will be treated unfairly and asks for everyone's cooperation. He stressed the importance of the product to the division.

Case 5–4
Duriron Company, Inc., Cookeville Valve Division (D)

John M. Burnham
David Lambert
Charles W. Smith, Jr.
John A. Welch
Dale A. Wilson

Overview

Beginning in 1988, the Duriron Company (DURCO) committed to becoming a world-class valve, pump, and fittings supplier to the worldwide process industries. Chemical, petroleum, and other processors of corrosive or exotic fluids had long been using DURCO products of ductile iron and other alloy materials, but the global market had brought global competition and a need to stay competitive. Since the WCM (world-class manufacturing) decision, the company has taken many steps to become more customer responsive. DURCO, as a mature organization, required significant changes. A series of substantial consulting assignments beginning in 1989 led to the strong recommendation to DURCO that the divisions move toward cell manufacturing rather than the traditional batch-job shop environment. This case follows the effects of this movement on marketing, field sales, and customer relations at the Cookeville Valve Division (CVD) located in Cookeville, Tennessee.

Background

Since corporate's directive to strive to WCM, CVD has taken steps to implement the philosophies of total quality, people involvement, and just-in-time manufacturing. The approach has been to focus on manufacturing cells as a means to incorporate these philosophies into the company. The process has been difficult, and there is a long way to go.

An action plan was developed in 1990 through a corporate agreement with Andersen Consulting. The

This case was developed by John M. Burnham, David Lambert, Charles W. Smith Jr., John A. Welch, and Dale A. Wilson *Tennessee Technological University,* Cookeville, TN. Copyright © 1994 by the National Consortium for Technology in Business, c/o the Thomas Walter Center for Technology Management, Auburn University, Auburn, AL.

plan called for a complete change to focused factories (cells) by October 1, 1992. CVD has not met the implementation schedule. In mid-1993 there were five cells in operation and another coming online soon.

CVD has brought two mature product lines into cells—first, smaller sizes of the G4 plug valve, followed by the T-Line valve. The Atomac ball valve, acquired from a German valve producer, is being produced in a focused factory as well. In addition, CVD developed a second-generation lined butterfly valve (BTV-2000) using concurrent engineering principles. All but the largest sizes of the BTV are produced in one cell. Recently, the BX butterfly valve was redesigned to improve cost through design for manufacturability. The BX is the most recent cell to be brought online.

The cells operate as true focused factories. All inventory is maintained within the cell. Cell team members are responsible for each facet of production, including scheduling and performance evaluation. All raw material and work-in-process inventories are maintained within the boundaries of each cell. The processes use a great deal of numerically controlled equipment and are designed for flexibility.

Marketing

The effects of WCM are not restricted to the shop floor. The marketing function also required changes in the pursuit of WCM.

As the manufacturing areas of the division progressed toward WCM, the marketing function was neglected. Historically weak in marketing, CVD has not documented marketing data well. Strong marketing will be key to the company's success in its WCM efforts, and good marketing function is necessary for ISO approval. It will be marketing's job to convey the importance of CVD's new programs to its customers.

Marketing currently makes decisions concerning the sizes of valves CVD should make based on the market and its growth potential. The vice president of sales and marketing and the marketing department handle order entry and customer relations. CVD recently formed two new marketing staff positions. One is a marketing product manager responsible for marketing all products and for organizing the marketing function. The second was recently acquired from corporate in order to bring in marketing research and analysis experience.

Marketing Research. Dennis Garber, who moved from corporate, is the new marketing staff person. The move was part of the effort to truly divisionalize the company. In the original division move, only operational marketing functions were brought to the new location. Company growth prompted the need to bring more developmental marketing functions to the division.

Garber's goal is to spread marketing awareness throughout the division. Everyone needs to realize that the job of each individual is to help meet the needs of an ever changing market.

Customer Service. Marketing its critical in forming customer relationships. Cellular manufacturing has greatly improved CVD's responsiveness to its customers. As a result, some customers and distributors have reduced inventories. CVD's customer relations staff has found that it must now educate its customers about its WCM program and its limits.

No set standards exist for field service quality. Product life varies with each application. Valve quality is judged by each individual customer. No warranty is given on valves unless they are defective from manufacturing or materials. Since the market is comprised of a few larger customers, however, CVD must be responsive to customer problems.

Cellular manufacturing has allowed the workers to visualize the customer better. Since valves are manufactured on an as-ordered basis, the workers know to which customer each valve is going. Occasionally cell team members have the opportunity to communicate with customers directly. Customer service measures have changed in the cellular areas and are now based on customer request dates.

With the recent poor economic climate, customer/supplier relations have changed, at least temporarily. CVD efforts to become a single-source supplier are pushed back as price has become the most important determinant of sales, making partnerships more difficult.

Sales. The sales force still provides the primary contact with customers. CVD is currently bringing applications engineers out of the six sales territories and back into the plant. These application engineers are to be assigned to two large regions. The marketing department is searching for ways to give salespeople information on specific valve applications. Because customers are becoming increasingly less technical, a knowledgeable sales staff is critical.

BTV-2000 Product Development. The BTV-2000 is a second-generation lined butterfly valve. Duriron introduced the first lined butterfly valve, the BL100, in 1965. When introduced, the BL was the state-of-the-art chemical service butterfly valve. Between 1966 and 1970 many improvements were made to the valve to maintain its position in the market. The product became a cash cow for CVD.

During the mid-1980s Duriron found the BL to be in the declining stage of its life cycle. The previous 24 years had seen major changes in the market, as well as innovative new designs that outperformed the BL. Sales volumes had remained flat over the past 10 years while unit volume had decreased significantly.

The segment of the lined butterfly valve market served by CVD contained three primary competitors. Customers in this segment chose suppliers primarily because of performance rather than cost.

Development. In 1985 CVD realized that a newly developed product would be needed to stay competitive in the market. At this time the industry was entering a recessionary period so any progress was delayed. In 1988 capital funds were obtained and development was started on the BTV.

A development team was formed of handpicked members of sales, marketing, engineering, quality engineering, manufacturing engineering, accounting, foremen, and hourly personnel. The team was pushed by corporate to bring the product online quickly.

The team sought to develop a high-quality, low-cost product through design for manufacturability. Toward this goal, the following four design requirements were considered:

1. To correct known weaknesses that existed in the lined butterfly valve.

2. To include key features and benefits from competitors.

3. To provide additional features and benefits that would differentiate the BTV from the competition.
4. To produce a cost-effective product using efficient design in conjunction with the cellular manufacturing concept.

The team incorporated two specific advantages into the design to set it apart from the competition. First, it was to be international in scope. The BTV was designed using both inch and metric measurements and using international valve standards. Second, the BTV addresses the stem sealing requirements that will be required of valves in the future.

To design a product that would meet customer needs, engineering staff contacted customers for constructive criticism on designs. Since the lined butterfly valve market was an existing market, Duriron knew it well. Much of the information came in the form of field performance reports. CVD also did competitive valve comparisons to locate the strengths and weaknesses of competitors' products.

The BTV project was finished on time and slightly under budget. Total redesign time was less than 18 months to market. The design team stayed with the cell until it was running smoothly.

The BTV-2000 cell operates on a make-to-order basis. Cell members can call customers from the floor in times of urgent customer needs. Processing rush orders is quick, and almost any order placed one day can go out the next. Needless to say, not *every* order can be treated as "rush!"

Forecasts for BTV sales have been extremely accurate. Actual sales have been within 3 percent of forecasts. The BTV exceeds the performance level of the competition and industry acceptance has been excellent. It has been difficult for CVD to keep up with domestic demand. European introduction of the valve has been just as good as in the United States. The BTV is seen as the cash cow of the future.

BX Redesign. The BX valve became a mature product in the late 1970s and early 1980s. The valve had matured to the point where it was no longer cost competitive. CVD had to decide whether to redesign the product or exit the market. Data showed the BX to be in a growing segment of the market. Duriron would also manufacture the redesigned BX for its recent acquisition—Valtek.

The BX was in the testing stages when the case writers attended a team meeting in early 1993. At the team meeting it was announced that the BX was scheduled for an almost immediate conditional release. This upset some team members as certain key issues had not been resolved. More discussion of the BX development and release can be found in Case 13.

G4 Product Development.   The G4 sleeve lined plug valve has been manufactured for over 22 years and has been a major source of revenue for the division. Currently, the G4 is in a declining market. The dollar sales are decreasing more slowly than unit sales, which has helped to mask the degree of the problem.

Reasons for the market decline are not apparent. Pricing is recognized as very critical in a declining market. CVD's new marketing staff is organizing efforts to listen to customer needs to see if new programs could be instituted to reverse the trend.

Competitor analysis has begun to evaluate competitor advantages. Only one major competitor exists in the G4 plug valve market. This competitor has a special products group, as well as the ability to do field modifications.

Product Development.   To replace shrinking G4 sales, the G5 Product Development Team was formed. The team is comprised of:

Dennis Garber, marketing.
Gerry McDermott, project engineering.
Mr. Shanks, engineering.
Joe Beaumont, manufacturing.
Patty Breig, materials engineering (Dayton).
Marv Grady, plant manager, engineered plastics (Dayton).
Jack Wiseman, chief engineer for plastics (Dayton).
Chief engineer from Atomac (Germany).

The G5 team first asked itself what things it should consider in designing a new valve. Team members looked at Valve Manufacturers Association (VMA) data and issued questionnaires to customers to find out what would be necessary to capture share in this competitive market. The G5 team then turned to its salespeople to ask how they felt customers made valve purchasing decisions.

The team is currently in the process of further customer questioning. This round of inquiry is looking for problems with the valves currently available. The survey is also searching for indications of the requirements for the year 2000.

From this point the team has plans to integrate the customer responses into initial design possibilities. The target is to have a product either as good as the competition at a lower price, or much better than the competition at the same price. They know from research that in this market the customer is not willing to pay a premium price for a premium product. This approach is expected to presage similar approaches for other project teams and products.

6 COSTING AND TECHNOLOGY

READING 6–1
TOOLS FOR COST-EFFECTIVE PRODUCT DESIGN AND DEVELOPMENT

Lakshmi U. Tatikonda
University of Wisconsin—Oshkosh

Mohan V. Tatikonda
University of North Carolina at Chapel Hill

"National prosperity is created, not inherited," says Michael Porter [3, p. 73]. The competitiveness of a nation depends on the capacity of its industry to innovate and upgrade. In order to succeed and prosper in intense global markets, firms need to develop strategies to achieve superior customer satisfaction. Three such strategies suggested by Porter [4] are: (1) *cost leadership,* which aims at achieving products with the same or similar attributes as the competitors', but at a lower cost; (2) *differentiation,* which tries to provide products with unique features such as higher quality or greater ease of use; and (3) *focus,* which aims to satisfy the needs of a single market in an exceptional manner.

In the past, companies often competed effectively by employing any one of these three strategies. However, to remain viable in today's intensely competitive global markets, companies need to achieve low cost along with differentiation and focus. For many U.S. companies, cost reduction is not a continuous, ongoing effort, but a one-time purge or crisis activity [5]. Failure to fully understand the nature of cost containment and the interdependencies of cost, focus, and differentiation often results in curing superficial symptoms while the underlying sickness spreads.

Traditional cost accounting and cost control techniques address tracking and reduction of costs once the product is in full-volume manufacturing. However, as shown in Figure 1, an extraordinary degree of a product's cost is committed during the design stage. According to General Motors executives, 70 percent of the cost of manufacturing truck transmissions is determined in the design stage [13]. Cost containment must also focus on efforts during the development of the product to minimize the final product cost. In this article, a number of tools are introduced which can be used early in the process to design and develop cost-effective products.

Source: Reprinted with the permission of APICS from *Production and Inventory Management Journal,* 2d quarter, 1994, pp. 22–28.

The product design and development process determines product attributes such as functional capabilities, appearance, reliability, and product life span. Product design affects ease of manufacture and product serviceability, and dictates the number and type of parts required and the manufacturing processes (such as tools and dies) that are needed to make and assemble them. The cost of engineering changes made after the design stage tends to increase in an exponential manner. As shown in Table 1, engineering change costs are estimated to increase 10-fold at each stage in the development of electronic products [9]. Fortunately, through use of appropriate tools, many of these changes can be avoided or made in earlier stages, thus either reducing or avoiding the costs altogether [6].

Simplifying product designs results in numerous benefits such as reduced costs, improved quality, and shorter product development lead times. For example, by redesigning its 2760 Point-of-Sale cash register, NCR reduced assembly time by 75 percent, parts by 80 percent, the number of supplies by 65 percent, and saved $1.1 million in direct labor alone [12].

Product Design Process

How products are designed has changed significantly over the years. Cross-functional teams are replacing functional areas working in isolation. Customer-focused product designs are replacing expensive, slow, and reactive engineering changes [7].

The Old Way of Designing Products.   In designing and manufacturing their products, many U.S. manufacturing companies follow a sequential or "relay-race" approach. As shown in Figure 2, different functional groups are involved, one at a time, with each group "handing off" to the next. In this approach, the product development effort is initiated by marketing, which

FIGURE 1

Cost Generators and Accounting Focus

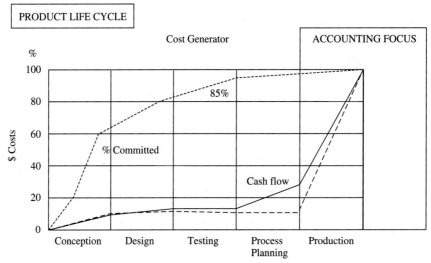

At the time of design completion, 5% of the budget has been spent, but 80% more is committed.

TABLE 1   Cost of Product Design Change

Change Made During	Estimated Cost
Design	$ 1,000
Design testing	$ 10,000
Process planning	$ 100,000
Test production	$ 1,000,000
Final production	$10,000,000

specifies the product functions, features, and approximate cost. Design engineering then designs a prototype and prepares documents detailing specifications of the desired product. These specifications are then used by manufacturing engineering to design and configure the needed tools, fixtures, and manufacturing equipment. Then, production manufactures the product in volume. Finally, the product becomes the responsibility of sales, distribution, and service groups.

This approach is inefficient, time-consuming, and expensive. Design engineers often work in virtual isolation with little or no knowledge of downstream opera-

tions and the impact of their product designs on manufacturing and servicing costs of the product.

The New Way of Designing Products.   To achieve competitive advantage, a number of firms now employ a product design and development process that involves several functional groups interacting simultaneously to identify and solve problems and take advantage of opportunities (see Figure 3). In this approach, products are developed in short, overlapping phases with interaction and feedback from multiple functional areas. Cost-containment tools play a vital role in this integrated approach.

Tools for Cost-Effective Product Design and Development

Cost-containment tools are methods employed individually or collectively to reduce or eliminate costs, and are particularly effective in controlling the costs of downstream operations. Target costing, value engineering, activity-based costing, cost tables, group technology, failure mode and effect analysis, and human factors engineering are some examples of cost containment techniques.

Figure 2

Traditional Product Development Process

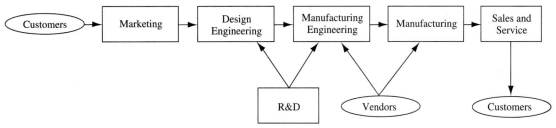

Figure 3

New Approach to Product Development

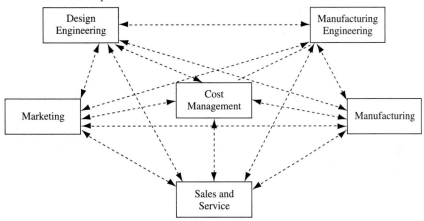

Target Costing.   The target cost of a product is the selling price less desired profit. In a competitive environment where the market determines the selling price, the desired profit can be earned only if companies learn to design and sell products to meet the target cost [8]. The target-costing process consists of two phases. The first phase includes planning and establishing the target cost. During this phase, the marketing or product planning department provides the engineering department with information about new products and/or model changes and the selling price at which the desired market share and volume can be achieved. The engineering department then prepares detailed product specifications along with specifications of materials, parts, tolerances, and assembly steps. The cost management department converts these specifications into cost estimates and checks whether the proposed design achieves the target profit levels [2].

Example 1: Developing the Target Cost.   Alpha Company estimates that they can sell 1,000,000 units at $100 per unit. Alpha expects to invest $100,000,000 in this product and desires to earn a return of 20 percent on investment. The following computations indicate that a target cost of $80 is needed to achieve this profit goal.

Target profit = 20% of $100,000,000 = $20,000,000

Revenue = Volume × Selling price
                  = 1,000,000 × $100 = $100,000,000

Target profit = Revenue − Cost

$$= \$100,000,000 - Cost = \$20,000,000$$

⇒ Target cost = $80,000,000

⇒ Target cost/unit

$$= \$80,000,000/1,000,000 = \$80/unit$$

If the estimated cost of the product as designed is higher than the target cost, then the second phase of the target-costing process is initiated. Cost reduction targets are set and creative ways to improve the product design to achieve these target reductions are explored. Target costing provides numerous benefits that are not available from traditional standard cost systems. Target costing is congruent with corporate strategic and profit planning, and unlike traditional cost systems, it measures and emphasizes cost reduction at the design stage.

Value Engineering. Oscar Wilde [14] said that "a cynic knows the cost of everything and the value of nothing," which is an important lesson in the context of product design. In a complex product design, all components add to both the cost and value of the total product. Value engineering (also known as value analysis, value control, and value manufacturing) provides a systematic approach to evaluating which design and manufacturing alternatives are essential to achieving product specifications.

In assessing the value of an alternative, both *functional value* and *esteem value* are considered. Functional value is the perceived value of the intended use (e.g., the primary purpose of an automobile is to provide transportation). To achieve maximum functional value is to achieve the lowest possible cost of providing the performance function.

Maximum esteem value is achieved by identifying the lowest possible cost of providing the necessary aesthetic features customers desire (e.g., sporty look, nice paint job). Table 2 shows relative functional and esteem values of some common consumer products.

Value engineering requires a cross-functional team to analyze the relative value of each product function. This entails determining the ratio of cost to perceived value for each function. It is conducted in two phases: analytical and creative. During the analytical phase, a team of experts from all relevant components of design and manufacturing investigates the functional value and esteem value. A series of questions such as the following are asked as each product function or feature is studied with respect to its cost and value.

TABLE 2 Estimated Functional and Esteem Value of Selected Products

Product	Functional Value	Esteem Value
Neck tie	10%	90%
Tie Clasp	20%	80%
Hammer	85%	15%
Shirt Button	90%	10%

- What is it?—A tie clasp.
- What will it do?—Hold tie in place.
- What is its cost?—$6.
- What is its value to the customer?—$15.
- Can something else accomplish the same function?—A paper clip can accomplish this function.
- What is the cost of the alternative?—$0.02.
- What is the value of the alternative to the customer?—$0.00, since this alternative is not aesthetically pleasing.

During the creative phase, the findings of the analytical stage are used by the team in seeking creative ways to eliminate any unnecessary functions or features or modify them to increase the value for customers. The team also tries to define novel design solutions that maintain the desired balance between functional value and esteem value [2].

Activity-Based Costing. The underlying concept of activity-based costing (ABC) is that products consume activities, and activities generate cost. Though initially designed to provide accurate product cost, ABC systems are extremely effective as cost-containment and communication tools. In addition to helping select design specifications to minimize material costs, the number of assembly steps, and so on, ABC also identifies activities that can be:

- Reduced—reducing the time and effort needed to perform tasks by using efficient procedures (e.g., replacing an expensive labor operation with automation).
- Eliminated—eliminating non-value-added tasks by altering design and procurement practices

(e.g., reducing unneeded material handling operations).

- Shared—reducing the cost and time it takes to design and produce a product (e.g., by using existing parts and standardizing components rather than creating new ones) [11].

Example 2.   To obtain more accurate product costing, the Beta Company used ABC-based overhead cost allocation. Accordingly, $6,000,000 in materials overhead (MOH) costs were allocated to products. The first stage of the allocation was based on the quantity of part numbers (10,000). The second stage of the allocation was based on the average usage of each part. The usage of an "active" part averages 10,000 units per year, while that of an "inactive" part averages only 100 units per year.

MOH applied/Part no. = $6,000,000/10,000 = $600

Active part: MOH applied/Part usage = $600/10,000 = $0.06

Inactive part: MOH applied/Part usage = $600/100 = $6.00

This information helps engineers understand the cost impact of using an inactive part ($6.00) compared with the cost of using an active part ($0.06). Accordingly, they may design or redesign products to contain stan-

dard parts. A part eliminated (or not designed in the first place) avoids the costs to design, document, procure, inspect, store, retrieve, fabricate, and assemble it.

Cost Tables.   Cost tables are computerized databases containing comprehensive and multidimensional information regarding the firm's major cost drivers [15]. Cost tables provide timely and relevant cost estimates regarding the impact of using different materials, components, product specifications, machinery, and manufacturing steps on product cost. This information helps design engineers and cost accountants in:

- Designing new products to achieve specific target costs.
- Modifying existing products to achieve target cost reductions.
- Selecting and maintaining desired product lines.

There are two types of cost tables: design cost tables, which assist in cost estimation of new products; and manufacturing cost tables, which assist in cost reduction of existing products. See Figure 4 and Table 3 for representation of the information in Example 3.

Example 3.   Gamma Company is considering design alternatives for a new staple gun. The options include three types of material (plastic, aluminum, and steel),

FIGURE 4

Gamma Company Estimated Product Cost

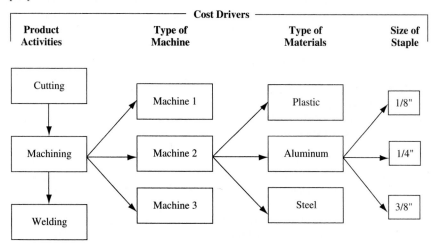

TABLE 3   **Gamma Company: Estimated Cost of Staple Gun When Using Machine 2**

Material Type	Staple Size											
	1/8"				1/4"				3/8"			
	DM	DL	OH	Total	DM	DL	OH	Total	DM	DL	OH	Total
Plastic	$3	$3	$6	$12	$4	$4	$6	$14	$5	$5	$7	$17
Aluminum	$6	$2	$5	$15	$9	$3	$6	$18	$9	$4	$6	$19
Steel	$8	$2	$5	$15	$9	$3	$6	$18	$9	$4	$6	$19

DM: Direct material.
DL: Direct labor.
OH: Overhead.

three sizes of staples (1/8", 1/4", and 3/8"), and three types of manufacturing processes. Cost tables were employed to estimate the cost of a staple gun under various input combinations.

Cost tables go beyond activity-based costing. ABC provides information based primarily on current and indirect costs, whereas cost tables contain information on direct and future costs in addition to indirect and current costs. Cost tables reflect an understanding of both the technological and financial aspects of the business.

Group Technology. Group technology identifies and exploits the similarity of products, parts, functions, and activities. Group technology classifies and codes parts according to their characteristics, such as material (aluminum, plastic, ceramic), shape (round, square, triangle), and size (small, medium, large). This classification and coding effort, manual or computerized, facilitates speedy retrieval of information since it simplifies the cumbersome job of sifting through numerous drawings to find a previously designed part. Design engineers identify the code for the desired part, and a search of the group technology database then reveals whether the same or a similar part exists. If one is found, the designer can simply modify the existing design or use the existing part.

Lack of such information leads to costly mistakes, such as designing the same part many times. For example, in General Dynamics an identical part was designed five different times by five different design engineers, drawn by five different draftspeople, and purchased by five different agents at prices ranging from

$0.22 to $7.50 per unit [1]. One midwestern firm employed group technology classification and coding and found that 50,000 parts could be classified into 3,500 families. Many families had duplication rates approaching 50 percent. The firm, in one situation, found 18 different part numbers and 11 different part names for one part [10].

Benefits from group technology in controlling part proliferation, eliminating redundant part designs, facilitating standardization, and improving productivity are phenomenal. For example, a reduction of a mere 10 percent of the new parts for a manufacturing company releasing 20,000 new parts a year, with annual costs per part ranging from $1,500 to $20,000, can easily result in savings of $3 million to $40 million.

Group technology benefits also extend to procurement. Fewer parts mean fewer vendors, smaller purchasing staff, larger purchase volumes, and quantity discounts. Even with a small discount of two cents per piece, one company saved $96,000 per year over a volume of 4.8 million pieces [1]. Further, design engineers and accountants can use group technology information to estimate product costs under alternative design and manufacturing approaches.

Failure Mode and Effect Analysis. Failure is the inability of a component or subsystem to perform its intended function. While some component or subsystem failures are hard to predict, many are often predictable. For example, switches fail to turn on or off, assemblies become loose, and components break. These patterns of failures are called failure modes.

Failure mode and effect analysis (FMEA) techniques provide the design team a systematic means of studying the causes and effects of product failures. Every possible malfunction of each component and assembly is studied individually and an estimate is made for each possible failure's frequency, technical and financial seriousness, and effect on the total system. Table 4 shows some failure modes for the electrical cord of a common household appliance such as a toaster. For each failure mode, the effect of the failure on the system and appropriate corrective actions are listed. This analysis allows the product design team to take appropriate corrective actions and redesign the product to prevent failures.

Human Factors Engineering.   The essence of human factors engineering is the application of engineering knowledge to design user-friendly products (i.e., products that are easy to use and have a minimal potential for human error). Many product design features, such as the shape and feel of the product or the location of its controls, influence its cost and operating and maintenance capabilities.

Poorly designed products are difficult and frustrating to use. A classic example is the videocassette recorder. For many individuals, the timed taping feature of a VCR is practically nonfunctional due to unintelligible instructions and numerous and confusing operating steps. Well-designed products take into consideration that it is easier to modify product characteristics to match human capability than to modify human capability to match the product characteristics. They contain visible clues to their operation that act as stimuli to the users of their intended function.

Designs devoid of human factor considerations often result in suboptimal use of the product, even to the point of making it functionally useless. For example, a high-speed hand drill cannot be used to its full capacity if its vibration makes it too painful to hold. Many accidents that are normally attributed to one's clumsiness or inability to operate the product can be traced to "user-hostile" design.

Human factors engineering rules are simple: design the product features and controls so that the user can look at them, understand them, and figure out how to use them in a reasonable amount of time. Products designed in such a way:

- Make erroneous actions practically impossible (e.g., automobiles that won't allow the doors to be locked unless the keys are removed from the ignition).
- Minimize the potential for error (e.g., automatic toasters that make it difficult to burn toast).
- Make it easy to reverse an erroneous action (e.g., a cancel button that overrides a previous command).
- Provide safety controls to eliminate potential injury (e.g., microwave ovens that automatically shut off power when the door is opened, eliminating possibility of radiation).

TABLE 4   Failure Mode and Effect Analysis: Electrical Cord of Household Appliance

Failure Mode	Cause of Failure	Effects of Failure on System	Corrective Actions	Potential Damage if Not Corrected
Loose wiring	Usage Vibration Improper handling	Electricity does not flow Generates excess heat	Molding the plug and wiring	Could cause fire
Broken or frayed wire	Improper insulation Fatigue	Electricity does not flow Generates excess heat Causes shock if touched	Using wire suitable for the appliance Adding proper insulation	Dangerous May result in death

- Provide a dialogue with the user (e.g., automatic teller machines that direct the user regarding how to operate it).

User-friendly product designs cut warranty and liability costs, create favorable product distinction, attract a larger customer base, and create significant competitive advantage, all of which translate into a larger bottom line.

Summary

Today's cost systems are often not in congruence with effective product development efforts. Rather than only tracking manufacturing costs and focusing on after-the-fact manufacturing variances, cost systems should consider the total cost of a product over its life cycle. The life-cycle cost of a product is significantly impacted by how it is designed. Design decisions include a complex array of diverse and often contradictory human and technological issues that differ with each product and continually change and evolve during the realization of the design. Thorough and careful consideration of design decisions and appropriate use of cost-containment tools, such as the ones described in this article, help ensure business success.

References

1. N. L. Hyer and U. Wemmerlöv, "Group Technology and Productivity," *Harvard Business Review,* September/October 1984, pp. 140–49.
2. Y. Monden and M. Sakurai, eds., *Japanese Management Accounting: A World Class Approach to Profit Management* (Cambridge, MA: Productivity Press, 1989).
3. M. E. Porter, "Competitive Advantage of Nations," *Harvard Business Review,* March/April 1990, pp. 73–93.
4. _____, *Competitive Strategy* (New York: Free Press, 1980).
5. P. Richardson, *Cost Containment: The Ultimate Advantage* (New York: Free Press, 1988).
6. S. R. Rosenthal and M. V. Tatikonda, "Competitive Advantage through Design Tools and Practices," in G. I. Susman, ed., *Integrating Design and Manufacturing for Competitive Advantage* (New York: Oxford University Press, 1992).
7. _____, "Time Management in New Product Development: Case-Study Findings," *IEEE Engineering Management Review* 21, no. 3 (1993), pp. 13–20.
8. M. Sakurai, "Target Costing and How to Use It," *Journal of Cost Management,* Summer 1989, pp. 39–50.
9. "A Smarter Way to Manufacture," *Business Week,* April 30, 1990, pp. 110–17.
10. M. V. Tatikonda and U. Wemmerlöv, "Adoption and Implementation of Group Technology Classification and Coding Systems," *International Journal of Production Research,* September 1992, pp. 2087–2110.
11. P. B. Turney, "How Activity-Based Costing Helps Reduce Cost," *Journal of Cost Management,* Winter 1991, pp. 29–35.
12. T. R. Welter, "Design for Manufacture and Assembly," *Industry Week,* September 4, 1989.
13. D. E. Whitney, "Manufacturing by Design," *Harvard Business Review,* July/August 1988, pp. 83–91.
14. Oscar Wilde, *Lady Windermere's Fan,* Act III (1892).
15. T. Yoshikawa, J. Innes, and F. Mitchell, "Cost Tables: A Foundation of Japanese Cost Management," *Journal of Cost Management,* Fall 1990, pp. 30–36.

CASE 6–1
EVALUATION OF OUTSOURCING OPTIONS AT STRATUS COMPUTER, INC.

Jeanne Ross
Sharon Johnson

In late February 1993, Gary Hartmann, manager of manufacturing operations at Stratus Computer, Inc., presented Mark Boissonneault, manufacturing controller, with sourcing proposals from two different subcontractors for the XA/R Model 10 power supply. The Model 10 had received enthusiastic reviews from industry publications when it was introduced seven months earlier, and internal forecasts were projecting sales of 1,200 units over the next year. By the end of the week, Boissonneault would submit both a financial analysis and a recommendation to Joe Sullivan, vice president of manufacturing, regarding the production of the power supply and its major subassembly. Stratus could continue to manufacture the power supply in-house, or the company could buy all or part of the power supply from subcontractors.

Historically, Stratus had often chosen to outsource the production of mechanical assemblies and electromechanical subassemblies for its computer lines. Management felt that outsourcing offered important benefits. As Hartmann noted:

> Our unique competency is the design and manufacture of powerful, reliable, high-quality computer systems. Subcontracting the production of parts permits us to focus on our core business. We don't want a shortage of $5 cables to prevent shipment of a $300,000 computer. Subcontractors have volumes that justify the investment in needed manufacturing facilities so they can produce parts costeffectively and also maintain the flexibility to respond to schedule changes.

Nonetheless, Stratus analyzed each make-or-buy decision independently, considering not only the financial

impact of outsourcing, but also the implications for quality, lead time, and flexibility. Having collected a variety of data, Boissonneault and Hartmann were prepared to weigh the merits of the two subcontractor proposals and the internal production option.

Background

Founded in 1980 by William Foster, Stratus Computer, Inc., ranked in 1993 as the world's second-largest manufacturer of fault-tolerant/continuous-availability computers. While generating only a quarter of the sales of market-leading Tandem Computers, in recent years Stratus had been the more profitable of the two, earning $49.7 million on sales of $448.6 in 1991 in contrast to Tandem's $66 million loss. Stratus also competed against Digital Equipment Corporation, the only large computer company to enter the fault-tolerant market, as well as several smaller companies such as Sequoia Systems, Inc.

By definition, fault-tolerant machines continue to operate even when they experience hardware problems. Continuous-availability machines offer even greater reliability, in that they survive not only hardware problems, but also operator errors, software problems, routine maintenance, and software upgrades. Because of their reliability, fault-tolerant/continuous-availability machines are of interest to any organization that has mission-critical computer operations. Initially, only life-and-death operations such as air traffic control and nuclear power facilities could justify the high premium for fault tolerance, but increasingly powerful chips and low-end machines were bringing prices down to where fault-tolerant computers were common in telecommunications operations and even more traditional data processing operations when companies felt they paid a high price for downtime.

In July 1992 Stratus introduced its line of 10 XA/R machines, which more than doubled the price/performance ratio of prior models. Ranging in price from $124,000 to $1.13 million, they offered improved levels of availability. Like prior Stratus computers, the XA/R machines' distinctive feature was that fault tolerance was built into the hardware. This design provided a

Professors Jeanne Ross and Sharon Johnson of Worcester Polytechnic Institute prepared this case as the basis for class discussion. Product names and costs have been disguised. The authors wish to thank Mark Boissonneault and Andrea Wilkinson of Stratus Computer, Inc., for their valuable input. Recipient of the "one of the best cases" award at the preconference workshop at the First National Conference on Business and Engineering Education, Auburn University, April 5, 1994. Copyright © 1993 by the National Consortium for Technology in Business, c/o the Thomas Walter center for Technology in Business, Auburn University, Auburn, AL.

key competitive advantage for Stratus because it offered a simpler programming environment than computers which achieve fault tolerance through joint hardware-software solutions. Competition in the fault-tolerant/continuous-availability industry was increasing, which led to shrinking gross margins (standard gross margins were currently in excess of 50 percent) and greater emphasis on quality and reliability. The telecommunications industry, in particular, was looking for even greater levels of availability (about three minutes of downtime per year), which none of the competitors could yet offer.

Stratus's manufacturing strategy was to cut cycle times and move toward just-in-time production processes. This would involve maintaining minimal inventories of raw materials, assemblies, and subassemblies. All Stratus machines were made-to-order, and Stratus intended to consistently reduce the time between receipt of an order and shipment of the machine. Because orders fluctuated greatly and tended to cluster around the end of each quarter, this strategy required considerable flexibility on the part of subcontractors. In addition, Stratus wanted subcontractors to start accepting responsibility for inspection. The shifting of responsibility would save time in the production cycle as long as Stratus could trust that a vendor was delivering high quality. Hartmann provided an example:

> Our sub(contractor)s accept responsibility for inspecting the housings for our power supplies. If we find a bad housing, we put the sub on notice. With a second unacceptable housing, we take the sub off the preferred vendor list. The only way to get back on is to work through a vendor quality inspector, which is a third party that inspects goods for us. This is slow and we prefer not to use this service.

Stratus's 2,700 employees were distributed among its Marlborough, Massachusetts, headquarters facility, its manufacturing plants in Marlborough and Dublin, Ireland, and its worldwide sales offices. William Foster carefully avoided hiring large numbers of managers, sensing that high fixed costs had been the undoing of many large computer companies. Stratus employed a flexible workforce in the manufacturing plants and exemplified cost consciousness in a variety of ways, including executive offices that were no larger or more glamorous than those of other Stratus managers.

Power Supply Production

The AS-301, the basic power supply for the Model 10, was manufactured in Marlborough, while the AP-300,

the controller board and key subassembly in the power supply, was assembled by a local subcontractor. The production process consists of three main activities: receiving and inspection, kitting, and assembly and testing. The sequence of activities is shown in Exhibit 1. First, the parts for both the controller board and the power supply are received, inspected, and stored. Employees then kit the parts for the controller board and ship them to a subcontractor for assembly. Returned controller boards are stored until all parts for the AS-301 power supply are kitted to the floor. Assembly and testing constitute the final stages in the production of the power supply.

The elapsed time between kitting parts for the AP-300 controller board and receipt of completed boards from the subcontractor was seven weeks. Once the controller board was received, the in-house assembly process for the AS-301 power supply took about two weeks. Typically, manufacturing costs were monitored by checking variances against standard costs (the 1993 standard cost summaries for the AS-301 and AP-300 are shown in Exhibit 2). Like many other organizations, Stratus sometimes considered standard costs in making managerial decisions, but Boissonneault was not comfortable with the financial analysis of make-buy decisions based on standard costs and traditional make-or-buy analysis techniques:

> There are different costs for different purposes. Frozen standard costs based on one plantwide overhead rate are adequate for valuing inventory and figuring out gross margins and cost of sales, but really not useful for analyzing sourcing decisions.

Boissonneault worked with manufacturing engineers and factory floor supervisors to learn more about the processes of producing the AP-300 and AS-301. The information he acquired is shown in Exhibit 3 and described below.

Receiving and Inspection. The bills of material for the AP-300 and the AS-301 are shown in Exhibit 4. Most of the raw materials for the two units are also used in other products. Only those with an asterisk in the "unique" column are ordered exclusively for manufacture of the controller board or power supply. The ABC designation refers to the frequency of orders. A parts are received twice per month. B parts are received once per month, and C parts are received once every two months. ABC designations are based on each part's inventory

EXHIBIT 1

AS-301 Production Process

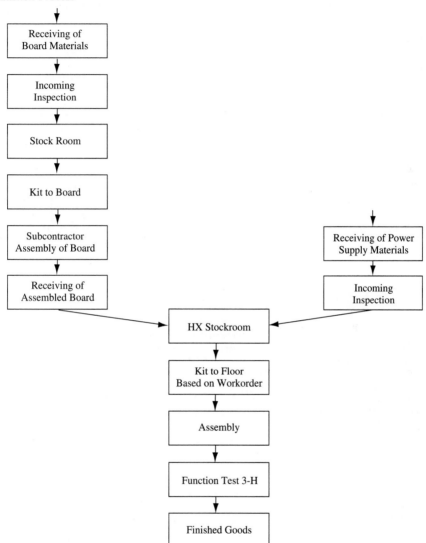

carrying costs relative to its order cost. Typically, higher-priced and bulky items are expensive to hold in inventory, so they are ordered more often than small and lower-priced items, which have relatively lower carrying costs.

The receiving and inspection activity involved visual inspection of parts, reviewing the packing slip, and transferring parts to the stockroom. Because parts were received at various times throughout the month, the time required to receive and inspect the parts for the AP-300 and AS-301, as shown in Exhibit 3, were estimates by the receivers. In the case of the AP-300, receiving and inspection occurred twice—once when the raw materials were received and again when the completed boards were returned from the subcontractor.

Exhibit 2

Total Standard Costs

	AP-300	AS-301*
Direct material	$98.75	$172.25
Subcontractor labor	78.25	
Component labor		78.25
Variable material overhead	10.27	17.91 @ 10.4% of direct material
Direct labor		9.58
Fixed overhead		28.75 @ 300% of direct labor
Total cost	187.27	306.75

*The AS-301 power supply cost includes the cost of the AP-300 printed circuit board (PCB), which is a component of the AS-301.

Exhibit 3

Breakdown of Variable Costs

Labor	Units	Time Taken per Unit (min.)	Parts per Unit	Standard Hourly Wage	Labor Cost per Unit
Receiving and inspection—assembled AP-300 (I)	Per assembly	20	3	$ 9.50	$3.17
Receiving and inspection—assembled AS-301 (I)	Per assembly	30	2	9.50	4.75
Kitting AP-300 (I)	Per component	20	3	10.25	3.42
Kitting AS-301 (I)	Per component	5	12	10.25	0.85
Assembly and testing AS-301 (D)	Per assembly	50	1.2	11.50	9.58
Receiving and inspection of components (I)	Per lot	15	4	9.50	2.38
Rework of AP-300 or AS-301 (I)	Per assembly			18.50	
Other Variable costs					
Subcontractor charge for AP-300		78.25			
Freight in—raw materials (AP-300)		0.90			
Freight in—raw materials (AS-301)		0.95			
Freight out—AP-300 kits		1.00			
Freight in—AP-300 assembled boards		1.00			

(I) = indirect or overhead labor.
(D) = direct labor operation.

Kitting Parts. Because many of the parts for the AP-300 controller board were very small and required hand-counting, kitting was a tedious and time-consuming process. Approximately 25 percent of the kits shipped to the subcontractor were in error—equally divided between overissues and underissues. Each overissue cost Stratus an additional 5 percent in material cost for the AP-300. Underissues were more expensive,

because the subcontractor would notify Stratus of missing parts and Stratus would respond by shipping the part by express delivery. Typically, these shipments cost about $8 per underissue. Time requirements for kitting of both AP-300 and AS-301 parts are shown in Exhibit 3. A kit for the AP-300 board included parts for 30 boards; a kit for the AS-301 included parts for 50 power supplies.

Assembly and Testing of the AS-301 Basic Power Supply.   Assembly of the AS-301 took place in four different stages, and Stratus had implemented quality checks at each step. The final 3-H test assured that the power supply performed to specifications. Following final test the power supply unit would be stored in finished goods, where it could be placed into a Model 10 or sold individually as a spare part. Direct labor hours associated with assembly and testing are shown in Exhibit 3.

Although the production process worked well, Stratus management felt that outsourcing might result in reduced cycle time, reduced cost, and greater quality and flexibility. For this reason they solicited bids for production of both the AP-300 controller board and the AS-301 power supply.

EXHIBIT 4

Bills of Material for AP-300 and AS-301

Unique	Part Number	Description	Quantity per Assembly	Extended Standard Cost (material only)	ABC	SC
AP-300						
*	CA-100	Cable	1	$ 5.00	B	P
	DI-400	Diode	14	0.50	C	P
	DI-500	Diode	1	0.06	C	P
	SC-009	Screw	1	0.07	C	P
	FU-002	Fuse	1	0.40	C	P
	RE-120	Relay	2	6.00	C	P
	LA-100	Label	1	0.02	C	P
*	LA-200	Label	1	0.15	C	P
*	PC-300	Printed circuit board	1	75.00	A	P
	VO-700	Voltage regulator	1	1.00	C	P
	RE-400	Resistor	1	0.25	C	P
*	TA-000017	Transformer	2	9.00	B	P
	OP-200	Optical couple	2	1.00	C	P
	IC-140	IC Transistor	2	0.20	C	P
	IC-500	IC Timing circuit	1	0.10	C	P
		Direct material total		98.75		
		Subcontractor labor		78.25		
@10.4% of direct material		Variable material overhead		10.27		
		Total standard cost		187.27		
AS-301						
	AP-300	Controller board	1	$ 98.75	A	S
	CI-900	Circuit breaker	2	31.00	B	P
*	CA-260	Cable	1	8.00	B	P
	SC-330	Screw	4	3.00	C	P
*	LA-210	Label	1	4.00	C	P
	CH-440	Chassis	1	25.00	A	P
	WI-100	Wire	3	2.50	C	P
		Direct material total		172.25		
		Component subcon labor		78.25		
@10.4% of direct material		Variable material overhead		17.91		
		Direct labor		9.58		
@300% of direct labor		Fixed DL overhead		28.75		
		Total standard cost		306.75		

SC = source code; P = purchased part; S = subcontracted assembly.

Outsourcing Alternatives

Stratus received bids from two subcontractors: Altec, a local Malcolm Baldrige Award finalist, and Hyko, a company based in Taiwan. Both companies were willing to produce either the AP-300 controller board or the entire AS-301 power supply. They would accept full responsibility for ordering, receiving, and inspecting parts, as well as assembly and testing of the completed unit. Altec and Hyko would both require Stratus to sign a one-year contract with a best estimate of total quantity for the year. Because both companies had extensive resources in terms of labor and equipment, Boissonneault sensed that both could respond to fairly broad fluctuations in demand over time. Although the initial contract would be for just one year. Stratus assumed that the part would be active for three years before new technologies would change power supply requirements.

Altec offered to produce the AP-300 controller board for $165 per unit. Incoming freight to Stratus would add $1.95 to the cost of each unit. Stratus would pay a one-time $4,000 charge for tooling and start-up costs. Altec would provide a one-year warranty on all parts and labor.

Altec also offered to produce the entire AS-301 at a per unit cost of $290.75 for the first 500, and $234.31 for all additional units. An additional tooling and start-up charge of $10,000 would be required. Freight on finished power supply assemblies would be about $13.95. Here too, Altec offered a one-year warranty.

Altec accepted all responsibility for inspection of goods shipped. It promised to deliver all orders with one week's lead time. Stratus had experience with Altec on a number of subassemblies for its computers and had been very pleased with the company's quality and reliability.

Hyko offered to produce the AP-300 controller board for $130 per unit. There would be no tooling or start-up charge. Freight expenses would be approximately $5.75 per unit, while customs and duty charges would add 7 percent of the value of the unit. Hyko offered a three-year warranty on any unit that failed.

Hyko would produce the entire AS-301 power supply at a cost of $200 per unit. Freight would add $40 to the cost, and the same customs and duty charges would apply. Hyko would offer a three-year warranty.

Hyko accepted all responsibility for inspection of goods shipped. It promised to deliver all orders seven weeks after they were placed. Hyko came highly recommended for its quality by two of its customers, although both references noted that delivery dates sometimes slipped by as much as two weeks.

Analyzing the Bids. In addition to the direct costs associated with producing the AP-300 and AS-301, a number of indirect costs were relevant to make-or-buy decisions. Exhibits 5 and 6 list some of the overhead pools that could be affected by decisions to outsource either or both units. Working with engineers and manufacturing floor supervisors Boissonneault collected the following data to help evaluate the bids:

- Stratus expected to produce 1,500 AS-301 power supplies and 1,500 AP-300 controller boards in the next fiscal year with 15% annual growth in production requirements the following two years.
- Within the first year, 0.5 percent of power supplies fail and must be returned to the factory for repair. Within two years the return rate increases to 2 percent, and 5 percent within three years. Sixty percent of the field failures are traceable to the AP-300 board. Typical direct labor required for rework of a failed power supply was six hours; material cost averaged $10. For a failed board the costs included four hours of direct labor and $2 of direct materials.

Exhibit 5

Material Overhead Pool

Department Description	Annual Budget
Purchasing	$ 210,000
Receiving	70,000
Incoming inspection	60,000
Stockrooms	55,000
Facilities	400,000
Management staff	300,000
Material planning	80,000
Freight	65,000
Total material overhead pool	$1,240,000

Projected direct material adds for the year = $11,923,076

Standard material overhead rate = $1,240,000/$11,923,076, or 10.4%

EXHIBIT 6

Direct Labor Overhead Pool

Department Description	Annual Budget
Stockrooms	$ 105,000
Facilities	700,000
Management staff	360,000
Production	65,000
Mechanical engineering	110,000
Electrical engineering	130,000
Quality programs	80,000
Traffic	55,000
Shipping	70,000
Total direct labor overhead pool	$1,675,000

Projected standard labor cost for the year = $558,333

Standard labor overhead rate = $1,675,000/$558,333, or 300%

- Savings in labor hours for receiving and inspecting, kitting, and assembly and testing would reduce overtime hours, which are paid at time and a half for all hours over 40.
- The following safety stock levels are assumed: A parts—2 weeks; B parts—9 weeks; C parts—13 weeks.
- An inventory carrying cost rate of 13 percent was used by the finance organization.

Boissonneault wanted to complete a thorough financial analysis of the Altec and Hyko bids as they compared to one another and to the existing production process. In addition, he wanted to make sure management considered the intangibles related to each alternative: "After all, what good is saving $5 per power supply if customer satisfaction suffers because of more frequent failures or longer delivery lead times?"

Technical Note
Accounting Measures of Manufacturing Costs

Jeanne W. Ross
Worcester Polytechnic Institute

Historically, accounting information has been used primarily to report the financial results of a firm. The goal has dictated what data is collected and how it is used. While some accounting data has been collected for purposes of helping managers understand the financial impacts of individual managerial actions and to assist with pricing decisions, support for these very important managerial decisions has been a secondary concern.

As the global economy becomes increasingly competitive, managers in organizations have a greater need to understand the impacts of their decisions on the cost and profitability of their organizations. They also need more precise information on costs in order to price products competitively. As a result, accounting information has become a strategic resource for many companies.

The reason understanding costs is so important is because the very competitive nature of business gives an edge to businesses that have cost-effective processes and that price products to maximize profits. Manufacturing facilities are extremely complex, so inefficiencies can be hidden. For example, managers have found cases where duplicate inspections are conducted in two different parts of a manufacturing plant. In other cases, machinery intended to increase output sits idle because bottlenecks further down the production line prevent utilization of the greater capacity of the new machines. Managers often must make decisions on whether to accept special orders at a discount, to reduce bids on certain kinds of contracts to generate new business in other areas, or to drop product lines. These kinds of decisions require that managers understand their costs and what causes those costs in order to make the most profitable decisions. A poor understanding of costs can actually lead to winning a contract that a business cannot afford to deliver on. Because understanding costs and how they behave is central to much managerial decision making, organizations are starting to collect accounting data that is not needed for financial reporting purposes.

This paper describes the kind of accounting information that has been available to managers. It then identifies the capabilities and limitations of typical managerial accounting systems. Finally, it reports on modern approaches to measuring manufacturing costs.

Financial Statements

Most accounting data that has been collected in organizations has focused on the need to report financial results. For-profit companies, in particular, provide quarterly reports to key stakeholders that indicate their profitability and financial soundness. At a minimum, companies will provide an income statement that summarizes the revenues and expenses the company incurred during a specified period of time, and a balance sheet that describes the assets, liabilities, and equity held by the company and its owners.

The income statement requires that companies match the revenues earned with the expenses required to generate those revenues. Thus, the income statement cannot simply state the dollar amounts that flowed into and out of the company. For a manufacturing company, this means that manufacturing costs (such as sawing, welding, and assembling) must be allocated to products on some reasonable basis.

Accountants calculate the cost of each product as a total of the material and labor incurred to manufacture that item, as well as overhead—costs incurred to support general factory operations. Thus, every product's cost includes a fraction of the plant manager's salary, property taxes on the facility, and other general operating expenses. The costs that are associated with the items that were sold during a specified period are reflected as an expense of that period (cost of goods or product sold). Costs that are associated with items that are in inventory and waiting to be sold are shown as an asset on the balance sheet. Examples of an income statement and balance sheet are shown in Exhibits A and B.

Example Income Statement

JOHNSON & JOHNSON AND SUBSIDIARIES
Consolidated Statement of Earnings
December 31, 1987, 1988, 1989
(dollars in millions except per share figures)

	1989	1988*	1987*
Sales to customers	$9,757	$9,000	$8,012
Cost of products sold	3,480	3,292	2,958
Selling, distribution and administrative expenses	3,897	3,630	3,228
Research expense	719	674	617
Other expense (income), net	93	(24)	(5)
	8,189	7,572	6,798
Earnings before interest and taxes on income	1,568	1,428	1,214
Interest income	87	72	95
Interest expense, net of portion capitalized	(141)	(104)	(116)
Earnings before provision for taxes on income	1,514	1,396	1,193
Provision for taxes on income	432	422	360
Net earnings	$1,082	974	833
Net earnings per share	$ 3.25	$ 2.86	$ 2.41

*Reclassified to conform to 1989 presentation.

Standard Costing Systems

Collecting manufacturing costs and allocating them to units for purposes of valuing cost of goods sold and inventory has never been an exact science. Companies are required to use consistent methods for valuing units over time, but due to the time and expense required to collect actual cost data, valuation relies on estimates rather than actual costs.

Most companies compute these estimated values by developing what are called standard costs. Standard costs are estimated costs of manufacturing a product. There are three components of standard costs: the expected raw materials costs (all the materials that are required to manufacture a single unit of a given product), the expected direct labor costs (average labor rate multiplied by the time required to manufacture the unit), and allocated overhead costs. Some overhead varies with production, such as utilities, lubricants, and supplies like nails and glue. Other overhead is required by a firm in order to stay in business. This includes property taxes, president's salary, legal department, and other expenses that are not directly attributable to a given product. This general overhead is totaled up and allocated to each product according to a predetermined cost base. Often, the cost base is direct labor costs. When labor costs are used to allocate overhead, products that require many direct labor hours absorb much of the general overhead costs.

As an example, if overhead is allocated based on direct labor hours, the standard cost of producing a tube of toothpaste would be a total of:

- Direct materials (budgeted cost of the ingredients and packaging).
- Direct labor (budgeted cost of the compensation to employees responsible for manufacturing the toothpaste multiplied by the amount of time spent on one tube.
- Overhead (total budgeted overhead cost divided by number of hours to be spent producing units multiplied by labor required for one unit).

For many years, standard costs were very useful. Materials and labor comprised the largest proportion of total costs, so the allocation of overhead costs, though

Exhibit B

Example Balance Sheet

JOHNSON & JOHNSON AND SUBSIDIARIES
Consolidated Balance Sheet
December 31, 1989, and January 1, 1989
(dollars in millions)

	1989	1988
Assets		
Current assets:		
Cash and cash equivalents	$ 452	$ 529
Marketable securities, at cost, which approximates market value	131	131
Accounts receivable, trade, less allowances $88 (1988, $71)	1,320	1,135
Inventories	1,353	1,273
Deferred taxes on income	196	183
Prepaid expenses and other receivables	324	252
Total current assets	3,776	3,503
Marketable securities, noncurrent, at cost, which approximates market value	254	188
Property, plant and equipment, net	2,846	2,493
Intangible assets, net	704	609
Deferred taxes on income	26	46
Other assets	313	280
Total assets	$7,919	$7,119
Liabilities and Stockholders' Equity		
Current liabilities:		
Loans and notes payable	$ 570	522
Accounts payable	622	651
Accrued liabilities	624	615
Taxes on income	111	80
Total current liabilities	1,927	1,868
Long-term debt	1,170	1,166
Certificates of extra compensation	85	77
Other liabilities	589	505
Stockholders' equity:		
Preferred stock—without par value		
(authorized and unissued 2,000,000 shares)	–	–
Common stock—par value $1.00 per share		
(authorized 540,000,000 shares; issued 383,670,000 shares)	384	384
Cumulative currency translation adjustments	(9)	(22)
Retained earnings	5,260	4,625
	5,635	4,987
Less common stock held in treasury, at cost		
(50,616,000 and 50,601,000 shares)	1,487	1,484
Total stockholders' equity	4,148	3,503
Total liabilities and stockholders' equity	$7,919	$7,119

inexact, did not result in large distortions. Managers could rely on standard costs as a starting point for determining prices and as a basis for understanding the efficiency of their operations. Efficiencies were determined by comparing total costs to budgets based on standard costs. Standard costs were inexpensive to develop and provided data for both managerial decision making and financial reporting.

Over time, changes in the business environment have made standard costs less valuable to management. Due to increasing automation, overhead consumes an ever larger portion of total cost, so that overhead allocations can result in significant cost distortions; thus, the bases for pricing products and evaluating operations are less reliable. At the same time, increasing competition has increased the need for a precise understanding of costs to enable profitable pricing and highly efficient operations.

Activity-Based Costing

To assist decision making, managers need better information on actual costs, and just as important, they need to understand how those costs come about. For example, if a pencil-making factory agrees to adjust equipment in order to add toothpicks to its production line, management will obviously need information on the impact of that change on equipment needs, additional labor, and additional materials. Management will also need a way to estimate how toothpick production will affect the maintenance of its machines, purchasing and shipping costs, customer accounting, human resource staff, computer services, and many other indirect services. Because standard costs provide no information on what drives costs, they do not support these kinds of decisions.

For this reason, organizations are starting to adopt activity-based costing approaches, which develop cost estimates from an understanding of the activities required to support each item that is manufactured. Activity-based costing approaches price each of an organization's key activities (which can number in the hundreds) and then build product costs by totaling the activities required to support each item.

Activity-based costing requires several steps for measuring product costs. The first step involves identifying all overhead activities and the drivers of those activities. Activities include such processes as placing purchase orders, inspecting incoming goods, sending invoices to customers, and hiring production line workers. Drivers of those activities are conditions that cause these activities to occur or determine the level of activity.

The second step involves determining the cost of each activity. This involves understanding the actual cost of a process, such as sawing a board, filling a tube of toothpaste, or completing a purchase order. In most organizations, data has not been collected in this manner, so determining the costs of activities requires very thorough analysis.

The third step requires identifying the appropriate measure for allocating the costs of activities. Some costs are related to the number of individual items produced, some are incurred with each process batch, regardless of the size of the batch, some result from the existence of a product line, and some support facilities. Some cost allocations are obvious, such as dividing warehouse property taxes among the space allocated to each product line, but often cost allocation is subjective, such as allocating depreciation expense when similar machines have different depreciation charges.

The final step involves developing a model that captures the interrelationships of costs, so that changes in a given activity can be tested to see their impact on other activities and costs. This is the most difficult part, because it demands a dynamic model, which is difficult to achieve.

The value of activity-based costing is that the analysis of processes can help identify where inefficiencies exist and can then provide fairly precise information on production costs. Thus, management better understands the impact on total operating costs of reducing activity in one area. The cost is significant, however, because most of the data required for activity-based costing models does not exist in company computers. Some organizations have implemented activity-based costing models that require manual input (often spreadsheet models are used). These have only short-term value, because the data input methods are too time-consuming. In the short term, manual calculation of activity-based costs can be worthwhile due to the insight it provides, but in the long term, activity-based costing requires computer support to be cost-effective.

Suggested Readings

R. Cooper and R. S. Kaplan, "Profit Priorities from Activity-Based Costing," *Harvard Business Review,* May–June 1991, pp. 130–35.

V. D. Hawks, M. P. Bonadies, A. B. Strong, and M. C. Reid, "Identifying Costs in Electronics Manufacturing Using Activity-Based Costing," *Journal of Applied Manufacturing Systems,* Winter 1992, pp. 70–81.

T. J. Stoffel, "Activity-Based Costing: The Competitive Advantage for the 1990s," *Journal of Applied Manufacturing,* Winter 1992, pp. 58–63.

CASE 6–2

AMERICAN SAW & MANUFACTURING COMPANY: CALCULATING COST PER CUT

Jeanne W. Ross
Christopher A. Brown

John Davis, president of American Saw & Manufacturing Company, expressed his frustration with potential customers who could not be convinced that low-cost saw blades were not a bargain.

> Sawing is one of the first operations in most metal working shops and it's not very glamorous. We've been in operations where saws are probably destroying millions of dollars worth of materials. These $25,000 machines have an incredible impact on the business. The guy running the saw knows this, but nobody listens.

To help demonstrate the cost-effectiveness of buying American Saw's Lenox brand saws, American Saw had developed SAWCALC, a personal computer software tool that offered recommended sawing parameters and comparisons of sawing costs between Lenox saws and competitors' brands. Davis felt that SAWCALC enhanced American Saw's commitment to "make products better than anyone else and to back up their quality with the world's finest technical services and customer support."[1] He hoped that business's increased awareness of total quality management concepts would make SAWCALC a more powerful marketing weapon and help customers obtain more value from their American Saw purchases.

Band Saw Blades

Band saw blades are required for industrial sawing machines in manufacturing operations that work with

---

[1] American Saw promotional literature, Catalog I-649-R, 1991.

This case was developed by Professors Jeanne W. Ross and Christopher A. Brown of Worcester Polytechnic Institute, Worcester, MA. Recipient of the "one of the best cases" award at the preconference workshop at the First National Conference on Business and Engineering Education, Auburn University, April 5, 1994. Copyright © 1994 by the National Consortium for Technology in Business, c/o Thomas Walter Center for Technology Management, Auburn University, Auburn, AL.

thousands of different materials, such as steel, fiberglass, graphite, aluminum castings, reinforced plastics, cast iron, and wood. Because blades can differ in their composition, gullet depth, and the form, angle, and spacing of their teeth, most band saw blade manufacturers offer hundreds of individual items. (See Exhibit 1 for the parts of a saw blade.) These blades are welded to length to fit specific machines and must be replaced when the blade breaks or the teeth become too dull. In general, blades would be replaced after approximately 80 hours of use.

Historically, most companies relegated responsibility for saw blade purchasing to purchasing managers. Many companies' standard costing systems calculated price variances as a measure of the purchasing department's effectiveness. This could result in the purchase of poor-quality saw blades that had to be changed more often, which hindered productivity, and ultimately increased manufacturing costs. Martin Kane, American Saw's director of corporate technology, described the problems created by poor quality blades at a company that bought the lowest-cost blades as part of its contract with the Defense Department:

> This company bought stuff that nobody else in the country bought because it was such terrible quality. Some manufacturers made these blades just for the aircraft industry. We call them "aircraft quality." I took some of their management people on a tour of the plant and we talked to the operators about the blades. The operators said they used one or two blades out of each coil. The rest they scrapped, because they were all snaky. They wouldn't weld properly. If you put one on a machine, it wouldn't cut straight. The guy doing the purchasing had never seen this operation. It was the cheapest blade in the world until operators started throwing them away.

The Saw Blade Industry

In early 1993 the United States dominated the $500 to $600 million global band saw blade manufacturing market with seven or eight manufacturers, but Germany,

EXHIBIT 1

Blade Basics

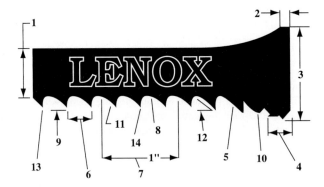

1. **Blade Back**—The body of the blade not including tooth portion.
2. **Thickness**—The thickness of the blade.
3. **Width**—The nominal dimension of a saw blade as measured from the tip of the tooth to the back of the band.
4. **Set**—The bending of the teeth to right or left to allow clearance of the back through the cut.
5. **Tooth**—The cutting portion of a saw blade.
6. **Tooth Pitch**—The distance from the tip of one tooth to the tip of the next tooth.
7. **T.P.I.**—The number of teeth per inch.
8. **Gullet**—The curved area at the base of the tooth.
9. **Gullet Depth**—The distance from the tooth tip to the bottom of the gullet.
10. **Tooth Face**—The surface of the tooth on which the chip is formed.
11. **Tooth Back**—The surface of the tooth opposite the tooth face.
12. **Tooth Back Clearance Angle**—The angle of the tooth back measured in relation to the cutting direction of the saw.
13. **Tooth Rake Angle**—The angle of the tooth face measured with respect to a line perpendicular to the cutting direction of the saw.
14. **Tooth Tip**—The cutting edge of the saw tooth.

Japan, and several other countries offered competition. A family business dating back to 1915, American Saw was the largest U.S. band saw blade manufacturer and probably the highest priced. It employed 700 people, mostly in its 500,000-square-foot headquarters plant in Springfield, Massachusetts. The company also owned a distribution center in Germany, which performed light manufacturing. Like other band saw blade manufacturers American Saw relied heavily on industrial distributors to sell and service its blades. Approximately 800 distributors in the United States and 55 other countries sold Lenox blades.

John Davis was an enthusiastic supporter of total quality management practices like employee empowerment and customer satisfaction. In one case, he had demonstrated his commitment to employee empowerment by sending four machine operators to a midwest trade show to select a major new piece of capital equipment. Promotional literature emphasized the company's commitment to customer satisfaction. Customer services included the Lenox Guaranteed Trial Order offer, a money-back guarantee that a Lenox blade would outperform the customer's current blade. In-plant seminars, machine tune-ups, hands-on demonstrations, and training manuals were all available to American Saw customers because Davis felt that effective use and maintenance of sawing machines was important to realizing the benefits of American Saw's high-quality blades. American Saw researchers developed products to improve sawing efficiency, such as the Traverse-Master, a precision electronic component that monitored the feeding rate of a saw blade to alert operators when the feed rate was above or below effective capacity. The Tension Meter monitored tension, and the Refractometer provided readings of a sawing operation's fluid to water ratio.

Sawing Costs

In most companies cost accountants allocate the cost of the sawing operation to product costs using standard costing techniques. This involves recording the direct materials and labor costs involved in sawing a particular product and attributing it directly to the cost of the product. All other costs associated with the sawing operation, such as depreciation of the machine, the cost of individual saw blades, the lubricants for running the machine, and the utilities powering the machines are incorporated into an overhead pool that may include costs associated with other operations. These are then allocated to individual products on some predetermined base, such as the direct labor hours or the machine hours required to produce a unit. A product's value in inventory (and eventually cost of goods sold) depends upon the total of its direct material and labor costs and its allocated overhead costs.

The standard cost of a product provides an estimate of the actual costs incurred throughout the production processes. The actual cost of a sawing operation depends upon a number of factors, including the following:

- Direct labor required to operate machinery.
- Machine costs, such as blades, depreciation, utilities, and other overhead costs.
- Cutting time.
- Blade changing time (downtime).
- Blade life.

These factors can be captured in equations that express sawing operations in terms of cost per cut. Through testing, American Saw management had determined that Lenox blades provided significantly longer blade life than low-cost blades. They felt that convincing clients to focus on cost per cut was the key to selling their higher-priced blades. Kane noted: "The cost per cut ultimately is the true measure of value. The Japanese know that, but we really have to preach it to American businesses."

Optimizing Sawing Operations

In theory, cost per cut calculations enable companies to optimize sawing operations. An optimatization model would consider tradeoffs between cutting time and blade life. Cutting time is a function of the cutting speed (how fast the blade moves), feed rate (how fast the material feeds into the blade), and the composition and geometry of the workpiece material. Blade life is a function of the cutting speed, the quality of the blade, the lubricant, the sawing machinery, and the workpiece material.

In practice, few, if any, companies attempt to calculate cost per cut. Although these calculations could potentially reduce the total cost of sawing operations, most companies would echo the sentiments of the prospective American Saw customer who said: "We're so busy mopping the floor, we don't have time to turn off the water."

Instead, customers typically rely upon manufacturers' literature that matches blades to cutting jobs and recommended cutting speeds. Manufacturers usually provide this information through slide charts that enable users to look up the materials they are cutting and identify the recommended cutting speed for each blade that might be used on the given material. Because customers use different machines, cut different sizes and shapes of materials, and vary in their expertise with regard to feeding materials into saws and calculating overhead, the optimum cutting speed actually differs by customer. So, the slide charts are based on performance specifications for the blades rather than optimization calculations. As a result, slide charts are conservative and ensure good utilization rather than optimum use.

Martin Kane observed that the slide charts never ensured effective use of blades. Machine operators sometimes used inappropriately fast cutting speeds, which often resulted in blades breaking before the teeth were worn. In some cases, poor cutting speed decisions were made by inexperienced or careless operators, but sometimes American Saw service technicians provided poor recommendations:

> We had service people who had been out there for years and their estimates of cutting speed kept going up. Depending upon how successful they were on their last account, they would go a little faster on the next one. Pretty soon, they were way out of range. They were getting failures and they didn't know why.

SAWCALC

To address concerns about inconsistent and unreliable recommendations and to improve customer information, Kane decided to computerize the slide chart. In 1985 he created SAWCALC, a proprietary piece of software intended to provide service technicians with consistent and reliable recommendations on choice of blade and cutting speed. The initial design was a lookup capability that provided slide chart information in an easy-to-read format. With the release of the first version, it became clear to Kane that the real potential for SAWCALC was to use it to calculate total cutting costs and compare the cost per cut of Lenox blades to those of competitors.

As he worked to revise the software, Kane enlisted a second researcher to help him study the performance of Lenox blades on different machines cutting workpieces of various sizes and shapes. By testing a variety of machines and materials they determined that cutting time for a given material of a specified size and shape was a function of three primary factors: cutting speed,

feed time, and tool. Kane noted that their research had implications for the entire organization: "When we discovered this correlation, I felt that it would change how we do business. It affects what tooth pitches we manufacture, how we sell the product, what tool we recommend for a job."

Following its introduction, SAWCALC was revised approximately every six months. Two researchers worked full-time to maintain the database, study interactions between key factors affecting cost per cut, adapt SAWCALC to new computing platforms, generate technical documentation, and train users. By 1992, SAWCALC could prescribe blade, cutting speed, and feed instructions given material composition and geometry and machine model (see Exhibit 2 for SAWCALC Recommendations screen). These recommendations varied according to the user's sawing objective. SAWCALC offered three alternative objectives: the fastest cutting parameters to minimize time, the longest life cutting parameters which would improve tool life at a reduced production rate, and a balanced option which provided

EXHIBIT 2

```
                    S A W C A L C ®  R E C O M M E N D A T I O N S

 Material:                      AISI 4140    Band speed (FPM):                    249
 Condition:               NOT HEAT TREATED.  Feed rates-
 Dimensions:          4" dia. SOLID ROUND      Entry / Exit (IPM):               4.25
 Area/piece (sq.in):               12.57       Max cross section (IPM):          3.34
    Pieces/cut:                        1        Average (IPM):                    3.85
 Total area (sq.in.):              12.57     Cutting rate (sq.in./min.):        12.10
 Machine:                    AMADA HA-400     Time per cut:                   00:01:02
 Feed system:                         D       Noncut cycle time:              00:00:20
 Blade size:               15' x 1-1/4"       Cycle time:                     00:01:22
 Tooth spec.:              3/4 Vari-tooth
 Blade type:                    MATRIX Z     OBJECTIVE: COST / CUT
 Blade tension (PSI):           30,000       PEP: 100.0%
 --------------------------------------------------------------------------------------
                           Break-in Instructions

               Start feed at 21% of normal feed and gradually increase
                     feed to normal over 72 sq.in. (5.7 cuts).




         F1:CHANGE MENU  F2:FINANCE MENU  F3:PRINTOUT  F7:OPTIONS
 E-SYS.   F8:LANGUAGE  F9:EXCHANGE  F10:ENGLISH/METRIC  ~A:HELP  ^E:EXIT <TAB> - CRT
```

parameters that balanced the other two objectives. It also provided cost per cut estimates for any combination of material, machine, labor and overhead costs, and setup time (see Exhibit 3).

SAWCALC recommendations for blade, cutting speed, and feed instructions resulted from cross-references to its database and then calculated results. The researchers at American Saw relied on their experience with existing blades and alloys as well as on new tests to develop parameters. The recommendations estimated probable conditions at their customers' sites, and the SAWCALC manual noted that individual operators might adjust recommended speeds based on their experience and conditions. SAWCALC had a database of 3,340 known alloys and 1,250 machine models with 20,000 cross-references. These were updated each time researchers learned of a new alloy or machine model.

The cost-per-cut calculations permitted users to manipulate 18 different cost factors (see Exhibit 4) and provided both the cost-per-part and the cost of a total job (as shown in Exhibit 3). It also permitted comparison with the cost per cut of a competitor's blade.

The software ran on both UNIX and DOS machines, and was leased to customers and distributors on an annual basis. American Saw's individual salespersons and service technicians were equipped with SAWCALC running on laptops to demonstrate cost-per-cut calculations for potential customers and to help existing customers judge cutting speeds and feed times. Davis, the president, reflected on the importance of putting SAW-CALC in the hands of customers, distributors, and company employees: "When we call on customers, they say that every manufacturer claims its blade is best. With SAWCALC we have data. The computer has a big impact on customers. Once they see the output, the war is won."

SAWCALC was useful in generating new customers, but it was perhaps even more valuable in supporting the efforts of existing customers. Responding to an open invitation, one company sent a team of engineers to

EXHIBIT 3

```
                         CUTTING COST ANALYSIS

Machine -
    cost ($):                 35,000.00   Cost per cut -
    depreciation (yrs.):            7.0       Labor:              0.23    (34.1%)
    Operation -                               Overhead:           0.34    (50.6%)
        Day/ year:                250         Total (Burden):             0.57  (84.7%)
        Shifts / day:               1         Blade:              0.06   (9.2%)
        Hours / shift:              8         Machine:            0.06   (8.4%)
        Total:                 2,000.00       Fluid:              0.006  (0.9%)
Metal cost ($/pound):             1.00        Total:                      0.68
Bar length:                       10'     Cost per piece:                 0.68
Blade change time:            00:10:00    Cost per square inch:           0.054
Labor cost ($/hr.):               7.50    Cost per part -
Fringe / tax: (35%)               2.63        Setup cost:                 0.01
Overhead cost ($/hr.):           15.00        Cut time cost:      0.52
Total burden ($/hr.):            25.13        Noncut time cost:   0.16
Blade cost:                      82.20        Cost per cycle:             0.68
Fluid cost ($/yr.):             558.32        Material cost:              3.56
Setup time:                   00:20:00        Kerf loss cost:             0.24
Total pieces required:           1,317        Total:                      4.48
Piece part length:               1.00"    Job cost:                   5,895.06




            F1:CHANGE MENU  F2:FINANCE MENU  F3:PRINTOUT  F7:OPTIONS
E-SYS.        F8:LANGUAGE  F9:EXCHANGE  F10:ENGLISH/METRIC  ^A:HELP  ^E:EXIT <TAB> - CRT
```

EXHIBIT 4

```
                    FINANCE OPTIONS MENU

    1. Labor rate                         7.50
    2. Overhead cost                      15.00
    3. Fringe / tax (percentage)          35.00
    4. Days worked per year               250
    5. Work shifts per day                1
    6. Hours per work shift               8
    7. Machine total cost                 35,000.00
    8. Machine depreciation (years)       7.00
    9. Fluid total cost                   558.32
    A. Setup time                         00:20:00
    B. Reloading time                     00:00:00
    C. Material cost per pound            1.00
    D. Work piece cut length              1.00"
    E. Stock length                       10
    F. Non-cut cycle time                 00:00:20
    G. Blade change time                  00:10:00
    H. Total pieces required              1,317
    I. Blade discount percent             0.00
  TAB. Apply changes / exit menu



            Press <F1> for change selections menu.
    E-SYS.      F8:LANGUAGE  F9:EXCHANGE  F10:ENGLISH/METRIC  ~A:HELP  ^E:EXIT
```

American Saw with a special steel alloy to test how cutting speed and quality varied on the different machines that American Saw maintained for testing purposes. American Saw checked SAWCALC recommended parameters prior to each test and found that the choice of the machine made a great difference in the quality of the cut even with the same blade. During the test process, the customer's engineers were impressed with the usefulness of SAWCALC and decided to lease a copy for applications in its plants. The company made it a habit to check SAWCALC recommendations prior to each sawing operation and to follow recommendations precisely. The company found SAWCALC recommended running its machines harder and shortening tool life slightly in order to minimize costs. Over a six-month period, the company reported that better utilization of the blades resulted in cost reductions of 30 percent per ton.

Distributors were enthusiastic about the value-added of SAWCALC. Tony Honig, president of Honig Industries, an industrial sales organization in Toronto, used SAWCALC in two ways. First, he found that SAWCALC provided starting points for tool, blade, and material combinations when testing new machines and materials. Second, he used it as a reference when customers called for help with machine settings. He noted that part of the value of SAWCALC derived from the knowledge of the user:

> Our knowledge is important to leveraging the value of SAWCALC. It's theoretically perfect, but when you get out in the field, the material isn't what they said, and the tool isn't running the way it's supposed to. SAWCALC tells us where to start and our experience takes it from there. Otherwise, we'd want to blow our brains out.

Despite very notable successes American Saw could not convince many potential customers to study SAW-CALC output. In particular, companies that focused on the price of the blade were not interested. Davis observed that the reluctance to buy higher-priced tools extended beyond the United States. "We took SAW-CALC to Israel to call upon some potential customers.

The thing that struck me about this was that here we are in another part of the world and the objections are no different here than if we were in Cleveland."

Honig also noted that he rarely used SAWCALC to calculate costs. "Customers don't think about costs in that way. Many feel that sawing has no cost, so they can't give the hourly rate that is needed to calculate the value of the blade."

Competitors had not yet developed comparable software products. Many had introduced lookup programs, similar to the original version of SAWCALC, but they had not attempted to generate cost per cut computations or to use software to help users apply their blades more effectively.

American Saw did not attempt to quantify either the costs or benefits of SAWCALC. Davis explained: "The value is hard to quantify. When you know the business, you know it works. It's really a strategic tool."

Future versions of SAWCALC would be developed on Windows so that operator instructions could be provided in pictures rather than words. These pictures would describe optimum cutting angles in addition to the currently available information. Recommendations would also become more precise as a result of computer modeling to better understand the interrelationships of the factors affecting cost per cut. In addition, American Saw planned to continue to update the database as soon as a new alloy was announced, or a new sawing machine model was placed on the market. Kane noted: "We're by no means done. We're doing tool life studies right now. Tool life is very nebulous because there are so many parameters. There's a ton of research that has to be completed."

Technical Note
Optimizing Cost per Cut

Christopher A. Brown
Worcester Polytechnic Institute

Objectives and Scope

These notes describe how to calculate and how to optimize the cost per cut in manufacturing. The ability to calculate the cost of a discrete manufacturing operation, on one component, is important to designing a manufacturing process, selecting tools and workpiece materials. Be aware that, while these notes are based primarily on machining (i.e., cutting, and the many variations thereof, such as, turning on a lathe, milling and sawing) it should be clear that this kind of calculation can be extended to other manufacturing operations.

One manufacturing operation may be composed of several steps (e.g., machining by turning requires that the part be loaded into the lathe, so there may be several individual machining steps once the part is loaded; then the part must be removed from the machine, chips may have to be cleared, and the tool may have to be changed). The cost of each of these steps may be influenced by the value selected for different manufacturing process variables. The costs can be calculated on a per part basis for a certain, limited portion of the entire manufacturing process, although this is not always done.

Calculating the cost of a manufacturing on this kind of discrete-operation basis is distinctly different than calculating the costs of manufacturing on a quarterly (three month) basis, a more common accounting procedure. The macroscopic view accorded by quarterly calculations is not detailed enough to be sensitive to the influence of many, or any, of the manufacturing process variables of interest. Therefore, the only way of optimizing these variables, and the optimum value may change with each lot of raw materials or tools, is to understand the cost of a discrete manufacturing operation on one component.

Optimization Options

The next issue is to identify what it is that should be optimized. Minimizing cost appears logical, however sometimes it is clear that maximizing the throughput could be more important. The importance of maximizing the throughput is usually linked to meeting a delivery, or keeping a transfer line in balance. There could be costs associated with missing the delivery or having the line out of balance, and with some effort these costs could be included in the equation, although accessing these costs is beyond the scope of this exercise.

Minimizing the manufacturing costs has appeal as an objective for processes design, and tool and workpiece selection. A more important goal is to maximize the profit rate. Developing this kind of strategy may require the assumption that the product containing the component will be sold, obviously an important, practical point. It might be simpler to assume that it is possible to put a value on the component at the end of the operation in question. Evaluating this value is problematic and beyond the scope of this exercise. In any event, one needs to be aware that minimizing costs is not the most important thing, and that the calculation of cost is an essential part of the profit calculation:

$$\text{Profit rate} = (\text{Value} - \text{Cost})/\text{Time}$$

where value implies selling, and is what the component is worth at the end of the operation. Cost is what will be calculated here, and time is the time to complete the operation in question. Note that since machine and labor costs are both based on time, the values of the process variables which result in the highest profit rate should be close to those that result in the lowest cost.

Rationale—Examples

A couple of examples can further support the rationale for studying ways for determining the cost per cut: One concerns a company which buys castings and then machines them into components. These components are assembled into valves. The company decided to purchase the castings at a lower price, from a new casting company. The castings from the new company are cheaper; however, they are more difficult to machine.

They require smaller feeds and lower speeds, tools wear faster, and tool holders break more frequently. There is a tendency to form long ribbonlike chips, which require the operator to stop and clear the chips, instead of the chips breaking up into small nines and sixes, which do not require operator intervention. The company's inability to calculate the cost of the machining operations means that they cannot assess which castings to use to make the components for the lowest cost. Another example concerns a large aerospace company, which purchases the least expensive saw blades it can find. This makes the purchasing department look good. When the blades get to the factory floor, however, many have to be discarded because the quality is so poor they cannot be loaded in the machines, cuts have to be made slowly, and the blades have to be changed frequently. Switching to a more expensive blade reduced the cost per cut significantly, because the cost of the blade is only one term in the cost equation and accounts for less than 20 percent of the cost of making the cut.

Manufacturing Cost Discretization

The methods for calculating cost should be understood in such a way that one will be capable of generalizing, that is, applying these methods to situations other than the machining operations used as examples here.

The classic equations for calculating the cost per cut in machining operations, which are found in manufacturing engineering texts, were developed by Taylor at the beginning of the 20th century (Taylor, 1907; Shaw, 1989, Chapter 19). They were developed in an age of mass production and manually operated machine tools. These classic equations provide a good starting point for our discussions, even though they may not be strictly applicable when industry uses computer-controlled machines and manufacturing cells and is moving toward mass customization. Variations of the classic equations to accommodate things like unattended operation of machines will be discussed.

The basic equation breaks the cost down into several components, for example:

$$C_{pc} = C_n + C_c + C_h + C_t + C_w \qquad (1)$$

where C refers to cost and the subscripts are defined as follows: pc is total per component, n is nonproductive, c is cutting, or machining, h is tool changing, t is tool, and w is material.

Nonproductive Cost

The nonproductive cost is cost intimately connected with the productive part of the process; however, no cutting is taking place while these costs are being incurred. The nonproductive cost can be expressed as a function of the nonproductive time:

$$C_n = x_1 T_1 \qquad (1.1)$$

where T_1 normally is the workpiece or part loading and unloading times, and x_1 is the labor plus machine cost per unit time. T_1 might also include a portion of the initial setup time for a production run and the time for tool positioning, loading software, filling out paperwork, or retrieving the parts from the previous operation. In these cases one should assign labor and machine costs appropriately, depending upon which are involved. Even while the machine is not operating, the cost of the machine time should somehow be attributed to a part. Some machines allow one part to be loaded while another is being machined; in these cases one could divide the machine portion of the part loading and unloading costs with the part being machined.

The nonproductive time is, in most cases, independent of any kind of cutting or processing speed. It is imaginable that the part-changing time could increase with processing speed. This can be the case with high-speed turning, where there may be significant nonproductive times required to stop a finished part and the time to spin a new workpiece up to the desired cutting speed.

Labor and Indirect Costs

The labor cost is the salary plus benefits for the machinist. The machine cost is based on the investment in the machine and the cost of the space on the factory floor. It is common to attribute indirect costs to some combination of the labor and the machine. Indirect costs are an important issue.

It can be argued that the total cost of running the factory, of developing the product and the manufacturing process, and of selling the goods should be reflected in the cost per part. When it is, then there is the issue of how to assign these costs in the production. The cost of running the factory includes the engineers, accounts, administrators, and managers, positions to which the students are probably aspiring. The more directly these costs can be associated with the goods in question, then the better the accounting will be. This is an important issue, because the best process parameters for a given optimization will depend on how the indirect costs are allocated to the production process. For example, if indirect costs are assigned to labor, then the apparent cost of labor goes up and the optimization will favor more expensive tooling and higher machining speeds. This is the same sort of difference one should find whenever the cost of labor changes, for whatever reason, as in manufacturing in Michigan versus in Mexico.

Machining Cost and Speed

The machining costs are the costs incurred when the tool is actually engaging the workpiece and removing a chip. In more general terms, this is when something is being produced—the production cost. The actual cost of making the cut is expressed as:

$$C_c = x_1 T_c \qquad (1.2)$$

where T_c is the cutting, or machining, time. Again x_1 is cost of the machine plus labor per unit of time. It may be necessary to account for these costs separately, as some machines are capable of unattended operation. As with the machine in the nonproductive term, one must ask what the machinist is doing when the machine is operating in the unattended mode. In this system, it could be argued that the machinist's time must be attributed to one part or another. In some operations the machinist loads a magazine of parts and then goes to another machine, or computer controls take over many of the functions once requiring operator attention. In these cases the operator may only be required occasionally and may be monitoring many machines simultaneously. And, in these cases the x_1 and T_c coefficient are broken down appropriately, so the proper percentage of the operator's effort is attributed to each part. For example if x_b is the labor cost, f is the portion of the cutting time that requires the operator, and x_m is the machine cost, then Equation (1.2) could be written:

$$C_c = fx_b T_c + x_m T_c \qquad (1.2.1)$$
$$\text{if } f = 1, \text{ then } x_b + x_m = x_1.$$

The cutting time, T_c, can be expressed as a function of the cutting speed, v, and the distance the tool must cover, r.

$$T_c = r/v \qquad (1.2.2)$$

In machining by turning, the cutting speed, v, is the vectorial sum of the components of the velocity of the tool over the surface; that is, feed velocity and the tangential, surface velocity due to rotation of the workpiece, and the distance to be covered, r, is the length of the helical path that the tool will cover. The speed, v, could be applied, with some modification, to any production rate; for example, the material removal rate, in a process like electric discharge machining, or the area to be cut in sawing, and the distance, r, would have to be adjusted accordingly. The speed and distance can be generalized and applied to any process where the output of the machine is adjustable as a function of some rate (i.e., time derivative). In cutting, there are other factors, feed and depth of cut, which can also influence the output of the machine. These factors can be optimized if the process is understood in sufficient detail. Most simply, Equation (1.2), expressed in terms of v and r, becomes:

$$C_c = x_1 r/v \qquad (1.2.3)$$

This equation represents an inverse relation of cost with speed or some manufacturing rate (i.e., the faster the cheaper). This is important. The next terms will have a direct relation.

Tool Costs and Tool Life

The terms for the cost of the tool itself and the cost of changing the tool both have coefficients of cutting time divided by tool life. The effect of this term is to proportion to each part its share of the tool and tool changing cost.

The tool changing cost is expressed most generally as follows:

$$C_h = x_1 T_h (T_c/T) \qquad (1.3)$$

where T is the tool life, T_h is the tool changing time, and T_c is still the cutting or processing time for one cut. On some machines, tool changing has been automated so that it does not require an interruption of the process time, or at least some of the tool changing time can be accomplished by the operator while the machine is processing another part with a fresh tool. In these cases then the labor and machine contributions to x_1 should be adjusted accordingly.

The cost of the tool can be expressed also as a function of the ratio of the cutting time for one part to the tool life:

$$C_t = y (T_c/T) \qquad (1.4)$$

where y is the cost of the tool. The tool cost may include more than the purchase price, as there are costs associated with selecting, ordering, stocking, and retrieving the tools.

Material Costs

The final term in Equation (1), C_w, material costs, is generally not related to cutting speed. It is worth considering three parts of material cost: that which is used in the part, that which is removed during cutting, and that which is scrapped because of errors. The first part clearly does not change with respect to speed; the part is the part. It is conceivable, although unlikely, that the material removed may increase with cutting speed (e.g., the kerf might be wider in some types of cutting). It is more likely that the amount of scrap produced would increase with speed, perhaps because of failure, on the part of operators or control systems, to correct errors, or to stop the machine after tool failure, in time to save the part.

Tool Life and Speed

Equations (1.3) and (1.4) normally both have inverse relations between the tool life and the cost. This is not surprising. At a given speed, the longer the tool life, the cheaper it is to use that tool. The Tc/T term shows how much of the cost of each tool, and of changing each tool, should be assigned to each part. The time to cut or produce a part is universally proportional to the cutting speed or processing rate. The tool life can also go down as the speed goes up. In general this can be explained because, as the speed is increased, the temperature of the tool increases, which permits wear by abrasion or by diffusion to occur at a higher rate, hence the total tool life is diminished. The number of parts that can be produced with a tool generally goes down as the tool speed goes up. This relation can be expressed as:

$$T = (c/v)^{1/n} \qquad (1.4.1)$$

where c and n are constants that describe the relation between the cutting speed and tool life from the Taylor equation. The Taylor equation expresses the relation between cutting speed and tool life. It was observed experimentally (Taylor, 1907) that the log of the tool life decreased linearly as the log of the cutting speed increased; $-n$ is the slope for this relation and c is the

log of the cutting speed which would give a tool life of one unit.

It appears, from discussions with engineers at several plants and with tool manufacturers, that the Taylor relation, Equation (1.4.1), is seldom used now. There are several difficulties with its current use. The most important one is probably related to training; the engineers have not been exposed to it in a way that makes its applicability in their context clear. A key issue is how to make its applicability clear in the context of current manufacturing practices. The following digression addresses this problem. And, by discussing the details of how the Taylor relation is used, it may become clear how to apply this type of approach in other manufacturing operations besides machining.

The constants in the Taylor relation, Equation (1.4.1), are evaluated by conducting machining experiments. While holding all other variables constant (e.g., workpiece, machine, feed per revolution, tool type), the influence of cutting, or tool, speed on tool wear is measured. It is necessary to establish a criterion for tool life which is based on some kind of measurement. The measurement can be the geometry of the tool directly (e.g., crater depth or wear land length) or something indirect, like power of the machine, machining force, or surface finish. Cutting is conducted at one speed until the wear criterion for the end of tool life has been met, and the time from the beginning of the cut is noted. Then the tool is changed, a new speed is selected, and the test is repeated until a sufficient number of trials have been run at the desired speeds (Figure 1, ANSI/ASME, 1985). The log of the tool life is plotted versus the log of the speed (Figure 2).

Note that the log-log plot has some interesting properties. The slope of the plot, which is used to determine n, is independent of the units. That is, it doesn't matter if the speed is measured in meters per minute or in feet per second, and the tool life measured in hours or shifts, the value of n will not change. The value of c, however, does depend on the units used for both speed and tool life.

The Taylor coefficients, n and c, are specific to one set of machining variables, including the obvious (e.g., feed and depth of cut in turning). One problem with the application of the Taylor relation to manufacturing costs is the sensitivity of the coefficients to the machine tool and variations in the tools and in the workpiece material. In some cases workpiece material will vary sufficiently even within one lot so that evaluation of the coefficients

FIGURE 1

Tool wear versus time for several speeds. These are representative of experimental curves, where some parameter used to describe tool wear is plotted on the vertical axis and the time for the measurements is plotted on the horizontal axis. A critical level of tool wear, used to define the end of tool life, is denoted by a line parallel to the horizontal axis

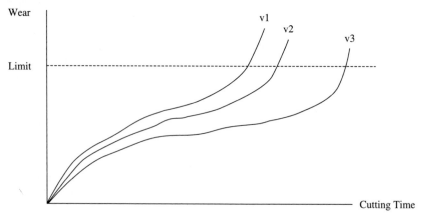

FIGURE 2

Tool life versus speed. The logs of the times corresponding to the end of tool life are plotted versus the logs of the speeds for each speed test, from Figure 1. The Taylor coefficient, n, is the negative of the slope, and c is the speed which gives tool life of one unit

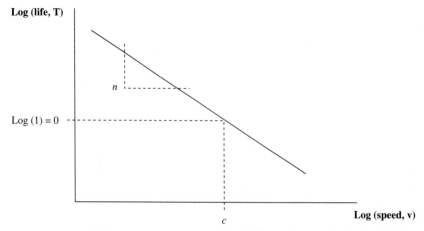

appears useless. In cases where the lots are sufficiently consistent and enough tools are used to machine one lot, evaluation of the Taylor coefficients and subsequent optimization of cutting speeds (addressed below) could be justified economically. The procedure of determining the coefficients and optimizing must itself be understood so that it can be optimized, and so that it is clear when it is beneficial to apply it. Much of the procedure could be performed by a computer attached to the machine tool and be transparent to the operator.

When n is less than one, which is the usual case, Equation (1.4.1) combined with the time-to-cut relation—distance divided by speed, Equation (1.2.2)—and substituted in (1.4) results in a term where the cost is proportional to a positive power of v, the production rate:

$$C_t = y \frac{(r/v)}{(c/v)^{1/n}}$$

which reduces to

$$C_t = y \frac{r}{c^{1/n}} v^{(1/n) - 1} \tag{1.4.2}$$

Since both C_h and C_t are independent of tool life, they may be combined as follows:

$$C_h + C_t = (x_1 T_h + y) \frac{r}{c^{1/n}} v^{(1/n) - 1} \tag{1.4.3}$$

When the exponent of v $[(1/n)-1]$ is positive this term represents increasing costs with increasing speed. The exponent will be positive whenever n is less than one. If n is greater than one, then the cost of the tool goes down as the machining speed goes up. Since n is the negative of the slope on the log-log plot of tool life versus cutting speed, then an n greater than one corresponds to a slope greater than negative one. The relation between n and the cost of the tool is illustrated in the following table:

Negative Slope, n, of Log of Tool Life versus Log of Cutting Speed	Cost (C_h) of the Tool and Tool Changing with Increasing Cutting Speed
$n < 1$	Increasing
$n = 1$	No change
$n > 1$	Decreasing

Values of n approaching one (slopes approaching negative one) are unlikely in metal cutting. If the slope equals zero, then there is only one value for tool life, and therefore the tool life and, hence, the wear rates do not change with respect to cutting speed. If the slope is greater than zero, the wear rate decreases with increasing speed, and tool life increases with increasing speed; this is unlikely in cutting, at least over any significant range of cutting speeds. This relationship can be shown by dividing Equation (1.4.1) by (1.2.2), to give the parts per tool as a function of speed.

In considering manufacturing operations other than cutting, the tool changing and tool cost terms, Equations (1.3) and (1.4), are not required to be a function of cutting tool life. Other elements of the manufacturing process change in cost as the production rate is increased, for example, scrap production, in which case a relation based on some other experimental study would be substituted for Equation (1.4.1).

There may be extra operations that are required at different speeds. There are a couple of examples in machining. The tendency to form a ribbony chip, which wraps around the tool or workpiece, can be a function of speed, although not necessarily high speeds. Burr formation, which requires a second operation to remove, can also be a function of speed. Whatever the process, the extra operations need to be considered as extra terms in Equation 1, and their dependency on speed included when processing speed is optimized to produce the lowest cost, highest throughput, or highest profit rate operation.

It is worthy of note that speed of processing is not the only parameter that might be optimized in manufacturing operations. Temperature or other rates (e.g., flow rate or quenching speed) may be studied. In these cases relations between the parameter and the outcome need to be identified, as has been done with speed.

Total Cost and Tool Life

The equations that give the details of the cost relations in the several terms of Equation 1 can be substituted into Equation 1:

$$Cpc = x_1 T_1 + x_1 T_c + x_1 T_h \frac{T_c}{T} + y \frac{T_c}{T} + C_w \tag{2}$$

At this point it should be made clear that a useful formula for the cost per cut has been developed. Different variations, which could make the development applicable to manufacturing processes other than machining, have been discussed. The equation, in this form, is valuable for computing the cost of manufacturing operations even if more detailed relations, such as Equation (1.4.1), are not known. Comparisons between different tools, workpieces, or processing parameters can be made on the basis of measurements of tool life, T; processing time, T_c; tool changing time, T_h; nonproductive time, T_1; and on the knowledge of the labor and machine costs, x_1, tool costs, y, and workpiece costs, C_w. These comparisons will allow an engineer to determine the options with the least cost, and, eventually, highest profit rate, for situations for which there is sufficient data. Clearly, this is an important thing to be able to do.

Optimizing Speed for Minimum Cost

The next step is to show how to optimize processing parameters to determine the values which give the lowest cost for situations for which there are not direct observations. For this it is necessary to rely on mathematical expressions, such as Equations (1.2.2) and (1.4.1), which define approximate relations between the tool life or machining time and a processing variable such as speed.

In order to find the value of a processing parameter which results in the lowest cost, it is necessary to express all the terms in the cost equation, Equation (2),

which can be, as a function of that processing parameter. In this exercise all the terms that can, have been written as a function of speed, v.

$$C_{pc} = x_1 T_1 + x_1 \frac{r}{v} + (x_1 T_h + y)rc^{-1/n}v^{(1/n)-1} \quad (3)$$

A graphic form of this relation is shown in Figure 3. In order to find the optimum value of the speed, the next step is to take the derivative of Equation (3) with respect to the cutting speed or processing speed, v. It should be pointed out that this is a relatively simple derivative to take. It is only necessary to keep track of the constant coefficients and adjust the exponents of the terms containing v. If the students are going to be able to generalize on the optimization portion of this exercise, then they must be comfortable with taking this derivative. Despite all their courses in calculus, many engineers, especially those that have been out of school for a few years, are not comfortable with taking even the simplest of derivatives. The derivative of the cost per cut, C_{pc}, with respect to cutting speed, v, is:

$$\frac{dC_{pc}}{dv} = -x_1 rv^{-2} + (x_1 T_h + y)rc^{-1/n}[(1/n) - 1]v^{(1/n)-2} \quad (4)$$

Note that the distance to be machined, r, is present in both remaining terms and can be divided out of the relation; hence, the optimum speed is not dependent on the distance to be cut (i.e., total material to be removed).

FIGURE 3

A composite graph for cost per cut versus speed, and several components of cost are plotted versus speed

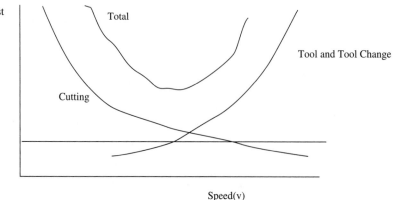

The optimum speed, v_{opt}, is found by setting the derivative to zero and solving for the speed. With some algebraic manipulation this becomes (Gilbert, 1950; Shaw, 1989):

$$v_{opt} = \{[x_1/(x_1 T_h + y)][(1/n) - 1]\}^n \qquad (5)$$

Based on labor, machine, and tool costs and on tool life, Equation (5) gives the optimum speed. It can be seen that greater tool cost, y, and greater tool changing time, T_h, correspond to slower optimum speeds; greater labor and machine costs, x_1, correspond to greater optimum speeds.

Applicability

It is not always clear when it makes sense to apply this procedure for calculating optimum values of process variables. Certainly the effort is favored by larger production runs. The use of such a procedure will depend on how easy it is to apply. Properly designed software should favor the application of this procedure, so that much of the sophistication can be transparent to the user. Currently some tool manufacturers supply software that calculates costs according to some version of Equation (2).

In many cases a cost equation does not have to be used precisely. It can be applied approximately. For example, if a new combination of tools and workpiece material results in greater tool life than previously, and if the speed had been optimized previously, then there will be a new optimum speed greater than the previous one. Additionally the basic ideas incorporated into this development can be applied to improve some industrial situations. It should be clear that efforts directed solely at minimizing one coefficient of one term (e.g., tool cost) will not, in general, result in an optimization of the cost of the product. In fact, it is likely that they will not.

It should also be clear that it is impossible to determine optimum values for manufacturing process parameters based on quarterly accounting alone. The application of the sort of discrete operation costing should, if it is effective, result in a lowering of manufacturing costs that should be evident on a quarterly basis.

There are some points which are only addressed here in passing, but need to be considered if the application of discrete operation accounting is to be effective. Labor savings may need to come in relatively large units, such as one person-quarter, before they can be recognized. Savings on machine time could be similar, in that unless an entire machine is eliminated and sold, no savings will be recognized. In fact, in some cases, where machine usage is measured, increasing the machining speed will mean that the machine is standing idle more of the time, which will look bad on machine utilization statistics. To make constructive use of less than one full unit savings may take some imagination on the part of the workers and management.

References

ANSI/ASME B94.55 M 1986, "Tool Life Testing with Single Point Tools," ASME, NY, 1986 (and ISO 3685-1977 (E)).

W. W. Gilbert, "Economics of Machining," in *Machining Theory and Practice* (Metals Park, OH: American Society for Metals, 1950), pp. 465–85.

M. C. Shaw, *Metal Cutting Principles* (New York: Oxford University Press, 1989), Chapter 19.

F. W. Taylor, *On the Art of Cutting Metals,* Transactions of the American Society of Mechanical Engineers, 1907, pp. 28–58.

7   Customized Case

CASE 7–1
THE LIVING CASE

Lori Franz
Cerry Klein

The Living Case Methodology

The living case methodology explained here is meant to guide interested faculty and students in developing one. An example of a living case is at the end.

The Limitations of Static Cases.   Case studies have long been seen as a mechanism to bring realism to the business and engineering classroom. Cases usually provide a richer student experience than found merely in working exercises. Cases usually include descriptions of the organization, along with a description of the situation or problem that decision makers face. In most cases, students must provide problem identification, analysis, and action.[1]

Unfortunately, most cases have limitations which impact their usefulness. While they bring a real-world flavor to courses by discussing the decision context, they are restricted by the following:

Case-life. A case is of greatest benefit the first time it is analyzed. Once students learn the angle of the case, this information is passed from student to student, as well as preserved in the "fraternity file" system. It is difficult to prevent students from taking short cuts in the analysis.

Problem identification. Textbook cases force students to identify problems from the narrative given. Further questions are not allowed, nor is a complete view of the history available. Unlike a real-world situation, where management can clarify where analysis is needed, students must guess rather than receive guidance from a boss or manager as is prevalent in the real world. This

limits a student's ability to learn how to analyze a problem and ask precise, relevant questions that lead to the actual problem needed to be solved.

Timeliness. Cases can become dated by changing environments, regulation, or changes in the company. Students may know the actual outcome of the problem situation from news or other readings.

Variety. Cases may be difficult to find which illustrate the desired points and provide the appropriate experiences for students. Solutions are kept and passed on by students via the fraternity file systems and other networks.

The Benefits of Living Cases.   Living cases have the advantage of overcoming the problems of case-life, problem identification, and timeliness that are associated with static textbook cases. Specifically, living cases are:

Up-to-date. The data can be changed each semester and during the semester according to the situation faced by the company at that time. A new analysis is necessitated by data change.

Company driven. The company can either send information to the professor or can send a manager to appear in the class to answer questions about the analysis desired or the problem to be addressed.

Motivational. Students are more interested in a case which involves a local firm. The company's problems seem more relevant, and the fact that company managers may evaluate their work provides pressure to perform.

The Requirements of the Living Case Methodology

Real-World Problems. Problems amenable to solution in living cases are those which have a boundary of decision making (i.e., they can be defined for a distinct unit where a single decision maker is primarily responsible). Problems may be of these types:

Secondary issue problems. These case problems may arise out of situations that are vexing but not

---

[1] P. A. Vatter, S. P. Bradley, S. C. Frey, and B. B. Jackson, *Teacher's Manual for Quantitative Methods in Management* (Burr Ridge, IL: Richard D. Irwin, 1978).

This case was prepared by Lori Franz and Cerry Klein, University of Missouri, Columbia, Missouri. Copyright © 1994 by the National Consortium for Technology in Business, c/o the Thomas Walter Center for Technology Management, Auburn University, Auburn, Alabama.

critical enough to warrant expending corporate resources to resolve the problem. It is attractive to company decision makers to "farm out" such problems to students, since any solution is of value.

Company benchmark problems. These may be routine problems currently under control by the company for which data can easily be supplied to students as a learning experience. Students or the instructor can then use the company solution as a benchmark against which to compare their own analysis.

Real problems. Companies may provide real problems to the class for student analysis, in an attempt to get a new view of solutions, or to generate new alternatives. They may look to the students and faculty as free consultants, willing to provide a high-quality recommendation.

Real-World Data. Data must be available for students to analyze with respect to applying the content of the course. Data may assume one of several forms.

One-shot or time-series. Data may be provided for a point in time upon which the analysis is to be conducted. For instance, a scheduling problem would include the data for the current demand and resources which could be analyzed for a recommendation. On the other hand, students studying statistical process control may receive daily or weekly data. Time-series data allows students to experience the *control and monitor* aspect of decision making, which is essential to technology management.

Clean or dirty. Data may be incomplete, inconsistent, or have missing values, requiring student decisions about how to prepare the data for analysis. Other data may already be clean and ready to process when given to students.

Raw or computerized. Data may be in the form of copies of machine logs, check sheets, or other employee records, or in the form of computer output, datasets, or as computer-ready input.

Real-World Communication via the Company Report. Student analysis results must be communicated in an appropriate form that is commonly used in companies. The following forms will be used unless another type of report is specified by the cooperating company. The purpose of the following types of communication-based assignments is to enhance the students' interpretation of results, the development of analytical and critical thinking skills, and to facilitate the students' communication and interpersonal skills, in addition to leading to better understanding of the subject matter.[2]

One-page memo to management. Results of smaller assignment problems can be presented in one-page memo format. Each memo can use tables and graphs to summarize analysis if appropriate. Memo reports should be concise and well written, with content carefully chosen.

Summary presentation. One student will be selected to prepare a five-minute summary of his or her analysis, with recommendations to the class, and/or to the company decision maker(s) if desired by the company. Visuals, such as transparencies, and handouts should be used to prepare an effective presentation.

Question-and-answer session. All presentations will be followed by a 5- to 10-minute question and answer session in which alternate analyses can be discussed and suggestions made for improved analysis, if needed.

Written reports to management. Each major case assignment should include a formal written report to management, complete with recommendations in appropriate managerial writing style.

Real-World Decision Making. The process used in analyzing and communicating results will mirror real-world decision making processes. The fact that current data from a local company is used, as well as the knowledge that the analysis will be made available to company management, provides a realism that cannot be captured in a static case. Likewise, the professor, because of the ongoing case cooperation with the company, will be able to provide much more of the story of the company during the course to add to the realism and be better prepared to effect appropriate analysis.

---

[2] Lori S. Franz, "Integrating Analysis and Communication Skills into the Decision Science Curriculum," *Decision Sciences* 20, pp. 830–43.

Real Partnership between University and Company. The living case approach requires a true partnership between the company and the university. The company develops an ongoing link with the faculty and the course, such that the faculty gain additional insight into practitioner concerns. This cooperation also allows the faculty to build an understanding of the company's environment over time and of the company's practices and operations. This improved understanding of industry practice enriches the instructor's teaching. Companies will see the value of the university and of the student analysis in terms of the identification and solution of actual problems. This relationship has obvious payoffs for both parties.

Developing an Ongoing Living Case. The process of developing an ongoing living case requires a large front end investment. However, as the case moves from semester to semester, the process becomes much easier as faculty and managerial participants become familiar with their roles. The steps are described in this section and are divided into two parts: those which are part of the initial setup of the case, a one time only effort, and those case responsibilities which are incurred each semester or term.

Initial Setup Tasks.

Soliciting cooperating companies. Companies interested in participating in an ongoing learning experience with the University are contacted. The long-term obligation is explained, in addition to the benefits for the students, the company, and society in general.

Matching company interests with courses. Company operations or specific departments which have links to courses are identified. Company personnel with an interest in participating in an educational experience are selected. Areas where companies could benefit by analysis of their secondary problems, and areas where data could be provided with very minimal cost in time or personnel are identified. Joint course and case projects are selected.

Commitment of level of company involvement. Company desires for involvement are discussed. Companies may choose to participate within a spectrum defined by the following two levels:

Low level: Cooperate with the development of the case history and the problem statement. Select the source for the data to be analyzed. Arrange for data to be collected and turned over to the university. Accept and comment on one or two selected student memos.

High level: In addition to low-level tasks, attend course at least once to present and discuss the managerial view of the problems and discuss with students, host class tour of facility, entertain student or faculty questions during analysis period, attend class discussion period where results are discussed, provide feedback to students on solution quality, implement attractive results and provide feedback.

Developing the case history. The company case history is a 2- to 10-page write-up describing the company and its operations. The history should emphasize the division and department of the company associated with the living case. The case history can be developed by the instructor or as an independent study by an interested student under the supervision of the faculty member.

Developing the problem statement for the living case. The problem statement write-up describes the particular situation which the living case will follow from semester to semester. It is prepared by the instructor or by the person writing the case history. It includes a detailed description of the operation or process which will be analyzed, the problems associated with the process, and a description of the data provided to facilitate the analysis.

Selecting the data to be analyzed. The data selection and handling mechanism will be determined. The faculty member will work with the company personnel to determine the data form and the method for transferring data to the instructor. If disguising of the data is necessary, a mechanism for doing this will be designed.

The analysis/communication assignment for company report. The assignment should contain two parts, a communication instruction sheet and a problem-specific instruction sheet.

Communications instructions. A generic sheet which includes the instructions for preparing the memo, the presentation, and the discussion. Objectives and grading criteria are also included.

Problem instructions. A brief statement requesting student recommendations with respect to the problem. This statement should be vague, requiring students to develop their own analysis of the problem.

Ongoing Tasks for Each Semester.

Determine if problem or data changes are necessary. Confer with the company representative to see if any changes have arisen in the problem environment. Adapt problem statement to accommodate changes in problem or in data description. Determine whether available data is sufficient.

Provide the current-semester data and story. The problem data which has been collected from the firm for that semester's analysis will be made available to the students, along with any changes in the company's situation or operations. Historical information about previous classes' analysis of the living case can be presented or made available, if beneficial.

The company report. Students analyze data and prepare company report (memo, presentation, and discussion).

The company feedback. Provide student analysis to company either via the presentation session or by sending selected high-quality memos to company decision makers. Make company feedback available to students if feedback is provided in a timely manner.

Maintaining the Living Case.

Revision. Each semester the case must be evaluated to see if it meets the learning objectives of the course, and if the problem situation requires changes to the case (see the discussion of ongoing tasks each semester in the preceding section).

Refocus of problem. In cases where the company is not highly interested in student recommendations, but is providing data as a learning tool for students, the instructors may wish to refocus the problem statement to look at different issues each semester. For instance, in a job shop problem environment, the focus of the problem may switch from scheduling jobs, to scheduling workers, to addressing bottlenecks with the same stream of data. Similarly, data could be used for static decisions, or several waves of data could be used for studying the problem over time for control purposes.

Appendix

A. B. Chance Company: A Living Case Example

Description of Company

A. B. Chance Company (ABC Co.), the main employer in the small mid-Missouri town of Centralia, was founded by Albert Bishop Chance in 1907. Mr. Chance also owned and managed the Home Telephone Company with his father, for which he invented and manufactured state-of-the-art telephone equipment. After a 1912 storm knocked over many of the company's telephone poles, Mr. Chance and his ABC Co. devised a quick and more secure way to install poles using earth anchors—metal bars screwed into the ground to which guy wires from the poles were attached. The product was a success and became ABC Co.'s best-selling product. In the 1930s, two related acquisitions expanded the product line of tools and hardware for the utilities industries.

Also during the 1930s, when many companies were going bankrupt due to the Great Depression, ABC Co. turned briefly to manufacturing piston rings for automobiles to keep the company afloat. During World War II, the company turned to making war equipment and machinery like many other mid-Missouri companies. After the war, ABC Co. returned its focus to providing equipment and tools to the utilities business, which it knew so well. As electricity was provided to all regions of the United States, an even larger market had emerged for ABC Company's products in the electric utilities industry. The worldwide electric industry is now the largest market for ABC Co. products.

In 1975, a merger was arranged and ABC Co. became a subsidiary of the Emerson Electric Company, a St. Louis–based national company. Twelve years later Emerson divested itself of ABC Co. through a leveraged management buyout which returned the company to private ownership.

Through the years ABC Co. made over a dozen related acquisitions to expand its sales and product lines. The company became successful by sticking to the industry it knew best. During the Emerson years, however, many of the less-profitable units were sold. Today, ABC Co. has over 1,200 employees and an annual payroll of over $25 million. The company complex in Centralia consists of a main headquarters, an engineering research center, and a 700,000-square-foot manufacturing facility. In addition, ABC Co. operates an insulator-manufacturing plant in West Virginia and two international subsidiaries (A. B. Chance of Canada and A. B. Chance of the United Kingdom), which are used mostly for assembly rather than manufacturing. The products and equipment tested, manufactured, and assembled at these facilities are sold in all 50 states and over 100 countries worldwide. ABC Co. promotes its products and services with sales representatives in over 50 countries.

Today, ABC Co. manufactures tools, equipment, and electrical apparatus used in the construction, maintenance, and operation of electric and telecommunication utilities. ABC Co.'s product lines include over 10,000 items and are divided into five major product categories: (1) electrical apparatus (which control and direct the flow of electric energy); (2) linesman's tools for repairs; (3) earth anchors used for securing power poles and other business, government, and home purposes; (4) insulators; and (5) hardware. ABC Co. is still the world's largest manufacturer of earth anchors. Anchors are the company's most widely used product in the greatest variety of markets, being used to secure such things as street lights, fence posts, highway signs, and large tents, in addition to still anchoring utility poles. Utility companies and contractors throughout the world who build high-voltage systems know of ABC Co.'s line of equipment.

ABC Co. is an extensive machine and assembly operator. The company is both a steel and nonferrous metal fabricator, a plastics manufacturer, and a major engineering researcher. ABC Co. operates the most comprehensive electrical and mechanical testing lab in a single site in the industry. Foreign visitors come to the Centralia headquarters to discuss electrical problems and to study the research and engineering facilities.

Current Quality Efforts

Total quality management (TQM) has become part of ABC Co.'s strategic objectives in recent years. Prior to 1985, the company's pursuit of quality in its products consisted of after-the-fact inspections designed to catch any defects before they went out the door. "Detection," according to Gene McKenzie, quality process control manager, "was our primary tool. Today, the key is prevention. We use state-of-the-art techniques to prevent defects before they occur, and we enlist more people in the first line of defense by giving them the tools they need to ensure that quality is built in." The main tool used in this effort is statistical process control (SPC), which allows workers to chart and control the critical factors affecting the manufacturing process. The workers can then recognize when the process is not in control, and they can make corrections so that the quality of the products is maintained.

TQM is a philosophy of management and a process for effecting change which emphasizes such things as participatory management to accomplish goals, identification of variables affecting satisfaction of both internal and external customers, measurement and display of data to assess the current process and product quality, and many other elements which focus the company on a road to continuous improvement of its products and services. ABC Co. currently has a TQM program with the following goals:

1. Effective utilization of the company's existing human resources.
2. Positive cooperation and integrated involvement by all services and employees in fulfilling mission.
3. Quality-designed products for optimum functionality, manufacturability, and reliability.
4. Total control of the manufacturing process through the use of SPC to ensure repetitive result with no scrap generation.
5. Use of TQM in administrative procedures to enable low-cost (not cheap) purchasing, minimum delay in order information, high inventory turnover, and reliable and flexible scheduling.
6. Sustained new product development.

According to Leif Lomo, ABC Co.'s chief executive officer, the mission of the company is the following: "to become the premier supplier to the electric utility industry, become globally competitive, and recognized as such." He states that designing and manufacturing top quality products is the company's top goal. "Quality

production is the low-cost way to operate," says Lomo. "Quality doesn't cost, it pays."

Lomo believes that being a world-class supplier to the electric utility and telecommunications industry requires improving the total quality process, and has included this as part of the company strategy. The goal for the total quality process at ABC Co. is a 10-fold increase in the traditional quality measures by 1994. This is to be accomplished by training the entire workforce in statistical process control; training managers, supervisors, and engineers in statistical problem-solving techniques; and defining specific processes as improvement projects. This will also require an improvement in the information management systems at ABC Co. In addition, the company wants to establish quantifiable reliability standards with progressive utility companies.

Ongoing Quality Assessment

ABC Co. is seeking to expand its markets outside the United States. Since the company is anxious to build on its already existing European market, part of the TQM program is to meet ISO accreditation.

ISO 9000. To do business with the European Community (EC) a company must be certified under the International Standards Organization (ISO) 9000 standards by 1993. The Geneva-based ISO has set quality standards for companies wishing to do business with the EC after 1993. A description of the standards is provided below:

Title	Standard
Quality management and quality assurance standards: guidelines for selection and use	ISO 9000
Quality systems: model for quality assurance in design/development, production, installation, and servicing	ISO 9001
Quality systems: model for quality assurance in production and installation	ISO 9002
Quality systems: model for quality assurance in final inspection and test	ISO 9003
Quality management and quality system elements: guidelines	ISO 9004

ISO 9000 is an overview and description of the standards. It suggests that suppliers and buyers decide upon either ISO 9001, 9002, or 9003 as the quality model to be used in contracts with each other based on the functional or organizational capability required of the supplier for a product or service. ISO 9004 provides general guidelines to suppliers on how to design and develop an integrated total quality management system.

In order for a company to supply products or services to an EC member, independent auditors approved by the ISO must certify that the supplier company's quality assurance is in conformance with the ISO standards. While Europeans are obviously aware of the importance of ISO certification, this fact seems to be eluding many U.S. firms. In Great Britain more than 20,000 facilities have been ISO-certified compared with only 400 in the United States.

ABC Co. Certification Efforts.   The company is already certified under ISO 9003. A program has been undertaken to certify under ISO 9001 in 1993. To gain the ISO's stamp of approval, companies must work through a 100-page, five-section guidebook that directs them to document how workers perform every function affecting quality, and to install controls to ensure that they follow through with the prescribed routines. Internal teams verify that procedures are being followed in 20 domains ranging from management responsibility to statistical techniques (see Appendix). Once management is satisfied with its compliance with the ISO standard, the independent auditors review the company for accreditation.

Problem Statement

This ongoing, living case used in cooperation with ABC Co. deals with the firm's efforts to conduct continual quality audits to assess progress and compliance with specific ISO 9000 standards. As a project, a student will choose one or more areas from the 20 domains of ISO 9001. The student will then be required to read the ISO 9000 standards to understand the requirements of the EC. After doing so, he or she will visit ABC Co.'s plant in Centralia to see how data dealing with the implementation and monitoring of total quality management is collected. Based on the questions and requests the student makes, ABC Co. will then provide data enabling the student to analyze the company's compliance with a specific area within ISO 9001.[1]

[1]*Editor's note:*
An example of a Compliance Report prepared by a student team is included in the Teacher's Manual accompanying this book.

8   APPENDIX

ENGINEERING/BUSINESS PARTNERSHIPS: AN AGENDA FOR ACTION

Summary Report of the First National Conference on Business and Engineering Education, April 5–7, 1994, Auburn University.

Objectives.

- **To bring together university faculty and administrators in engineering and business** who are leaders in developing linked business and engineering curricula, with the participation of industry, responding to the need for improved management of rapidly evolving technologies in a global economy and the shift of federal technology policy from defense to commercial needs.

- **To share approaches, methods, successes and failures** experienced to date in developing engineering/business partnership curricula, especially models using case-based courses conducted in close cooperation with industry.

- **To develop recommendations** to universities, industry and government that will provide an agenda for action to improve the capabilities of engineering and business graduates to meet industry needs for competing in the global marketplace.

Process.

- **A preconference workshop** reviewing partnership course projects based on industry cases and carried out at 10 universities under sponsorship of National Consortium for Technology in Business, with results reported to conference participants by Ed Ernst (University of South Carolina), William Boulton (Auburn University), and Gary Scudder (Vanderbilt University).

- **Presentations by representative leaders** in engineering/business partnership programs at major universities—John White (Georgia Tech), Robert Laessig (Drexel University), Edward Magrab (University of Maryland), Richard Lewis (N.C. State University), Dayne Aldridge, and Paul Swamidass (Auburn University).

- Keynote address by Al Pense (Lehigh University).

- **An intensive Socratic discussion** led by Joe Morone (Rensselaer Polytechnic Institute), with input from representatives of industry and government, followed by a **small group process** work and **general session discussion** to evaluate situation and formulate recommendations.

Results.

- **The preconference workshop was attended by 70** business and engineering faculty; the **cases and teaching notes** will be published for use in engineering and business courses at undergraduate and graduate levels.

- **Conference participants totaled 106,** representing 48 universities and several national organizations and industries, including Frank Huband (ASEE), George Peterson (ABET), Charles Hickman and Jacqueline Harrington (AACSB), and Jon Paugh (U.S. Dept. of Commerce). Faculty numbered 58 (35 engineering), with 26 deans of engineering and business.

Recommendations for Universities.

Universities should institute undergraduate and graduate programs and curricula in schools of business and engineering that facilitate cross-disciplinary learning consistent with the long-term goals of relevant industry and the university.

Criteria should be developed for faculty reward systems and performance review, especially for promotion and tenure, that reward and encourage faculty who work with topics and programs at the intersection of traditional engineering and business programs.

The ASEE and AACSB should jointly conduct faculty development workshops for both engineering and business faculty to encourage cross-disciplinary educational activities.

Recommendations for Industry.

Industrial firms should enter into joint long-term programs with schools of business and engineering for the purpose of nurturing partnership projects that benefit both parties, helping faculty and students learn about current industrial practice and facilitating an ongoing flow of university developed concepts, technology, and expertise to the industrial partner.

Industrial firms should work closely with schools of business and engineering to help faculty members develop cross-disciplinary curriculum criteria and materials that will better prepare graduates to meet both immediate and evolving industrial needs.

Industry should articulate its educational needs on local, regional, national, and international levels in new ways that provide specific guidance to the education community.

Recommendations for Government.

The federal government should provide funding for development of cross-disciplinary business and engineering projects and for programs to stimulate continued interaction and coordination of effort between industry and schools of business and engineering.

The National Science and Technology Council should assure that new federal technology policy supports infrastructure development in universities in ways that integrate business and technology issues that are fundamental to global competitiveness.

State, regional, and local governments should form partnerships and establish policies that support interactions between engineering and business schools and industry.

Conference Recommendations—Summary of Discussion

The following sections outline the conference context and background of the discussion process resulting in the recommendations issued by the conference to universities, industry, and government. Numerous specific recommendation proposals were offered by participants, with discussion on each. Recommendations in each area were ranked by a priority-weighting vote process, and the top recommendations formulated and adopted after further discussion.

Recommendations for Universities.   The consensus viewpoint among participants from all sectors was that cross-disciplinary teaching methods with industry participation have significant demonstrated value and should be further explored and more widely (although not exclusively) adopted. Discussion noted a possible trend in universities, acknowledged in public statements by administrators at many institutions, to shift from primary emphasis on research to a balance of instruction and research. However, faculty participants especially perceived single-investigator research reported through peer-reviewed journals as continuing to dominate promotion and tenure decisions and thus blocking serious improvement of teaching programs, and especially of cross-disciplinary efforts.

The top two recommendations for universities therefore focus on the twin goals of formalizing cross-disciplinary programs and curricula and revamping faculty reward systems to encourage participation in such activities. Participants saw these as primarily responsibilities of university administrators, but also noted the relevant roles that could be played by professional organizations and by faculty through faculty governance procedures.

Discussion also noted culture differences between engineering and business schools as a difficulty in implementing partnership courses, and noted a lack of technical engineering depth in many of the case projects presented at the conference. The recommendation for joint faculty development workshops sponsored by ASEE and AACSB was in part a response to these perceived problems.

Other specific proposals discussed included recognition by accrediting bodies of the legitimacy of cross-disciplinary curricula, establishment by universities of a network of regional centers to facilitate interaction between industry and engineering/business faculty (similar to the SBDC concept), creation by ASEE and AACSB of an electronic information clearing-house concerning opportunities for business and engineering faculty to participate in joint research and curriculum development programs, and joint AACSB and ABET involvement, with industry input, in better defining the objectives of business and engineering partnership curricula.

Recommendations for Industry.   Conference participants were unanimous in calling for closer teamwork and improved communication between industry and schools of business and engineering. The forms envisioned for such interaction ranged widely, from involvement of specific firms with particular courses and faculty at a given university to regional and national linkings of universities and university associations with industrial consortia, trade associations, professional organizations, and so on. A common perception voiced in conference discussion was that development of closer industry/university partnerships would be critical for both parties in coping with the challenges presented by national and global economic, technological, social, and environmental change processes.

The most commonly noted obstacle to improving industry/university relationships was a perceived difference in perspective: the universities seeing their primary role as providing students with knowledge basic to a career of life-long learning, and industry, while acknowledging the value of this long-term perspective, feeling driven to meet current technological and market requirements and thus in practice demanding graduates more specifically trained to be productive early in their first job. Conference recommendations for industry were therefore formulated with a view toward reducing this gap, proposing continuing partnership arrangements to bring faculty and students into closer contact with current industrial needs and at the same time inviting industry to undertake closer examination and articulation of its needs and to participate in development of curricula with appropriate balance for achieving near-term and long-range goals of both parties.

Effective partnership arrangements between industry and schools of business and engineering were seen to depend on close interaction at the working level, involving faculty, students, managers, engineering personnel, and the like. However, participants also noted the critical importance of ongoing contracts and relationships at the senior level in both the university and industry.

Specific kinds of interactions discussed in addition to the industry case-based engineering/business course models presented at the conference included increased or expanded school/corporation advisory councils, industry-sponsored internship programs at national and international levels, programs involving mentors and executives in residence, and use of industry associations and roundtables to identify and communicate needs to the university. Also discussed as worth exploring was modeling on the agricultural extension system, especially that system's role in establishing ongoing interrelationships between university programs and industry, including small business.

Recommendations for Government.   The conference recognized the shift in emphasis in federal technology policy from defense to commercial needs as representing both a challenge and an opportunity. One effect of the shift is that the federal system for funding basic and applied university research is undergoing a major transition. Faculty as well as administrators in engineering and business have become aware of the changes underway, and especially in engineering have begun seriously considering fundamental changes in the university culture, including faculty reward systems, appropriate to the new environment.

The conference recommendations reflect traditional thinking in proposing that government should play a major role in sponsoring university programs and projects. However, conference participants saw the new environment as also inviting a stronger role for business and engineering education interests in the crafting of innovative partnerships between government, industry, and higher education capable of responding to new business and technology realities.

The thrust of the recommendations is therefore to call on government to recognize and support the kinds of cross-disciplinary programs and the corresponding university infrastructure changes now needed, as well as assisting in creation of effective industry/university interrelationships. Discussion noted the need for coordinated participation in these efforts by all relevant government agencies, including the National Science Foundation, National Science and Technology Council, Department of Commerce, the Department of Defense, and so forth.

The conference also called for participation of state, regional, and local governments, which have their own interests involved as well as serving as conduits for federal funds. One of the specific proposals discussed was governmental support for a network of regional and local university-based centers for integrating engineering and business issues, possibly patterned after the agriculture extension service, bringing together engineering/business faculty teams with industry and small business.